Readings in

Object-Oriented Systems and Applications

David C. Rine

IEEE Computer Society
Readings in series

Each volume in the *Readings in* series is coordinated with
a special-interest issue of *Computer* magazine,
the IEEE Computer Society's flagship periodical.
Readings in volumes consolidate both
tutorial and intermediate material to deliver
the most up-to-date information on
developing areas in
computer science and engineering.

Readings in titles

Readings in

Object-Oriented Systems and Applications

David C. Rine

George Mason University

IEEE Computer Society Press
Los Alamitos, California

Washington • Brussels • Tokyo

Library of Congress Cataloging-in-Publication Data

Readings in object-oriented systems and applications /
   [edited by] David C. Rine.
            p.   cm.
   Includes bibliographical references.
   ISBN 0-8186-6222-0 (case) — ISBN 0-8186-6221-2 (fiche).
   1. Object-oriented programming (Computer science) 2. Computer software — Development.
   I. Rine, David C.
QA76.64.R44   1995
      005.1' 1—dc20   94-10044
                                                                                CIP

IEEE Computer Society Press
10662 Los Vaqueros Circle
P.O. Box 3014
Los Alamitos, CA 90720-1264

IEEE Computer Society Press Order Number 6222-04
Library of Congress Number 94-10044
IEEE Catalog Number EH0396-2
ISBN 0-8186-6222-0 (case)
ISBN 0-8186-6221-2 (microfiche)

Additional copies may be ordered from:

IEEE Computer Society Press	IEEE Service Center	IEEE Computer Society	IEEE Computer Society
Customer Service Center	445 Hoes Lane	13, Avenue de l'Aquilon	Ooshima Building
10662 Los Vaqueros Circle	P.O. Box 1331	B-1200 Brussels	2-19-1 Minami-Aoyama
P.O. Box 3014	Piscataway, NJ 08855-1331	BELGIUM	Minato-ku, Tokyo 107
Los Alamitos, CA 90720-1264	Tel: +1-908-981-1393	Tel: +32-2-770-2198	JAPAN
Tel: +1-714-821-8380	Fax: +1-908-981-9667	Fax: +32-2-770-8505	Tel: +81-3-3408-3118
Fax: +1-714-821-4641			Fax: +81-3-3408-3553
Email: cs.books@computer.org			

Technical Editor: Jon T. Butler
Production Editor: Bob Werner
Book design: Edna Straub
Additional layout: Chris Patterson
Cover: Toni Van Buskirk, VB Designs
Printed in the United States of America by Braun-Brumfield, Inc.

  The Institute of Electrical and Electronics Engineers, Inc.

Contents

Part 1
Principles of Object-Oriented Systems

Chapter 1: Theory of Object-Oriented Systems

Chapter 2: Object-Oriented Software Development

Part 2
Software for Object-Oriented Systems

Chapter 3: Object-Oriented Language System Architecture

Chapter 4: Object-Oriented Database Management
System Architecture

Part 3
Object-Oriented Applications

Papers marked with an asterisk have been revised and expanded especially for this series.

Foreword

This is the fourth of our *Readings in* volumes, a series published by the IEEE Computer Society Press. Our intent is to provide, in one text, tutorial and intermediate material on developing areas in computer science and engineering. A unique aspect of this series is its origin. Each volume is developed from a special issue of *Computer* magazine, the IEEE Computer Society's flagship periodical. That is, the editors have chosen papers to produce both a special issue of *Computer* and, subsequently, a *Readings in* volume. The papers in *Computer* provide a tutorial introduction to the subject matter and target an audience with a broad background. The papers in our *Readings in* series provide a wider perspective of the subject and significantly greater coverage.

The *Readings in* series is appropriate for (1) students in senior- and graduate-level courses, (2) engineers seeking a convenient way to improve their knowledge, and (3) managers wishing to augment their technical expertise. The guiding principle motivating this series is the delivery of the most up-to-date information in emerging fields. Because computer scientists and engineers deal with rapidly changing technology, they need access to tutorial descriptions of new and promising developments. Our *Readings in* texts will satisfy that need.

Papers chosen for this volume were judged on their technical content, quality, and clarity of exposition. As with other Computer Society Press products, this text has undergone thorough review. In addition, all of the previously published papers had to pass *Computer* magazine's strict review process.

We wish to thank all who have contributed to this effort: the authors, who devoted substantial effort to produce the high quality required for their papers to be selected, and our referees, who donated their expertise and time to evaluate the manuscripts and provide feedback to the authors. A special acknowledgment is due the editor, David C. Rine, whose time and energies were required to read the papers, direct an extensive administrative effort, coordinate referee reports, select final papers, and secure timely and high-quality revisions.

Jon T. Butler

Preface

This book got its start with a collaboration that created a special issue of *Computer*, published by the IEEE Computer Society in October 1992. In that issue, entitled "Object-Oriented Systems and Applications," began the regular *Computer* section devoted to the subject. A number of the authors who contributed to the special issue also appear as coauthors in this book, along with others who published on the subject during 1992 and 1993. The book contains three parts, which cover principles of object-oriented systems, object-oriented systems software, and object-oriented applications, and includes a comprehensive list of contributing authors and their affiliations. We are indebted to the authors, the reviewers, and the IEEE Computer Society for making it possible to publish these works.

David C. Rine

Introduction

The volume of literature on developing object-oriented software has mushroomed in the past ten years. As the topic begins to mature, fundamental ideas take shape, methodologies are embodied in new practice, and we now see many interesting systems and applications. To help get this wealth of material under control without compiling an encyclopedia, we limit this book to some of the indispensable facts about object-oriented development and present in detail some of the systems and applications conceived in an object-oriented way. Thus, we divide the book into three parts: Principles of Object-Oriented Systems, Software for Object-Oriented Systems, and Object-Oriented Applications.

Within Chapter 1, "Introduction to Object-Oriented Systems and Applications" provides an overview and historical perspective of object-oriented systems and applications. Chapters 2–10 consist of reprinted papers published in 1992 and 1993, and need no further introductory descriptions.

Part 1

Principles of
Object-Oriented Systems

Chapter 1

Theory of Object-Oriented Systems

Introduction to Object-Oriented Systems and Applications

David C. Rine

George Mason University

As in studying any technical discipline, before we discuss object-oriented systems and applications, we need a working vocabulary. In this section we provide a first glossary of language commonly used in describing these systems and applications. This is followed by an example that will further clarify our concept of object orientedness.

Objects terminology: A brief glossary

Object	an abstraction that stands for a real-world entity.
Class	a set or collection of objects having like features.
Feature	a routine, activity, or attribute serving as part of the definition for an object or class.
Method (routine)	a feature performing an operation on an object.
Instance variable (attribute)	an attribute or feature of an object.
Execution-time creation	the dynamic or runtime creation of an object or instance of a class.
Message	a protocol comprising a method or routine and an object reference or address.
Relationship	a defined association between one or more classes and objects.
System	a collection of classes and objects with defined relationships among them.
Object-oriented language	a well-defined notation that supports object-oriented properties and specifies object-oriented systems.

Object-oriented programming	a method of object-oriented design and implementation that leads to a software system based on the objects every system and subsystem manipulates, rather than the function it is meant to ensure.

Object-oriented properties:

Information hiding	separating details about implementation of an object, class, or system from details in its application domain.
Abstraction	separating unnecessary details from systems requirements or specifications so as to reduce complexities in understanding requirements or specifications.
Dynamic binding	instantiating an identifier or variable, defined by using an object-oriented language with an object during execution of a system.
Inheritance	a relationship between two classes of objects in which one of the classes, the child, takes on all relevant features of the other class, the parent.

Example: A world view and a world model

Consider a model of our world in which each person is an object, persons are members of class structures, and systems are created as related classes of people. People (persons) *as objects* can be placed in a situation in which we can apply specific kinds of sentences and methods to process them. The situation may involve an entire class of people as objects, such as a computer-science class or a basketball team. By learning and experience, however, each people object (person) has inherited other sentences and methods for processing them and may therefore be able to deal with other unexpected situations (such as changing the topic of conversation from computer science to basketball).

People as objects may be combined and integrated into classes for purposes such as carrying on a conversation in some domain, performing a task requiring teamwork, having parties, or playing games with different teams. These combination and integration activities are called *object-oriented development*. If such development is carried out in a predefined metalanguage of instruction, then the activities are called *object-oriented programming*.

People as objects 1) use their native ability to deal with ideas, facts, knowledge, and sentences imprecisely and abstractly; 2) can process ideas and messages by hiding much of the implied information associated with these ideas and messages; and 3) can send, receive, and adapt to ideas and messages dynamically in real time. These three statements are associated with three technical expressions: *abstraction, information hiding, and dynamic binding*.

Consider a world view in which people are thought of as objects. In this frame of reference, people as objects

1. have ideas, facts, knowledge, sentences.
2. have methods for processing facts and sentences such as

    understanding,
    reducing,
    changing,
    remembering.

3. communicate with each other by sending messages back and forth, and these may be understood or not understood (for example, remember when <sentence phrase>, change the <sentence phrase>).
4. may be placed in a situation in which specific kinds of sentences and methods for processing them are used, and an entire class of instances of such people objects may be involved; however, because each people object, from learning and experience, has inherited other ideas and facts and methods for processing them, a people object may be able to deal with other situations (the topic of conversation may change from computer science to basketball).

Let us summarize. People as objects may be combined and integrated into groups of people objects so as to

1. carry on a conversation in some domain.
2. carry out some task involving teamwork.
3. carry out games or have parties.
4. carry out games involving different teams.

These activities are called *object-oriented development*. If such development is carried out in a predefined metalanguage of instruction, then the activities are called *object-oriented programming*.

People as objects use their native ability to 1) deal with ideas, facts, and sentences vaguely, imprecisely, and abstractly; 2) process ideas and messages by hiding a lot of the implied information that is really associated with these ideas and messages; and 3) send, receive, and adapt to messages and ideas dynamically in real time. These actions are described as abstraction, information hiding, and dynamic binding.

We represent, model, or simulate people-object activities in the computer by

1. analyzing the people objects and their activities.
2. devising ways of representing people objects in the computer — their ideas or methods — and enabling us to use the features called *information hiding, data abstraction, dynamic binding,* and *inheritance*.
3. developing design techniques for grouping and integrating the computer-represented people objects in productive ways.

We can also represent people as objects mathematically with finite-state automata and formal logic. An automaton can be an object, a class, or a system. The states of an automaton are represented by the set of its instance-variable (attribute) values, and applying its transition function represents an application of a message to objects. The output function, along with the transition function, produces a new object. With formal logic, logic assertions, and predictions one represents the semantics of a class or system. One set of assertions may be used to represent the state of a system or object that must exist before a method or feature can be applied to it; these are *preassertions*. A second set of assertions may be used to represent the state of a system or object that must exist after a method or feature is applied to it; these are *postassertions*. A third set of assertions may be used to represent the invariants of a system or object — that is, properties or laws that must always be true of the system or object; these are *axioms*. In a system of people as objects, a preassertion for voting would be the eligibility requirements for people. A postassertion for voting would be the election results. An axiom would be a law of the land. A paradigm for the formal-logic approach is presented in Chapter 2.

Thoughts on developing systems in science and engineering

Object-oriented systems are as old as the record of human thought. The Book of Genesis organizes the Creation and presents the first genealogies. Early Greek writing distinguishes *phusis* — the kind, or natural constitution of emphasis, from *genos* — the hierarchy of ancestors and descendants.

In his early writings on genetics, Gregor Mendel, Benedictine monk and scholar in a German monastery, considered how to use his records of plant genetic characteristics to classify and breed plants. Later in the nineteenth century, Darwin extended Mendel's work, but he chose another direction, seeking rational ways of classifying species of insects and animals by their attributes.

All through the history of human thought, classification and relationships between classes have been a fundamental way of representing knowledge. Only late in the twentieth century, however, have engineers and computer scientists sought to apply these paradigms to form modern systems.

The fundamental activity for those of us working in science and engineering is *problem solving*, which has two aspects: process and structure. Problem-solving begins as we prepare our definition and arrive at a *problem statement* (set of requirements) and ends with a *solution statement* (set of specifications), which may be further realized by some tangible product. The procedure we follow is generally called *reasoning*, and the result of reasoning is *structure*. Solution statements take on structure so that we can understand the result of reasoning. The many reasoning processes include *inductive reasoning, deductive reasoning, eductive reasoning, intensive reasoning, extensive reasoning, reasoning under uncertainty*, and so on.

Although we have various ways of presenting structure — the result of reasoning — two are considered here: function and form. We can represent *function* as a set of rules by which someone or something behaves. We can represent *form* by classifying someone's or something's features. These two ways of representing structure (function and form), have been around since ancient times. The Book of Genesis tells us about form and the classifying of that which has been created into *kinds,* another word for *class* or *type.* Thus one result of reasoning or thinking about something or someone is *rules,* and another result is *classes.*

A way of thinking about something is sometimes called a *paradigm.* Hence, the first result of reasoning or thinking is the *rule-based paradigm,* and the second is the *class-based paradigm* or, because classes comprise objects, the *object-oriented paradigm.* Do we know other fundamental paradigms that cannot be covered by these two? Both scientists and engineers are quite interested in what happens to structures, whether function or form, under eduction, further reasoning, by (for example) induction or deduction, while changes are taking place. Dealing with eduction is at the heart of our ability to maintain and reuse, by reasoning, previously resulting structures, whether function or form. In this reading we conjecture that eductive reasoning, calling for maintaining and reusing previous structures, can be more effective if we use the object-oriented paradigm.

To motivate the practice of solving problems with the object-oriented paradigm, let us consider a simple example. Suppose we are given this paragraph, which is a problem statement representing requirements of a software system that keeps an inventory or count of used parts removed from junked cars:

> Keep a working used-parts bin with the parts of a used car that have not yet been counted. Initially, get a used car from the junkyard and assign it to an empty, working used-parts bin; the count of the indecomposable parts (those which customers will later be interested in buying) is initially set to zero. As long as the working used-parts bin is not empty, repeatedly take a used part from the working used-parts bin and examine it. If the part consists of one indecomposable part, then increment the part counter and throw the part in a final-supply bin. If the part is not one indecomposable part but instead consists of several parts, split the part into its subparts and put them back into the working used-parts bin. Once the working used-parts bin is empty and the final-supply bin is filled with parts from the used car, display the count of the indecomposable parts.

To arrive at an object-oriented solution structure that is derived from this problem statement, we may carry out this strategy:

- identify objects or classes that are of interest.
- identify and associate attributes with objects or classes.
- identify and associate routines with objects or classes.
- identify structure relationships between objects or classes.
- present a specification for system solution.

One way to identify objects is to associate them with nouns in the problem statement, and one way to identify attributes and routines associated with these objects is to associate them with adjectives and verbs. Let us highlight noun parts with *italics* and verb parts with <u>underscoring</u>. For the problem statement above, we get this paragraph:

Keep a working used-parts bin with the parts from a used car that have not yet been counted. Initially, get a used car from the junkyard and assign it to an empty, working used-parts bin; the count of the indecomposable parts (those which customers will later be interested in buying) is initially set to zero. As long as the working used-parts bin is <u>not empty</u>, repeatedly <u>take</u> a *used part* from the working *used-parts bin* and <u>examine</u> *it*. If the *part* consists of <u>one indecomposable</u> *part*, then <u>increment</u> the *part counter* and <u>throw</u> the *part* into a *final-supply bin*. If the *part* is not one <u>indecomposable</u> *part* but instead consists of several *parts*, <u>split</u> the *part* into *sub-parts*, and <u>put</u> *them* back into the working <u>used-parts bin</u>. Once the working *used-parts bin* is <u>empty</u> and the *final-supply bin* is <u>filled</u> with the *parts* from the *used car*, display the *count* of the <u>indecomposable</u> *parts*.

The next step — and this requires some thought — is to select good nouns from those highlighted in *italic* type. We would probably identify these as *used-parts bin*, *supply bin*, *used car*, *part*, and *count*. Other nouns are either redundant or not considered good. As you can see, natural-language analysis comes into play here.

The next step is to identify relationships among the selected nouns. This is another task requiring thought, and some of these relationships may not necessarily be explicitly stated in problem-statement words, but may instead be inferred. Let us identify words in the problem statement that identify relationships explicitly.

Keep a working used-parts bin with the parts from a used car that have not yet been counted. Initially, get a used car from the junkyard and assign it to an empty, working used-parts bin; the count of the indecomposable parts (those which customers will later be interested in buying) is initially set to zero. As long as the working used-parts bin is not empty, repeatedly take a used part from the working used-parts bin and examine it. If the part consists of one indecomposable part, then increment the part counter and throw the part into a final-supply bin. If the part is not one indecomposable part but instead <u>comprises</u> several parts, split the part into its subparts and put them back into the working used-parts bin. Once the working used-parts bin is empty and the final-supply bin is filled with the parts from the used car, display the count of the indecomposable parts.

Various other relationships can be inferred among objects :

used-parts bin is a bin, *supply bin* is a bin, *count* is associated with indecomposable part, *used car* is a part, *used-parts bin* comprises parts, *supply bin* comprises indecomposable parts, and *indecomposable part* is a part.

Notice that in the problem-statement text *consists of* is not good English because an indecomposable part *is* a part. Moreover, a subpart is a part. Hence the structure of our solution to this problem comprises these seven object relationships:

used-parts bin is a bin, *supply bin* is a bin, *used-parts bin* comprises parts, *used car* is a part, *supply bin* comprises indecomposable parts, *count* is associated with indecomposable parts.

To make the solution structure into a complete system one must add at least two object relationships. To do so we add a final root object associated with the concept *program*. Let us name this object *parts-counting program*. These are the two additional object relationships:

> parts-counting program uses used-parts bin, and
> parts-counting program uses supply bin.

Finally, these nine relations and eight objects are a solution in object-oriented form to our stated problem.

Notice that much of this solution can be reused in deriving other used-parts programs, and this solution can evolve or be extended, eductively, into parts-counting programs having other features.

If we were to implement our solution using common object-oriented languages such as C++, Eiffel, or Smalltalk, the entities we have been calling *objects* would be called *classes*, where a class conveys the concept *module* in object-oriented programming. In programming theory these classes would be called *abstract data types*. When we implement our parts-counting program in an object-oriented language, an important, nontrivial task is to decide how the object relations will be implemented. For the example above *is-a* relationships probably would be implemented with *inheritance*. With Eiffel, *comprising* probably would be implemented with the client-server Eiffel relationship between classes. A similar implementation is available in C++.

The example above informally illustrates a kind of methodology for object-oriented analysis and for designing systems. In Chapter 2, we look into alternative methodologies for analysis and design and compare object-oriented analysis with conventional methodologies for analysis and design.

Expanding the terminology: Adding to our glossary

Over the past several years, numerous models and much terminology have been introduced to describe object-oriented approaches to development. Discussion has usually been focused on components of the targeted software, including basic objects, concepts, ideas, links or relationships, trials or tests of relationships, and applications. Informal discussions, models, and terminology reported in recent articles make it seem necessary to propose standard terminology for discussing object-oriented development. Let us therefore expand our brief glossary of object-oriented language with words that represent ideas necessary in developing object-oriented software systems and applications.

Object	entity, instance of a defined set of services.
Class	definition of a set of services, set of instances, set of ordered pairs of entities or instances.
Relationship	a defined association between one or more classes, including but not limited to an *inheritance* relationship, a *client-server* relationship, a *defined request for services*, an *is-a* relationship, an *is-part-of* relationship, and an *implies* relationship.

Link	a defined association between one or more objects, including but not limited to a *controls* link, a *responds to* link, an *influences* link, an *associates with* link, a *depends upon* link, and a *supplies to* link.
Class	(revised definition): a set of ordered pairs of entities or instances, each of which is a link, and denoted (O, R), R a subset of the Cartesian product $O \times O$.
Kinds of classes	R is reflexive, R is symmetric, R is transitive, R is reflexive and symmetric (cover), R is symmetric and transitive (islands), R is reflexive, symmetric, and transitive (equivalence).
Specialization	a defined relationship between a class and an object (usually not containing that object), the object is the specialist in the class of which it is a member.
Delegation	defined relationship between an object and a class (usually not containing that object); the object is the delegate of the class of which it is a member.
System	an integrated collection of objects and classes connected by relationships, links, specializations, and delegations.
Law	a set of policies, rules, or constraints determining which objects or classes (in a universe of discourse) may be related, linked, delegated, or specialized.
Assembly	the activity or proposed plan or methodology by which objects or classes are integrated into a system, A.
Laws-governed assembly	an assembly that is defined according to a set of laws, L, A/L.
Protection-governed assembly	a computational (usually computer-language) implementation, I, of a laws-governed assembly, $I(A/L)$.
Enforced assembly	a protection-governed assembly that is implemented from a laws-governed assembly so that some relationships in the implementation correspond to laws, the correspondence being denoted by E.
Sound assembly	an enforced assembly such that every relationship of L that is not to be enforced, is prevented, in the implementation, $I(A/L)$; conversely, every relationship derivable in $I(A/L)$ corresponds to, by E, a truly allowable member of L.
Complete assembly	an enforced assembly such that every relationship of L, truly allowable, corresponds, by E, to an enforced relationship in $I(A/L)$.
Theory	these notions of soundness and completeness come from logic, which states that a theory is sound if everything that is provable is true, and a theory is complete if everything that is true is provable.

Test	an activity for determining whether or not an assembly is laws-governed, enforced, sound, or complete.
Test plan	a strategy for carrying out a test.
Requirements specification	includes a set of laws, *L*.
Metric	a measure associated with a requirement and instantiated to one or more tests.
Assembly quality control	an activity to determine by testing if an important percentage of an assembly is sound or complete.
Consistent assembly	an activity whereby a laws-governed assembly is produced so that the services used are not conflicting.
Coordinated assembly	an activity whereby a laws-governed assembly is produced so that services may be carried out concurrently and sequentially.
Abstract data type	specifying the syntax, usage, and semantics of a class, i.e., a set of services.
Abstract system	specifying an assembly of abstract data types that is axiomatically sound, complete, consistent, and coordinated.

Real-time systems and language applications

Temporally or dynamically, two very different kinds of objects are named *passive* and *active*. Let us illustrate the difference between them with a few examples. Consider the sentence, "The boy threw the ball and then the girl caught the ball." By grammatical rules the sentence has three common nouns: "boy," "girl," and "ball." Moreover, by grammatical rules two of these common nouns, "boy" and "girl," are subject nouns because they use the verbs "threw" and "caught." On the other hand the common noun "ball" is an object noun because it is used in "threw" and "caught." "Threw" is associated with an action that "boy" performs, and "caught" is associated with an action that "girl" performs. By example, this sentence illustrates that "boy" and "girl" are classes of objects that are *active*, and "ball" is a class of objects that are *passive*. Hence you can see how easy it is in simple sentences to pick out the classes of active and passive objects. Notice also that the two classes of active objects, "boy" and "girl," share a passive class of objects "ball" as a resource. So far we have ignored the important temporal word "then," which illustrates a controlled ordering of the active object classes. "Then" defines in which order the events "threw" and "caught" of active classes of objects must appear, first "threw," then "catch." Indeed, we can analyze this sentence at three levels of abstraction. The first and most abstract is the *functional level*. At this level the function is playing catch. That activity is described is the *function* of playing catch.

The next level down, or second level of abstraction, is the *activity level*. At this level the active classes of objects are identified; here the *active* classes of objects are "boy" and "girl" associated with the *activities* "threw" and "caught."

The third level of abstraction is the *process (task) level*. At this level the temporal ordering of the events associated with the active-objects classes is identified. With each class of active objects one or more *processes* or *tasks* are associated, representing threads of activity that must take into account orders by which passive classes of objects are used or shared. In our example the temporal word "then" defines how we order the two *processes* "threw" and "caught," which are associated with use of the resource "ball" by the classes of active objects "boy" and "girl." This third level, or process or task level, takes into account that verbs associated with active classes of objects are *concurrent*. This example helps illustrate how we can extract the three kinds of *requirements* — functional, activity, and process — from a *problem statement*. Here the simple problem is how to play catch. The example can be repeated with the proper nouns "John" and "Mary," which are *instances of classes* of active objects "boy" and "girl." The class of passive objects "ball" can also be replaced by a proper noun, "the white baseball of John's," represented by an instance of the class of passive objects "ball."

We pursue this temporal perspective of object-oriented applications in more detail in Chapter 7, looking at further real-time systems examples and concepts developed by an object-oriented approach, as well as how to implement them in object-oriented, real-time programming languages.

Computing and science: Past, present, and future

Object-oriented programming has been around for some time. Its history comprises object-oriented structures as they have appeared in science and in early object-oriented thought related to computing. Object-oriented systems development in science and engineering is briefly outlined in Table 1.

The principles underlying object-oriented systems development build on the informational entities called *objects*, which are identified, along with their informational and functional features, and grouped into identifiable classes. These classes, in turn, are integrated into a system of the world in which the objects live. This classification scheme goes back hundreds of years; such classification schemes appeared early in modern science and engineering.

In the 1960s, leading thinkers in experimental programming, especially in artificial intelligence, introduced the class–system idea into the representation of knowledge. Soon computer languages such as Simula picked up the idea and it was clear that computer systems could be built around it and that a more visually oriented user interface could be added. Early in the 1970s, personal computers were designed to support environments for object-oriented problem solving, and computer environments such as Smalltalk were introduced.

Department of Defense interest in significantly improving Ada-oriented software-development methodologies led to a marriage of necessity between the AI community's little-known use of these object-oriented thoughts and the more widely publicized Ada/software engineering. Object-oriented techniques experienced a quantum leap in interest following this union.

Table 1: Systems development in science and computing — a historical outline (including suggestions for further reading).

I. Object-oriented structures in science. The story begins with theories and applications of classifications and knowledge-representation strategies, as discussed in

> Newman, J., "The Growth of Mathematical Science in Ancient Times," *The World of Mathematics*, Vol. 1, Ch. 1; "Classification of Men According to Their Natural Gifts," Vol. II, part VI, Ch. 2; "The General and Logical Theory of Automata," Vol. IV, part XIX, Ch. 1; Simon and Schuster, New York, 1956.
>
> Wegner, P., "The Object-Oriented Classification Paradigm," in *Research Directions in Object-Oriented Programming*, B. Shriver and P. Wegner, eds., MIT Press, Cambridge, 1987.

II. Early object-oriented thought in computing: the 1960s and 1970s

   A. Programming environments: Simula, Smalltalk
   B. Artificial intelligence: concept formulations
   C. Software systems design: modularity, abstraction

> Birman, K., et al., "Implementing Fault-Tolerant Distributed Objects," *IEEE Trans. Software Eng.*, June 1985.
>
> Cox, B., "Message/Object Programming: An Evolutionary Change in Programming Technology," *IEEE Software*, Jan. 1984.
>
> Mudge, T., "Object-Based Computing and the Ada Language," *Computer*, Mar. 1985.
>
> Ungar, D., and D. Patterson, "What Price Smalltalk?" *Computer*, Jan. 1987.

III. Recent developments in object-oriented analysis and design

   A. Design methods: software-engineering methods
   B. Programming environments: user interfaces, object-management systems, dynamically typed languages, statically typed languages, distributed systems
   C. Domain modeling: domain analysis, modeling
   D. System-development metrics: cost models, reliability models
   E. Management approaches: contractual representations

> Albert, S., et al., "Object-Oriented Programming in AI," *IEEE Expert*, Dec. 1990.
>
> Almes, G., and C. Holman, "Edmas: An Object-Oriented, Locally Distributed Mail System," *IEEE Trans. Software Eng.*, Sept. 1987.
>
> Booch, G., "Object-Oriented Development," *IEEE Trans. Software Eng.*, Feb. 1986.
>
> Chidamber, S., and C. Kemerer, "A Metrics Suite for Object-Oriented Design," *IEEE Trans. Software Eng.*, June 1994.
>
> Coleman, D., J. Dyck, and S. Bear, "Introducing Objectcharts or How to Use Statecharts in Object-Oriented Design," *IEEE Trans. Software Eng.*, Jan. 1992.
>
> Jones, C., "Gaps in the Object-Oriented Paradigm," *Computer*, June 1994.
>
> Lieberherr, K., and C. Xiao, "Object-Oriented Software Evolution," *IEEE Trans. Software Eng.*, Apr. 1993.
>
> Meyer, B., "The Case for Object-Oriented Design," *IEEE Software*, Mar. 1987.
>
> Mohan, L., and R. Kashyap, "An Object-Oriented Knowledge Representation for Spatial Information," *IEEE Trans. Software Eng.*, May 1988.
>
> Song, X., and L. Osterweil, "Experience with an Approach to Comparing Software Design Methodologies," *IEEE Trans. Software Eng.*, May 1994.
>
> Ward, P., "How to Integrate Object Orientation with Structured Analysis and Design," *IEEE Software*, Mar. 1989.
>
> Wiederhold, G., "Views, Objects, and Databases," *Computer*, Dec. 1986.
>
> Wilde, N., and R. Huitt, "Maintenance Support for Object-Oriented Programs," *IEEE Trans. Software Eng.*, Dec. 1992.
>
> Wyatte, B., K. Kavi, and S. Hufnagel, "Parallelism in Object-Oriented Languages: A Survey," *IEEE Software*, Nov. 1992.

IV. New disciplines using object-oriented thought

   A. Economics: property rights, agoric open systems
   B. Software business: management-constrained design
   C. Legal aspects: law-governed design, contractual design

> Miller, M., and E. Drexler, "Markets and Computation: Agoric Open Systems," *The Ecology of Computation*, 1988.

V. Progress made by object-oriented computing in performance and user friendliness

   A. Speed and memory considerations
   B. Tools

What lies ahead in reuse technology?

Object-oriented systems are a maturing technology that will continue to evolve in supporting human-software reuse, maintenance, openness, and quality. We list here some exciting new areas in which this technology will engage. Some of these issues (listed in [1]) deserve attention not just because they are new:

- scalability (success with large information systems)
- manageability (standards, library tools for users, methodologies, metrics, evolution)
- performance (memory management, processing management)

These issues also point toward new subjects to which object-oriented technology will be applied. In this book we promote these and other new applications.

Problems in applying the technology

Object-oriented technology has had successes in developing domain-specific reuse libraries and has been a catalyst in questioning how our cultures address the economic, marketing, and social aspects of software. In the information revolution we experience a problem undreamed of in the industrial revolution, reusing software systems, components, and knowledge in many applications. The problem has been attacked from many angles.

Reuse methodology, supported by object-oriented technologies, must build on paradigms beyond those applied in developing past software. We must identify and solve at least three types of problems: ways of dealing with reuse, technology that will support reuse, and techniques for handling institutional reactions to reusability.

A critical problem is failure to understand the conceptual framework necessary for reuse. One example is the object-oriented software components necessary to support reuse. Because the components must be adaptable to different applications, it is tempting to derive families of components by extensively applying, say, parameterization, specialization, and generalization. Another conceptual challenge is defining a method for understanding how the component behaves so that it can be properly reused.

A second problem is lack of technology that would support reuse. Technological problems include lack of 1) techniques for building and maintaining component libraries [2]; 2) tools for promoting reuse; and 3) methodologies supporting modification and use of reusable components, especially for maintaining software.

Hence, a technological problem is how to implement procedures for modifying and reusing components. To reuse components requires more than splicing them into the new application. The other part is modifying the component so that it can be spliced in. This aspect of reuse methodology is also dangerous. Any change may induce side-effects in the component or application and may harm the component's later evolution. The authors of Chapters 1 and 6 further address some of these problems.

Software difficulties further defined

Computer software has been successfully reused in recent years [3]. Such successes, however, do not point the way toward a unifying concept for treating reusable software components.

These inadequacies now make reusing and maintaining software a problem:

- stability
- traceability
- timely reachability
- modifying reuse components
- software reuse as capital

The effort to meet new or modified requirements provides the value added to the entire procedure of maintaining software. This component's relative cost heavily depends on *stability* in the application domain of the software. A domain that changes little will necessitate few alterations in the software to meet new or modified requirements. As the application domain's functions, objects, and relationships evolve, we must make corresponding changes in the software. In a relatively stable domain, such as mathematical subroutine libraries, changes in the domain's functions, objects, or relationships over many years may have been few. In this domain the cost for maintaining components should be minimal.

Another inadequacy in today's practice in reusing software is the ability to trace (traceability) adequately and define the impact of a proposed change in maintenance on the other components in the software-application system. We need a satisfactory impact analysis of such proposed changes — that is, how much time and effort such a change will require.

Yet another inadequacy in software reuse practice as it affects a system's maintainability is being able to reach (reachability) the software system quickly by human intervention to make the change. This inadequacy is directly related to a major problem we address in this section. We illustrate with two examples.

Consider the difficulty of maintaining software on unmanned flights in very deep space. If wear and tear degrade the spacecraft's hardware or the craft enters a new physical environment necessitating modifications, two problems arise: 1) the craft is too far away to allow timely human interaction (as by uplinking new changes), and 2) the software is not designed to rebuild itself.

Now for the second example. The usual procedure with modern computerized automotive systems is to bring the car to the shop for tuneup and maintenance. Two problems now appear: the service may be needed when the auto is distant from a service facility, and the owner faces inconvenience and cost in bringing the car to the shop. Of course the second example has another economic cost: if automotive computer systems can be made somewhat self-maintaining, then maintenance shops as we know them could be out of business. New kinds of services supplying software maintenance might be introduced, however; it's all part of an unregulated free-enterprise system.

Software reuse components generally are not completely stable and eventually need to evolve or be modified. To provide for modifiability in reuse software that is not reachable, I propose that we introduce a retrainable software component [4] or system as a software component — a system that is reusable and has built-in capability, knowledge, or intelligence that will allow it to reconfigure itself to meet new requirements. That is, it has some capacity for self-maintenance, in the sense of perfective software maintenance. In principle, these new requirements may come from a regulated or restricted (bounded) domain of allowable activities, or it may not be regulated or restricted. We've been entertained by problems with unrestricted activities in such stories as HAL's unpredicted behavior in the classic movie *2001: A Space Odyssey*. And the newest world-class chess programs may reach the point of human unpredictability. The Deep Thought generations of computer chess programs may give us a positive experience by mastering any human world-champion chess player. The human player may no longer be able to see the plan such a powerful program follows because for many challenges the program self-adapts. It would create appalling problems, though, to install that kind of unplanned and unpredictable power in an automobile, airplane, or military system. The outcome would no longer be positive but potentially disastrous.

Future software requirements and specifications for any component or system, though different from those we know, should be flexible but restricted by regulations. Software should be able to discern and react to new situations in its environment, but its reactions should be planned in some way. More formally, we would like the specified domain of possible activities to be logically sound: the software must always perform under restrictions, adhering to specified, though possibly evolving, policies.

Now that we have reusable components, we add another order of capital goods to the software capital structure. Software components are working capital for programmers [5] to apply in constructing software tools. When they have such components on the shelf, they need not build those inputs from scratch; they can take advantage of work done by specialists who have built the inputs for them. In a reuse environment the capital goods available to programmers steadily improve in range and quality. As software systems take form, and reusable components derived from them are made generally available, the software capital structure is added to directly. When an organization or market shares these components, programmers stand on each other's shoulders.

Object-oriented technology supports reusing knowledge and intelligence, evolving tools and systems, reusing components by applying principles of modularity, and replenishing an infrastructure of capital goods by supplying software. Moreover, with object-oriented programming, programmers independently rediscover the virtues of property rights. These rights combine software by contract [6], [7] (see Chapter 2 of this book) with incentives for developing reusable software components.

Software engineering versus knowledge engineering

During its frenetic evolution, computer technology has branched into the computer-science and engineering disciplines. Among these are software engineering and knowledge engineering, respectively built on experience and intelligence. The software engineer and knowledge engineer may have been used to talking about completely different things, but lately their subjects have begun to sound similar, such as software maintenance [8]. At this stage, many feel it is beneficial to stress the interplay between the two, for both software engineering and knowledge engineering work at developing and maintaining software.

Software engineering is the technology developing high-quality software products within budget and on time. It has been through at least two revolutions, including structured programming in the 1970s [9] and object-oriented programming in the 1980s [7]. Its issues usually deal with the life-cycle model, which, simply described, consists of only two parts, development and maintenance.

Object-oriented design has frequently been applied in both software engineering and knowledge engineering, but the latter is younger. The expression "knowledge engineering" was coined in the mid-1970s (about ten years after "software engineering"), specifically referring to inserting an expert's (nonalgorithmic, empirical) knowledge, including experience and intelligence, into an expert system [10]. Among issues often discussed are acquisition and representation of knowledge. An expert system, which uses engineered knowledge, can be implemented in many ways, using conventional or unconventional paradigms. An expert system implemented in a conventional paradigm differs little from a conventional system, because everything is coded or represented procedurally, although knowledge may be acquired in a different way.

RBP: Another way of thinking

The rule-based paradigm (RBP) or way of thinking applies to production-system architecture. Unlike the object-oriented paradigm, it was first used in knowledge engineering. A system implemented in RBP is a rule-based system (RBS), and it typically consists of a database, a rule base, and a generic-inference engine. The database comprises a collection of data, reflecting the status of the application domain. The rule base comprises a set of rules, which is the knowledge (experience, intelligence) extracted from a domain expert and coded declaratively. The domain-independent inference engine controls the entire system by deciding which rule to apply under a specific circumstance.

Perhaps one of the best-known advantages of the RBP is that it does not distinguish between development and maintenance. Whether you are developer or maintainer, all you need do is add, delete, or modify rules. Unfortunately, reality has failed to justify this advantage. Experience shows that maintaining an RBS is just as difficult as, if not more difficult than, maintaining many conventional systems. Davis [11] described a clear limitation of the RBS as one who is expert at being a knowledge czar, a statement with two implications. First, one RBS, more specifically one rule base, should incorporate, by nature, one expert's expertise to avoid any possible conflict or inconsistency caused by different types of expertise provided by multiple experts. Second, RBS performance is determined mainly by the quantity and quality of knowledge the expert provides. Practically, rather than saying that one expert is crucial, this limitation implies that only one knowledge engineer should be responsible for constructing and maintaining a rule base. From the software-engineering point of view this limitation is fatal, because in reality the developer usually is not the maintainer, and often more than one person will be involved in the life cycle of an RBS.

Very few design issues come up in developing an RBS. Moreover, the RBP has simply failed to provide mechanisms vital for securing successful evolution for an RBS over a reasonable period. Meta-rules were introduced as an additional control to compensate for this inadequacy, but its drawbacks include system transparency, which makes the system hard to test and maintain.

Many researchers quickly spotted limitations in expert-system technology, especially the RBP. Facing such an unpleasant conclusion, a cynic might believe that nothing could be done with these complex problems that the RBP has been attempting to solve. To resolve the problem, two directions seem possible: extend software engineering to address the RBP's problems, or abandon the RBP completely.

Programming with the object-oriented paradigm

Unlike the RBP, the object-oriented paradigm (OOP) is a general-purpose programming method good for many applications. By definition, the system seems as revolutionary as the RBP, though perhaps evolutionary would be the more appropriate description. As a programming paradigm the OOP is perhaps more procedural than declarative, because one of the major issues in OOP is sharing and reusing attributes and data-manipulating routines among objects by inheritance, and these routines are often implemented in the same way as conventional programming. Inheritance is a relationship between objects or classes of objects allowing an object or a class to share or reuse resources previously developed for another object or class. Just as structured programming was two decades ago, OOP is inclusive.

Object-oriented programming is a newer way of programming than the traditional structured technique. Structured programming has been associated exclusively with functional design methods such as functional-decomposition design, data-flow design, and data-structure design. In OOP, objects are first categorized in classes and organized hierarchically according to the dependency and similarity [12], [13], [14], [15]. Often, objects are categorized in classes in three stages or tiers: classification by functionality and architectural aesthetics, further classification by features, and still further classification by objects. The consequent classes of objects have greater functional and feature cohesion. Each class definition comprises attributes reflecting the object's generally static properties and routines (methods in Smalltalk) that manipulate these attributes to achieve dynamics. Then relationships between classes, such as inheritance, are designed, often from the natural domain-dependent relations between classes found during domain analysis.

Although we have advocated, by experience and observation, that the OOP may be the best programming paradigm available for implementing some types of systems, such as expert systems, including experience-based systems, we do not suggest that OOP is a panacea solving all our problems in software maintenance, reuse, reliability, and quality. In fact, software engineering still has no silver bullet [16], even with appropriate marketing and economic incentives such as reuse incentives. According to Cox [17], however, a silver bullet may be had if one is willing to treat reusable software much as one does other utilities (for example, water, electricity, phones) — with meters.

Fast evolution is observed in many applications in the real world today, and it is a growing challenge for many software systems because of adaptability or, more broadly, maintainability. Software maintenance too is growing into a dominant issue in knowledge engineering. Many RBP problems are fatal, and appropriate real-world applications for this paradigm probably are very few. On the other hand, OOP is perhaps the best programming paradigm available for implementing some types of systems, such as expert systems, including experience-based systems, because OOP conforms to conventional wisdom. Therefore, we see that expanded, intelligent management-information systems need development and maintenance to adapt to rapid and significant changes in the application [18], [19]. Because adaptation and maintenance have been major stumbling blocks for enterprises with which we work, we propose to use OOP, not alternatives such as RBP.

Languages and performance

As object-oriented programming languages like C++, Smalltalk, and Eiffel win acceptance, OOP is coming into the mainstream of computing. Moreover, object-based languages such as Ada are moving into new object-oriented languages such as Ada9X. One major consideration in deciding whether or not to commit to OOP and such languages as C++, Smalltalk, Eiffel, or Ada9X is how programs written in these languages perform compared to computationally equivalent programs written in earlier languages such as C, Pascal, or FORTRAN. Bjarne Stroustrop, who created C++, said he wanted something that ran like greased lightning and allowed easy interfacing with the rest of the world [20].

One observation from looking at object-oriented programs in general and C++ in particular [21] is that the object-oriented programming discipline tends to create many objects, each with several relatively small member functions. If most procedures are small compared to non–object-oriented programs, it seems that object-oriented programs will cross substantially more procedure boundaries in getting the same task accomplished. This factor may increase the importance of procedure-call overhead in C++ programs. But C++ has introduced the inline feature to reduce this overhead, and good future C++ optimizing compilers will do such inlining as a standard feature. For those interested in doing their own benchmarking for C++ programs, a C++ version of the Dhrystone Benchmarks is available [22]. A main reason that some versions of C++ do not yet execute as fast as computationally equivalent C is that the algorithms available in some commercial C++ class libraries are not yet as mature as comparable algorithms written for C libraries. These C++ class library algorithms can be reprogrammed to run as fast as or faster than C algorithms, and sometimes that has been done. With many newer C++ class libraries, performance has been primary, and their algorithms have been made to run as fast as or faster than comparable C algorithms.

How do we categorize object-oriented computer languages? We can choose, first, *binding time*, which connects types or classes to program identifiers. The two binding categories are: 1) static-typed object-oriented languages; and 2) dynamic-typed languages. In the first category binding is fixed between types or classes and program identifiers when the source code is written, and at compile time. In the second category, binding between classes and identifiers is not known until the program is executing. C++ and Eiffel are in the first category, and Smalltalk is in the second. Both categories can have advantages and disadvantages. In object-oriented languages, polymorphism can be harmful in category 2 programs [23]. Polymorphism, though a powerful and flexible mechanism for programming, like many other structure mechanisms, presents opportunities for abuse. The problem with polymorphism in category 2 languages such as Smalltalk is similar to that of unrestricted gotos with variable destinations. Both problems can be addressed by disciplined programming, such as using type assertions to inform readers about the range of possible date types.

In Chapter 3, we address recent language enhancements that dramatically improve performance for Smalltalk-like languages. Optimizing compilers have also been prepared for Eiffel (see Chapters 2 and 6) to compete in speed with C and C++ languages. Eiffel generates C, and this code can be optimized with C optimizers. The performance forecast is not yet in on Ada9X, but we conjecture that its performance too will be addressed. In summary, object-oriented programs can be made to execute as fast as non–object-oriented programs.

Maintaining the software

During the past decade it has been conjectured that principles associated with process and products used in developing object-oriented software systems significantly influence later maintenance of software products. At least in the details, common sense about designing software generally supports such a conjecture. Suppose that during a program's design phase I am to decide whether to use a function-oriented design method. How will I reason so that I will make an appropriate choice? One thing I will probably do is look at requirements for the program and project later patterns of maintenance that will be required for both data and function. If in time requirements for data change much more frequently than requirements for function, I may well decide on a function-oriented method for design, speculating that with such structure it will be easier to modify some data requirements. Conversely, if I find every time that function requirements change more often than data requirements, I may choose an object-oriented method of design because that structure will make it easier to modify some function requirements. In many data-processing applications such as accounting and mailing, function requirements do change more often than data requirements. On the other hand, users are prone to assess their needs according to what they feel their application is supposed to *do* rather than what the application is supposed to *do it to*. Hence the paradigm shift to object-oriented thought is new to many potential users.

Traditionally, software maintenance is of three types [24]: perfective maintenance, adaptive maintenance, and corrective maintenance; a fourth is preventive maintenance. A survey by Lientz and Swanson [25] reports that 65 percent of software maintenance is perfective. Ideally, perfective-maintenance changes should add functionality to the software system without compromising its original functionality. Furthermore, such system changes at either the user's view (abstract level) or at the systems view (representation level) should be made without compromising its original functionality. Because at least half the effort may be devoted to maintaining a system, we need to better understand software maintenance, and especially perfective maintenance.

Perfective maintenance: From specification to application

Perfective maintenance traditionally covers changes demanded by users at the applications end or by systems support at the representation end. These changes may come as stated new requirements and are dealt with during change-control procedures. The effect of such changes may appear at either the specification level or the algorithmic level. These traditional views of perfective maintenance can also include an entire set of software requirements that are initially specified but not all initially implemented. Implementing additional specified requirements may be left to a later need for these requirements that is invoked by intelligence or evolutionary programming technologies (for example, genetic algorithms) built into the initial software system and triggered by events in the changing environments in which the system is running. Of course such newly evolved implementation features must always remain within the scope of the initially defined specifications so that their operation remains sound. This is the framework within which we think about perfective software maintenance.

Does object-orientedness promote reusable software?

During the decade just past some suggested that principles applied to the process and products of object-oriented software systems development significantly influence later reuse of software product entities such as code components, modules, and templates. Many of these ideas remain conjectural for now because they lack empirical, statistically oriented evidence. On the other hand, recent studies [26] give some evidence that using specific software-quality metrics in designing objects influences their later patterns of reuse.

Planning and supporting economical reuse

The elementary notion of reusing software has been around for a long time, beginning, for instance, with the early subroutine, which in turn led to the software module, as well as numerous ideas about subroutine libraries and using modules in developing modern languages. A reuse methodology will not succeed, though, if it is merely based upon notions supporting past paradigms for developing software. Problems need to be identified and solutions proposed in at least three areas: concepts for dealing with reuse, technology to support reuse, and reaction by institutions to reusability. Here, we deal with some of the factors in the first two only.

As we have seen, a critical problem is failure to understand the conceptual framework necessary for reuse. One example is the object-oriented computer software component, such as classes and templates, necessary to support reuse. Because these components must be adaptable to fit different applications, it is tempting to derive families of components by extensive use of such techniques as parameterization. Another conceptual challenge is defining a method for understanding how the component behaves so that it can be reused.

Finally, a most important influence on the cost of developing software is the number of instructions. Ways of reducing instructions include constructing simpler products and reusing components [27]. If done correctly, the cost of software would drop precipitately as developers included in their bids software-reuse paradigms and many nonproprietary software components [28].

We have therefore generally reviewed some of these factors affecting reuse of software:

- economics
- technical features
- management, method, and metric features
- characteristics of reuse

To further help us analyze the possibilities in generating technology with which we can efficiently prepare and apply reusable software, we have devised taxonomies, one of which appears in Table 2.

Traditional examples of modules are C++, Smalltalk, and Eiffel classes. Examples of templates are C++ templates, Eiffel generic classes, SNAP templates (SNAP is a product of Template Software, Inc., Herdon, Virginia; SNAP templates are reusable software architectures that afford high productivity gains), and OLEs from Microsoft, Digital Equipment, and Sun [29].

Some current examples of software development indicate that gains in productivity may be higher when one starts with templates instead of object classes. New studies in domain engineering and experience, however, point out that both templates and object classes are necessary parts of the domain model. Stability is crucial in developing software templates and architectures because later changes with templates or architectures at higher levels can strongly affect many parts of the software product.

New metrics for developing applications

Pfleeger and Fonash have made significant contributions in measurements for development of reusable software.

Table 2. A taxonomy to help guide reuse technology.

I.   Programs
II. Building blocks
    A. Components
        1. Code segments and modules
        2. Packages
    B. Composition
        1. Object-oriented
        2. Architectures
III. Patterns
    A. Designs
        1. Templates
        2. Transformers
        3. Architectures
    B. Generators
        1. Application
        2. Language-based
IV. Data
    A. Interchange
    B. Abstract types

Making software pay: The Pfleeger COSTTOOL

Pfleeger [30] has devised a statistically verified cost-and-effort tool called COSTTOOL for estimating the effort it takes to create object-oriented software. Pfleeger evaluated his model by comparing it to the more conventional, non–object-oriented COCOMO and AdaCOCOMO estimators of effort. The statistical results indicated that COSTTOOL performed more accurately than COCOMO and AdaCOCOMO working with objects instead of lines of source code. Next tackling reusable computer-software components, Pfleeger [30] showed how a payoff point can be identified in preparing a code component for reusable computer software. An elementary equation helps determine how often the component needs to be used to pay the cost invested in reuse production. This payoff arrives when the savings from reuse can cover the extra cost of engineering the component so that it can be reused. The equation accounts for both the producer's cost for developing the reusable component and the consumer's cost for integrating it.

Measuring successful code reuse: The Fonash criterion

Fonash [26] has prepared a statistically verified criterion for developing code components for reusable object-oriented software. The criterion also covers other metrics proposed in current literature. These are the general categories of reusable code components assembled by an object-oriented method: reused without modification, reused after modification, and developed as new components. The general categories for metrics of code component reuse include quality, complexity, general purpose, coupling, and cohesion, and it is shown that Fonash's metric categories cover other proposed categories that were not yet statistically verified. This work also suggests that successful reuse usually is associated with highly domain-specific efforts having an extensive base of support from organizations and consumers.

Modeling domains: Limiting the system

Principles devised for object-oriented systems deeply influence domain modeling. A vital step in successfully dealing with software-requirements specifications (SRS) in constructing domain-specific software is to create a domain model. Here is one definition for that model. In mathematics a domain model is, functionally, a set or representation of objects to which a mathematical variable or logical variable is limited. Dynamically this set may be considered a sphere of influence or activity of such functionality. Similarly, from a systems point of view, a domain model represents a set of systems whose influence or activity is limited. Either way, the domain model should enable us to purposefully select, parametrically, a member or subcollection of such systems. In applications software a domain model supports development of SRSs for a specific application system or systems when using either a traditional approach to writing SRSs or an automated, interactive, acquisition approach between user and development system. Either way, a domain model represents important knowledge and features of the application area in question, such as missile software systems.

In this paper we treat a domain model as an automated, classification-oriented representation and a system as a purposeful and possibly active set of structural relationships founded on this classification. The domain model should be used in such a way that communicative cohesion will be very close between SRSs and specification design of a system after the initial phase in a software life cycle (as in the transformational paradigm).

Let us say you're preparing a software-domain model for the application or domain consisting of missile software dealing with such problems as the missile's guidance, trajectory, and signal communications. Experts and specialists in representing knowledge have prepared a taxonomy of knowledge and experience about such a domain. Ultimately you seek information so classified that this representation of knowledge would rely on fundamental, standardized, stable, indecomposable building blocks (assuming that here we would use building blocks instead of patterns) that we would call *domain primitives*. In our example these domain primitives at the SRS level would correspond to such primitive functional requirements as computed sine, cosine, and tangent. These and others are the primitives used in solving problems dealing with guidance, trajectory, and signaling. Domain primitives here obviously have the characteristics that users desire — stability and standardization.

At the representation or environments level, however, those ways of implementing and automatically computing these domain primitives would vary: they would not remain stable or standardized but would depend on the characteristics of hardware processors, operating systems, and run-time environments. We must therefore distinguish between domain primitives and *environment primitives,* or as Harandi and Lubars [31] do, between domain-oriented SRSs and implementation-oriented details of the target software system. In our example, environment primitives would include the target system's arithmetic processors, registers, and precision characteristics.

Prior to mapping the domain-oriented SRSs into an implementation-oriented target representation that is executable by a software system, we consider in this paper one additional step after mapping SRSs to the specified design: mapping design to a formal specification. The formally specified representation will allow software engineering to examine mathematically, analytically, or logically important properties of both the domain model and the software-solution model or the target-system model. Once we have examined the formal specification and selected precise parameters, coefficients, and assertions, we follow with mapping to computer-processable form. The next question is whether or not formal specifications should be executable [7]. Another issue is whether or not we should use a formal specification or a related prototype in developing the target system.

Figure 1 summarizes our procedure in constructing software with the transformational paradigm [32], [33], including elicitation of requirements, SRSs, specifications for design, and formal specification. In this paradigm each of these steps interacts with part of the software-domain model. An additional step is generating and executing the prototype from the formal specification to acquire from the user's end additional requirements that are not yet part of the software-domain model or its system members. As we will see, formal specification and design of the target system is refined by finding correct sets of coefficients associated with domain primitives. Related prototyping can help identify the actual values of these coefficients and domain primitives. If in the latter step important requirements are found that are not part of the software-domain model, then we must invoke the management step for the software-domain model to update that model, which becomes an evolutionary model. Once we recognize no further requirements, software construction proceeds to the optimization-design step. Even now, however, some optimization can proceed at the formal-specification level. We next discuss how this paradigm applies to software-domain model, domain primitives, formal specification, and prototyping.

In other engineering disciplines, creating a mathematical model and mathematical methods helps one understand structure and processes. We propose that mathematical methods and models can also give us insight and understanding if we apply them to software-domain modeling and engineering. Little work has been done on mathematical models and methods required for software. A fundamental problem is coping with changes demanded by users at the applications end or by systems support at the representation end.

These changes may come as stated new requirements and are dealt with during change-control procedures. Such changes may be felt at either the specification level (SRS) or the algorithmic level. The notion of describing or constructing an application or function from a *basis* is old and important in mathematics, physics, and engineering. Fourier analysis, linear algebra, and functional analysis in applied mathematics have used the notion to describe a class or set of applications or functions. Physics and engineering have used the notion extensively to characterize, analyze, and synthesize wave forms.

The transformation paradigm of the software life cycle includes: requirements, software requirements specifications, specification design, formal specification, prototype generation, prototype, optimization design, and completed product.

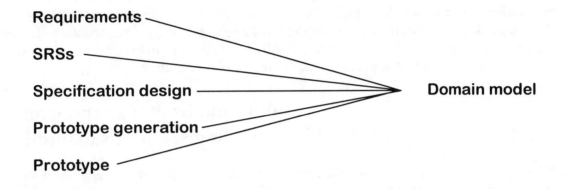

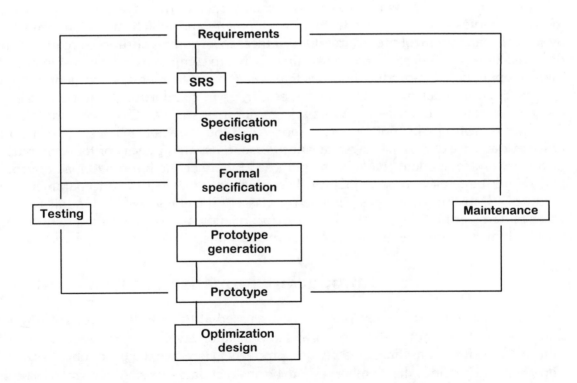

Figure 1. Software life cycle: Transformational paradigm.

The basis idea, however, has not so obviously been included within the formal software-engineering framework. Here we show how this approach can also be a powerful formal framework in domain modeling for software engineering.

Therefore, we illustrate how the formalism known as a basis, common to many applied-mathematics and engineering applications, can be applied to software engineering, using an object-oriented approach. This formalism will erect a relationship between domain primitives and basis elements. We propose this formalism as a mathematical model for software-domain modeling activities. Theorems and properties about the model are presented as guides to software-domain modeling. The model and formal software-domain modeling techniques have been applied to a software system in management information systems to demonstrate this approach to domain-modeling requirements [34].

Baseline and basis: Components or specifications to build on

A *basis* in a universe of discourse or a problem domain is a linearly independent subset that generates (spans) the whole domain (space).

The basis is an abstraction of the software-engineering *baseline*, which is founded on the important idea of reusable, stable, standardized software components. The baseline is also [35] a specification which has been formally reviewed and agreed upon, which thereafter serves as the basis for further development, and which can be changed only by formal change-control procedures. One of these incorporates additional requirements that arise during software-domain modeling. Software companies have invested heavily in developing baseline-product libraries that will support further development of applications. Such libraries are often domain-specific, as in standardized science and engineering subroutine libraries or Ada package libraries such as Common Ada Missile Packages (CAMP) [36]. Another is Common APSE Interface Set [37], a standardized library or database of Ada packages meant for use in developing sets of tools. Standardized software components have been composed by either the building-block approach [24] or the patterns approach [32]. Such components may be generic parameterized modules [7], abstract data types [7], deferred classes [7] metaviews [38], modules [39], or other patterns or building blocks. Here a direct relationship is established between the idea of domain primitives and that of basis and baseline.

Introductory formalism: Basis for software

The domain-primitives concept previously discussed at the SRS level we can now formalize as the concept of basis at the formal-specification level. Let $E = \{e_1, e_2, ..., e_n\}$ denote a basis for a baseline of software products. Here we take an object-oriented approach and consider the members of E to be abstract data types (ADTs) or ADT representations after Meyer [7]. Hence we address the issue of configurations from the basis by means of inheritance and other related structure operations. The symbol + denotes inheritance of exported features only, the symbol * denotes class or ADT intersection (features in common), and the symbol . denotes class with additional features. For example, using Eiffel language syntax from Meyer [7], let us consider this structural assembly of classes:

class GRAPHICS
export — Graphics interface, including c_1, c_2, and c_3
inherit POINTS; LINES; TRIG — Exported features from POINTS, LINES,
                     and TRIG become features
                     for GRAPHICS as well
feature — Section for features defined explicitly in GRAPHICS
c_1;
c_2;
c_3;
end — class GRAPHICS

In our notation we represent this assembly by this expression:

GRAPHICS $= c_1$.POINTS $+ c_2$.LINES $+ c_3$.TRIG

where c_1, c_2, and c_3 are the additional features that must be incorporated with baseline components $E = \{$POINTS, LINES, TRIG, ...$\}$ to construct GRAPHICS. Assuming c_1, c_2, c_3 to be relative constants, GRAPHICS then becomes a function of baseline components POINTS, LINES, and TRIG, and is denoted GRAPHICS(POINTS, LINES, TRIG), assuming that E comprises only POINTS, LINES, and TRIG. Notice also that we do not use parentheses because GRAPHICS (POINTS, LINES, TRIG) $= (c_1 \cdot$ POINTS $+ c_2 \cdot$ LINES$) + c_3 \cdot$ TRIG $= c_1 \cdot$ POINTS $+ (c_2 \cdot$ LINES $+ c_3 \cdot$ TRIG$)$. That is, the object-oriented inheritance operation + is associative. Inheritance, +, is the important systems-integration function in this paper. Notice also that $(c_1 \cdot$ POINTS $+ c_2 \cdot$ LINES$)$ and $(c_2 \cdot$ LINES $+ c_3 \cdot$ TRIG$)$ are possible noncomponent-level subsystems of GRAPHICS(POINTS, LINES, TRIG). When we speak, in the context of this paper, of $E = \{$POINTS, LINES, TRIG$\}$ as a formal baseline, we refer to baseline software components POINTS, LINES, and TRIG as formally specified components, which are then ADTs as defined in Meyer (1988).

Theorem 1. Let $E = \{e_1, e_2 ..., e_n\}$, n positive integer, represent a formal baseline; and let $A(E) = A(e_1, e_2, ..., e_n) = c_1 \cdot e_1 + c_2 e_n + ... + c_n \cdot e_n$ denote an integrated software system where c_i (i in $(1,n)$) are relative constant lists of additional features. Then

1) $A(E)$ is a well-defined function; and
2) The sum total of all formally specified features of $A(E)$ is the set union of all the features in each of the c_i (i in $(1,n)$), and exported features of each of the e_i (i in $(1,n)$).

Proof. 1) is proved simply by using mathematical induction on n. 2) is proved from the definition of inheritance.

Theorem 2. (Rine 1990). Let 0 denote the null class with no features. Let $E = \{e_1, e_2, ..., e_n\}$ represent an abstraction of a baseline that is a proper subset of possible components such that none of the e_i (i in $(1,n)$) is the null class. Then E is a basis.

Proof. Consider $c_1, c_2, ..., c_n$ as arbitrary features or subcollections of features, and suppose that $c_1 \cdot e_1 + c_2 \cdot e_2 + ... + c_n \cdot e_n = 0$. Thus the result of inheriting exported features from $e_1, e_2, ..., e_n$ and adding features $c_1, c_2, ..., c_n$ is the null class of features. This statement can be true only if each of the $c_i \cdot e_i$ is the null class of features, $c_i \cdot e_i = 0$ (i in $(1,n)$). Now e_i is not the null class and has features. Therefore c_i has no features to contribute to the assembly. Hence, $c_i = 0$ (i in $(1,n)$). Hence, E is a linearly independent subset. Because E is a baseline it spans the specified domain space. Hence, E is a basis.

Notice that we assumed E to be an abstraction of a baseline. This is a rather strong assumption.

Bases and databases

As we have mentioned, a primary step in developing a modern software-reuse program and improving productivity and flexibility in software manufacturing is to create a domain model. An important part of the domain model is a base of domain primitives. Using object-oriented technology, we represent domain primitives as fundamental classes, and consider the base a standard repository of parts from which software applications are manufactured. Because this parts repository, including object-oriented software classes, is an integrated, shared resource from which various kinds of applications are derived, we must apply proper management and control in using it. The technology with which we manage and control this shared repository comes from database systems concepts and principles. Important materials describing how this managing is done appear in Chapters 4 and 9.

Finally, software-engineering practice in using the domain model above and object-oriented database repository of domain primitives and software parts, represented as classes for developing various applications, is carried out in a client-server computing environment. That environment is a distributed system of software-engineering workstations and tools, using the repository like those in other modern, flexible assembly-line manufacturing systems. In Chapter 5, we discuss some major concepts in such object-oriented distributed systems.

Manufacturing software with GUI

We apply this notion of a manufacturing capability based on domain-modeling and object-oriented technologies to produce software products. Each engineer or scientist using such a capability needs a user-friendly way of interacting with the tools in software manufacturing. Today this tool is the graphical user interface (GUI), and we discuss some of these graphics capabilities in Chapter 8. All these ideas are pulled together to support computer aided design and manufacturing (CAD/CAM) with an object-oriented technology. Some of these aspects of CAD/CAM are presented in Chapter 10.

Better business with the product-family approach

The business rationale we are also proposing is based on the one recently introduced by Chrysler Corporation (as part of our broad attempt to compete more favorably with the Japanese automotive industry and others). This plan requires that far greater flexibility and reliability be built into the initial manufacturing plant for new product lines than has been done.

We have observed that individual products are the offspring of product platforms that are gradually enhanced. Product families and their successive platforms are themselves the applied result of a firm's underlying capabilities. In a well-managed firm, such abilities last much longer and are broader than single-product families or individual products. We recommend a long-run focus on enhancing capabilities, identifying them, and determining how they are synthesized and applied to make new products. These capabilities include a domain model, common architecture, common libraries of software components, and common GUI. All are built on object-oriented technological support where the software-code components are classes and the guide for making them reusable is the one recently devised by Fonash [26]. The software-engineering procedure we follow to derive these new capabilities is domain engineering and comprises domain analysis, domain modeling, and development of design tools. We are deliberately building product families for the applications domain rather than following the old science-and-engineering FORTRAN mentality of making one product at a time, which has failed in the past. But this innovation will require managing future maintenance of a company's new core capabilities, a function we also address in this section, using object-oriented technologies.

What is a product family? We adopt the expression *product platform* in its usual meaning, encompassing the design and components shared by a set of products. A robust platform is at the heart of a successful product family, serving as the foundation for a series of closely related products.

Not long ago, Chrysler released three new lines of cars — the Chrysler Concorde, Eagle Vision, and Dodge Intrepid—based on one platform, sharing the same basic frame, suspension, and drive train. New products are refinements or extensions of the platform. Our example is a family of products derived from common domain features, and our proposed flexible assembly line, using object-oriented technology, comprises the domain model and common architecture, product templates, a software-components set of integrated libraries (called *repository*), all managed by object-oriented database systems technology, maintenance tools, and assembly tools via a GUI.

We call products which share a platform but which have specific features and functionality required by different customers a *product family*. A typical company's product family usually addresses a market segment, and specific products or groups of products within the family target niches within that segment.

The technology embodied in a product family has two parts: the design and its implementation. Design groups dedicated to new-product platform research create basic designs, standard components, and norms for integrating subsystems. Implementation teams create different product models integrating component technologies to achieve specific product goals. Individual products are therefore the offspring of product platforms that are gradually enhanced. Product families and their successive platforms are themselves the applied result of a company's underlying core capabilities. We believe that, as with Chrysler Corporation, the product family built on common domain features can be used as a basis for assessing the dynamics of that company's capabilities — in other words, how these capabilities grow, decline, and integrate with one another over extended periods. In summary, object-oriented technology will, as it matures, have a significant supporting role in this evolution of new software products.

References

1. J.M. Grochow, "Developing Strategic Business Systems Using Object-Oriented Technology," *Hotline on Object-Oriented Technology*, Vol. 3, No. 11, Sept. 1992, pp. 1–12.

2. J. Gold, "Reusability Promise Hinges on Libraries," *IEEE Software*, Vol. 13, No. 1, Jan. 1993, pp. 86–92.

3. R. Comerford, "Technology 1993: Software," *IEEE SPECTRUM*, Jan. 1993, pp. 32–33.

4. D. Rine, "Software Perfective Maintenance: Including Retrainable Software in Software Reuse," *Information Sciences, An International J.*, Vol. 75, No. 1, Dec. 1993.

5. P. Wegner, "Capital-Intensive Software," *IEEE Software*, Vol. 1, No. 3, July 1984.

6. B. Meyer, "Reusability: The Case for Object-Oriented Design," *IEEE Software*, Vol. 4, No. 2, Mar. 1987.

7. B. Meyer, *Object-Oriented Software Construction*, Prentice-Hall International Series in Computer Science, Prentice-Hall, Englewood Cliffs, N.J., 1988.

8. V. Barker and E. O'Connor, "Expert Systems for Configuration at Digital," *Comm. ACM*, Mar. 1989.

9. T. DeMarco, *Structured Analysis and System Specification*, Yourdon Press, Prentice-Hall, Englewood Cliffs, N.J., 1979.

10. *Building Expert Systems*, F. Hayes-Roth, D. Waterman, and D. Lenat, eds., Addison-Wesley, Reading, Mass., 1983.

11. R. Davis, "Expert Systems: Where Are We? And Where Do We Go from Here?" *AI Magazine*, Summer 1982.

12. P. Coad and E. Yourdon, *Object-Oriented Analysis*, Yourdon Press, Prentice-Hall, Englewood Cliffs, N.J., 1990.

13. R. Prieto-Diaz, "Domain Analysis for Reusability," *Proc. CompSAC 87*, IEEE CS Press, 1987.

14. R. Prieto-Diaz, "Classifying Software for Reusability," *IEEE Software*, Jan. 1987.

15. *Research Directions in Object-Oriented Programming*, B. Shriver and P. Wegner, eds., MIT Press, Cambridge, Mass., 1987.

16. F. Brooks, "No Silver Bullet: Essence and Accidents of Software Engineering," *Computer*, Sept. 1987.

17. B. Cox, "There Is a Silver Bullet," *Byte*, Oct. 1990.

18. D. Rine, "Retrainable Software: Software Engineering and Machine Learning," *Digest of Papers AIDA-88 Conference*, George Mason University, 1988.

19. D. Rine and H. Wechsler, "Object-Oriented Programming and Its Relevance to Designing Intelligent Software Systems," *Proc. 1988 Int'l Conf. Computer Languages*, IEEE CS Press, 1988.

20. L. Sing, "Interview with Bjarne Stroustrop," *C++ J.*, Vol. 1, No. 3, 1991.

21. A. Koenig, "Why I Use C++," *J. Object-Oriented Programming*, Vol. 1, No. 2, June 1988.

22. R. Weicker, "Dhrystone Benchmark," *Comm. ACM*, Vol. 27, No. 10, Oct. 1984.

23. C. Ponder and B. Bush, "Polymorphism Considered Harmful," *Software Eng. Notes*, Vol. 19, No. 2, Apr. 1994.

24. M. Lenz, H.A. Schmid, and P.F. Wolf, "Software Reuse through Building Blocks," *IEEE Software*, July 1987.

25. B. Lientz and E. Swanson, *Software Maintenance Management*, Addison-Wesley, New York, 1980.

26. P. Fonash, *Characteristics of Reusable Software Code Components*, doctoral dissertation, George Mason University, Fairfax, Va., 1993.

27. B. Boehm, "Improving Software Productivity," *Computer*, Vol. 20, No. 9, Sept. 1987.

28. M. Lubars, "Code Reusability in the Large versus Code Reusability in the Small," *ACM SIGSOFT Software Eng. Notes*, Vol. 11, No. 1, Jan. 1986.

29. J. Udell, "Component Ware," *Byte*, May 1994.

30. S. Pfleeger, *An Investigation of Cost and Productivity for Object-Oriented Development*, doctoral dissertation, George Mason University, Fairfax, Va., 1989.

31. M. Harandi and H. Lubars, "Automating Software Specification and Design," in *Artificial Intelligence and Software Eng.*, D. Partridge, ed., Ablex Publishing, Norwood, N.J., 1991.

32. R. Balzer, T.E. Cheatham, and C. Green, "Software Technology in the 1990s: Using a New Paradigm," *Computer*, Vol. 13, No. 11, Nov. 1983.

33. A. Partsch and R. Steinbruggen, "Program Transformation Systems," *ACM Computing Surveys*, Vol. 15, No. 3, 1983.

34. D. Rine, "Domain Modeling Requirements of an Expanded MIS Using a Formal Approach," Tech. Report, CS Department, George Mason University, 1991.

35. *IEEE Software Eng. Standards*, IEEE, New York, 1984.

36. "CAMP: Common Ada Missile Packages: Reusable Software Parts," Tech. Report MDAC-STL, McDonnell-Douglas Astronautics Co., St. Louis, Missouri, 1987.

37. "CAIS, Military Standard Common APSE Interface Set," US Department of Defense, MIL-STD-CAIS, 1985.

38. A. Van Lamsweerde et al., "The Kernel of a Generic Software Development Environment," *Proc. ACM SIGSOFT and SIGPLAN Symp.*, ACM, New York, 1986.

39. D.L. Parnas, "On the Criteria to Be Used in Decomposing Systems into Modules," *Comm. ACM*, Vol. 5, No. 12, Dec. 1972.

Dimensions of Object-Oriented Modeling

Peter Wegner, Brown University

Reprinted from *Computer*, October 1992, pp 12–20.
Copyright © 1992 by The Institute of Electrical and
Electronics Engineers, Inc. All rights reserved.

Encapsulation and reactiveness are essential dimensions of object orientation; they support decentralized abstraction, interaction, and evolution of individual objects. Distribution is a strong (two-way) form of encapsulation, while concurrency reduces computation time and enhances modeling power. These four dimensions — encapsulation, reactiveness, distribution, and concurrency — provide a framework for exploring the object-oriented paradigm and a basis for distinguishing it from other programming-language paradigms.

The object-oriented and logic programming paradigms can be distinguished in terms of reactiveness. Object-oriented programming is a modeling paradigm that supplements the raw modeling power of objects with the management flexibility of classes and inheritance. Logic programming is a reasoning paradigm that focuses primarily on processes of deduction and only secondarily on processes of computation. Reactiveness precisely captures informal differences between the problem-solving style associated with object-oriented modeling and that associated with deductive reasoning: Object-oriented programs are quintessentially reactive, pure logic programs are nonreactive, while concurrent logic programs abandon nonreactiveness (and their logical integrity) in favor of a reactive, object-oriented style of computation.

Fundamentals of object-oriented programming

In the object-oriented paradigm, *objects* are the atomic units of encapsulation, *classes* manage collections of objects, and *inheritance* structures collections of classes. Languages that support only objects are called *object-based*, while languages that additionally support classes and inheritance are called *object-oriented*.[1] Object-oriented systems derive their modeling power from a seamless integration of object functionality and object management. Object-based and object-oriented languages have a fundamentally similar structure, but their program structures are entirely different because of differences in their modeling methodologies.

Objects. Objects partition the state of a computation into encapsulated chunks. Each object has an interface of operations that control access to an encapsulated state (see Figure 1). The operations determine the object's behavior, while the state serves as a memory of past invocations that can influence future actions. An object named Point with state variables (instance variables) x, y and four opera-

> The author explores the problem-solving power of object-oriented and logic programming in terms of the dimensions of encapsulation, distribution, concurrency, and reactiveness.

tions for reading and changing them can be defined as follows:

```
Point: object
x := 0; y := 0;
read-x: return x;
read-y: return y;
change-x(dx): x := x + dx;
change-y(dy): y := y + dy;
```

By accepting messages only through read and change operations, the object Point protects its instance variables x, y from access by other objects. The operations of an object share its state. Therefore, state changes by one operation can be seen by subsequently executed operations. For example, read-x and change-x share the variable x, which is nonlocal to these operations although local to the object.

An object's operations can access instance variables only through nonlocal variables (nonlocal to operations though local to the object). The sharing of instance variables by local procedures is a direct consequence of the strong protection objects have against access by other objects. Autonomy at the level of objects is realized at the expense of the autonomy of component operations. This distinction between private, internally communicating subsystems and public, contractual interfaces to the outside world arises in any organization or organism.

Procedure- and object-oriented languages differ sharply in their patterns of resource sharing. Procedure-oriented languages encourage autonomy at the level of procedures, while discouraging interaction through nonlocal variables. In contrast, object-oriented languages discourage procedure autonomy, organizing procedures instead into collections of operations that share an object's state through their nonlocal variables. An object's operations share its state, sacrificing autonomy and reusability to achieve higher granularity autonomy for objects and classes. Encapsulation at the level of objects derives its power by abandoning encapsulation at the level of procedures.

Classes. Classes specify the behavior of collections of objects with common operations. For example, points with read and change operations may be specified by a class Point with two instance variables x, y and four operations as follows:

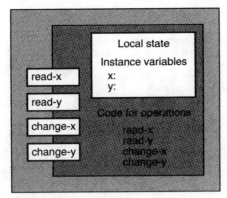

Figure 1. Point object.

```
Point: class
x := 0; y := 0;
read-x: return x;
read-y: return y;
change-x(dx): x := x + dx;
change-y(dy): y := y + dy;
```

Classes specify the set of messages accepted by objects of the class: They define an encapsulation interface. Classes also serve as templates for creating objects with the specified interface and implementation behavior. Two instances p1, p2 of the class Point can be created as follows:

```
p1 := create Point;
p2 := create Point;
```

Each of the two point instances p1, p2 is an encapsulated chunk of state whose behavior is determined by the class operations. In a shared-memory implementation, class operations are represented by a single shared copy in the class template, while instance variables are represented by private copies for each instance. Languages that are generally implemented in a shared memory, like Smalltalk and C++, represent class operations by a single copy in a class template.

However, in a distributed implementation, where communication between an instance and its class template is potentially expensive, each instance could in principle have a local copy of the class operations. If all shared information in the class template is unmodifiable, then the shared-memory implementation can be viewed as a space-saving optimization of the distributed implementation. Programmers should avoid putting modifiable information, such as class variables, in class templates because it destroys the equivalence between the shared and distributed implementation of class operations (see the sidebar on class variables).

Classes help manage collections of objects by uniformly defining class-wide operations such as creation, assignment, and parameter passing. In "class-based" languages that require every object to

Class variables

Class variables shared by all instances of a class are useful and natural for representing dynamically changing properties of classes, like the number of instances of a class. Though easy to implement in a shared memory, they are hard to implement for classes whose instances are physically distributed. Factoring out information common to all objects of a class into a shared class template works well for unchanging information but breaks down when templates contain dynamically changing class variables.

Any kind of resource sharing inevitably weakens object autonomy, but shared read-only types or operations do not disrupt autonomy nearly as much as shared modifiable data. Classes and inheritance support the sharing of unmodifiable resources while avoiding the sharing of data. Both of these forms of sharing greatly increase the expressive power of object-oriented programs. Shared behavior represented by unmodifiable (read-only) code can trivially be converted to an equivalent nonshared representation. Object-oriented programming realizes conceptual sharing of behavioral properties of objects and classes without materially sacrificing autonomy.

Object-oriented systems without class variables balance autonomy and sharing. They support controlled sharing of data by procedures within objects and read-only sharing of object and class properties among objects.

Class variables are an acceptable optimization for nondistributed implementations but not for physically distributed implementations. Object-oriented systems without class variables are logically distributed, while object-oriented systems with class variables are not.

belong to a class, objects are "first-class" values with three properties: They can be components of data structures, they can be passed as parameters, and they can be pointed to by pointer variables. However, in languages like Ada that are object-based but not object-oriented,[1] objects are not first-class values: Packages, the Ada counterpart of objects, cannot be passed as parameters or be components of records.

Classes enhance modeling power by describing behavior explicitly and independently of its realization in specific objects. For example, a class can model the behavior of a collection of points by an abstract notion of pointhood. In this respect, classes are like Platonic ideals. The ability to use finite sets of attributes to model abstract concepts like point-

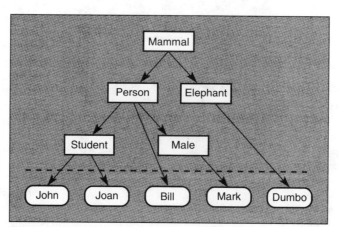

Figure 2. Example of an inheritance hierarchy.

hood, cathood, and even happiness substantially extends object-oriented modeling power.

But classes can only approximate Platonic ideals, because classes of real objects such as cats are generally *natural kinds* that cannot be completely charac-

terized by a finite set of attributes. There is no finite set of properties that precisely specifies the collection of all real and potential cats. An object-oriented cat class can at best approximate the class of cats. Real cats are therefore not object-oriented.[2]

Inheritance. Inheritance is a mechanism for sharing the code or behavior common to a collection of classes. It factors shared properties of classes into superclasses and reuses them in the definition of subclasses. Programmers can therefore specify incremental changes of class behavior in subclasses without modifying already specified classes. Subclasses inherit the code of superclasses, to which they can add new operations and possibly new instance variables.

Classifying classes by inheritance

Inheritance classifies classes like classes classify objects. It is a *second-order classification* mechanism for classes that complements the *first-order classification* of objects. The ability to classify classes as well as values is uniquely object oriented and greatly enhances conceptual modeling power.

Classes facilitate the sharing of behavior among a collection of objects, while inheritance raises the level of sharing so that behavior can be shared by other behavior. There is a close relation between classification and sharing: Classes and inheritance are both behavior-sharing and behavior-classification mechanisms. Tree structure can represent both the classification of high-level categories into subcategories and the sharing of the properties of ancestor classes by descendant classes.

Both block-structure and inheritance hierarchies can be viewed as either sharing or classification hierarchies. But there is a difference between sharing of updatable variables in block-structure languages and sharing of read-only operations (behavior) in inheritance hierarchies. Sharing unmodifiable operations is in principle equivalent to a distributed implementation that creates copies of superclass operations for each subclass. Though similar tree structures represent inheritance and block structure superficially, shared superclasses can be transformed in principle into equivalent distributed structures, while sharing updatable variables in block-structure languages is not compatible with a distributed implementation.

Multiple inheritance

Multiple inheritance arises in designing a new artifact from several previous artifacts, such as designing PL/I from Fortran, Algol, and Cobol, or an object-based concurrent language from object-based and concurrent languages. The conceptual difficulty of multiple inheritance is due in large measure to problems of combining inherited traits from several ancestors. For example, the attempt to combine inherited language features of Fortran, Algol, and Cobol in the design of PL/I resulted in duplicate features and poor design. New designs that compromise among competing inherited ideas are often unaesthetic and perhaps unusable hybrids.

These problems of the real world spill over into computer-based multiple inheritance. It is not easy to create uniform mechanisms that usefully combine the methods of multiple inherited classes, since new features are usually a complex synthesis rather than a simple combination of inherited features. Multiple inheritance of a class T from superclasses T1, T2, . . . , TN may be specified as follows:

class T inherits(T1, T2, . . . , TN) in body-of-T

Each of the classes T, T1, T2, . . . , TN has a finite set of operations (methods). The methods that objects of the class T can invoke are specified by combining methods inherited from T1, T2, . . . , TN with the methods directly defined by T. To simplify method combination, some multiple inheritance systems flatten inheritance hierarchies, for example, by ordering inherited classes T1, T2, . . . , TN in a left-to-right linear order.

Figure 2 describes a class of mammals with persons and elephants as its subclasses. The class of persons has mammals as its superclass, and students and males as its subclasses. Each instance — John, Joan, Bill, Mark, and Dumbo — has a unique base class. An instance's membership in more than one base class, such as John's being both a student and a male, cannot be expressed.

Inheritance plays an important role in modeling because it can express relations among behaviors such as classification, specialization, generalization, approximation, and evolution (see the sidebar on classifying by inheritance). Figure 2 *classifies* mammals into persons and elephants. Elephants *specialize* the properties of mammals, and mammals conversely *generalize* the properties of elephants. The properties of mammals *approximate* those of elephants. Moreover, elephants *evolved* from early species of mammals.

Multiple inheritance supports the incremental evolution of artifacts from several ancestors, but transforms inheritance from a classification and specialization mechanism to a complex relation among interacting behaviors (see the sidebar on multiple inheritance).

Inheritance supports the incremental specification and composition of behavior chunks. It allows the combination of these chunks into composite classes from which instances can be created. Classes that must be composed from subclasses before they can be instantiated are called abstract classes. For example, the class of mammals in Figure 2 is an abstract class: The attributes of the class "mammals" must be supplemented by behavioral attributes of specific mammals (persons or elephants) before instances like Joan and Dumbo can be created. Abstract classes are chunks of partial behavior; other chunks of behavior must supply the missing attributes before objects can be instantiated.

Nonabstract classes have the open/closed property.[3] They are open when subclasses use them for extending behavior by inheritance, but closed when objects use them to execute messages. Classes are a good example of open/closed software components; they are open for clients wishing to extend them and closed for clients wishing to use them. The circumstances under which components can be both open and closed and the more general use of open/closed mechanisms in designing extensible systems are interesting topics for further research.

Distribution

A distributed computing system can be defined as a system of multiple autonomous processors that do not share primary memory, but cooperate by sending messages over a communication network.[4] This definition captures the behavior of physically separated components and logically autonomous modules communicating via messages.

Alternatively, a distributed system can be defined as a system whose components have encapsulation boundaries that are opaque in both directions. That is, both client access to component resources and component access to client resources are inaccessible except through messages mediated by the component interface.

The abstraction concerns of logically and physically distributed systems are very different. Physically distributed systems supplement the logical autonomy requirements of object-oriented systems by physical requirements for failure tolerance, migration transparency, replication transparency, and location transparency[5] (see the sidebar on transparency). Such system requirements add considerable implementation burdens to the requirements of sequential object-oriented systems, and greatly increase the physical robustness of distributed components but do not affect user-level functionality.

Thus, providing robust, failure-tolerant autonomy for physically distributed systems increases the complexity and cost of communication by several orders of magnitude without increasing the level of logical autonomy. For example, remote procedure call can be implemented in shared memory as a simple transfer of control to a new execution environment, but in distributed

Transparency (distributed abstraction)

The distributed programming community uses the term *transparency* (invisibility) as a close synonym for *encapsulation* (enclosure). Distributed programming is concerned with the following kinds of transparency[5]:

• *Failure transparency* conceals the failure of processors, allowing users and application programs to complete their tasks despite hardware failures.
• *Access transparency* enables the use of identical operations to access local and remote files and other objects.
• *Location transparency* enables access to objects without knowledge of their location.
• *Concurrency transparency* enables concurrent implementation of services without the knowledge of clients that use them.
• *Replication transparency* enables the use of multiple instances of files and other data to increase reliability and performance without the knowledge of users.
• *Migration transparency* allows the movement of objects within a system without affecting the operation of users or application programs.
• *Performance transparency* allows reconfiguration of the system to improve performance as loads vary.
• *Scaling transparency* allows the system and applications to expand in scale without change to the system structure or the application algorithm.

The object-oriented concerns of reusability and incremental modifiability are absent from this list. In turn, object-oriented language design does not address failure transparency and techniques for its realization, such as replication and migration transparency. However, language designers should be familiar with both the transparency concerns of distributed computing and the abstraction concerns of component-based software technology, since both are relevant to the design of future computing systems.

systems it involves elaborate precautions against processor and communication failure.

Extending the notion of a distributed system to include logical as well as physical distribution requires a corresponding extension of network communication. Physical communication over network wires must be supplemented by a logical notion of conceptual communication over abstract channels whose properties are defined by their send and receive protocols. Static interconnection is modeled by naming channels explicitly, while dynamic interconnection is realized by channel variables (sockets) that take channel names as their values.

Channels replace shared variables as the mechanism for sharing data among processes. Send and receive operations are analogous to store and fetch operations for shared variables but have greater communication and synchronization overhead. To complete the analogy with channels, variables should be viewed as streams or buffers with unlimited capacity for asynchronous communication and zero capacity for synchronous communication (that is, they block pending message receipt).

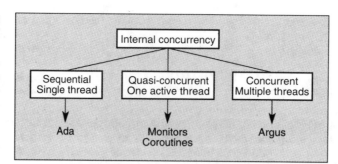

Figure 3. Internal concurrency within processes.

Since physically distributed components may execute concurrently, concurrency is sometimes included as a necessary property of distributed systems. But sequential object-based systems are distributed and not concurrent, while shared-memory multiprocessors are concurrent but not distributed. Distribution focuses on the robust autonomy of components, while concurrency focuses on very different concerns relating to parallel execution.[6]

Concurrency

Concurrency is described in terms of multiple threads that can be executed in parallel by multiple processes or simulated sequentially by a single process.

Creation of a thread increases a program's degree of concurrency, while termination or suspension of a thread by synchronization decreases concurrency.

The granularity of concurrency is independent of the granularity of encapsulation and distribution; it can be coarser or finer than that of distributed components. Sequential object-oriented programs have a coarser granularity of concurrency than of encapsulation. Internally sequential processes have the same granularity of concurrency and encapsulation, while quasi-concurrent and fully concurrent processes have a finer granularity of concurrency (see Figure 3).

Internally sequential processes permit only a single sequential execution thread within a process. This limitation simplifies internal process structure but complicates interprocess communication, because concurrency cannot be encapsulated within processes and must be modeled entirely by message disciplines. Sequential processes require two levels of program structure with different rules for internal and interprocess specification. Expressive power within sequential processes is further limited

---

Monitors

Monitors, like objects, have an interface of operations that clients can invoke:

Monitor M
    hidden local variables
    operations (entry points) that clients can invoke
    wait and signal commands for suspending and
        resuming operations
endmonitor

At any given time a monitor may have one active process, a number of partially executed suspended processes, and a number of waiting processes in its entry queue.

Executing processes are suspended when conditions for their execution are not satisfied. For example, consider a buffer with Append and Remove operations and internal wait queues Empty and Full. An attempt to execute a Remove when the buffer is empty causes the thread to be suspended and placed on the Empty wait queue. An attempt to execute an Append when the buffer is full causes the thread to be suspended and placed on the Full wait queue.

A distributed mail system

Consider a distributed mail system with Mailer, Maildrop, and Registry processes that can be replicated at many physical locations.[7] Mailer provides the user interface, allowing users to send and receive mail and the system to add users. Maildrop contains a subset of the mailboxes and is invoked by Mailer to deliver mail to those mailboxes. Registry specifies the maildrop for each user and must be updated when users are added to or deleted from the system.

Mailer can execute multiple threads freely, since there is no shared-data structure to worry about. Maildrop must synchronize for delivery and removal from a given mailbox but can concurrently interact with different mailboxes. Registry can permit concurrent lookup but must synchronize when adding or removing users. Concurrency can be increased by delaying synchronization until the time of access to shared data within Maildrop and Registry processes, rather than on entry to each process. But the concurrency model becomes more complex, requiring fine-grain concurrency within processes to be superimposed on a large granularity of encapsulation and distribution.

because an executing thread must run to completion before a second thread can enter the process. Executing threads can call a subtask or return to the caller, but they cannot be suspended in favor of another thread and later resumed.

Quasi-concurrent processes have at most a single active executing thread, but they can have many passive suspended threads in one or more wait queues. They provide more flexible concurrency control than internally sequential processes like Ada tasks, without sacrificing internal sequentiality. For example, job-shop simulation of tasks whose execution time differs from their arrival time can be handled adequately by sequential processes but easily by quasi-concurrent processes that suspend entering tasks until they are ready to execute.

Monitors are quasi-concurrent processes[7] (see the sidebar on monitors). They are internally sequential, guaranteeing each client exclusive access to shared data, but client operations may suspend and later resume (like coroutines). A wait command suspends the current thread and places it on the named wait queue, from which a resume command can remove (reawaken) it. Monitors have an entry queue for incoming monitor calls and wait queues associated with each condition name for suspended monitor calls. When a thread suspends, a reawakened waiting thread or an entering thread may commence execution.

Quasi-concurrent processes do pay a price for their extra flexibility. Suspended threads have no control over their shared data and may, like Rip Van Winkle, find that the world has changed beyond recognition when they reawaken. This can be avoided by using transactions that lock sensitive data while tasks are suspended. However, this both increases the complexity and reduces the concurrency of quasi-concurrent processes.

Fully concurrent processes are illustrated by Argus guardians.[8] Guardians do not synchronize incoming threads on entry, so when a thread enters a Guardian it simply increases the number of executing threads. Synchronization is lazy, occurring only when an executing thread within a Guardian attempts to access shared data (see the sidebar on a distributed mail system).

Fully concurrent processes are internally much more complex than sequen-tial processes, but they provide the same concurrent environment within the processes as outside them. They can hide concurrency from process users. In concealing lower level concurrency issues, they simplify higher level architecture. In contrast, sequential processes must specify all concurrency at the outer level.

In spite of their greater internal complexity, fully concurrent processes are more compatible with the principles of modular programming than sequential processes are. Therefore, they appear to be a desirable goal for next-generation object-oriented systems.

Dimensions of modularity

Encapsulation, distribution, and concurrency play independent though coordinated roles in determining module boundaries (see Figure 4).

The *encapsulation boundary* is the interface a component presents to its clients. It determines the form in which an object's resources can be accessed (invoked). It is an information-hiding boundary encountered by a client looking inward to the component. It limits what the client can see, hiding local data from client access. It is the unit of encapsulation and the fundamental unit of object granularity.

The *distribution boundary* is the boundary of accessible names visible when looking outward from within an object. The encapsulation boundary is encountered by a client looking inward, while the distribution boundary is encountered by an internal agent looking outward.

The distribution boundary is coarser than the abstraction boundary in block-structure languages, since blocks are transparent when looking outward and opaque when looking inward. It is finer when a large abstraction (say, an airline reservation system) is implemented on several distributed components. When the abstraction and distribution boundaries coincide, a component is called *distributed*. (This corresponds precisely to human intuition.) Abstraction for distributed components is symmetric; the receiver's view of the sender is as abstract as the sender's view of the receiver. Message communication has the property of symmetric two-way abstraction required by our definition.

The *concurrency boundary* of a component is the boundary at which threads entering a component synchronize with its ongoing activities. For sequential processes, the concurrency boundary is also the encapsulation boundary, while for concurrent processes, the concurrency boundary is finer than the encapsulation boundary. Conversely, the unit of encapsulation can be coarser than that for concurrency (for example, when the address space associated with a single thread can contain many encapsulated objects).

The boundaries for encapsulation, distribution, and concurrency are in general independent. However, the special case when the three boundaries coincide is interesting. Such processes are called *distributed sequential processes*. They are distributed because their abstraction and distribution boundaries coincide, and they are sequential because their encapsulation and concurrency boundaries coincide.

Distributed sequential processes are attractively simple. However, insisting

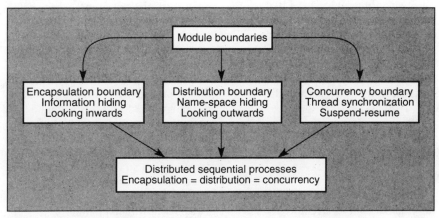

Figure 4. Encapsulation, distribution, and concurrency boundaries.

on the same granularity for encapsulation, distribution, and concurrency can reduce efficiency or expressive power. For example, large abstractions such as airline reservation systems need finely grained synchronization at the level of individual flights or even individual seats to execute efficiently. Conversely, a network of sequential computers with multiple objects at each node is naturally modeled by a unit of concurrency coarser than its unit of encapsulation.

Open systems

A software system is said to be open if its behavior can be easily modified and extended. Systems can achieve openness dynamically through reactiveness or statically through modularity.

• A *reactive (interactive)* system that can react to stimuli by modifying its state and emitting a response is an open system.
• A *modular (encapsulated)* system whose number of components and/or functionality can be statically extended by an external agent, such as a programmer, is an open system.

Reactive openness is the natural mechanism of biological evolution and human learning, but modular openness is the preferred practical mechanism for software evolution. While either one is sufficient to qualify a system as open, the most flexible open systems are both reactive and modular.

Object-oriented systems are strongly open, being both reactive and modular. Objects are reactive subsystems that respond to a message by changing their internal state, returning an output, then waiting for another message. They are also encapsulated modules that can be statically extended by modifying already defined objects or by introducing new objects. Classes and inheritance enhance the inherent modularity of objects by supporting the systematic, incremental modification of objects and classes.

Reactive control structures

Objects realize their reactiveness by an implicit control structure for selecting among their interface operations

---

Object-oriented systems are strongly open, being both reactive and modular.

op1, op2, . . . , op*N*. A select statement can explicitly specify this structure as follows:

select(op1, op2, . . . , opN)

This statement specifies selection of the operation of the first arriving message. It allows objects to react flexibly to potential stimuli. Select statements are the fundamental reactive control structure of both sequential and concurrent object-oriented programming. They capture the reactive essence of object-based modeling, being a prototype for Dijkstra guarded commands.[6] The select statement of concurrent objects specifies selection among operations op*i* of a set of waiting messages having a true guard G*i* ($i =$ 1, 2, . . . , N):

select(G1‖op1, G2‖op2, . . . ,
GN‖opN)

Ada has select statements of precisely this kind for selecting alternative messages at an entry point, while CSP (communicating sequential processes) makes use of a generalized version based on Dijkstra guarded commands.[6] They are also the fundamental selection mechanism for finite automata, where selection of the next input symbol for execution is governed by an implicit select statement similar to that for sequential objects.

Guards act as conditions that prevent operations from executing until the condition specified by G*i* is satisfied. For example, the operation for appending an element to a buffer is guarded by the condition notfull, while the operation for removing an element is guarded by the condition notempty:

select(notfull‖Append,
notempty‖Remove)

Committed-choice nondeterminism

Viewed as isolated subsystems, objects are not deterministic; they do not know which operation will be executed next. This uncertainty, called *input nondeterminism or indeterminism*,[1] is resolved when the object commits itself to the operation op*i* of the first arriving message.

Processes, like objects, are indeterministic subsystems. When idle, they commit themselves to the action specified by the first arriving message. Because processes operate in a concurrent environment, waiting messages may accumulate at entry points.

When messages are waiting for several operations, the select statement makes a nondeterministic choice among them. The nondeterminism of both sequential and concurrent objects is called *committed-choice nondeterminism*, since it irrevocably commits the object (process) to a particular choice. There is no later backtracking.

Committed-choice nondeterminism is fundamental in realizing reactive flexibility, but it is neither necessary nor sufficient for concurrency. Reactive access by multiple messages and multiple clients does not require concurrent module execution. Sequential object-based systems are reactive but not concurrent, while concurrent nonreactive systems have fewer constraints on efficient concurrent execution than concurrent reactive systems do. Reactiveness and concurrency are orthogonal properties of computing systems.

Don't-know nondeterminism

The distinction between reactiveness and concurrency is particularly critical in logic programming. Logic programs can be highly concurrent, but they cannot be reactive without losing their logical integrity. This is because logic programs rely on backtracking—a powerful control structure that allows sequential exploration of tree-structured logical solution spaces, thus guaranteeing logical completeness. Backtracking precludes irrevocable commitment to interactive actions until a complete solution has been found, and its requirement for failed computation paths to be unobservable (that is, to have no irreversible side effects) is incompatible with reactiveness.[9]

Consider the set of all clauses of a Prolog program whose clause heads have the form P(Ei), where P is a given predicate and Ei is an expression that may contain logical variables:

P(E1) if B1
P(E2) if B2
. . . .
P(EN) if BN

This program states that the clause head P(Ei) can be proved by proving the body Bi. To prove a goal P(E), it is sufficient to prove any clause for which E unifies with Ei. This rule for proving a goal P(E) can be specified by a nondeterministic choice statement of the form:

choice (E1|B1, E2|B2, . . . , EN|BN)

To prove the goal P(E) in this statement requires nondeterministically choosing a body Bi for which P(E) unifies with P(Ei); if this clause cannot be proved, backtrack and select other alternatives Bi for which P(E) unifies with P(Ei) until an alternative succeeds or all alternatives have been tried unsuccessfully.

A nondeterministic choice statement whose alternatives Bi are guarded by patterns Ei can capture the implicit control structure of logic programs. The nondeterminism of choice statements is called *don't-know nondeterminism* because the programmer need not know which inference paths lead to successful inference of the goal. Prolog programs explore all alternatives until a successful inference path is found and report failure only if all inference paths fail.

Don't-know nondeterminism requires backtracking from failed inference paths so that the effects of failed computations become unobservable. Since programs cannot commit to irrevocable input or output until a proof is complete, don't-know nondeterminism cannot be used as a computational model for reactive systems.[9]

Concurrent logic programs

Concurrent logic programs have a clause structure similar to that of se-

---

Logic programs cannot be reactive without losing their logical integrity.

---

quential logic programs, but have an entirely different control structure. Each predicate P has an associated set of classes of the form "P(Ei) if Gi|Bi," where Ei is an expression, Gi is a guard that must be satisfied, and Bi is a sequence of subgoals executed if the system commits to execution of this clause. A goal P(E) triggers nondeterministic execution of those bodies Bi for which E unifies with Ei and the guards Gi are satisfied. But instead of trying all possible alternatives, a concurrent Prolog computation commits irrevocably to one alternative. This form of nondeterminism, called *don't-care nondeterminism* because the program behaves as though it does not care which alternative is selected, is equivalent to committed-choice nondeterminism. The execution rule for proving a goal P(E) can therefore be represented by a select statement whose alternatives are bodies Bi guarded by a unification requirement and a traditional guard condition:

select((E1;G1)||B1, (E2;G2)||B2, . . . , (EN;GN)||BN)

Commitment versus logical integrity

Both the choice and the select statements require choosing among guarded alternatives. They differ only in that choice statements permit later selection of alternatives, while select statements irrevocably commit to the first chosen alternative. This difference has fundamental consequences: Choice statements sacrifice reactiveness to permit the complete search of logical solution spaces, while select statements sacrifice completeness to realize reactiveness. The inherent incompatibility between deductive reasoning and flexi-

ble reaction to unpredictable stimuli is a fundamental limitation of logic.

Surprisingly, the fundamental control structure for concurrent logic programs is precisely the same as that for object-oriented programming — namely, committed choice to a guarded alternative. This reflects the common goal of achieving reactive flexibility in choosing among potential actions.

Committed-choice nondeterminism in logic programs realizes reactiveness and keeps the number of nondeterministic alternatives explored to a manageable size. But it may cause commitment to an inference path not containing a solution at the expense of paths possibly containing solutions. Logic programs employing committed-choice nondeterminism are incomplete in the sense that they may fail to prove true assertions that would have been derivable by don't-know nondeterminism from the same set of clauses. It becomes the programmer's responsibility to make sure that programs do not yield different results for different orders of don't-care commitment.

The "dimensions" of encapsulation and reactiveness provide a framework for distinguishing modeling paradigms based on objects from deductive reasoning paradigms based on logic. Object-oriented systems are both encapsulated and reactive while logic programming systems are nonencapsulated and nonreactive. Concurrent logic programs are reactive but not encapsulated. Advocates of concurrent logic programming feel that this compromise combines the advantages of logic with the power of reactiveness, while skeptics feel that the compromise falls between two stools by compromising the integrity of logic without providing a systematic framework for programming in the large (see Wegner[10] for further discussion).

Encapsulation, the fundamental mechanism for partitioning into components with abstract interfaces, provides a static partitioning into objects. Reactiveness, which supports flexible incremental access to procedures of the interface on the basis of need, adds a temporal incrementality that complements the spatial incrementality of encapsulation.

Closer semantic analysis reveals that encapsulated interfaces specify objects (nouns) by the set of all potential procedures (verbs) that the object may execute, while reactiveness ensures flexible incremental access to the procedures that collectively define the object. The characterization of entities by the set of all their potential actions is a common interdisciplinary scientific modeling technique in physics (operationalism) and psychology (behaviorism). Objects adapt this general scientific modeling technique to computation by specifying modeled entities through a reactive interface of all possible actions (reactions, interactions) in which the entities might become involved. The specification of entities by their effects is a fundamental domain-independent principle of operational modeling. Like all profound ideas, the harnessing of this principle for the purpose of object-oriented modeling appears in retrospect to be simple and obvious.

Reactiveness, encapsulation, and modeling power stand in the following relation:

$$\text{reactiveness} + \text{encapsulation} \rightarrow$$
$$\text{modeling power} \rightarrow \text{open system.}$$

By making the stronger assumption that these implications are two-way — equating the notion of openness, modeling power, and reactiveness + encapsulation — the argument can be made that formalisms lacking reactiveness and encapsulation, like logic programming, also lack modeling power and openness. The incompatibility of reactiveness with deductive reasoning provides a technical basis for the widespread intuitive perception that deductive reasoning realizes rigor at the expense of flexibility. It also provides a rationale for choosing the object-oriented paradigm over the logic programming paradigm as a framework for modeling. ∎

References

1. P. Wegner, "Concepts and Paradigms of Object-Oriented Programming," *OOPS Messenger*, Vol. 7, No. 7, Aug. 1990, pp. 7-84.

2. R. King, "My Cat is Object-Oriented," in *Object-Oriented Concepts, Databases, and Applications*, W. Kim and F. H. Lochovski, eds., Addison-Wesley, Reading, Mass., 1989.

3. B. Meyer, *Object-Oriented Software Construction*, Prentice-Hall, Englewood Cliffs, N.J., 1988.

4. H. Bal, J. Steiner, and A. Tanenbaum, "Programming Languages for Distributed Computing Systems," *Computing Surveys*, Vol. 21, No. 3, Sept. 1989, pp. 261-322.

5. G.F. Colouris and J. Dollimore, *Distributed Systems: Concepts and Design*, Addison-Wesley, Reading, Mass., 1988.

6. G.R. Andrews, *Concurrent Programming: Principles and Practice*, Benjamin Cummings, Redwood City, Calif., 1991.

7. G.R. Andrews and F.B. Schneider, "Concepts and Notations for Concurrent Programming," *Computing Surveys*, Vol. 15, No. 1, 1983, pp. 3-43.

8. B. Liskov and R. Scheifler, "Guardians and Actions, Linguistic Support for Robust Distributed Programs," *TOPLAS*, Vol. 5, No. 3, 1983, pp. 381-404.

9. E. Shapiro, "The Family of Concurrent Programming Languages," *Computing Surveys*, Vol. 21, No. 3, Sept. 1989, pp. 413-510.

10. P. Wegner, "Object-Based Versus Logic Programming," *Proc. Int'l Fifth-Generation Computing Conference*, Tokyo, June 1992.

Peter Wegner is a professor of computer science at Brown University. His research interests include programming languages and software engineering. His interest in the comparison of object-oriented modeling and logic-based reasoning paradigms led to his participation in June 1992 in the Fifth-Generation Computing Conference in Tokyo and the Simula 25th anniversary meeting in Oslo. The final sections of this article are influenced by presentations prepared for these two conferences.

Wegner was educated at London and Cambridge Universities, and taught at Cornell, Penn State, and the London School of Economics before going to Brown. He published the first book on Ada in 1980 and has since contributed to object-oriented programming in the areas of type theory, concurrency, and language design issues. He is a member of the IEEE Computer Society and ACM.

Readers can contact the author at the Department of Computer Science, Brown University, Providence, RI 02912; e-mail pw@cs.brown.edu.

Chapter 2

Object-Oriented
Software Development

Object-Oriented and Conventional Analysis and Design Methodologies

Comparison and Critique

Robert G. Fichman and Chris F. Kemerer

Massachusetts Institute of Technology

Reprinted from *Computer*, October 1992, pp. 22–39. Copyright © 1992 by The Institute of Electrical and Electronics Engineers, Inc. All rights reserved.

Although the concepts underlying object-orientation as a programming discipline go back two decades, it's only in the last few years that object-oriented analysis (OOA) and object-oriented design (OOD) methodologies have begun to emerge. Object orientation certainly encompasses many novel concepts, and some have called it a new paradigm for software development. Yet, the question of whether object-oriented methodologies represents a radical change over such conventional methodologies as structured analysis remains a subject of much debate.

Yourdon has divided various object-oriented methodologists into two camps, *revolutionaries* and *synthesists*.[1] Revolutionaries believe that object orientation is a radical change that renders conventional methodologies and ways of thinking about design obsolete. Synthesists, by contrast, see object orientation as simply an accumulation of sound software engineering principles that adopters can graft onto their existing methodologies with relative ease.

On the side of the revolutionaries, Booch[2] states

> Let there be no doubt that object-oriented design is fundamentally different from traditional structured design approaches: it requires a different way of thinking about decomposition, and it produces software architectures that are largely outside the realm of the structured design culture.

Coad and Yourdon[3] add

> We have no doubt that one could arrive at the same results [as Coad and Yourdon's OOA methodology produces] using different methods; but it has also been our experience that the thinking process, the discovery process, and the communication between user and analyst are fundamentally different with OOA than with structured analysis.

On the side of the synthesists, Wasserman, Pircher, and Muller[4] take the position that their object-oriented structured design (OOSD) methodology is essentially an elaboration of structured design. They state that the "foundation of OOSD is structured design" and that structured design "includes most of the necessary

> **The question of whether emerging object-oriented analysis and design methodologies require incremental or radical changes on the part of prospective adopters is being vigorously debated.**

concepts and notations" for OOSD. Page-Jones and Weiss[5] take a similar position in stating that

> The problem is that object orientation has been widely touted as a revolutionary approach, a complete break with the past. This would be fascinating if it were true, but it isn't. Like most engineering developments, the object-oriented approach is a refinement of some of the best software engineering ideas of the past.

Factors to consider. One of the most important assessments a company must make in considering the adoption of a technical innovation is where the innovation falls on the incremental-radical continuum in relation to its own current practice. Incremental innovations introduce relatively minor changes to an existing process or product and reinforce the established competencies of adopting firms. Radical innovations are based on a different set of engineering and scientific principles, and draw on new technical and problem-solving skills.

If object-oriented analysis and design comes to be regarded as a radical change by most organizations, then a strong, negative impact on the ultimate rate of adoption of the technology can be expected. Compared with incremental change, implementation of radical change involves greater expense and risk, and requires different management strategies. Many development groups have already invested considerable resources in conventional methodologies like structured analysis/structured design or information engineering. These investments can take many forms, including training in the specifics of the methodology, acquisition of automated tools to support the methodology, and repositories of analysis and design models accumulated over the course of employing the methodology.

On an industry-wide level, vendors have been actively developing more powerful tools to support conventional methodologies, and a growing pool of expertise now exists in the use of these tools. To the extent that object orientation is a radical change, investments in conventional methodologies will be lost: Staff will have to be retrained, new tools will have to be purchased, and a likely expensive conversion process will be necessary.

Implementation of radically new technologies also involves a much greater element of risk because the full range of impacts is typically unknown. Moreover, the implementation of a radically new methodology requires different strategies to manage this risk and to overcome other implementation barriers (such as resistance to change).

The radical-versus-incremental debate is crucial to assessing the future of object orientation and formulating a transition strategy, but unfortunately no comprehensive analyses have been performed comparing leading object-oriented methodologies with conventional methodologies. Two surveys of object-oriented methodologies have been compiled, but these only cover either analysis[6] or design,[7] and neither draws specific comparisons with conventional methodologies. Loy[8] provides an insightful commentary on the issue of conventional versus object-oriented methodologies, although no specific methodologies are compared.

The current research fills the gap left by other surveys by analyzing several leading conventional and object-oriented analysis and design methodologies, including a detailed point-by-point comparison of the kinds of modeling tools provided by each. A review (described below in greater detail) was performed that resulted in the selection of six analysis methodologies and five design methodologies. The analysis methodologies were

- DeMarco structured analysis,
- Yourdon modern structured analysis,
- Martin information engineering analysis,
- Bailin object-oriented requirements specification,
- Coad and Yourdon object-oriented analysis, and
- Shlaer and Mellor object-oriented analysis.

The design methodologies were

- Yourdon and Constantine structured design,
- Martin information engineering design,
- Wasserman et al. object-oriented structured design,
- Booch object-oriented design, and
- Wirfs-Brock et al. responsibility-driven design.

Incremental or radical? We conclude that the object-oriented analysis methodologies reviewed here represent a radical change over process-oriented methodologies such as DeMarco structured analysis but only an incremental change over data-oriented methodologies such as Martin information engineering. Process-oriented methodologies focus attention away from the inherent properties of objects during the modeling process and lead to a model of the problem domain that is orthogonal to the three essential principles of object orientation: encapsulation, classification of objects, and inheritance.

By contrast, data-oriented methodologies rely heavily on the same basic technique — information modeling — as each of the three OOA methodologies. The main differences between OOA and data-oriented conventional methodologies arise from the principle of encapsulation of data and behavior: OOA methodologies require that all operations be encapsulated within objects, while conventional methodologies permit operations to exist as subcomponents of disembodied processes. At the level of detail required during analysis, however, we conclude that expert information modelers will be able to learn and apply the principle of encapsulation without great difficulty.

Regarding design methodologies, we conclude that object-oriented design is a radical change from *both* process-oriented and data-oriented methodologies. The OOD methodologies we review here collectively model several important dimensions of a target system not addressed by conventional methodologies. These dimensions relate to the *detailed* definition of classes and inheritance, class and object relationships, encapsulated operations, and message connections. The need for adopters to acquire new competencies related to these dimensions, combined with Booch's uncontested observation that OOD uses a completely different structuring principle (based on object-oriented rather than function-oriented decomposition of system components), renders OOD as a radical change.

Conventional methodologies

A systems development methodology combines tools and techniques to guide the process of developing large-scale information systems. The evolution of modern methodologies began in the late 1960s with the development of the concept of a systems development life cycle (SDLC). Dramatic increases in hardware performance and the adoption of high-level languages had enabled much larger and more complicated systems to be built. The SDLC attempted to bring order to the development process, which had outgrown the ad hoc project control methods of the day, by decomposing the process into discrete project phases with "frozen" deliverables—formal documents—that served as the input to the next phase.

Structured methodologies. The systems development life cycle concept gave developers a measure of control, but provided little help in improving the productivity and quality of analysis and design per se. Beginning in the 1970s, structured methodologies were devel-

oped to promote more effective analysis and more stable and maintainable designs. Early structured methodologies were largely *process-oriented*, with only a minor emphasis on modeling of entities and data. This emphasis on processes seemed natural, given the procedural programming languages and batch, file-based applications commonplace at the time. Although many authors contributed to the so-called structured revolution, our review concentrates on the critical contributions of Yourdon and Constantine,[9] DeMarco,[10] and Ward and Mellor.[11]

Yourdon and Constantine structured design provided a method for developing a system architecture that conformed to the software engineering principles of modularity, loosely coupled modules, and module cohesion. The structure chart (see the sidebar, "Tools for structured methodologies") was the primary tool for modeling a system design. (Al-

though the emphasis of structured design was on creating a module architecture, the methodology also suggested dataflow diagrams for modeling processes and hierarchy diagrams for defining data structure.)

DeMarco's seminal work enlarged the structured approach to encompass analysis. DeMarco prescribed a series of steps for performing structured analysis, flowing from modeling of existing systems (using dataflow diagrams) to modeling of the system to be developed (using dataflow diagrams, mini-specifications, and a data dictionary). Although modeling of data was not ignored, the emphasis was on modeling processes. The ultimate goal of structured analysis and design was to create a top-down decomposition of the functions to be performed by the target system.

Continuing in the structured tradition, Ward and Mellor recommended significant extensions to structured analysis to better support modeling of real-time systems. Their methodology added entity-relationship diagrams and state-transition diagrams to the structured analysis toolset. Entity-relationship diagrams illustrate the structure of entities and their interrelationships, while state-transition diagrams focus on system and subsystem states and the events that caused transitions between states.

In recognition of the evolution of systems, languages, and tools over the past two decades, Yourdon[12] updated structured analysis under the name *modern structured analysis*. Modern structured analysis differs from DeMarco's original work in several respects: It no longer recommends modeling of current implemented systems; it adds a preliminary phase to develop an "essential model" of the system; it substitutes a technique known as "event partitioning" for top-down functional decomposition as the preferred technique for constructing dataflow diagrams; it places more emphasis on information modeling (via entity-relationship diagrams) and behavior modeling (via state-transition diagrams); and it encourages prototyping.

These updates have served to blur somewhat the one-time clear distinctions between structured methods and the data-oriented methods that we describe next.

Information engineering. In the late 1970s and early 1980s, planning and modeling of data began to take on a more central role in systems development, culminating in the development of data-oriented methodologies such as information engineering. The conceptual roots of data-oriented methodologies go back to the 1970s with the invention of the relational database model and entity-relationship modeling, although it took several years for mature data-oriented methodologies to emerge.

The data-oriented approach has two central assumptions:

(1) Organizational data provides a more stable foundation for a system design than organizational procedures.

(2) Data should be viewed as an organizational resource independent of the systems that (currently) process the data.

One outgrowth of the data-oriented approach was the creation of a new information systems subfunction, data administration, to help analyze, define, store, and control organizational data.

Martin[13] information engineering is a comprehensive methodology that extends the data-oriented approach across the entire development life cycle. While structured methods evolved backwards through the life cycle from programming, information engineering evolved forward through the life cycle from planning and analysis. Martin defines information engineering as consisting of four phases:

(1) Information strategy planning,
(2) Business area analysis,
(3) System design, and
(4) Construction.

Information engineering distinguishes activities that are performed on the level of a business unit (planning and analysis) from those that are project-specific (design and construction). Compared with structured methods, information engineering recommends a much broader range of analysis techniques and modeling tools, including enterprise modeling, critical-success-factors analysis, data modeling, process modeling, joint-requirements planning, joint-applications design, time-box methodology, and prototyping (see the sidebar, "Tools for Martin information engineering").

Information engineering describes planning as an organization-wide activity that develops an enterprise model and a high-level data architecture. Business area analysis attempts to capture a more detailed understanding of business activities and their interdependencies, using such tools as data-model diagrams, decomposition diagrams, process-dependency diagrams, and entity-process matrices. The design phase builds on the results of prior phases and produces a detailed model of a target

Tools for Martin information engineering

Action diagram — Used to depict detailed procedural logic at a given level of detail (for example, at a system level or within individual modules). Similar to structured English, except graphical constructs are used to highlight various control structures (condition, sequence, iteration, and selection).

Bubble chart — A low-level diagram used as an aide to normalization of relational tables. Shows attributes (depicted as bubbles) and the functional dependencies between them (depicted as directed arcs).

Dataflow diagram (DFD) — Conforms to the conventional notation and usage for dataflow diagrams (see the sidebar, "Tools for structured methodologies").

Data-model diagram — Depicts data entities (boxes) and their relational connections (lines). Shows cardinality and whether the connections are optional or mandatory. Similar to the entity-relationship diagram.

Data-structure diagram — Shows data structures in a format appropriate to the database management system to be used for implementation.

Encyclopedia — A more comprehensive version of the data dictionary that serves as an integrated repository for modeling information from all development phases, including the enterprise model; organizational goals, critical success factors, strategies, and rules; data models and data definitions; process models and process definitions; and other design-related information. Automated support is assumed.

Enterprise model — A model that defines, at a high level, the functional areas of an organization and the relationships between them. It consists of text descriptions of functions (usually an identifiable business unit such as a department) and processes (a repetitive, well-defined set of tasks that support a function).

Entity-process matrix — Cross-references entities to the processes that use them.

Process-decomposition diagram — A hierarchical chart that shows the breakdown of processes into progressively increasing detail. Similar to the conventional tree diagram, except a particularly compact notation is used to fit many levels on one page.

Process-dependency diagram — A diagram consisting of processes (depicted by bubbles) and labeled arcs. It shows how each process depends on the prior execution other processes. Similar to a dataflow diagram, except conditional logic and flow of control is also depicted.

State-transition diagram — Conforms to the conventional notation and usage for state-transition diagrams (see the sidebar, "Tools for structured methodologies").

system consisting of process-decomposition diagrams, process-dependency diagrams, dataflow diagrams, action diagrams, and data-structure diagrams. System construction, the last phase of information engineering, consists of translating the models from the design phase to an operational system — ideally using a code generator.

Object-oriented analysis methodologies

As with traditional analysis, the primary goal of object-oriented analysis is the development of an accurate and complete representation of the problem domain. We conducted a literature search to identify well-documented, broadly representative OOA methodologies first published in book form or as detailed articles in refereed journals from 1980 to 1990. This search resulted in the selection of three methodologies from Coad and Yourdon,[3] Bailin,[14] and Shlaer and Mellor.[15,16] Numerous OOA methodologies have emerged in recent years. Since no more than a few methodologies could be compared in depth, two criteria — maturity (first published prior to 1990) and form of publication (book or refereed journal) — were used to select among them. Several methodologies were identified that did not meet these criteria (see Fichman and Kemerer[17]) although this should not be taken to mean they are inferior to those that did. Object-oriented analysis is, of course, quite young; it is much too early to predict which (if any) of the current methodologies will come to be recognized as standard works in the field. The goal here is to provide a detailed comparison of representative methodologies at a single point in time, not a comprehensive review.

The three methodologies are presented in the order of their similarity to conventional methodologies. Bailin's methodology is viewed as most similar, followed by Coad and Yourdon's, and then Shlaer and Mellor's.

Bailin object-oriented requirements specification. Bailin developed object-oriented requirements specification (OOS) in response to a perceived incompatibility between conventional structured analysis and object-oriented design. Outwardly, the method resembles structured analysis in that a system decomposition is performed using a dataflow diagram-like notation. Yet, there is an important difference: Structured analysis specifies that functions should be grouped together only if they are "constituent steps in the execution of a higher level function," while OOS groups functions together only if they "operate on the same data abstraction."[14] In other words, functions cannot exist as part of disembodied processes, but must be subordinated to a single entity. (Bailin uses the term entity rather than object for stylistic reasons only; the terms are assumed to be interchangeable.) This restriction is used to promote encapsulation of functions and data.

Two distinctions are central to OOS. First, Bailin distinguishes between *entities*, which possess underlying states that can persist across repeated execution cycles, and *functions*, which exist solely to transform inputs to outputs and thus have no underlying states remembered between cycles. Entities can be further decomposed into subentities or functions, but functions can only be decomposed into subfunctions.

Second, Bailin distinguishes between two classes of entities, *active* and *passive*. Active entities perform operations (on themselves or other entities) important enough to be considered in detail during the analysis phase, while passive entities are of lesser importance and can therefore be treated as a "black box" until the design phase. These distinctions are important because, as we show below, active entities, passive entities, and functions are each modeled differently during the analysis process.

The OOS methodology consists of a seven-step procedure:

(1) *Identify key problem domain entities.* Draw dataflow diagrams and then designate objects that appear in process names as candidate entities.

(2) *Distinguish between active and passive entities.* Distinguish between entities whose operations are significant in terms of describing system requirements (active entities) versus those whose detailed operations can be deferred until design (passive). Construct an entity-relationship diagram (ERD).

(3) *Establish dataflows between active entities.* Construct the top-level (level 0) entity-dataflow diagram (EDFD).

Designate each active entity as a process node and each passive entity as a dataflow or data store.

(4) *Decompose entities (or functions) into subentities and/or functions.* This step is performed iteratively together with steps 5 and 6. Consider each active entity in the top-level EDFD and determine whether it is composed of lower level entities. Also consider what each entity does and designate these operations as functions. For each of the subentities identified, create a new EDFD and continue the decomposition process.

(5) *Check for new entities.* At each stage of decomposition, consider whether any new entities are implied by the new functions that have been introduced and add them to the appropriate EDFD, reorganizing EDFDs as necessary.

(6) *Group functions under new entities.* Identify all the functions performed by or on new entities. Change passive to active entities if necessary and reorganize EDFDs as appropriate.

(7) *Assign entities to appropriate domains.* Assign each entity to some application domain, and create a set of ERDs, one for each domain.

The end result of OOS is an entity-relationship diagram, together with a hierarchy of entity-dataflow diagrams (see the sidebar "Tools for Bailin object-oriented requirements specification"). Bailin's methodology conforms to the essential principals of object orientation, although explicit object-oriented terminology is not used. (Loy[8] lists three principles that distinguish object orientation from other approaches: encapsulation of attributes, operations, and services within objects; classification of object abstractions; and inheritance of common attributes between classes.) The entity-relationship diagrams capture a classification of objects as well as opportunities for inheritance, and Bailin's functions map to the object-oriented concept of encapsulated services.

Coad and Yourdon object-oriented analysis. Coad and Yourdon[3] view their OOA methodology as building "upon the best concepts from information modeling, object-oriented programming languages, and knowledge-based systems." OOA results in a five-layer model of the problem domain, where each layer builds on the previous layers. The layered model is constructed using a five-step procedure:

(1) *Define objects and classes.* Look for structures, other systems, devices, events, roles, operational procedures, sites, and organizational units.

(2) *Define structures.* Look for relationships between classes and represent them as either general-to-specific structures (for example, employee-to-sales manager) or whole-to-part structures (for example, car-to-engine).

(3) *Define subject areas.* Examine top-level objects within whole-to-part hierarchies and mark these as candidate subject areas. Refine subject areas to minimize interdependencies between subjects.

(4) *Define attributes.* Identify the atomic characteristics of objects as attributes of the object. Also look for associative relationships between objects and determine the cardinality of those relationships.

(5) *Define services.* For each class and object, identify all the services it performs, either on its own behalf or for the benefit of other classes and objects.

The primary tools for Coad and Yourdon OOA are class and object diagrams and service charts (see the sidebar, "Tools for Coad and Yourdon object-oriented analysis"). The class and object diagram has five levels, which are built incrementally during each of the five analysis steps outlined above. Service charts, which are "much like a [traditional] flow chart," are used during the service definition phase to represent the internal logic of services." In addition, service charts portray state-dependent behavior such as preconditions and triggers (operations that are activated by the occurrence of a predefined event).

Coad and Yourdon explicitly support each of the essential principles of object orientation. The class and objects diagram (levels 1, 2, and 4) provides an object classification and identifies potential inheritance relationships. In addition, encapsulation of objects is modeled through the concept of exclusive services. Coad and Yourdon OOA is similar to modern structured analysis (MSA) and information engineering in its emphasis on information modeling, but differs in providing constructs for

modeling exclusive services and message connections.

Shlaer and Mellor object-oriented analysis. Shlaer and Mellor developed their object-oriented analysis methodology over the course of several years of consulting practice in information modeling. Although information modeling forms the foundation of the method, two other views of the target system are prescribed as well: a state model and a process model. This three-way view of

the system, contained in interrelated information, state, and process models, is proposed as a complete description of the problem domain. Shlaer and Mellor advocate a six-step procedure:

(1) *Develop an information model.* This model consists of objects, attributes, relationships, and multiple-object constructions (based on is-a, is-part-of, and associative relationships). (The term object, as used by Shlaer and Mellor, is equivalent to the conventional notion

Tools for Shlaer and Mellor object-oriented analysis

Action-dataflow diagram (ADFD) — Similar to DFDs, except ADFDs are used to model elementary "action" processes rather than to create a top-down functional decomposition of the entire system. Standard DeMarco notation is used, except additional notations are provided to show control flows and to show conditionality in the execution of dataflows and control flows.

Domain chart — A simple diagram that illustrates all domains relevant to the implementation of an OOA model. Domains are enclosed within bubbles and are connected by directed arcs. These arcs represent bridges between domains. Four types of domains are identified: application, service, architectural, and implementation.

Information structure diagram — A variant on the entity-relationship diagram that shows objects (boxes) connected by relationships (labeled arcs). Attributes are listed within object boxes. Relationship conditionality and multiplicity are also shown.

Object and attribute description — A text description of an object, including object name, object description, object identifier, a list of attributes, and descriptions of each attribute.

Object-access model — Shows the synchronous interactions between state models at the global system level. Synchronous interactions occur when one state model accesses the instance data of another object via an accessor process. State models (enclosed in ovals) are connected to each other by directed arcs labeled with the accessor process.

Object-communication model — Shows the asynchronous interactions between state models and external entities at the global system level. State models (enclosed in ovals) are connected to each other and to external entities (enclosed in boxes) by directed arcs labeled with communicating events.

Process description — A narrative description of a process. A process description is needed for every process appearing on an action-dataflow diagram.

Relationship specification — A text description of each relationship, including the name of the relationship (from the point of view of each object), conditionality (required or optional), multiplicity (one-to-one, one-to-many, many-to-many), a general description of the relationship, and identification of the attributes (foreign keys) through which the relationship is formalized.

State model — State models conform to the conventional notation for state-transition diagrams (see the sidebar, "Tools for structured methodologies"), except they are used to model the states of problem domain entities. (Traditional STDs, by contrast, model the states of a system, system component, or process.)

Subsystem access model — Shows synchronous interactions between object-access models (one OAM exists for each subsystem). Directed, labeled arcs represent synchronous processes flowing between OAMs (enclosed in boxes).

Subsystem communication model — Shows asynchronous interactions between object-communication models (one OCM exists for each subsystem). Directed, labeled arcs represent asynchronous events flowing between OAMs (enclosed in boxes).

Subsystem relationship model — Shows relationships between information models (where each subsystem has exactly one information model). Information models (enclosed in boxes) are connected by undirected arcs (labeled with relationships).

of an entity, that is, a person, place, thing, or event that exists in the real world.)

(2) *Define object life cycles.* The focus here is on analyzing the life cycle of each object (from creation through destruction) and formalizing the life cycle into a collection of states (some predefined condition of an object), events (signals that cause transitions from state to state), transition rules (which specify the allowable transitions between states), and actions (activities or operations that must be done by an object upon arrival in a state). This step also defines *timers*, mechanisms used by actions to generate a future event. The primary tool during this step is the state model. (See the sidebar, "Tools for Shlaer and Mellor object-oriented analysis.")

(3) *Define the dynamics of relationships.* This step develops a state model for those relationships between objects that evolve over time (dynamic relationships). For each dynamic relationship, an associative object is defined in the information model. Special assigner state models are defined for relationships in which there may be contention between object instances for resources of another object instance.

(4) *Define system dynamics.* This step produces a model of time and control at the system level. An object-communication model (OCM) is developed to show asynchronous control (akin to simple message passing). An object-access model is developed to show synchronous control (instances where one object accesses the instance data of another through an accessor process). Shlaer and Mellor also describe a procedure for tracing threads of control at a high level (by following events on the OCM) and at a more detailed level (by creating a thread-of-control chart for individual actions).

(5) *Develop process models.* For each action, an action-dataflow diagram is created that shows all of the processes for that action, and the data flows among the processes and data stores. (Standard DeMarco notation for DFDs is used, except additional notations are provided to show control flows and to show conditionality in the execution of dataflows and control flows.) OOA defines four types of processes (accessors, event generators, transformations, and tests) and provides guidelines for de-

composing actions into these constituent processes.

(6) *Define domains and subsystems.* For large problems, it can be useful to decompose the subject matter into conceptually distinct domains. Four types of domains are identified: application, service, architectural, and implementation. In addition, it is sometimes useful to decompose the application domain into multiple subsystems.

Shlaer and Mellor provide implicit, rather than explicit, support for the three essential principles of object orientation — classification, inheritance, and encapsulation. The objects and relationships contained in the information structure diagram, while not identical to object-oriented concepts of classification and inheritance, can easily be mapped to these concepts during design. (Regular entities and parent entities engaged in is-a style relationships correspond to classes and superclasses, respectively, and identify candidate inheritance relationships. The is-part-of style relationships correspond to whole-to-part class relationships.) The requirement that each action process (and associated dataflow diagram) be associated with exactly one object preserves encapsulation of those operations.

Comparison of analysis methodologies

The conventional and OOA methodologies reviewed here can be compared along 11 modeling dimensions; these dimensions represent the superset of dimensions supported by the individual methodologies (see Table 1). Since the various methodologists tend to use widely divergent terminology and notations for similar concepts, Table 1 presents the dimensions at a level that captures essential similarities and differences between the methodologies. We examined the concepts and notations advocated by each methodology in detail to determine those that were variants on the same basic idea. (For example, Coad and Yourdon's concept of a generalization-specialization relationship between objects is viewed as essentially the same as the is-a style or subtype/supertype entity relationships described in the other analysis methodologies. When used as part of an OOA methodology, gener-

alization-specialization and is-a relationships are both intended to identify candidate opportunities for inheritance.)

Object-oriented versus conventional analysis. As Table 1 shows, object-oriented analysis covers many of the same dimensions as Yourdon MSA and Martin information engineering, although there is a marked contrast between OOA and DeMarco structured analysis. MSA, information engineering, and all of the object-oriented methodologies provide a variety of tools for modeling entities. These include tools for defining entity relationships and attributes (see Table 1, rows 1 through 4) and partitioning large models by grouping naturally related entities (row 5). MSA, Coad and Yourdon OOA, and Shlaer and Mellor OOA support modeling of states (row 6), although within MSA states are modeled at the level of a system or system component, while in the OOA methodologies states are modeled at the level of problem domain entities (objects). DeMarco structured analysis, MSA, Coad and Yourdon OOA, and Shlaer and Mellor OOA provide tools for defining the detailed logic within functions or services (row 7).

The most important differences between object-oriented and conventional analysis methodologies ultimately stem from the object-oriented requirement of encapsulated operations. Conventional methodologies provide tools to create a functional decomposition of operations (row 8) and to model end-to-end processing sequences (row 9). A functional decomposition of systems violates encapsulation because operations can directly access a multitude of different entities and are not subordinated to any one entity; so it is appropriate that no object-oriented methodology provides support here. It is less clear why none of the OOA methodologies as reviewed here provide an explicit model of end-to-end processing sequences, since there is no inherent incompatibility between this view of a system and object orientation. This issue is discussed further in the concluding section.

All the OOA methodologists recognize a need to develop some sort of model of system operations, albeit in a way that preserves encapsulation. As a result, each methodology provides new tools, or variants on conventional tools, for modeling operations as exclusive services of objects (row 10). Row 11

illustrates a further distinction between object-oriented and conventional analysis that arises from the need in object orientation for active communication between entities. (Entities communicate explicitly in an object-oriented system, whereas in a conventional system, entities are passive data stores manipulated by active, independent procedures.)

OOA methodology similarities. The three OOA methodologies illustrated in Table 1 overlap significantly, although different notations and terminology are used for essentially the same concepts. These stylistic differences obscure the fact that, in each of the three methodologies, entities (objects) and relationships establish a foundation for later stages of analysis. Bailin uses a standard ERD notation, which includes the idea of subtype/supertype relationships, as well as any number of user-defined relationships. Shlaer and Mellor's information structure diagrams are similar in terms of content to ERDs. While neither of these methodologies specifically mentions such object-oriented notions as inheritance and object classification, ERDs do, in fact, capture candidate instances of these sorts of relationships using subtype/supertype constructs.

Dynamic entity connections and using-style relationships are also captured in ERDs through such relationship types as creates, destroys, uses, and modifies. Unlike the other two methodologies, Coad and Yourdon refer explicitly to object-oriented concepts such as inheritance and object decomposition. Nonetheless, layers 1, 2, and 4 of the class and objects diagram can easily be mapped to an ERD notation, and these three layers serve essentially the same purpose as an ERD. (The objects and classes identified in level 1 map to the ERD concept of an entity. The generalization-specialization relationships defined in level 2 correspond to subtype/supertype relationships in an ERD. The whole-part structures defined in level 2 and the associative relationships identified in layer 4 correspond to general relationships in an ERD.)

OOA methodology differences. The clearest differences between the methodologies occur in three areas:

(1) depiction of entity states,

Table 1. Comparison of analysis methodologies.

Component	DeMarco Structured Analysis	Yourdon Modern Structured Analysis	Martin Information Engineering	Bailin Object-Oriented Requirements Specification	Coad and Yourdon Object-Oriented Analysis	Shlaer and Mellor Object-Oriented Analysis
1. Identification/ classification of entities*	*Not supported*	Entity-relationship diagram	Data-model diagram	Entity-relationship diagram	Class and objects diagram layer 1	Information-structure diagram
2. General-to-specific and whole-to-part entity-relationships	*Not supported*	Entity-relationship diagram	Data-model diagram	Entity-relationship diagram	Class and objects diagram layer 2	Information-structure diagram
3. Other entity-relationship (creates, uses, etc.)	*Not supported*	Entity-relationship diagram	Data-model diagram	Entity-relationship diagram	Class and objects diagram layer 4	Information-structure diagram
4. Attributes of entities	Data dictionary	Data dictionary	Bubble chart	*Not supported*	Class and objects diagram layer 4	Information-structure diagram
5. Large-scale model partitioning	Dataflow diagram	Event-partitioned dataflow diagram	Subject databases	Domain-partitioned entity-relationship diagrams	Class and objects diagram layer 3	Domain chart; subsystem communication, access, and relationship models
6. States and transitions**	*Not supported*	State-transition diagram	*Not supported*	*Not supported*	Object-state diagram; service chart	State model
7. Detailed logic for functions/ services	Mini-specification	Mini-specification	*Not supported*	*Not supported*	Service chart	Action dataflow diagram; process descriptions
8. Top-down decomposition of functions***	Dataflow diagram	Dataflow diagram	Process-decomposition diagram	*Not Supported*	*Not Supported*	*Not Supported*
9. End-to-end processing sequences	Dataflow diagram	Dataflow diagram	Process-dependency diagram	*Not supported*	*Not supported*	*Not supported*
10. Identification of exclusive services	*Not supported*	*Not supported*	*Not supported*	Entity-dataflow diagram	Class and objects diagram layer 5	State model, action-dataflow diagram
11. Entity communication (via messages or events)	*Not supported*	*Not supported*	*Not supported*	Entity-dataflow diagram	Class and objects diagram layer 5	Object communication model; object-access model

* For stylistic reasons, the term entity, when it appears in this column, is intended to encompass the terms entity (as used in conventional methodologies and by Bailin), object (as used by Shlaer and Mellor), and class (as used by Coad and Yourdon).

** Conventional STDs as used in Yourdon's MSA describe the states of a system or system component, whereas Shlaer and Mellor's state model and Coad and Yourdon's object-state diagram describe the states of problem domain entities. STDs are not an integral part of information engineering because they are thought to be too detailed for the analysis phase, although Martin allows that they may be used occasionally.

*** Bailin does provide some support for decomposition of functions via entity-dataflow diagrams, but functions are decomposed only at the lowest levels of the diagram rather than at all levels.

(2) definition of exclusive services, and
(3) attention to attribute modeling.

Shlaer and Mellor place the most emphasis on modeling entity states and devote an entire phase of their methodology to defining entity life cycles and depicting them in state models. Coad and Yourdon also model entity states, although this does not appear to be a significant component of the methodology. (Coad and Yourdon's service chart contains much of the same information as Shlaer and Mellor's state model, although it also contains procedural logic unrelated to entity states and transitions. Coad and Yourdon recommend the use of an object-state diagram where helpful, but this diagram does not explicitly name the events that trigger transitions. The object-state model is referred to only sparingly, and does not appear to be a significant component of the final system model.) Bailin has no formal means of depicting entity states and transitions, although he notes that state-transition diagrams are being considered as one possible extension of the method.

Coad and Yourdon and Shlaer and Mellor provide the most detailed representations of exclusive services. In Coad and Yourdon, exclusive services are assigned to objects in layer 5 of the class and objects diagram, and the procedural logic contained in each service is defined in detail in an associated service chart. Shlaer and Mellor also identify exclusive services, which they term *actions*. Actions are identified on state models (object specific) and are defined in detail in the action-dataflow diagram (ADFD) and corresponding process descriptions. The primary tool for modeling Bailin's functions — the entity-dataflow diagram — contains much less detail than Coad and Yourdon's service chart or Shlaer and Mellor's ADFD with process descriptions.

The methodologies differ substantially in their level of attention to attribute modeling. Bailin places a very low emphasis on defining attributes of entities; in fact, he makes no mention of attribute modeling at all. Coad and Yourdon devote a phase to identifying attributes, although not to the extent of ensuring that attributes are normalized within entities. Shlaer and Mellor provide the most emphasis on attribute modeling of the three methodologies, including extensive guidance for describing and normalizing attributes.

Finally, Shlaer and Mellor support some concepts not addressed by Coad and Yourdon or Bailin. These include

(1) a distinction between asynchronous and synchronous control,
(2) the use of timers to generate future events, and
(3) the concept of a dynamic relationship and its role in handling contention between concurrent processes.

OOA: Incremental versus radical change. With regard to the incremental versus radical debate, object-oriented analysis does represent a radical departure from older process-oriented methodologies such as DeMarco structured analysis, but is only an incremental change from data-oriented methodologies like Martin information engineering. Table 1 shows that OOA methodologies typically model six dimensions of the problem domain not contained in a structured analysis model (see rows 1-3, 6, 10-11) and do not model two process-oriented dimensions (rows 8-9) that form the foundation of a De Marco structured analysis model. OOA decomposes the problem domain based on a classification of entities (objects) and their relationships, while structured analysis provides a decomposition based on processes. Developers schooled in DeMarco structured analysis will find the competencies they developed in the construction of hierarchies of DFDs to be, for the most part, irrelevant. Meanwhile, a whole new set of competencies relating to the classification and modeling of entities will have to be developed.

The revolutionaries quoted in the introduction rightly observe that object orientation is fundamentally at odds with the process-oriented view of systems favored by structured methodologies during the 1970s. However, they ignore important changes in these same methodologies over the course of the 1980s towards a more balanced view of data and processes. OOA methodologies only model two dimensions of the problem domain not modeled by Yourdon MSA or Martin information engineering (see Table 1, rows 10-11).

All the OOA methodologies reviewed here contain a heavy information modeling component, and potential adopters with a strong information modeling background should require only limited exposure to absorb the notational differences between conventional information modeling diagrams and the variants developed by OOA methodologists. The idea of shifting from disembodied processes (modeled in dataflow diagrams) to encapsulated services will be more challenging. However, at the level of detail required for analysis, this conceptual shift can probably be absorbed without great difficulty. Shlaer and Mellor OOA, with its emphasis on modeling object life cycles, appears to represent the most significant change of the three OOA methodologies.

Object-oriented design methodologies

Design is the process of mapping system requirements defined during analysis to an abstract representation of a specific system-based implementation, meeting cost and performance constraints. As was done with OOA methodologies, we conducted a literature search to identify broadly representative OOD methodologies first published in book form or as detailed articles in refereed journals from 1980 to 1990. This resulted in the selection of three methodologies from Booch,[2] Wasserman et al.,[4] and Wirfs-Brock et al.[18] Implementation-specific methodologies, such as those targeted at real-time systems using the Ada language, were excluded from consideration.

We present the methodologies in an order based on their similarities to conventional methodologies. Wasserman et al. draws most heavily on structured design and is presented first, followed by Booch, and Wirfs-Brock et al.

Wasserman et al. object-oriented structured design. Object-oriented structured design (OOSD) was developed by Wasserman, Pircher, and Muller. The methodology provides a detailed notation for describing an *architectural design*, which they define as a high-level design that identifies individual modules but not their detailed internal representation. Wasserman et al. state that the overall goal of OOSD is to provide a standard design notation that can support every software design, including both object-oriented and conventional approaches.

OOSD offers a hybrid notation that

Object-oriented structure chart — An updated version of the classical structure chart that adds notations for objects and classes ("information clusters"), methods, visibility, instantiation, exception handling, hidden operations, generic definitions (abstract classes), inheritance, and concurrency. The charts can also be used to show multiple inheritance, message passing, polymorphism, dynamic binding, and asynchronous processes.

incorporates concepts from previous work from several areas, including structure charts from structured design; Booch's notation for Ada packages and tasks; hierarchy and inheritance from object orientation; and the concept of monitors from concurrent programming. However, as Wasserman et al. observe, OOSD does not provide a detailed procedure for developing the design itself.

The primary tool for OOSD is the object-oriented structure chart (see the sidebar, "Tools for Wasserman et al. object-oriented structured design"). This chart takes the symbols and notations from conventional structure charts, including modules, data parameters, and control parameters, and adds notations for such object-oriented constructs as objects and classes (called "information clusters" by the authors), methods, instantiation, exception handling, generic definitions (similar to abstract classes), inheritance, and concurrency. Object-oriented structure charts can be used to show multiple inheritance, message passing, polymorphism, and dynamic binding. OOSD also supports the concept of a monitor, which is useful in depicting the asynchronous processes typically found in real-time systems.

Although OOSD is intended primarily for architectural design, the authors state that OOSD provides a foundation for representing design decisions associated with the physical design. The authors recommend that annotations be used to reflect the idiosyncrasies of individual implementation languages, while preserving the generic character of basic symbols. For example, OOSD includes optional Ada language-specific annotations to provide for packages, sequencing, and selective activation.

Booch object-oriented design. Booch

pioneered the field of object-oriented design. As originally defined in the early 1980s, Booch's methodology was Ada language specific, but it has been significantly expanded and generalized since then. Booch views his methodology as an alternative to, rather than an extension of, structured design.

Although Booch describes a host of techniques and tools to assist design, ranging from informal lists to formal diagrams and templates, he is reluctant to prescribe a fixed ordering of phases for object-oriented design. Rather, he recommends that analysts work iteratively and incrementally, augmenting formal diagrams with informal techniques as appropriate to the problem at hand. Nevertheless, Booch does delineate four major steps that must be performed during the course of OOD:

(1) *Identify classes and objects.* Identify key abstractions in the problem space and label them as candidate classes and objects.

(2) *Identify the semantics of classes and objects.* Establish the meaning of the classes and objects identified in the previous step using a variety of techniques, including creating "scripts" that define the life cycles of each object from creation to destruction.

(3) *Identify relationships between classes and objects.* Establish class and object interactions, such as patterns of inheritance among classes and patterns of cooperation among objects. This step also captures visibility decisions among classes and objects.

(4) *Implement classes and objects.* Construct detailed internal views of classes and objects, including definitions of their various behaviors (services). Also, allocate objects and classes to modules (as defined in the target lan-

guage environment) and allocate programs to processors (where the target environment supports multiple processors).

The primary tools used during OOD are

- class diagrams and class templates (which emphasize class definitions and inheritance relationships);
- object diagrams and timing diagrams (which stress message definitions, visibility, and threads of control);
- state-transition diagrams (to model object states and transitions);
- operation templates (to capture definitions of services);
- module diagrams and templates (to capture physical design decisions about the assignment of objects and classes to modules); and
- process diagrams and templates (to assign modules to processors in situations where a multiprocessor configuration will be used).

(See the sidebar, "Tools for Booch object-oriented design.")

Booch OOD provides the widest variety of modeling tools of the OOD methodologies reviewed here. Although he does not prescribe a fixed sequence of design steps, Booch does provide a wealth of guidance on the design process by describing in detail the types of activities that must be performed and by working through the design of five hypothetical systems from different problem domains.

Wirfs-Brock et al. responsibility-driven design. Wirfs-Brock, Wilkerson, and Wiener developed their responsibility-driven design (RDD) methodology during several years of internal software development experience in various corporate settings. RDD is based on a client-server model of computing in which systems are seen as being composed of collections of *servers* that hold private responsibilities and also render services to *clients* based on contracts that define the nature and scope of valid client-server interactions.

To map these terms to more conventional object-oriented terminology, clients and servers are different kinds of objects, while services and responsibilities correspond to methods. Contracts and collaborations are metaphors for the idea that, to preserve encapsulation, some objects must be willing to perform certain tasks (such as modifying the values of their own internal variables) for the benefit of other objects, and that some kinds of services require several objects to work together to achieve the desired result.

Their methodology is responsibility driven because the focus of attention during design is on contracts between clients and server objects. These contracts spell out what actions each object is responsible for performing and what information each object is responsible for sharing. Wirfs-Brock et al. contrast their approach with what they term data-driven object-oriented design methodologies (they cite no specific authors), which are said to emphasize the design of data structures internal to objects and inheritance relationships based on common attributes. In contrast, the responsibility-driven approach is intended to maximize the level of encapsulation in the resulting design. Data-driven design is said to focus more on classes and inheritance, while responsibility-driven design focuses more on object interactions and encapsulation.

Like Booch, Wirfs-Brock et al. recommend an incremental/iterative approach to design, as opposed to rigid phases with fixed deliverables. RDD provides for a six-step procedure spread across two phases. An exploration phase finds candidate classes, responsibilities, and collaborations. A second analysis phase builds hierarchies, defines subsystems, and defines protocols. The steps are

(1) *Find classes.* Extract noun phrases from the requirements specification and build a list of candidate classes by looking for nouns that refer to physical objects, conceptual entities, categories of objects, and external interfaces. Attributes of objects and candidate superclasses are also identified.

(2) *Find responsibilities and assign to classes.* Consider the purpose of each class and examine the specification for action phrases to find candidate responsibilities. Assign responsibilities to classes such that system intelligence is evenly distributed, behaviors reside with related information, and responsibilities are shared among related classes.

(3) *Find collaborations.* Examine responsibilities associated with each class

and consider which other classes are needed for collaboration to fulfill each responsibility.

(4) *Define hierarchies.* Construct class hierarchies for kind-of inheritance relationships such that common responsibilities are factored as high as possible and abstract classes do not inherit from concrete classes. Construct contracts by grouping together responsibilities used by the same clients.

(5) *Define subsystems.* Draw a collaborations graph for the complete system. Look for frequent and complex collaborations and identify these as candidate subsystems. Classes within a subsystem should support a small and strongly cohesive set of responsibilities and should be strongly interdependent.

(6) *Define protocols.* Develop design detail by writing design specifications for classes, subsystems, and contracts. Construct the protocols for each class

(the signatures for the messages to which each class responds).

Tools used throughout the design process include

- Class cards (steps 1, 2 and 3);
- Hierarchy diagrams (step 4);
- Venn diagrams (step 4);
- Collaborations graphs (steps 4 and 5);
- Subsystem cards (step 5);
- Class specifications (step 6); and
- Subsystem specifications (step 6).

(See the sidebar, "Tools for Wirfs-Brock et al. responsibility-driven design.")

In advocating an approach that emphasizes the dynamic behavior and responsibilities of objects rather than their static class relationships, RDD provides a significant contrast to Booch OOD and to the OOA methodologies reviewed earlier. Unlike these other meth-

Tools for Booch object-oriented design

Class diagram/template — Shows the existence of classes (enclosed in dotted-line "clouds") and their relationships (depicted by various kinds of directed and undirected arcs) in the logical design of a system. Relationships supported include uses, instantiates, inherits, metaclass, and undefined.

Module diagram/template — Documents the allocation of objects and classes to modules in the physical design of a system. Only needed for languages (such as Ada) that support the idea of a module as distinct from objects and classes.

Object diagram/template — Used to model some of dynamics of objects. Each object (enclosed in solid line "clouds") represents an arbitrary instance of a class. Objects are connected by directed arcs that define object visibility and message connections. Does not show flow of control or ordering of events.

Operation template — Structured text that provides detailed design documentation for operations.

Process diagram/template — Used to show the allocation of processes to processors in the physical design of a system. Only for implementations in multiprocessor environments.

State-transition diagram — Shows the states (depicted by circles) of a class, the events (directed arcs) that cause transitions from one state to another, and the actions that result from a state change.

Timing diagram — A companion diagram to the object diagram, shows the flow of control and ordering of events among a group of collaborating objects.

odologies, the initial steps of RDD do not focus on establishing a hierarchy of classes, but rather attempt to construct a close simulation of object behaviors and interactions.

Comparison of design methodologies

Object-oriented design versus conventional design. The distinctions between conventional and object-oriented development, some of which were identified in the discussion of analysis methodologies, are amplified during design due to the growing importance of implementation-specific issues (see Table 2). None of the conventional methodologies support the definition of classes, inheritance, methods, or message protocols, and while it may not be necessary to consider these constructs

explicitly during object-oriented analysis, they form the foundation of an object-oriented design (Table 2, rows 6 through 10). In addition, while conventional and object-oriented methodologies both provide tools that define a hierarchy of modules (row 1), a completely different method of decomposition is employed, and the very definition of the term module is different.

In conventional systems, modules — such as programs, subroutines, and functions — only contain procedural code. In object-oriented systems, the object — a bundling of procedures and data — is the primary unit of modularity. Structured design and information engineering both use function-oriented decomposition rules, resulting in a set of procedure-oriented program modules. OOD methodologies, by contrast, employ an object-oriented decomposition resulting in collections of methods encapsulated within objects.

The greatest overlap between conventional and object-oriented design methodologies is between Booch OOD and information engineering. Both methodologies provide a tool for defining end-to-end processing sequences (row 4), although Booch's timing diagram contains much less detail than information engineering's data-dependency diagram. Both methodologies provide for a detailed definition of procedural logic.

Booch recommends the use of a generic program definition language (PDL) or structured English, while information engineering recommends the use of a graphical action diagram for this purpose. Finally, for information-intensive applications, Booch recommends that a normalization procedure be used for designing data. This normalization procedure is very similar to the one employed by information engineering.

OOD methodology differences. The most notable differences among the three OOD methodologies have to do with

(1) data design,
(2) level of detail in describing the process of OOD, and
(3) level of detail provided by diagram notations.

Booch, as mentioned above, employs a detailed procedure (where appropriate) for designing the data encapsulated within objects. In fact, Booch[2] sees many parallels between database design and OOD:

> In a process not unlike object-oriented design, database designers bounce between logical and physical design throughout the development of the database... The ways in which we describe the elements of a database are very similar to the ways in which we describe the key abstractions in an application using object-oriented design.

Wasserman et al. and Wirfs-Brock et al., by contrast, say little on the issue of data design or normalization.

Wirfs-Brock et al. provide a very thorough description of the design process, which they break into 26 identifiable design activities spread across six steps. Booch offers less in the way of explicit, step-wise design procedures, although he does provide a wealth of implicit guidance, using a detailed description of five hypothetical design projects.

Table 2. Comparison of design methodologies.

Component	Yourdon and Constantine Structured Design	Martin Information Engineering	Wasserman et al. Object-Oriented Structured Design	Booch Object-Oriented Design	Wirfs-Brock et al. Responsibility-Driven Design
1. Hierarchy of modules (physical design)	Structure chart	Process-decomposition diagram	Object-oriented structure chart	Module diagram	*Not supported*
2. Data definitions	Hierarchy diagram	Data-model diagram; data-structure diagram	Object-oriented structure chart	Class diagram	Class specification
3. Procedural logic	*Not supported*	Action diagram	*Not supported*	Operation template	Class specification
4. End-to-end processing sequences	Dataflow diagram	Dataflow diagram; process-dependency diagram	*Not supported*	Timing diagrams	*Not supported*
5. Object states and transitions	*Not supported*	*Not supported*	*Not supported*	State-transition diagram	*Not supported*
6. Definition of classes and inheritance	*Not supported*	*Not supported*	Object-oriented structure chart	Class diagram	Hierarchy diagram
7. Other class relationships (instantiates, uses, etc.)	*Not supported*	*Not supported*	Object-oriented structure chart	Class diagram	Class specification
8. Assignment of operations/ services to classes	*Not supported*	*Not supported*	Object-oriented structure chart	Class diagram	Collaborations graph; class specification
9. Detailed definition of operations/ services	*Not supported*	*Not supported*	*Not supported*	Operations template	Class specification
10. Message connections	*Not supported*	*Not supported*	Object-oriented structure chart	Object diagram and template	Collaborations graph

Wasserman et al., by contrast, assume that the particulars of an implementation environment will dictate what kinds of procedures and quality metrics are best; they do not offer a procedural description of OOSD.

Wasserman et al. and Booch both provide a comprehensive and rigorous set of notations for representing an object-oriented design. Wirfs-Brock et al. provide a less detailed notation in their RDD methodology, and do not address such concepts as persistence, object instantiation, and concurrent execution. The authors claim that RDD is appropriate for object-oriented and conventional development projects alike; this may explain the lack of attention to implementation issues that are more closely associated with object orientation.

OOD: Incremental versus radical change. Regarding the incremental-versus-radical debate, object-oriented design is clearly a radical change from both process-oriented methodologies and data-oriented methodologies (Yourdon and Constantine structured design and Martin information engineering, respectively). Table 2 shows that the number of modeling dimensions on which conventional and object-oriented methodologies overlap ranges from a maximum of four out of 10 (information engineering and Booch OOD) to as few as one out of 10 (structured design and Wirfs-Brock OOD). Although conventional methodologies such as information engineering support a data-oriented view in modeling the problem domain during analysis, they use a function-oriented view in establishing the architecture of program modules during design. As a result, not only is the primary structuring principle for program code different — functions versus objects — but at least half of the specific dimensions of the target system model are different.

Object-oriented design requires a new set of competencies associated with constructing detailed definitions of classes and inheritance, class and object relationships, and object operations and message connections. The design trade-offs between maximizing encapsulation (by emphasizing object responsibilities) versus maximizing inheritance (by emphasizing commonalties among classes) are subtle ones. Designing classes that are independent of the context in which they are used is required to maximize reuse, and here again, very subtle design decisions must be made.[19] As mentioned in the introduction, the important point is not whether object-oriented concepts are radically new in some absolute sense, but rather whether they are radically new to the population of potential adopters. The idea of building systems devoid of global-calling programs, where everything literally is defined as an object, will certainly

be a radical concept to designers schooled in conventional design methodologies.

Transition from analysis to design

Analysis is usually defined as a process of extracting and codifying user requirements and establishing an accurate model of the problem domain. Design, by contrast, is the process of mapping requirements to a system implementation that conforms to desired cost, performance, and quality parameters. While these two activities are conceptually distinct, in practice the line between analysis and design is frequently blurred. Many of the components of an analysis model have direct counterparts in a design model. In addition, the process of design usually leads to a better understanding of requirements, and can uncover areas where a change in requirements must be negotiated to support desired performance and cost constraints. In recognition of these realities, most current methodologies recommend that analysis and design be performed iteratively, if not concurrently.

One of the frequently cited advantages of object orientation is that it provides a smoother translation between analysis and design models than do structured methodologies. It is true that no direct and obvious mapping exists between structured analysis and structured design:

> Anyone involved with [structured design] knows that the transition from the analysis model to the design model can be tricky. For example, in moving from a dataflow diagram view of the system to creating design-structure charts the modeler is forced to make a significant shift in perspective. There are strategies to assist in the matter (transform analysis, transaction analysis, etc.), but it remains a difficult task because the mapping is not truly isomorphic.[6]

With object orientation, the mapping from analysis to design does appear to be potentially more isomorphic, as a comparison of Tables 1 and 2 reveals. Every analysis model component supported by at least one OOA methodology can be mapped to a similar (albeit usually more detailed) component supported by at least one design methodology. Rows 1-3, 4, 5, 6, 7, 10, and 11 in

Table 1 correspond to rows 6-7, 2, 1, 5, 9, 8 and 10 in Table 2, respectively.

Only two object-oriented methodologists provided detailed procedures encompassing both analysis and design (Coad and Yourdon[20] and Rumbaugh et al.[21]). Shlaer and Mellor also briefly describe a procedure for translating OOA into OOD. Development groups that do not elect to adopt a single methodology spanning analysis and design will face the problem of matching up incompatible terminology and notations from different methodologists. The blurring between analysis and design is a particularly acute issue because the somewhat arbitrary line between analysis and design is drawn in different places by different methodologists. Of the OOA methodologies, Coad and Yourdon's and Shlaer and Mellor's seem to encroach the most on design. Coad and Yourdon explicitly identify inheritance relationships (usually considered a design activity) and provide for a formal and detailed specification of the logic within services. Shlaer and Mellor provide for complete normalization of attributes and advocate detailed modeling of entity life cycles. Of the design methodologies reviewed here, Wirfs-Brock et al. RDD appears to encroach the most on analysis in that it assumes that only an English-language specification (rather than a full-analysis model) is the input to the methodology.

Overall critique

Object-oriented methodologies are less mature than conventional methodologies, and may be expected to undergo a period of expansion and refinement as project experience uncovers gaps in modeling capabilities or misplaced assumptions. Three areas currently stand out as candidates for further development work. To begin with, a rigorous mechanism is needed for decomposing very large systems into components, such that each component can be developed separately and subsequently integrated. Second, tools for modeling end-to-end processing sequences that involve multiple objects are either cumbersome or wholly lacking. Third, in the area of reuse, much is made of designing in reuse ("sowing" reuse), but no more than passing mention is made of techniques or procedures for finding and exploiting existing models, domain

58

knowledge, or components ("harvesting" reuse). The first two areas are ones where object-oriented methodologies lack functionality provided by conventional methodologies, while the third area lacks support in both object-oriented and conventional methodologies.

System partitioning/object clustering. Traditional methodologies, such as structured analysis and information engineering, provide mechanisms for creating a natural, coarse-grained decomposition of systems (nested processes in the case of structured analysis, and subject databases in the case of information engineering). This decomposition is essential because many projects are too large to be developed by a single team within the desired time frame and, hence, must be divided into components and assigned to multiple teams working in parallel. To be most beneficial, the decomposition must be performed early in the development process, which also suggests it must be created in top-down fashion rather than bottom-up. In addition, the decomposition must create natural divisions between components and allow for a rigorously defined process of subsequent reintegration of the components.

The most coarse-grained, formally defined entities in object orientation are objects and classes. While objects and classes certainly provide a powerful mechanism for aggregating system functionality, they are usually defined in a bottom-up fashion as common characteristics get factored to ever higher levels in an inheritance structure. In addition, very large systems, even after this factoring process has been completed, may still consist of hundreds of top-level classes. De Champeaux[22] notes

> While the analysis of a toy example like the popular car cruise control system yields only a "flat" set of objects [classes], the analysis of ... an airline system or a bank will yield "objects" [classes] at different abstraction levels.

The objects and classes, even at the highest level, are too fine-grained and defined too late in the development process to provide a basis for partitioning large development projects. This limitation has apparently been recognized by several methodologists; they have responded by inventing high-level constructs for clustering related object classes. These constructs include subject areas,[3] domains,[16] systems,[16,18] and ensembles.[22]

Two of these constructs — Coad and Yourdon's subject areas and the Wirfs-Brock et al. subsystems — appear to be very similar conceptually and provide a starting point for partitioning object-oriented models. Yet they are quite informally defined, and they provide little indication of how individually developed system components might interact. Shlaer and Mellor's concepts of domains and subsystems are better developed, and four of the methodology's diagrams are devoted to modeling the interactions between domains and between application domain subsystems (domain chart, subsystem relationship model, subsystem communication model, and subsystem access model).

De Champeaux's *ensembles* and *ensemble classes*[22] are the most rigorously defined of the clustering mechanisms. Ensembles are analogous to conventional objects, while ensemble classes are analogous to conventional classes. An ensemble is a flat grouping of objects (or other ensembles) that naturally go together — usually because they participate in whole-to-part relationships. An automobile, for example, is an ensemble consisting of an engine, doors, wheels, etc. Ensembles have many of the same characteristics as conventional objects, including attributes, states and transitions, and the capability of interacting with other objects and ensembles.

De Champeaux distinguishes ensembles from objects on this basis: Ensembles can have *internal parallelism* while objects cannot. That is, ensembles may consist of subordinate objects or ensembles that each exhibit behaviors in parallel during system execution. Objects, by contrast, are assumed to exhibit only sequential behaviors (for example, as modeled in a finite-state machine.)

De Champeaux distinguishes ensembles from other clustering mechanisms (such as, the Wirfs-Brock et al. subsystems) in that they are more than just conceptual entities; they exist during system execution and may have persistent attributes. It is less clear how ensembles differ from the conventional notion of a compound or composite object,[2] except that ensembles seem to be a more general concept than composite objects. That is, an ensemble might refer to a cluster of related entities, such as a fleet of ships that would not ordinarily be viewed as a composite object in the real world.

Yet, in terms of how they behave, ensembles and composite objects appear to be quite similar. De Champeaux notes that the constituents of an ensemble only interact directly with each other or with the encompassing ensemble. An ensemble hides the details of constituents that are irrelevant outside of the ensemble, and acts as a gateway that forwards messages or triggers to external objects and ensembles. Likewise, Booch recommends that when using composite objects, the encapsulating object should hide the details of the constituent objects and mediate between constituent objects and external objects.[2]

Although De Champeaux's use of ensembles seems promising on a conceptual level, actual project experiences will tell whether or not ensembles provide a practical basis for partitioning large projects. An interesting question for language designers is whether ensembles, or some similar construct, should be explicitly supported, for example, through mechanisms that limit the allowable patterns of interaction between ensembles, their constituents, and external objects to just those envisioned by de Champeaux.

End-to-end process modeling. Many problem domains contain global processes that impact many objects and involve the serial or parallel execution of numerous intermediary steps between initiation and conclusion. Examples of such processes include the ordering process for a manufacturer, daily account reconciliation in a bank, and monthly invoice processing by a long-distance telecommunications carrier. Conventional methodologies provide well-established tools such as dataflow diagrams (see the "Tools for structured methodology" sidebar) and process-dependency diagrams (see the sidebar, "Tools for Martin information engineering") for modeling these sorts of processes.

None of the object-oriented methodologies reviewed here provide a specific model for describing global processes end to end, although individual parts of the process are modeled piecemeal using such concepts as operations,[2,4] services,[3] actions and processes,[16] and responsibilities.[18] (Shlaer and Mellor describe a procedure for following threads of control, but this procedure spans several different diagrams and seems rather cumbersome. In any case, no distinct view of end-to-end processing — devoid of extraneous information — is provided.)

Bailin supports the idea of using data-flow diagrams (and presumably, global process modeling as well) during analysis, but only to help achieve a better understanding of objects. The resulting diagrams serve only as an intermediate representation and are not part of the object-oriented specification.[14]

Booch's timing diagram (see the sidebar, "Tools for Booch object-oriented design") is the closest that any of the methodologies come to supporting a distinct view of end-to-end process modeling. Yet this diagram contains very little expressive power compared with, for example, information engineering's process-dependency diagram. A timing diagram only shows flow of control information, whereas a process-dependency diagram shows flow of control, flow of data, and conditional execution. Bailin also recognizes the need for end-to-end process modeling and has listed composition graphs (similar to timing diagrams in terms of expressive power) as a possible extension of his methodology. (Note that the most recent Bailin methodology refers to compositions graphs as "stimulus-response diagrams.")

This lack of support for global processes is not surprising since the concept of a global process, not subordinated to any individual object, seems to be at odds with the spirit of object orientation. In fact, Booch[2] and de Champeaux[22] both warn against the use of even throwaway dataflow models, for fear that it will irrevocably bias subsequent object modeling towards a "function" orientation.

Still, there is no reason to believe that complicated business processes and the system components that automate them will no longer exist simply because one adopts object orientation. Nor is elimination of end-to-end processes listed by any methodologist as a precondition for adopting object orientation. Thus, it would seem that a separate tool is needed to arrange the mosaic of encapsulated services into a model that illustrates sequencing, conditional execution, and related ideas for certain key global processes.

Harvesting reuse. One of the most persistently claimed advantages of ob-

ject orientation is that it enables pervasive levels of software reuse. If properly applied, object-oriented mechanisms such as encapsulation, inheritance, polymorphism, and dynamic binding certainly obviate many technical barriers to reuse of program code. In addition, it has been claimed that object orientation opens the way to reuse of design models, or frameworks,[7] and even analysis models from relevant problem domains.[6] At the level of analysis and design, reuse can take two basic forms: reuse of components from previously developed analysis and design models, and reuse of abstractions of previously implemented program components.

Even within an object-oriented implementation environment, achieving high levels of reuse is by no means automatic; virtually all object-oriented methodologists emphasize that reuse must be designed into an application from the start. This emphasis on sowing reuse is not surprising; however, it is curious how little attention object-oriented methodologists pay to harvesting reuse during analysis and design. Analysis and design consume more resources than programming, and perhaps more importantly, development budgets and management decisions — both of which should be strongly influenced by anticipated levels of reuse — are set early in the development process.

Of the methodologies described here, only two address the issue of harvesting reuse from beyond the confines of the project at hand. Coad and Yourdon refer to the need to examine previous analysis models for reusable components and also provide a procedure for merging existing design or program components with new applications.[20] Like Coad and Yourdon, Booch emphasizes the importance of seeking reusable software components from existing class libraries during design. Yet, neither author provides specific guidance on how to find or evaluate existing components.

De Champeaux and Faure[6] and Caldiera and Basili[19] discuss the issue of harvesting reuse at the level of analysis and design. De Champeaux and Faure recommend a repository-based approach to managing reuse. They suggest that the software development process can be seen as a process of creating and modifying three cross-referenced repositories with analysis, design, and implementation components. In this

view, the analysis components serve as annotations to the design and implementation components and may point to alternative realizations of the same requirements (for example, with different performance parameters). They further suggest that these annotations could be the basis for a smart library transversal mechanism. This mechanism could assist in identifying candidate reusable components.

Caldiera and Basili provide a much more thorough examination of the issue of harvesting reuse, especially in the areas of identifying and qualifying software components. They suggest a model for project organization where application developers are segregated from "reuse specialists." Reuse specialists work in a "component factory" and are responsible for the development and maintenance of a repository of reusable components. The component factory is responsible for identifying, qualifying, and tailoring reusable components for subsequent integration — by application developers — into ongoing applications development projects.

O bject-oriented analysis and design methodologies are rapidly evolving, but the field is by no means fully mature. None of the methodologies reviewed here (with the possible exception of Booch OOD) has — as of this writing — achieved the status of a widely recognized standard on the order of the conventional methodologies of Yourdon and Constantine or DeMarco. Object-oriented methodologies will continue to evolve, as did conventional methodologies before them, as subtler issues emerge from their use in a wide array of problem domains and project environments. As discussed above, three areas — system partitioning, end-to-end process modeling, and harvesting reuse — appear to be especially strong candidates for further development work. In the meantime, adopters of current object-oriented methodologies may need to develop their own extensions to contend with these issues, or alternatively, limit application of the methodologies to problem domains where these issues are of lesser importance.

Compared with object-oriented methodologies, conventional methodologies fall at different places along the incremental-radical continuum. Developers schooled only in structured analysis circa 1978 can be expected to have great difficulty making the transition to OOA, while those with an information modeling background will find much of OOA to be based on familiar concepts.

During design, all conventional methodologies revert to a process-oriented view in establishing the architecture of program modules, and as a result, object orientation will likely be viewed as radical change by developers schooled in any of the conventional design methods reviewed here. Since organizations will have to adopt object-oriented design methodologies to end up with object-oriented implementations, a move to an object-oriented environment in general may be seen predominantly as a radical change.

Object orientation is founded on a collection of powerful ideas — modularity, abstraction, encapsulation, reuse — that have firm theoretical foundations. In addition, trends in computing towards complex data types and complex new forms of integrated systems seem to favor the object model over conventional approaches.

Although little empirical evidence exists to support many of the specific claims made in favor of object orientation, the weight of informed opinion among many leading-edge practitioners and academics favors object orientation as a "better idea" for software development than conventional approaches. Organizations that are able to absorb this radical change may well find themselves in a significantly stronger competitive position vis-a-vis those incapable of making the transition. ∎

References

1. E. Yourdon, "Object-Oriented Observations," *Am. Programmer*, Vol. 2, No. 7-8, Summer 1989, pp. 3-7.

2. G. Booch, "What Is and What Isn't Object-Oriented Design?" *Am. Programmer*, Vol. 2, No. 7-8, Summer 1989, pp. 14-21.

3. P. Coad and E. Yourdon, *Object-Oriented Analysis*, 2nd edition, Prentice Hall, Englewood Cliffs, N.J., 1991.

4. A.I. Wasserman, P.A. Pircher, and R.J. Muller, "An Object-Oriented Structured Design Method for Code Generation," *Software Eng. Notes*, Vol. 14, No. 1, Jan. 1989, pp. 32-55.

5. M. Page-Jones and S. Weiss, "Synthesis: An Object-Oriented Analysis and Design Method," *Am. Programmer*, Vol. 2, No. 7-8, Summer 1989, pp. 64-67.

6. D. De Champeaux and P. Faure, "A Comparative Study of Object-Oriented Analysis Methods," *J. Oriented-Oriented Programming*, Vol. 5, No. 1, 1992, pp. 21-33

7. R.J. Wirfs-Brock and R.E. Johnson, "Surveying Current Research in Object-Oriented Design," *Comm. ACM*, Vol. 33, No. 9, Sept. 1990, pp. 104-124.

8. P.H. Loy, "A Comparison of Object-Oriented and Structured Development Methodologies," *ACM SIGSoft Software Eng. Notes*, Vol. 15, No. 1, Jan. 1990, pp. 44-48.

9. E. Yourdon and L. Constantine, *Structured Design: Fundamentals of a Discipline of Computer Programming and Design*, 2nd edition, Prentice Hall, New York, 1979.

10. T. DeMarco, *Structured Analysis and System Specification*, Yourdon Inc., New York, 1978.

11. P.T. Ward and S.J. Mellor, *Structured Development of Real-Time Systems*, Yourdon Press, Englewood Cliffs, N.J., 1985.

12. E. Yourdon, *Modern Structured Analysis*, Yourdon Press, Englewood Cliffs, N.J, 1989.

13. J. Martin, *Information Eng., Books I, II, and III*, Prentice Hall, Englewood Cliffs, N.J., 1990.

14. S.C. Bailin, "An Object-Oriented Requirements Specification Method," *Comm. ACM*, Vol. 32, No. 5, May 1989, pp. 608-623.

15. S. Shlaer and S.J. Mellor, *Object-Oriented Analysis: Modeling the World in Data*, Yourdon Press, Englewood Cliffs, N.J., 1988.

16. S. Shlaer and S.J. Mellor, *Object Life Cycles: Modeling the World in States*, Yourdon Press, Englewood Cliffs, N.J., 1992.

17. R.G. Fichman and C.F. Kemerer, "Object-Oriented Analysis and Design Methodologies: Comparison and Critique," MIT Sloan School of Management, Center for Information Systems Research Working Paper No. 230, Nov. 1991.

18. R. Wirfs-Brock, B. Wilkerson, and L. Wiener, *Designing Object-Oriented Software*, Prentice Hall, Englewood Cliffs, N.J., 1990.

19. G. Caldiera and V. Basili, "Identifying and Qualifying Reusable Software Components," *Computer*, Vol. 24, No. 2, Feb. 1991, pp. 61-70.

20. P.Coad and E. Yourdon, *Object-Oriented Design*, Prentice Hall, Englewood Cliffs, N.J., 1991.

21. J. Rumbaugh et al., *Object-Oriented Modeling and Design*, Prentice Hall, Englewood Cliffs, N.J., 1991.

22. D. De Champeaux, "Object-Oriented Analysis and Top-Down Software Development," *Proc. European Conf. Object-Oriented Programming, Lecture Notes in Computer Science*, P. America, ed., Springer-Verlag, Geneva, 1991, pp. 360-376.

Robert G. Fichman is a PhD student in the Information Technologies group at the MIT Sloan School of Management. Previously, he was an applications development supervisor at Williams Telecommunications. His research interests include software engineering management, software development methodologies and tools, and technology diffusion.

Fichman received his BS and MS degrees in industrial and operations engineering at the University of Michigan-Ann Arbor in 1982 and 1983, respectively.

Chris F. Kemerer is the Douglas Drane Career Development Associate Professor of Information Technology and Management at the MIT Sloan School of Management. His research interests are in the measurement and modeling of software development for improved performance, and he has published articles in leading academic journals on these topics. He serves on several editorial boards, including *Communications of the ACM*.

Kemerer received his BS degree in economics and decision sciences from the Wharton School of the University of Pennsylvania and his PhD from the Graduate School of Industrial Administration at Carnegie Mellon University. He is a member of the IEEE Computer Society, the ACM, and the Institute for Management Sciences.

Readers can contact the authors at the Massachusetts Institute of Technology, E53-315, Cambridge, MA 02139, fax (617) 258-7579.

Applying "Design by Contract"

Bertrand Meyer

Interactive Software Engineering

Reprinted from *Computer*, October 1992, pp. 40–51. Copyright © 1992 by The Institute of Electrical and Electronics Engineers, Inc. All rights reserved.

As object-oriented techniques steadily gain ground in the world of software development, users and prospective users of these techniques are clamoring more and more loudly for a "methodology" of object-oriented software construction — or at least for some methodological guidelines. This article presents such guidelines, whose main goal is to help improve the reliability of software systems. *Reliability* is here defined as the combination of correctness and robustness or, more prosaically, as the absence of bugs.

Everyone developing software systems, or just using them, knows how pressing this question of reliability is in the current state of software engineering. Yet the rapidly growing literature on object-oriented analysis, design, and programming includes remarkably few contributions on how to make object-oriented software more reliable. This is surprising and regrettable, since at least three reasons justify devoting particular attention to reliability in the context of object-oriented development:

- The cornerstone of object-oriented technology is reuse. For reusable components, which may be used in thousands of different applications, the potential consequences of incorrect behavior are even more serious than for application-specific developments.
- Proponents of object-oriented methods make strong claims about their beneficial effect on software quality. Reliability is certainly a central component of any reasonable definition of quality as applied to software.
- The object-oriented approach, based on the theory of abstract data types, provides a particularly appropriate framework for discussing and enforcing reliability.

The pragmatic techniques presented in this article, while certainly not providing infallible ways to guarantee reliability, may help considerably toward this goal. They rely on the theory of *design by contract*, which underlies the design of the Eiffel analysis, design, and programming language[1] and of the supporting libraries, from which a number of examples will be drawn.

The contributions of the work reported below include

- a coherent set of *methodological principles* helping to produce correct and robust software;
- a systematic approach to the delicate problem of how to deal with abnormal cases, leading to a simple and powerful *exception-handling* mechanism; and

Reliability is even more important in object-oriented programming than elsewhere. This article shows how to reduce bugs by building software components on the basis of carefully designed contracts.

62

- a better understanding of *inheritance* and of the associated techniques (redeclaration, polymorphism, and dynamic binding) through the notion of subcontract, allowing a systematic approach to using these powerful but sometimes dangerous mechanisms.

Most of the concepts presented here have appeared elsewhere. They were previewed in the book *Object-Oriented Software Construction*[2]; and a more complete exposition was presented in a recent book chapter,[3] from which this article has been adapted. More profoundly, this work finds its root in earlier work on systematic program development[4,5] and abstract data types.[6-8] This article focuses on the central ideas, introducing them concisely for direct application by developers.

Defensive programming revisited

Software engineering and programming methodology textbooks that discuss reliability often emphasize the technique known as *defensive programming*, which directs developers to protect every software module against the slings and arrows of outrageous fortune. In particular, this encourages programmers to include as many checks as possible, even if they are redundant with checks made by callers. Include them anyway, the advice goes; if they do not help, at least they will not harm.

This approach suggests that routines should be as general as possible. A partial routine (one that works only if the caller ensures certain restrictive conditions at the time of the call) is considered dangerous because it might produce unwanted consequences if a caller does not abide by the rules.

This technique, however, often defeats its own purposes. Adding possibly redundant code "just in case" only contributes to the software's complexity — the single worst obstacle to software quality in general, and to reliability in particular. The result of such blind checking is simply to introduce more software, hence more sources of things that could go wrong at execution time, hence the need for more checks, and so on ad infinitum. Such blind and often redundant checking causes much of the complexity and unwieldiness that often characterizes software.

Obtaining and guaranteeing reliability requires a more systematic approach. In particular, software elements should be considered as implementations meant to satisfy well-understood specifications, not as arbitrary executable texts. This is where the contract theory comes in.

The notion of contract

Assume you are writing some program unit implementing a task to be performed at runtime. Unless the task is trivial, it involves a number of subtasks. For example, it might appear as

```
my_task is
    do
        subtask₁ ;
        subtask₂ ;
        ...
        subtaskₙ ;
    end
```

a form that suffices for this discussion, although in many cases the control structure linking the various subtasks is less simple than the mere sequencing shown here.

For each of these subtasks, you may either write the corresponding solution in line as part of the body of *my_task*, or rely on a call to another unit. The decision is a typical design trade-off: Too much calling causes fragmentation of the software text; too little results in overcomplex individual units.

Assume you decide to use a routine call for one of the subtasks. This is similar to the situation encountered in everyday life when you decide to contract out for a certain (human) task rather than doing it yourself. For example, if you are in Paris and want an urgent letter or package delivered to another Paris address, you may decide to deliver it yourself, or you may contract out the task to a courier service.

Two major properties characterize human contracts involving two parties:

- Each party expects some benefits from the contract and is prepared to incur some obligations to obtain them.
- These benefits and obligations are documented in a contract document.

Table 1 shows an imaginary roster of obligations and benefits for the courier service of the example.

A contract document protects both sides:

- It protects the client by specifying *how much* should be done: The client is entitled to receive a certain result.
- It protects the contractor by specifying how *little* is acceptable: The contractor must not be liable for failing to carry out tasks outside of the specified scope.

As evidenced by this example, what is an obligation for one party is usually a benefit for the other.

This example also suggests a somewhat more subtle observation, which is important in the following discussion (and in studying the application of these ideas to concurrent computation). If the contract is exhaustive, every "obligation" entry also in a certain sense describes a "benefit" by stating that the constraints given are the only relevant ones. For example, the obligation entry for the client indicates that a client who satisfies all the constraints listed is *entitled* to the benefits shown in the next entry. This is the No Hidden Clauses rule: With a fully spelled out contract between honest parties, no requirement

Table 1. Example contract.

Party	Obligations	Benefits
Client	Provide letter or package of no more than 5 kgs, each dimension no more than 2 meters. Pay 100 francs.	Get package delivered to recipient in four hours or less.
Supplier	Deliver package to recipient in four hours or less.	No need to deal with deliveries too big, too heavy, or unpaid.

other than the contract's official obligations may be imposed on the client as a condition for obtaining the contract's official benefits.

The No Hidden Clauses principle does not prevent us from including references, implicit or explicit, to rules not physically part of the contract. For example, general rules such as the relevant laws and common business practices are implicitly considered to be part of every contract of a certain kind, even if not explicitly repeated in the text of each contract. They apply to both client and supplier and will lead below to the notion of class invariant.

Assertions: Contracting for software

It is not difficult to see how the preceding ideas apply to software construction. If the execution of a certain task relies on a routine call to handle one of its subtasks, it is necessary to specify the relationship between the client (the caller) and the supplier (the called routine) as precisely as possible. The mechanisms for expressing such conditions are called assertions. Some assertions, called preconditions and postconditions, apply to individual routines. Others, the class invariants, constrain all the routines of a given class and will be discussed later.

It is important to include the preconditions and postconditions as part of routine declarations (see Figure 1).

In this Eiffel notation, the Require and Ensure clauses (as well as the header comment) are optional. They introduce assertions — respectively the precondition and the postcondition. Each

```
routine_name (argument declarations) is
              -- Header comment
    require
              Precondition
    do
              Routine body, i.e. instructions
    ensure
              Postcondition
    end
```

Figure 1. A routine equipped with assertions.

```
put_child (new: NODE) is
              -- Add new to the children of current node
    require
              new /= Void
    do
              ... Insertion algorithm ...
    ensure
              new.parent = Current;
              child_count = old child_count + 1
    end -- put_child
```

Figure 2. Assertions for child insertion routine.

assertion is a list of Boolean expressions, separated by semicolons; here a semicolon is equivalent to a Boolean "and" but allows individual identification of the assertion clauses.

The precondition expresses requirements that any call must satisfy if it is to be correct; the postcondition expresses properties that are ensured in return by the execution of the call.

A missing precondition clause is equivalent to the clause Require True, and a missing postcondition to the clause Ensure True. The assertion True is the least committing of all possible assertions. Any possible state of the computation will satisfy it.

Consider, for example, in a class *TREE* describing tree nodes, a routine *put_child* for adding a new child to a tree node *Current*. The child is accessible through a reference, which must be attached to an existing node object. Table 2 informally expresses the contract.

This is the contract enforced by *put_child* on any potential caller. It contains the most important information that can be given about the routine: what each party in the contract must guarantee for a correct call, and what each party is entitled to in return. Because this information is so crucial to the construction of reliable systems using such routines, it should be a formal part of the routine's text (see Figure 2).

A few more details about the rules of object-oriented programming as embodied in Eiffel should help make this example completely clear:

• A reference such as *new* is either void (not attached to any object) or attached to an object. In the first case, it equals the value *Void*. Here the precondition expresses that the reference *new* must not be void, as stated informally by the corresponding entry in Table 2.

• In accordance with Eiffel's object-oriented principles, the routine will appear in the text of a class describing trees, or tree nodes. This is why it does not need an argument representing the node to which the routine will add the reference *new* as a child; all routines of the class are relative to a typical tree node, the "current instance" of the class. In a specific call such as *some_node.put_child* (*x*), the value before the period, here *some_node*, serves as the current instance.

• In the text of the class, the predefined name *Current* serves, if necessary, to refer to the current instance. Here it is used in the postcondition.

• The notation Old *child_count*, appearing in the postcondition of *put_child*, denotes the value of *child_count* as captured on entry to a particular call. In

Table 2. The *put_child* contract.

Party	Obligations	Benefits
Client	Use as argument a reference, say *new*, to an existing node object.	Get updated tree where the Current node has one more child than before; *new* now has Current as its parent.
Supplier	Insert new node as required.	No need to do anything if the argument is not attached to an object.

other words, the second clause of the postcondition expresses that the routine must increase *child_count* by one. The construct Old may appear only in a routine postcondition.

The role of assertions

You may well be wondering what happens if one of these conditions fails to be satisfied during execution. This question will be answered by whether assertions are monitored at runtime, depending on programmer wishes. But this is not a crucial question at this point. The prime goal of this discussion is to find ways of writing reliable software — systems that work. The question of what happens when they do *not* work, al-

```
if new = Void then
        ... Take care of special case ...
else
        ... Take care of standard case ...
end
```

Figure 3. Handling a special case.

though practically significant, comes only after achieving that more fundamental goal.

Another way of expressing this observation is to notice that assertions do *not* describe special but expected cases that call for special treatment. In other words, the above assertions are not a way to describe (for example) the handling of void arguments to *put_child*. If we wanted to treat void arguments as an acceptable (although special) case, we would handle it not through assertions but through standard conditional control structures (see Figure 3).

Further sources

One of the two primary sources of inspiration for this work is the research on program proving and systematic program construction pioneered by Floyd,[1] Hoare,[2] and Dijkstra.[3] Other well-known work on the application of proof methods to software construction includes contributions by Gries[4] and Mills.[5] The other major influence is the theory of abstract data types (see references in the body of the article).

The use of assertions in an object-oriented language and the approach to inheritance presented here (based on the notion of subcontracting) appear original to Eiffel. The exception-handling model and its implementation are also among Eiffel's contributions. These mechanisms, and the reasoning that led to them, are discussed in detail in references 1 and 2 of the main bibliography at the end of the article.

The notion of class invariant comes directly from Hoare's data invariants.[6] Invariants, as well as other assertions, also play an important role in the VDM software specification method, as described by Jones.[7] The transposition of data invariants to object-oriented software development, in the form of class invariants, appears to be new with Eiffel.

Nonobject-oriented research languages that support assertions have included Euclid[8] and Alphard[9]; see also the Ada-based specification language Anna.[10] CLU, cited in the text, includes nonformal assertions.

The view of programs as mechanisms to compute partial functions is central in the mentioned VDM method.

Another view of exceptions can be found in Cristian.[11] Eiffel's notion of a rescue clause bears some resemblance to Randell's recovery blocks,[12] but the spirit and aims are different. Recovery blocks as defined by Randell are alternate implementations of the original goal of a routine, to be used when the initial implementation fails to achieve this goal. In contrast, a rescue clause does not attempt to carry on the routine's official business; it simply patches things up by bringing the object to a stable state. Any retry attempt uses the original implementation again. Also, recovery blocks require that the initial system state be restored before an alternate implementation is tried after a failure. This appears impossible to implement in any practical environment for which efficiency is of any concern. Eiffel's rescue clauses do not require any such preservation of the state; the only rule is that the rescue clause must restore the class invariant and, if resumption is attempted, the routine precondition.

The rescue clause notion was actually derived from a corresponding formal notion of surrogate function, also called doppelgänger, which appeared in the specification method and language M,[13] a direct successor to Abrial's original Z language.[14] Like Z and unlike Eiffel, M was a formal specification language, not an executable language. Functions in an M specification may be partial. A surrogate is associated with a partial function and serves as a backup for arguments that do not belong to that function's domain.

References

1. R.W. Floyd, "Assigning Meanings to Programs," *Proc. Am. Math. Soc. Symp. in Applied Math.*, Vol. 19, J.T. Schwartz, ed., American Mathematical Society, Providence, R.I., 1967, pp. 19-31.

2. C.A.R. Hoare, "An Axiomatic Basis for Computer Programming," *Comm. ACM*, Vol. 12, No. 10, Oct. 1969, pp. 576-580, 583.

3. E.W. Dijkstra, A *Discipline of Programming*, Prentice Hall, Englewood Cliffs, N.J., 1976.

4. D. Gries, *The Science of Programming*, Springer-Verlag, Berlin and New York, 1981.

5. H.D. Mills et al., *Principles of Computer Programming: A Mathematical Approach*, Allyn and Bacon, Boston, 1987.

6. C.A.R. Hoare, "Proof of Correctness of Data Representations," *Acta Informatica*, Vol. 1, No. 4, 1972, pp. 271-281.

7. C.B. Jones, *Systematic Software Development Using VDM*, Prentice Hall, Englewood Cliffs, N.J., 1986.

8. B.W. Lampson et al., "Report on the Programming Language Euclid," *SIGPlan Notices*, Vol. 12, No. 2, Feb. 1977, pp. 1-79.

9. Mary Shaw et al., *Alphard: Form and Content*, Springer-Verlag, Berlin and New York, 1981.

10. D. Luckham and F.W. von Henke, "An Overview of Anna, a Specification Language for Ada," *IEEE Software*, Vol. 2, No. 2, Mar. 1985, pp. 9-22.

11. F. Cristian, "On Exceptions, Failures, and Errors," *Technology and Science of Informatics*, Vol. 4, No. 4, July-Aug. 1985.

12. B. Randell, "System Structure for Software Fault Tolerance," *IEEE Trans. Software Eng.*, Vol. SE-1, No. 2, June 1975, pp. 220-232.

13. B. Meyer, "M: A System Description Method," Tech. Report TRCS85-15, Computer Science Dept., Univ. of California, Santa Barbara, 1986.

14. J.-R. Abrial, S.A. Schuman, and B. Meyer, "A Specification Language," in *On the Construction of Programs*, R. McNaughten and R.C. McKeag, eds., Cambridge University Press, England, 1980.

Assertions (here the precondition) are something else: ways to describe the conditions on which software elements will work, and the conditions they will achieve in return. By putting the condition *new /= Void* in the precondition, we make it part of the routine's specification; the last form shown (with the If) would mean that we have changed that specification, broadening it to include the special case *new = Void* as acceptable.

As a consequence, any runtime violation of an assertion is not a special case but always the manifestation of a software bug. To be precise:

• A precondition violation indicates a bug in the client (caller). The caller did not observe the conditions imposed on correct calls.

• A postcondition violation is a bug in the supplier (routine). The routine failed to deliver on its promises.

Observations on software contracts

In Table 2, the bottom-right entry is particularly noteworthy. If the precondition is not satisfied, the routine is not bound to do anything, like a mail delivery company given a parcel that does not meet the specification. This means that the routine body should *not* be of the form mentioned above:

if *new = Void* **then**
 ...
else
 ...
end

Using such a construction would defeat the purpose of having a precondition (Require clause). This is an absolute rule: Either you have the condition in the Require, or you have it in an If instruction in the body of the routine, but never in both.

This principle is the exact opposite of the idea of defensive programming, since it directs programmers to avoid redundant tests. Such an approach is possible and fruitful because the use of assertions encourages writing software to spell out the consistency conditions that could go wrong at runtime. Then instead of

Figure 4. An invariant for binary trees.

checking blindly, as with defensive programming, you can use clearly defined contracts that assign the responsibility for each consistency condition to one of the parties. If the contract is precise and explicit, there is no need for redundant checks.

The stronger the precondition, the heavier the burden on the client, and the easier for the supplier. The matter of who should deal with abnormal values is essentially a pragmatic decision about division of labor: The best solution is the one that achieves the simplest architecture. If every routine and caller checked for every possible call error, routines would never perform any useful work.

In many existing programs, one can hardly find the islands of useful processing in oceans of error-checking code. In the absence of assertions, defensive programming may be the only reasonable approach. But with techniques for defining precisely each party's responsibility, as provided by assertions, such redundancy (so harmful to the consistency and simplicity of the structure) is not needed.

Who should check?

The rejection of defensive programming means that the client and supplier are not both held responsible for a consistency condition. Either the condition is part of the precondition and must be guaranteed by the client, or it is not stated in the precondition and must be handled by the supplier.

Which of these two solutions should be chosen? There is no absolute rule; several styles of writing routines are possible, ranging from "demanding" ones where the precondition is strong (putting the responsibility on clients) to "tolerant" ones where it is weak (increasing the routine's burden). Choosing between them is to a certain extent a matter of personal preference; again, the key criterion is to maximize the overall simplicity of the architecture.

The experience with Eiffel, in partic-

ular the design of the libraries, suggests that the systematic use of a demanding style can be quite successful. In this approach, every routine concentrates on doing a well-defined job so as to do it well, rather than attempting to handle every imaginable case. Client programmers do not expect miracles. As long as the conditions on the use of a routine make sense, and the routine's documentation states these conditions (the contract) explicitly, the programmers will be able to use the routine properly by observing their part of the deal.

One objection to this style is that it seems to force every client to make the same checks, corresponding to the precondition, and thus results in unnecessary and damaging repetitions. But this argument is not justified:

• The presence of a precondition *p* in a routine *r* does not necessarily mean that every call must test for *p*, as in

if *x.p* **then**
 x.r
else
 ... Special Treatment ...
end

What the precondition means is that the client must *guarantee* property *p*; this is not the same as *testing for* this condition before each call. If the context of the call implies *p*, then there is no need for such a test. A typical scheme is

x.s; *x.r*

where the postcondition of *s* implies *p*.

• Assume that many clients will indeed need to check for the precondition. Then what matters is the "Special Treatment." It is either the same for all calls or specific to each call. If it is the same, causing undue repetition in various clients, this is simply the sign of a poor class interface design, using an overly demanding contract for *r*. The contract should be renegotiated and made broader (more tolerant) to include the standard Special Treatment as part of the routine's specification.

• If, however, the Special Treatment is different for various clients, then the need for each client to perform its own individual test for *p* is intrinsic and not a consequence of the design method suggested here. These tests would have to be included anyway.

The last case corresponds to the frequent situation in which a supplier simply lacks the proper context to handle abnormal cases. For example, it is impossible for a general-purpose STACK module to know what to do when requested to pop an element from an empty stack. Only the client — a module from a compiler or other system that uses stacks — has the needed information.

Class invariants

Routine preconditions and postconditions may be used in non-object-oriented approaches, although they fit particularly well with the object-oriented method. Invariants, the next major use of assertions, are inconceivable outside of the object-oriented approach.

A class invariant is a property that applies to all instances of the class, transcending particular routines. For example, the invariant of a class describing nodes of a binary tree could be of the form shown in Figure 4, stating that the parent of both the left and right children of a node, if these children exist, is the node itself. (The Implies operator denotes implication. Eiffel operator precedence rules make the parentheses un-

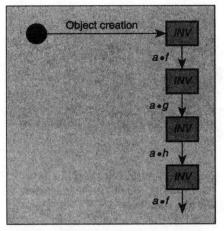

Figure 5. The invariant in an object's life cycle.

necessary here; they have been added for clarity.)

The optional class invariant clause appears at the end of a class text:

class *BINARY_TREE* [*T*] **feature**

... Attribute and routine declarations ...

invariant
... As shown above ...
end — class *TABLE*

Two properties characterize a class invariant:

• The invariant must be satisfied after

the creation of every instance of the class (every binary tree in this example). This means that every creation procedure of the class must yield an object satisfying the invariant. (A class may have one or more creation procedures, which serve to initialize objects. The creation procedure to be called in any given case is specified in the creation instruction.)

• The invariant must be preserved by every exported routine of the class (that is to say, every routine available to clients). Any such routine must guarantee that the invariant is satisfied on exit if it was satisfied on entry.

In effect, then, the invariant is added to the precondition and postcondition of every exported routine of the class. But the invariant characterizes the class as a whole rather than its individual routines.

Figure 5 illustrates these requirements by picturing the life cycle of any object as a sequence of transitions between "observable" states. Observable states, shown as shaded rectangles, are the states that immediately follow object creation, and any states subsequently reached after the execution of an exported routine of the object's generating class. The invariant is the consistency constraint on observable states. (It is not necessarily satisfied in between these states.)

The invariant corresponds to what

```
put_child (new: NODE)
                -- Add new to the children of current node
    require
            new /= Void
    ensure
            new.parent = Current;
            child_count = old child_count + 1
```

Figure 6. The short form of a routine.

was called "general conditions" in the initial discussion of contracts: laws or regulations that apply to all contracts of a certain category, often through a clause of the form "all provisions of the XX code shall apply to this contract."

Documenting a software contract

For the contract theory to work properly and lead to correct systems, client programmers must be provided with a proper description of the interface properties of a class and its routines — the contracts.

Here assertions can play a key role, since they help express the purpose of a software element such as a routine without reference to its implementation.

The *short* command of the Eiffel environment serves to document a class by extracting interface information. In this approach, software documentation is not treated as a product to be developed and maintained separately from the actual code; instead, it is the more abstract part of that code and can be extracted by computer tools.

The *short* command retains only the exported features of a class and, for an exported routine, drops the routine body and any other implementation-related details. However, pre- and postconditions are kept. (So is the header comment if present.) For example, Figure 6 shows what the *short* command yields for the *put* routine. It expresses simply and concisely the purpose of the routine, without reference to a particular implementation.

All documentation on the details of Eiffel classes (for example, the class specifications in the book on the basic libraries[9]) is produced automatically in this fashion. For classes that inherit from others, the *short* command must be combined with another tool, *flat*, which flattens out the class hierarchy by including inherited features at the same level as "immediate" ones (those declared in the class itself).

Monitoring assertions

What happens if, during execution, a system violates one of its own assertions?

In the development environment, the answer depends on a compilation option. For each class, you may choose from various levels of assertion monitoring: no assertion checking, preconditions only (the default), preconditions and postconditions, all of the above plus class invariants, or all assertions. (The difference between the last two follows from the existence of other assertions, such as loop invariants, not covered in the present discussion.)

For a class compiled under the "no assertion monitoring" option, assertions have no effect on system execution. The subsequent options cause evaluation of assertions at various stages: routine entry for preconditions, routine exit for postconditions, and both steps for invariants.

Under the monitoring options, the effect of an assertion violation is to raise an exception. The possible responses to an exception are discussed later.

Why monitor?

As noted, assertion violations are not special (but expected) cases; they result from bugs. The main application of run-time assertion monitoring, then, is debugging. Turning assertion checking on (at any of the levels previously listed) makes it possible to detect mistakes.

When writing software, developers make many assumptions about the properties that will hold at various stages of the software's execution, especially routine entry and return. In the usual approaches to software construction, these assumptions remain informal and implicit. Here the assertion mechanism enables developers to express them explicitly. Assertion monitoring, then, is a way to call the developer's bluff by checking what the software does against what its author thinks it does. This yields a productive approach to debugging, testing, and quality assurance, in which the search for errors is not blind but based on consistency conditions provided by the developers themselves.

Particularly interesting here is the use of *preconditions* in library classes. In the general approach to software construction suggested by the Eiffel method, developers build successive "clusters" of classes in a bottom-up order, from more general (reusable) to more specific (application-dependent). This is the "cluster model" of the software life cycle.[10] Deciding to release a library cluster *l* for general use normally implies a reasonable degree of confidence in its quality — the belief that no bugs remain in *l*. So it may be unnecessary to monitor the postconditions of routines in the classes of *l*. But the classes of an application cluster that is a client of *l* (see Figure 7) may still be "young" and contain bugs; such bugs may show up as erroneous arguments in calls to routines of the classes of *l*. Monitoring preconditions for classes of *l* helped to find them. This is one of the reasons why precondition checking is the default compilation option.

Introducing inheritance

One of the consequences of the contract theory is a better understanding and control of the fundamental object-oriented notion of inheritance and of the key associated techniques: redeclaration, polymorphism, and dynamic binding.

Through inheritance, you can define new classes by combining previous ones. A class that inherits from another has all the features (routines and attributes) defined in that class, plus its own. But it is not required to retain the exact form of inherited features: It may *redeclare* them to change their specification, their implementation, or both. This flexibility of the inheritance mechanism is central to the power of the object-oriented method.

For example, a binary tree class could provide a default representation and the corresponding implementations for search and insertion operations. A descendant of that class may provide a representation that is specifically adapted to certain cases (such as almost full binary trees) and redeclare the routines accordingly.

Such a form of redeclaration is called a *redefinition*. It assumes that the inherited routine already had an implementation. The other form of redeclaration, called *effecting*, applies to features for which the inherited version, known as a deferred (or abstract) feature, had no implementation, but only a specification. The effecting then provides an implementation (making the feature effective, the reverse of deferred). The subsequent discussion applies to both forms of redeclaration, although for simplicity it concentrates on redefinition.

Redeclaration takes its full power thanks to polymorphism and dynamic binding. Polymorphism is type adaptation controlled by inheritance. More concretely, this means that if you have *b* of type *BINARY_TREE* and *sb* of type *SPECIAL_BINARY_TREE*, the latter class a descendant of the former, then the assignment

$$b := sb$$

is permitted, allowing *b* to become attached at runtime to instances of *SPECIAL_BINARY_TREE*, of a more specialized form than the declaration of *b* specifies. Of course, this is only possible if the inheritance relation holds between the two classes as indicated.

What happens then for a call of the form

$$t.insert (v)$$

which applies procedure *insert*, with argument *v*, to the object attached to *t*? Dynamic binding means that such a call always uses the appropriate version of the procedure — the original one if the object to which *t* is attached is an instance of *BINARY_TREE*, the redefined version if it is an instance of *SPECIAL_BINARY_TREE*. The reverse policy, static binding (using the declaration of *b* to make the choice), would be an absurdity: deliberately choosing the wrong version of an operation.

The combination of inheritance, redeclaration, polymorphism, and dynamic binding yields much of the power and

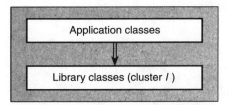

Figure 7. Library cluster and application cluster.

flexibility that result from the use of the object-oriented approach.[2] Yet these techniques may also raise concerns of possible misuse: What is to prevent a redeclaration from producing an effect that is incompatible with the semantics of the original version — fooling clients in a particularly bad way, especially in the context of dynamic binding? Nothing, of course. No design technique is immune to misuse. But at least it is possible to help serious designers use the technique properly; here the contract theory provides the proper perspective.

What redeclaration and dynamic binding mean is the ability to *subcontract* a task; preventing misuse then means guaranteeing that subcontractors honor the prime contractor's promises in the original contract.

Consider the situation described by Figure 8. *A* exports a routine *r* to its clients. (For simplicity, we ignore any arguments to *r*.) A client *X* executes a call

$$u.r$$

where *u* is declared of type *A*. Now *B*, a

The concurrency issue

The theory of design by contract raises important questions regarding the application of object-oriented ideas to concurrent computation. In discussing contracts, this article mentions that clients may view the precondition of a routine not just as an obligation but also in part as a benefit, since the contract implicitly indicates that a call satisfying the precondition will be serviced correctly. This is the No Hidden Clause rule. For example, if the insertion routine *put* for a *BOUNDED_QUEUE* class has the precondition

not *full*

to state that an insertion operation requires a queue that is not full, then a protected call of the form

```
q: BOUNDED_QUEUE [T];
x: T;
...
if not q.full then
    q.put (x)
end
```

will succeed, since the client executing this call has taken the trouble to check the precondition explicitly.

In parallel computation, however, things are not so nice. The bounded queue in this example may be used as a bounded buffer, accessible to several processors. The processor in charge of the client, which will carry out the above instructions, and the processor in charge of *q*, which will carry out the execution of *put*, could be different processors. Then, even if the test for *q.full* yields false, between the time the client executes this test and the time it executes the call *q.put (x)*, quite a few events may have occurred. For example, another client may have made the queue full by executing its own call to *put*.

In other words, a different semantic interpretation may be necessary for preconditions in the context of parallel computation. This observation serves as the starting point for some of the current work on models for concurrent object-oriented programming.[1,2]

References

1. B. Meyer, "Sequential and Concurrent Object-Oriented Programming," in *TOOLS 2* (Technology of Object-Oriented Languages and Systems), Angkor/SOL, Paris, June 1990, pp. 17-28.

2. J. Potter and G. Jalloul, "Models for Concurrent Eiffel," in *TOOLS 6* (Technology of Object-Oriented Languages and Systems), Prentice Hall, Englewood Cliffs, N.J., 1991, pp. 183-192.

descendant of *A*, redeclares *r*. Through polymorphism, *u* may well become attached to an instance of *B* rather than *A*. Note that often there is no way to know this from the text of *X* alone; for example, the call just shown could be in a routine of *X* beginning with

some_routine (*u*: *A*) **is** ...

where the polymorphism only results from a call of the form

z.*some_routine* (*v*)

for which the actual argument *v* is of type *B*. If this last call is in a class other than *X*, the author of *X* does not even know that *u* may become attached to an instance of *B*. In fact, he may not even know about the existence of a class *B*.

But then the danger is clear. To ascertain the properties of the call *u*.*r*, the author of *X* can only look at the contract for *r* in *A*. Yet, because of dynamic binding, *A* may subcontract the execution of *r* to *B*, and it is *B*'s contract that will be applied.

How do you avoid "fooling" *X* in the process? There are two ways *B* could violate its prime contractor's promises:

- *B* could make the precondition stronger, raising the risk that some calls that are correct from *X*'s viewpoint (they satisfy the original client obligations) will not be handled properly.
- *B* could make the postcondition weaker, returning a result less favorable than what has been promised to *X*.

None of this, then, is permitted. But the reverse changes are of course legitimate. A redeclaration may weaken the original's precondition or it may strengthen the postcondition. Changes of either kind mean that the subcontractor does a *better* job than the original contractor — which there is no reason to prohibit.

These rules illuminate some of the fundamental properties of inheritance, redeclaration, polymorphism, and dynamic binding. Redeclaration, for all the power it brings to software development, is not a way to turn a routine into something completely different. The new version must remain compatible with the original specification, although it may improve on it. The noted rules express this precisely.

These rules must be enforced by the

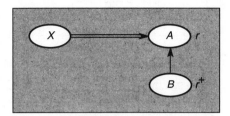

Figure 8. Redefinition of a routine under contract.

language. Eiffel uses a simple convention. In a redeclaration, it is not permitted to use the forms *require*... and *ensure*.... The absence of a precondition or postcondition clause means that the redeclared version retains the original version's assertion. Since this is the most frequent situation, the class author is not required to write anything special in this case. A class author who does want to adapt the assertion will use either or both of the forms

require else
　　new_pre

ensure then
　　new_post

which yield the following as new precondition and postcondition:

new_pre **or else** *original_precondition*

new_post **and then**
　　original_postcondition

where Or Else and And Then are the noncommutative versions of the "or" and "and" operators (evaluating their second argument only if necessary). In this way, the new precondition is guaranteed to be weaker than or equal to the originals, and the new postcondition is guaranteed to be stronger than or equal to the originals.

Invariants and dynamic binding

In addition to the rules on preconditions and postconditions, another constraint ties assertions with inheritance: Invariants are always passed on to descendants.

This is a direct result of the view that inheritance is (among other things) classification. If we want to consider every instance of a class *B* as being also an instance of *B*'s ancestors, we must ac-

cept that consistency constraints on a parent *A* also apply to instances of *B*.

For example, if the invariant for a class *TREE*, describing tree nodes, includes the clause

child.parent = Current

expressing that the parent of a node's currently active child is the node itself, this clause will automatically apply to instances of a class *BINARY_TREE*, which inherits from *TREE*. As a result, the language specification defines "the invariant of a class" as the assertion obtained by concatenating the assertion in the invariant clause of the class to the invariants of all parents (obtained recursively under this definition).[1]

As a result, the invariant of a class is always stronger than or equal to the invariants of each of its parents.

These rules lead to a better understanding of why static binding would be, as previously stated, such a disaster. Assume again the declaration and call

u: *A*;
...
u.*r*

where a descendant *B* of *A* redefines *r*. Call r_A and r_B the two implementations. Then r_A must preserve INV_A, the invariant of *A*, and r_B must preserve INV_B, the invariant of *B*, which is stronger than or equal to INV_A.

There is, of course, no requirement that r_A preserve INV_B. In fact, class *A* may have been written long before *B*, and the author of *A* does not need to know anything about eventual descendants of this class.

If *u* dynamically becomes attached to an instance of *B*, dynamic binding requires the execution of r_B for this call. Static binding would trigger r_A. Since this version of the routine is not required to preserve INV_B, the result would yield a catastrophic situation: an object of type *B* that does not satisfy the consistency constraint — the invariant — of its own class. In such cases, any attempt at understanding software texts or reasoning about their runtime behavior becomes futile.

A simple example will make the situation more concrete. Assume a class *ACCOUNT* describing bank accounts, with the attributes shown in Figure 9a and a procedure to record a new deposit shown in Figure 9b.

With this version of the class, obtaining an account's current balance requires a computation expressed by a function. Figure 10 shows how the *balance* function could appear, assuming the appropriate function *sum* in class *TRANSACTION_LIST*.

In a descendant class *ACCOUNT1*, it may be a better space-time trade-off to store the current balance with every account object. This can be achieved by redefining the function *balance* into an attribute (a process that is indeed supported by the language). Naturally, this attribute must be consistent with the others; this is expressed by the invariant of *ACCOUNT1*, shown in Figure 11.

For this to work, however, *B* must redefine any routine of *A* that modified deposits or withdrawals; the redefined version must also modify the *balance* field of the object accordingly, so as to maintain the invariant. This is the case, for example, with procedure *record_deposit*.

Now assume that we have the declaration and call

    a: ACCOUNT;
    ...
    a.record_deposit (1_000_000)

If in a certain execution, *a* happens to be attached to an object of type *ACCOUNT1* at the time of the call, static binding would mean applying the original, *ACCOUNT* version of *record_deposit* — which fails to update the *balance* field. The result would be an inconsistent *ACCOUNT1* object and certain disaster.

Dealing with abnormal situations

The Design by Contract theory has one more immediate application to the practice of reliable software development: exception handling.

Exceptions — abnormal cases — have been the target of much study; and several programming languages, notably Ada, PL/I, and CLU, offer exception-handling mechanisms. Much of this work is disappointing, however, because it

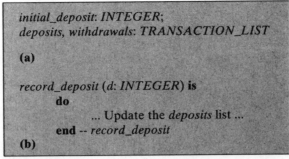

Figure 9. Features of a Bank Account class.

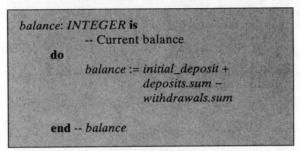

Figure 10. Computing the balance.

    invariant
        balance = initial_deposit + deposits.sum
            − withdrawals.sum

Figure 11. Invariant of the Account class.

fails to define precisely what an abnormal case is. Then exception handling often becomes a kind of generalized, interroutine "goto" mechanism, with no clear guidelines for proper use.

To understand the issue better, I performed a study (reported elsewhere[3]) of Ada and CLU textbooks, looking for examples of exception handling and methodological principles. The results were disappointing, as the books showed many examples of *triggering* exceptions but few of how to *handle* them. Furthermore, some of the latter were hair-raising. For example, one textbook proposed an example of a square root routine which, when confronted with a negative argument, triggers an exception. The exception handler prints a message and then simply returns to the caller without notifying the caller that something wrong has occurred — fooling the caller, as it were, into believing that everything is going according to plan. Since a typical use for square roots in a typical Ada program is a missile trajectory computation, it is easy to foresee the probable consequences.

Beyond the bad taste of such individual examples, one may fault the design of the exception mechanism itself for failing to encourage, or even to define, a proper discipline for handling abnormal cases.

The contract theory provides a good starting point for a more rational solution. If a routine is seen not just as some "piece of code" but as the implementation of a certain specification — the contract — it is possible to define a notion of *failure*. Failure occurs when an execution of a routine cannot fulfill the routine's contract. Possible reasons for a failure include a hardware malfunction, a bug in the implementation, or some external unexpected event.

"Failure" is here the basic concept. "Exception" is a derived notion. An exception occurs when a certain strategy for fulfilling a routine's contract has not succeeded. This is not a failure, at least not yet, because the routine may have an alternative strategy.

The most obvious example of exception is the failure of a called routine: *r*'s strategy for fulfilling its contract involved a call to *s*; the call failed; clearly, this is an exception for *r*. Another example, previously mentioned, is a runtime assertion violation, if assertions are monitored. It is also convenient to treat as exceptions the signals sent by the operating system or the hardware: arithmetic overflow, memory exhaustion, and the like. They indeed correspond to failures of calls to basic facilities (arithmetic operations, memory allocation).

Equipped with this notion of failure and exception, we can define a coherent response to an exception. The exception occurs because the strategy used to achieve the routine's contract did not work. Only three possible responses then make sense:

(1) Perhaps an alternative strategy is available. We have lost a battle, but we have not lost the war. In this case the routine should put the objects back into a consistent state and make another attempt, using the new strategy. This is called *resumption*.

(2) Perhaps, however, we have lost the war altogether. No new strategy is

```
get_integer_from_user: INTEGER is
        -- Read an integer (allow user up to five attempts)

    local
            failures: INTEGER
    do
            Result := getint
    rescue

            failures := failures + 1;

            if failures < 5 then
                    message ("Input must be an integer. Please enter again: ");
                    retry
            end

    end -- get_integer_from_user
```

Figure 12. Reading an integer with an unsafe primitive.

available. Then the routine should put back the objects in a consistent state, give up on the contract, and report failure to the caller. This is called *organized panic*.

(3) A rare but possible third case is the *false alarm*. This may occur only for operating-system or hardware signals. On some multiwindowing systems, for example, a process receives a signal (transformed by the runtime into an exception) when its window is resized. In most cases, the process should be able to continue its execution, possibly after taking some corrective actions (such as registering the new window dimensions for use by editors and other tools).

The description of both resumption and organized panic mentions putting back the objects "in a consistent state." This is essential if further executions (after an eventual resumption) will use the objects again. The notion of consistent state should be clear from the preceding discussion: Any exception handling, whether for resumption or for organized panic, should restore the invariant.

A disciplined exception-handling mechanism

It is not hard to devise an exception mechanism that directly supports the preceding method for handling abnormal cases.

To specify how a routine should behave after an exception, the author of an Eiffel routine may include a "rescue" clause, which expresses the alternate behavior of the routine (and is similar to clauses that occur in human contracts, to allow for exceptional, unplanned circumstances). When a routine includes a rescue clause, any exception occurring during the routine's execution interrupts the execution of the body (the Do clause) and starts execution of the rescue clause. The clause contains zero or more instructions, one of which may be a Retry. The execution terminates in either of two ways:

• If the rescue clause terminates without executing a Retry, the routine fails. It reports failure to its caller by triggering a new exception. This is the organized panic case.
• If the rescue clause executes a Retry, the body of the routine (Do clause) is executed again.

As an example, here is a solution to a problem found in many Ada textbooks: Using a function *getint*, which reads an integer, prompt a user to enter an integer value; if the input is not an integer, ask again, unless the user cannot provide an integer after five attempts, in which case a failure occurs. It is assumed that *getint* is an external routine, perhaps written in C or assembly language, and we have no control over it. It triggers an exception when applied to input that is not an integer; the routine should catch that exception and prompt

the user again. Figure 12 shows a solution.

The first five times the interactive user enters a wrong input, the routine starts again, thanks to the Retry. This is the direct implementation of resumption.

The local entity *failures* serves to record the number of failed calls to *getint*. Like any integer local entity, it is automatically initialized to zero on routine call. (The Eiffel language definition[1] specifies simple initialization values for every possible type.)

In this example, only one type of exception is possible. In some cases, the rescue clause might need to discriminate between possible types of exceptions and handle them differently. This is made possible through simple features of the kernel library class *EXCEPTIONS*, although it isn't necessary to look at the (straightforward) details here. This class also provides mechanisms for handling the false alarm case by specifying that for certain signals execution may be allowed to resume.

What happens after five successive failures of *getint*? The rescue clause terminates without executing a Retry and the routine execution fails (organized panic). The key rule in this case is that the caller of *get_integer* will get an exception, which it will have to handle by using the same policy, choosing between organized panic, resumption, and false alarm.

In a typical system, only a handful of routines have an explicit rescue clause. What if an exception occurs during the execution of a routine that has no such clause? The rule is simple: An absent clause is considered equivalent to an implicit clause of the form

rescue
        default_rescue

where *default_rescue* is a general-purpose procedure that, in its basic form, does nothing. Then an exception simply starts the rescue clause, which, executing the empty *default_rescue*, causes failure of the routine; this triggers the rescue clause, explicit or implicit. If exceptions are passed in this manner all the way back to the "root object" that started the execution, that execution halts after printing an exception history table that clearly documents the sequence of recorded abnormal events. But, of course, some routine in the call chain may have a rescue clause, even one containing a Retry that will attempt a resumption.

Why define the default behavior as a call to *default_rescue* rather than just as an empty rescue clause? The reason comes from the methodological discussion. In the case of organized panic, it is essential to restore the invariant before conceding defeat and surrendering. A null action would not achieve this for a class with a nontrivial invariant.

The solution is provided once again by the coalesced forces of inheritance and assertions. Procedure *default_rescue*, in its default null form, appears as a procedure of the general-purpose class *ANY*. This library class, as defined by the language rules,[1] is automatically an ancestor of all possible developer-defined classes. So it is the responsibility of designers of a class *C*, if they are concerned about possible exceptions occurring in routines that do not have specific rescue clauses, to redefine *default_rescue* so that it will ensure the class invariant of *C*.

Often, one of the creation procedures may serve as a redefinition of *default_rescue*, since creation procedures are also required to ensure the invariant.

This illuminates the difference between the body (the Do clause) and the rescue clause:

- The body must implement the contract, or ensure the postcondition. For consistency, it must also abide by the general law of the land — preserve the invariant. Its job is made a bit easier by the assumption that the invariant will hold initially, guaranteeing that the routine will find objects in a consistent state.
- In contrast, the rescue clause may not make any such assumption; it has no precondition, since an exception may occur at any time. Its reward is a less-demanding task. All that it is required to do on exit is to restore the invariant. Ensuring the postcondition — the contract — is not its job.

A useful analogy is the contrast between the grandeur and servitude of two equally respectable professions — cook and fire fighter. A cook may assume that the restaurant is not burning (satisfies the invariant) when the workday begins. If the restaurant is indeed nonburning, the cook must prepare meals (ensure

Status of Eiffel

The definition of the Eiffel language, used as the vehicle for this article, is in the public domain. The language evolution is under the control of an organization of users and developers of Eiffel technology: the Nonprofit International Consortium for Eiffel (NICE). Membership in NICE is open to any interested organization. The address is PO Box 6884, Santa Barbara, CA 93160.

the postcondition). It is also a part of the cook's contract, although perhaps an implicit one, to avoid setting the restaurant on fire in the process (to maintain the invariant).

When the fire fighter is called for help, in contrast, the state of the restaurant is not guaranteed. It may be burning or (in the case of a wrong alert) not burning. But then the fire fighter's only duty is to return the restaurant to a nonburning state. Serving meals to the assembled customers is not part of the fire fighter's job description. ∎

Acknowledgments

I have been greatly influenced by the originators of the classical work on systematic software development, mentioned in the "Further sources" sidebar. With his usual thoroughness, Kim Walden read the text and pointed out errors and possible improvements. The anonymous referees made several useful comments.

Eiffel is a trademark of the Nonprofit International Consortium for Eiffel.

References

1. B. Meyer, *Eiffel: The Language*, Prentice Hall, Englewood Cliffs, N.J., 1991.

2. B. Meyer, *Object-Oriented Software Construction*, Prentice Hall, Englewood Cliffs, N.J., 1988.

3. B. Meyer, "Design by Contract," in *Advances in Object-Oriented Software Engineering*, D. Mandrioli and B. Meyer, eds., Prentice Hall, Englewood Cliffs, N.J., 1991, pp. 1-50.

4. C.A.R. Hoare, "An Axiomatic Basis for Computer Programming," *Comm. ACM*, Vol. 12, No. 10, Oct. 1969, pp. 576-580, 583.

5. E.W. Dijkstra, *A Discipline of Programming*, Prentice Hall, Englewood Cliffs, N.J., 1976.

6. J.A. Goguen, J.W. Thatcher, and E.G. Wagner, "An Initial Algebra Approach to the Specification, Correctness, and Implementation of Abstract Data Types," in *Current Trends in Programming Methodology*, Vol. 4, R.T. Yeh, ed., Prentice Hall, Englewood Cliffs, N.J., 1978, pp. 80-149.

7. J.V. Guttag, "Abstract Data Types and the Development of Data Structures," *Comm. ACM*, Vol. 20, No. 6, June 1977, pp. 396-404.

8. B. Meyer, "La Description des Structures de Données," *Bulletin de la Direction des Etudes et Recherches d'Electricité de France*, Série C (Informatique), No. 2, Paris, 1976.

9. B. Meyer, *Eiffel: The Libraries*, Prentice Hall, Englewood Cliffs, N.J., (to appear in 1993).

10. B. Meyer, "The New Culture of Software Development," *TOOLS 1* (Technology of Object-Oriented Languages and Systems), SOL, Paris, Nov. 1989, pp. 13-23. Slightly revised version in *Advances in Object-Oriented Software Engineering* (see reference 3).

Bertrand Meyer is president of Interactive Software Engineering Inc. and Société des Outils du Logiciel, Paris. His areas of interest include formal specification, design methods, programming languages, interactive systems, software development environments, and various aspects of object-oriented technology.

Meyer holds an engineering degree from Ecole Polytechnique, an MS from Stanford University, and a PhD from the University of Nancy. He is the author of a number of technical books and articles, editor of the Prentice Hall Object-Oriented Series, and chairman of the TOOLS (Technology of Object-Oriented Languages and Systems) conference series.

The author can be contacted at Interactive Software Engineering, 270 Storke Rd., Suite 7, Goleta, CA 93117.

Part 2

Software for
Object-Oriented Systems

Chapter 3

Object-Oriented Language System Architecture

Object, Message, and Performance: How They Coexist in SELF

David Ungar, Randall B. Smith, Sun Microsystems Laboratories, Inc.

Craig Chambers, University of Washington, Seattle

Urs Hölzle, University of California, Santa Barbara

Applying object-oriented techniques to the art of computer programming confers many benefits, and like an older discipline, structured programming, is most effective when applied uniformly throughout a program. The SELF programming language distills object-oriented computation down to a simple story based on copying prototypes to create objects, inheriting from objects to share their contents, and passing messages to invoke methods. SELF programs even send messages to alter the flow of control, access variables, and perform arithmetic. As a result, methods are oblivious to the representations of objects and are therefore easier to reuse.

Last year you might have written a routine to sort an array of numbers. It was a method defined for arrays that works by sending the less-than (<) message to the numbers. Today, you may need to sort an array of strings. In a pure object-oriented language, you can just call the same sort method. The old sort method still works, because the objects in the array (now strings) respond to the < message. The code run for < is decided at runtime according to the type of the receiver, and so the sort method works for any object that implements a < method. When the same code can be used for different types of objects, it is said to be *polymorphic*. With this kind of polymorphism, you do not have to explicitly parameterize the sort routine when you write it—it just works! This quality of unanticipated reusability may be one of the reasons programmers feel empowered by pure object-oriented languages.

Unlike structured programming, however, pure object-oriented programming cannot be implemented efficiently with traditional compilation techniques because traditional optimizations rely on static declarations of representation types. In this chapter we present the novel implementation techniques that recapture much of the efficiency that seems lost in a pure

object-oriented language. For some of the benchmarks we have measured, these techniques provide a fivefold speedup, enabling SELF to come within a factor of two or three of optimized C.

SELF: A simple, pure, object-oriented programming language

SELF was initially designed at Xerox PARC by authors Ungar and Smith (32). The designers employed a minimalist strategy, striving to distill an essence of object and message. The subsequent design evolution and implementation were undertaken by authors Chambers, Hölzle, and Ungar, and by Bay-Wei Chang at Stanford University. In 1991, the SELF project moved to Sun Microsystems Laboratories. Today SELF is a fairly large system, has hosted a few sizable projects, and has been tried at several hundred sites (most of them academically curious).

The basic notion in SELF is an object consisting of slots. A slot has a name and a value. Slot names are always strings, but slot values can be any SELF object. Slots can be marked with an asterisk to show that they designate a parent. In Figure 1, an object represents a two-dimensional point with x and y slots, a parent slot called p, and two special-assignment slots, x: and y:, which are used to assign to the x and y slots. The object's parent has a single slot called *print* (containing a method object).

When sending a message, if a no slot name matches within the receiving object, its parent's slots are searched, and then slots in the parent's parent, and so on. Thus our point object can respond to the messages x, y, x:, y:, and p, plus the message *print*, because it inherits the *print* slot from its parent. In SELF, any object can potentially be a parent for any number of children, or a child of any object. This provision gives the language unusual uniformity and flexibility.

In addition to slots, a SELF object can include code. Such objects are called *methods*; they correspond to subroutines in other languages. For example, the object in the *print* slot above includes code and thus serves as a method. When an object is found in a slot as a result of a message send it is *run*: an object without code runs by simply returning itself, but a method runs by invoking its code. Thus when the *print* message is sent to our point object, the code in the print slot's method will run immediately. The assignment slots, *x*: and *y*:, contain a special method (symbolized by the arrow), which takes an argument (in addition to the receiver) and stuffs it in either the *x* or the *y* slot.

Messages can have arguments in addition to the receiver. For example, 3 + 4 sends the message + to the object 3 with 4 as argument. Because languages like Smalltalk or SELF do arithmetic by sending messages, programmers are free to add new numeric data types to the language, and the new types can inherit and reuse all the existing numeric code. Adding complex numbers or matrices to the system would be straightforward: after defining a + slot for matrices, the user could have the matrix freely inherit code that sends +, and this code would then work for matrices as well as for integers. The cost in performance will be severe, however, if sending + to integers cannot be expressed efficiently as simple operations in the CPU (such as a single-cycle add instruction). Again, extreme adherence to the object-oriented paradigm confers benefits, but raises issues about performance.

In addition to messages with arithmetic symbols, messages with textual names can have arguments. The message *ifTrue: False:* takes two arguments, one for each word ending with a colon. For convenience, the arguments are sprinkled among the pieces of a multiple-argument message name, and so we write (*a* < *b*) *ifTrue: case1 False: case2*. Here, the result of the (*a* < *b*) message send (in practice, either the object *true* or *false*) is sent the message *ifTrue: False:* with two arguments. The arguments of *ifTrue: False:* are typically "blocks" or "closures"—bundles of SELF expressions that can be evaluated by sending the *value* message. That flow-of-control

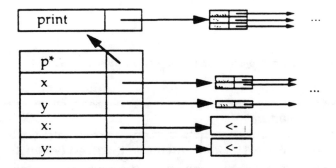

Figure 1.

statements such as *ifTrue:False:* are done with message sending has its benefits, such as adding fuzzy logic to the system by redefining the *ifTrue:False:* method is relatively straightforward, as is adding any sort of user-defined control structure. This is yet another performance challenge, however: the compiler had better figure out how to replace the message sends with compare-and-branch machine instructions.

More can be said about the language SELF: new SELF objects are made simply by copying—there are no special class objects for instantiation. Our current implementation allows multiple inheritance, which requires a strategy for dealing with multiple parents. It has block-closure objects and threads. SELF also has mirrors, for "structural reflection," so that, for example, a slot can be deleted, or set to contain a method.

SELF might be called an extremely object-oriented language, because what other languages do with special flow-of-control mechanisms, or special variable scoping and accessing mechanisms, or special primitive types and operations, is all done with objects and messages in SELF. This extreme devotion to the object–message paradigm has forced us to develop the techniques described in the following sections.

Why objects hinder performance: the price of passing messages

We have shown how a pure object-oriented language like SELF replaces many conventional language idioms with message passing. But exactly why are messages slow? Message passing is a two-stage procedure:

- *Finding the method.* The system must search the message's receiver and its ancestors for a slot that matches the message name. Conceptually, this task involves searching many objects, and straightforward implementation would be slow. Almost all systems optimize this lookup, however: a hash table may be used to cache the results of prior lookups (6). Alternatively, message names can be encoded as offsets into function tables referenced from object headers (10, 28, 29). Or the call instruction can be backpatched with the result of a prior lookup, as long as methods include a prologue to verify the caching (9, 15, 31). But even the fastest of these approaches (an indexed indirection through a function table) takes two loads. Typical implementations used for C++ require three loads and an addition, about eight cycles (11).
- *Calling the method.* Once found, if a matching slot contains a data object, the slot contents must be loaded and returned. Or, if the matching slot contains a method object, the method must be invoked. This step resembles conventional procedure invocation and includes saving the PC and other registers, allocating a stack frame, passing any parameters, branching to the first instruction of the new method, executing the method, returning the result, restoring the PC and other registers, and popping the stack frame. Even on a CPU with register-window architecture, a nontrivial procedure call typically requires four instructions.

By summing the cost of each step, we can estimate the total cost of sending a message: at least ten cycles. When taken to its logical conclusion, object-oriented programming requires that a message be sent

Table 1. Procedural and object-oriented implementations of the "min" function.

	Procedural	Object-Oriented	
Source Code	**self = 7, x = 11**	**methods involved (when self = 7, x = 11)**	**as inherited by**

	int min(int self, int x) {
	  if (self < x)
	    return self;
	else
	    return x;
	}
		min: x = (self < x ifTrue: self False: x)[a]	many objects

		< x = (IntLTPrimitive: x IfFail: ...)[a]	integers
		ifTrue: truePart False: falsePart = (truePart value)[a].	the **true** object
Works on	**32-bit integers only**	**any object that inherits a "<" method** **(integers, floats, complex numbers, strings, ...)**	

Object Code (for Integers)

	Traditional Optimizing Compilation		Traditional Optimizing Compilation			Customizing, Inlining, & Splitting	
source	object code	cycles	source	object code	cycles		cycles
			<	send **<** message to **self**	10		
			IntLTPrim	check receiver's type	2		
				check x's type	2	check x's type	2
<	cmp self, x	1		cmp self, x	1	cmp self, x	1
if	branch LT	1		branch LT	1	branch LT	1
				return true	2		
			ifTrue:False:	send **ifTrue:False:** to **true**	10		
			value	send **value** to **self**	10		
	mov self, result	1		mov self, result	1	mov self, result	1
				return from value	2		
				return from ifTrue:False	2		
	rough total:	**3**		**rough total:**	**43**	**rough total:**	**5**

a. A word about syntax: the ". . . = (. . .)" form simply mean that the contents of the parentheses are the source code for the message in front of the equals sign.

for each arithmetic operation, control operation, or even access operation—which should be simple one-cycle operations. When common single-cycle primitive operations are replaced by ten-cycle method invocations, programs run much slower: pure objects resist efficient implementation.

Consider a simple routine for computing the minimum of two quantities. Table 1 compares the object code for a procedural, monomorphic minimum routine with the object code for an object-oriented, polymorphic minimum routine. (It assumes throughout that the receiver, *self*, is 7, and the argument, *x*, is 11). On the left is the integer-specific C code. It executes three instructions and runs in 3 cycles. On the right is the SELF version. The example in the table is detailed in coming sections. For now, notice that the SELF source code works on any objects that understand <. As shown in the lower middle section, a traditional implementation would be forced to include three dynamic calls, and the result would be about a 40-cycle execution time. With the techniques described in this chapter, the compiler can inline all the calls, reducing execution time to about 5 cycles. For object-oriented systems to be fast, they must *pretend* to send most messages instead of actually sending them.

Traditional ways to achieve performance in object-oriented languages

Before examining the new techniques of customizing, inlining, and splitting, it will be helpful to consider more traditional strategies for optimizing object-oriented programs.

Special-purpose hardware. Hardware designers have tried to cater to object-oriented programming by adding architectural support for message passing (8). For example, the Smalltalk-on-a-RISC (SOAR) project designed a special-purpose microprocessor for Smalltalk, which ran quite efficiently for its time (31). When each of its special features was evaluated, however, only register windows, byte manipulation, integer tagging, and one-cycle call instructions contributed more than 10 percent each to performance. Now, each of these effec-

tive features is available on various stock processors (e.g., all are found in the SPARC). Furthermore, recent advances in compilation tend to diminish the importance of register windows and integer tagging. Also, many users are not willing to buy special hardware to run an object-oriented programming language.

Object-oriented extensions to procedural languages: creating a dilemma. Many pre-object-oriented languages, including C and Lisp, have received object-oriented extensions. The resulting hybrid object-oriented languages such as C++ (11) and CLOS (22) provide message passing but retain statically bound procedure calls and primitive, non-object-oriented data types such as integers, arrays, and cons cells. These data types are accessed via built-in operators or procedure calls that are automatically inlined by the compiler to achieve good performance. Users of a hybrid language enjoy a choice of expressive media, but the down side is that they must deal with a kind of schizophrenia, for two mindsets are needed to read and write code. Languages like C++ and partly object-oriented Lisps offer a choice between speed and generality: a routine can employ primitive types or procedural mechanisms and run fast (but have restricted reusability), or it can employ more versatile objects and run slower but be reusable. Traditional implementation techniques cannot provide both the speed of primitive operations and the reusability of message passing at the same time.

Static typing: not necessarily sufficient for high performance. Even statically typed (but fairly pure) object-oriented languages like Trellis/Owl (30) and Eiffel (26) must overcome the overhead of dynamically dispatched message passing, and even these languages restrict common built-in types like integer and boolean to get better performance. Static typing allows the compiler to check that an object will understand every message sent to it, and as a result the compiler can use a somewhat faster dispatching mechanism. Because an instance of a subclass can always be substituted for an instance of a superclass, however, and because subclasses can provide alternate method implementations, static type-checking cannot in general determine if a single method will be invoked by a message at runtime, and thus it cannot further opti-

mize the call. For example, if min's arguments were declared to be a general type like ComparableObjects, then the compiler could guarantee that there would be some definition of < (less-than), but it could not statically determine which version of < would be needed. Therefore min would have to pay the price of a dynamic dispatch for <. For a statically typed language to optimize min, its arguments will have to be statically typed as, say, 32-bit integers, but such specificity will prohibit min's reuse with other types. Because conventional static typing alone does not enable static binding and inlining of messages, it cannot significantly reduce the overhead of message passing.

Dynamic compilation: the Deutsch-Schiffman Smalltalk System. When the first Sun Workstation was announced, Peter Deutsch and Alan Schiffman set about the task of devising a high-performance Smalltalk-80 system for this machine (9). As the price and physical size of main memory shrank, it became possible to include a simple compiler and a compiled code cache in main memory, along with the application. Their Smalltalk-80 system exploited a combination of dynamic compilation, compiled code caching, peephole optimization, hard-wiring a few messages, stack-allocated activation records, and inline caching (backpatching call instructions) to achieve better runtime performance than an interpreter while reducing compile-time and code-space costs compared to those of a conventional static compiler. As diagrammed in Figure 2, when a programmer types in a method, a parser translates it into a simple byte-coded intermediate representation. A compiler compiles the method and performs peephole optimization. The space needed to store all the compiled code, and the time needed to recompile all the code affected by a small change can be considerable. Consequently, the compilation step is deferred until runtime, when the method is actually invoked, and the resulting object code is cached for future use.

This system doubled performance over that of the fastest Smalltalk interpreter. It executed code approximately 24 times faster than an earlier and more straightforward interpreter (12), whose implementors despaired of gaining practicality like that of pure object-oriented languages. But it was still an order of magnitude slower than optimized C.

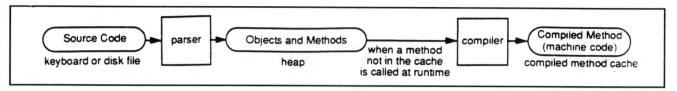

Figure 2.

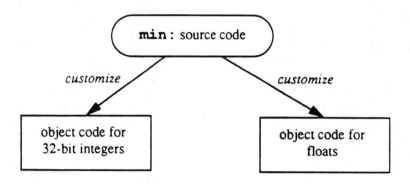

Figure 3.

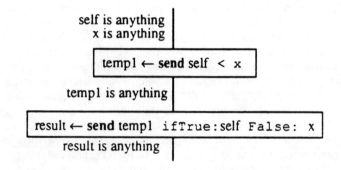

Figure 4.

Customizing, inlining, and splitting: global optimizations for dynamically compiling methods

In the past few years, new techniques have been discovered for statically binding and inlining methods for realizing high performance for dynamically bound message sending. A motif runs through all these techniques: creating multiple versions of machine code for a piece of source code, each version specialized for one situation. The generated code can thus be optimized for a specific context, even though the source code is completely general. In other words, it is the compiler, not the programmer, which creates specialized versions of a general-source method to achieve better efficiency. This automatic customizing not only saves programming time, it avoids source-code redundancy: if the general-source method (such as our sorting method) needs to be changed, all customized compiled code can be updated automatically. If the programmer had created customized sort routines by hand (for example, one version for integers and another one for strings), all versions would have to be updated manually, and one or more versions could accidentally be forgotten.

Customized compilation. In Smalltalk, the min: method is defined in a general class (Magnitude), and the Deutsch-Schiffman system compiles one machine-code routine for it. Because many classes may inherit this method, the Smalltalk compiler cannot know the exact class of the receiver. Consequently, when min sends less-than, the target routine may be any less-than method in the system, and so a ten-cycle dynamically dispatched call is needed to invoke a one-cycle compare instruction.

A customizing compiler, on the other hand, compiles a different machine-code method *for each type of receiver* that runs a given source method. The advantage of this approach is that it gives the compiler precise information about the exact type of the receiver. As a result, the compiler can usually generate much better code for each specific version than it could for one general-purpose compiled method.

Creating all possible versions after every source change would waste space and effort on many versions that will never run. Consequently, as with the Deutsch-Schiffman technique, compiled machine code is created on demand, at runtime. Dynamic compilation is essential to the SELF implementation. The technique for dynamically compiling multiple specialized versions of one source-code method is *customized compilation* (see Figure 3.).

Consider the min: method defined in a slot inherited by many objects:

min: x = (self < x ifTrue: self False: x)

This notation means that there is a slot named "min:" and the code in the parentheses defines the method in that slot. Figure 4 is a general flow-graph representation for this code (expensive operations are in boldface), including information about types (in this case for self, x, temp1, and result) at various points along the flow graph:

This method could be invoked on integers, floating-point numbers, strings, or any other objects that can be compared using <. Like other dynamic compilation systems, the SELF system waits until the min: method is first invoked before com-

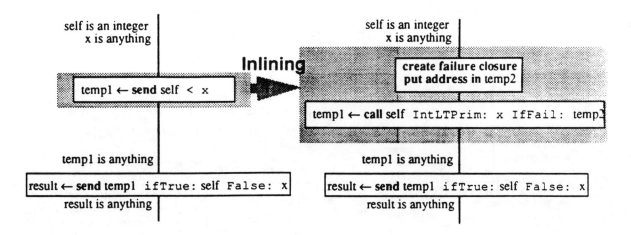

Figure 5.

piling any code for this method. Because the SELF compiler generates a separate version for each type of receiver, it can customize the version to that specific receiver type. In our example, it can use the newly found type information about the receiver (self) to optimize the < message by using the *message-inlining* technique.

Message inlining. If the type of a message's receiver is known at compile-time, the message lookup can be performed at compile-time rather than runtime. Because the compiler can then examine the slot found by the lookup, it can perform these critical optimizations:

- If the slot contains a method, the compiler can inline the body of the method at the call site, if the method is short and nonrecursive.
- If the slot is a constant-data slot, the compiler can replace the message send with the value of the slot (a constant known at compile-time).
- If the slot is an assignable-data slot, the compiler can replace the message send with code to fetch the contents of the slot (e.g., a load instruction).
- If the slot is an assignment slot, the compiler can replace the message send with code to update the contents of the slot (e.g., a store instruction).

Let us trace the operations of the SELF compiler to evaluate the expression *i* min: *j* for the case in which *i* is an integer. Assuming this is the first time min: has been sent to an integer, the compiler will generate code for a version of min: that is customized for integer receivers. In this case, the SELF compiler can statically look up the definition of < for integers:

< *x* = (IntLTPrim: *x* IfFail: [... code for handling failure.*s*..] .)

This method simply calls the integer less-than primitive and supplies a failure closure (whose code is omitted here for brevity). The compiler inlines the < method to transform the flow graph (see figure 5).

The overhead for sending the < message has been eliminated, but calling a procedure to compare two integers is still expensive. We next explain how a compiler can open-code primitive built-in operations to eliminate this call overhead.

Primitive inlining. Primitive inlining can be considered a simpler form of message inlining. Calls to primitive operations are normally implemented by calling an external function in the virtual machine. Like most other high-performance systems, however, the SELF compiler replaces calls of common primitives such as integer arithmetic, comparisons, and array accesses with equivalent in-line instruction sequences. This substitution significantly improves performance because some of these primitives can be implemented in only two or three machine instructions if the procedure call's overhead is removed. If the arguments to a side-effect-free primitive, such as an arithmetic or comparison primitive, are known at compile-time, the compiler can even call the primitive at compile-time, replacing the entire computation with the result of the primitive; this is how our compiler can do *constant folding*.

In our continuing min: example, the compiler inlines the *IntLTPrim:IfFail:* call (the definition of the integer less-than *primitive,* but not the integer less-than *method,* is hard-wired into the compiler)

to get the Figure 6 flow graph.

The first test is a compare-and-branch sequence verifying that the argument to the *IntLTPrim:IfFail:* call is also an integer (the receiver is already known to be an integer because the method is being customized for integer self); if not, the failure closure is created and invoked. Thus this optimization not only eliminates the call overhead but also saves considerable time by not creating the failure closure unless really needed. On the commonest branch (the argument is an integer), the two integers are compared, and either the true object or the false object is returned as the result of the < message.

Lazy compilation of uncommon cases. Here a dynamic compiler can bring to bear an unorthodox optimization first suggested to us by John Maloney. If a specific primitive rarely fails, the compiler can save some time and improve its chances of producing better code by delaying compilation of the failure branch. Instead of actually generating code, the compiler merely leaves a stub that will call the compiler to generate the failure code on demand if it is ever needed. The failure code will be an entirely different chunk of instructions and will not merge back into the main code. Consequently, the compiler need not determine the effect of the failure code on the types of variables in this method, and the resulting code can therefore run faster. The receiver of *ifTrue:False:* must now be one of two objects: the true object or the false object. Normally, this stricture would prevent inlining of the *ifTrue:False:* message because the type of its receiver cannot be uniquely determined. By splitting the single call of *ifTrue:False:* into two

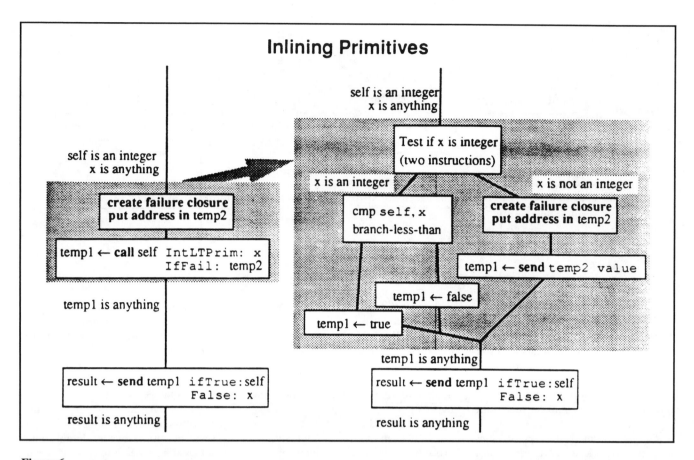

Figure 6.

calls, however, one for each statically known receiver type, a compiler can handle and optimize each case separately. This technique is called *message splitting* (see Figure 7).

Message splitting. When several branches of the control-flow graph merge, type information may be lost. In the min: example, for instance, a merge comes just prior to the *ifTrue:False:* message, which loses type information about temp1. With message splitting, a compiler can postpone the merge until after the *ifTrue:False:* message send by duplicating this message send on both paths. Along each path, the compiler has more type information, and can perform compile-time message lookup and message inlining to improve performance. In general, there may be a path for which the receiver type remains unknown, but the compiler can preserve the semantics of the original unsplit message by generating a real message send on this path.

Message splitting can be thought of as an extension to customized compilation, because the compiler customizes individual message sends along specific control-flow paths, with similar improve-

ments in runtime performance. For the min: example, the SELF compiler will split the *ifTrue:False:* message into two separate versions (see Figure 8).

Now the compiler can inline the definition of *ifTrue:False:* for the true object:

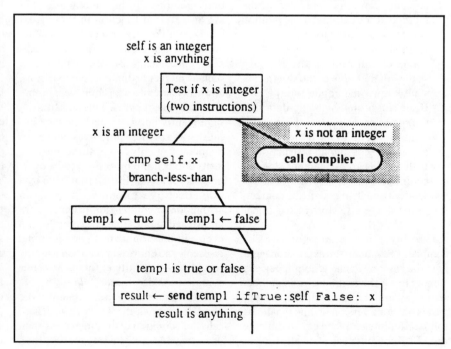

Figure 7.

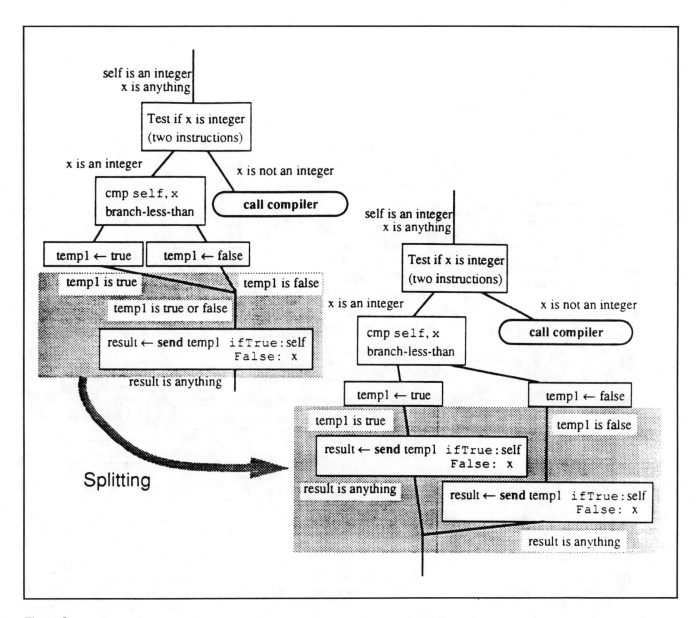

Figure 8.

ifTrue: truePart False: falsePart = (*truePart value*) (see Figure 9).
and for the false object:

ifTrue: truePart False: falsePart = (*falsePart value*)
to get to the following flow graph. Because the compiler knows that here both self and *x* must be integers, it can look up the value method. Integers inherit a general value method that just returns the *receiver: value = (self)*. This method is so short that the compiler can inline it and replace it with a register-move instruction. Thus, in the common case of taking the minimum of two integers, the customized version of *min:* executes only two simple compare-and-branch sequences and a (register) move instruction. Similar savings will also be seen if

the user calls *min:* on two floating-point numbers or two strings, because customizing, inlining, and splitting can also optimize special versions for each of these receiver types. Even though these compilation techniques can dramatically improve performance, they still preserve the message-passing semantics of the original source code.

Other optimization techniques. Besides customizing and inlining, many more optimization techniques are possible. All those listed here have been adopted in the SELF-91 system:

• *Type prediction.* Sometimes the compiler does not know the type of a message's receiver, but can make a

good guess from the name of the message. For example, studies of Smalltalk code show that when the message is named +, -, <, and so on, the receiver is an integer 90 percent of the time (31). Accordingly, a compiler can predict the types of receivers for these messages by inserting a type test into the control-flow graph and assigning a high probability to the integer branch. Then splitting and inlining can take over to produce very fast code for the common case, and lazy compilation can save the compiler the trouble of compiling the noninteger case. Additionally, if the same objects are sent more messages later in the method, the compiler need not insert more type

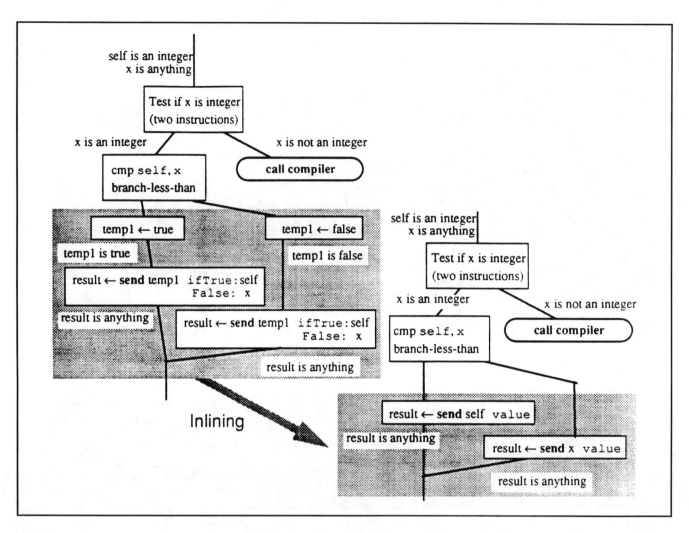

Figure 9.

tests, for the objects are known to be integers along the common-case branch. Type prediction can, without adding much complexity, optimize the sort of integer-intensive code that many would expect to be fast. It was first used by Deutsch and Schiffman in their Smalltalk system (9).

- *Eliminating block (closure).* We have simplified discussion of the optimization techniques by ignoring issues raised by blocks. In a language like SELF that implements all control structures with blocks, however, creation and invocation of blocks must be optimized away to achieve reasonable performance. This optimization is more difficult in SELF than, say, Scheme for two reasons: First, Scheme does not use blocks for if-s, but instead has a built-in construct, *cond*. Second, Scheme functions are easier to inline because function invocation does not perform dynamic-dispatching on user-defined

types. Despite the difficulty of eliminating blocks in a pure object-oriented language, the techniques outlined in this chapter are equal to the task; they can keep track of which variables are bound to which blocks, and the same inlining techniques can inline-expand the code in the block. The compiler will also defer creating blocks as long as possible. For example, the failure block for a primitive invocation is not created until the primitive actually fails.

- *Extended splitting.* In the min example, the compiler split the *ifTrue:False:* message because the preceding node was a merge that lost type information. Other examples might have had other messages between the merge and the would-be consumer of the lost information. Extended splitting allows the compiler to split whole paths instead of single messages (2). Of course, the amount of code being copied needs to be balanced against

the potential savings in execution time to avoid explosion in code size. Therefore, extended splitting usually is profitable only if just a few instructions need to be copied (See Figure 10.)

- *Loops.* Once it can split whole paths, a compiler need take only a short step to split off whole loops. This optimization can make a dramatic difference by hoisting type tests and message sends out of tight loops. In a loop that increments an integer index, the compiler can generate a separate loop without type tests by splitting on the type of the index.
- *Supporting the programming environment.* Although customizing, inlining, and the other techniques move the object code farther from the source code, it is still possible to hide their existence to provide source-level debugging and allow the programmer to change programs while they are running. The SELF compiler

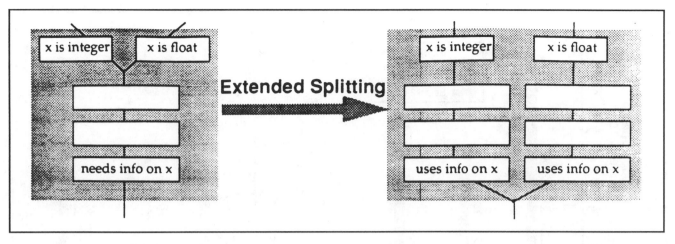

Figure 10.

outputs debugging information about the layout of stack frames to hide the effects of inlining and splitting. It also maintains dependency lists to invalidate compiled code when a source method is changed, and it can deoptimize code and stack frames to provide singlestepping. Consequently, for the user, the system behaves exactly like an extremely fast interpreter: for debugging, all optimizations are invisible to the user (16).

Performance. To measure how effective our optimizing techniques were, we ran small C-like benchmark programs (traditionally, pure object-oriented languages perform worst on this kind of program). The standard Sun C compiler with optimization enabled (using the -O2 option) established a goal for runtime performance.

To compare our approach to implementing a pure object-oriented language with competing approaches, we measured the ParcPlace Smalltalk-80 system (version 4), which incorporates the Deutsch–Schiffman techniques (9). As far as we know, this is the fastest implementation of any system in which nearly every operation is performed by sending a dynamically dispatched message. (In Smalltalk-80, unlike SELF, variable accesses and some common control structures do not use messages.)

To compare our techniques against other (non-object oriented) systems supporting generic arithmetic, we also measured the ORBIT compiler (version 3.1) (23) for T, a dialect of Scheme. ORBIT is respected as a good optimizing compiler for a Scheme-like language. In addition

to the normal T program, we measured a hand-optimized version of the benchmarks that uses unsafe integer-specific arithmetic (e.g., *fx+* and *fx<*) instead of the general + function and contains explicit directives to the compiler to inline specified functions. These data are labeled T/ORBIT (integer only). Compilation time includes the time to read and write files but not the time to load the generated file into the running T system.

In some ways, comparing these systems is like comparing apples to oranges. The SELF system, unlike the C or T compilers, includes support for message passing at the basic levels (including user-defined control structures), generic arithmetic, robust error-checking primitives (e.g., test for overflow in integer addition), and full source-level debugging of the optimized code. We have directed much of our effort toward developing optimization techniques that coexist with the advantages of the SELF language and environment so that programmers need not choose between clean semantics and performance.

We measured the eight Stanford integer benchmarks and the Richards operating-system simulation benchmark. The C version of the Richards benchmark is actually written in C++ version 1.2 (using inline functions whenever reasonable), translated into C using the standard cfront filter, and then optimized using the Sun C compiler. Compilation time for optimized C includes the time to read and write files but not the time to link the resulting .o files. The execution speeds we report for SELF do not include the cost of compiling, and so they reflect performance after the methods have been optimized. In the charts below, we

report the geometric mean for the seven small Stanford integer benchmarks and puzzle and Richards separately; this sorting separates the benchmarks into rough "equivalence classes" based on benchmark size. All times were measured on a lightly loaded SPARCstation-2. Raw data for each benchmark may be found in Appendix A.

The graphs in Figure 11 show the execution speed and compilation speed for our benchmarks, normalized to optimized C (taller bars are better).

Comparing Smalltalk to SELF suggests that the new compilation techniques provide a three- to sixfold improvement in performance on these programs. They even do a better job of eliminating the generic-primitives overhead than do unsafe type declarations in the T systems. A two- to threefold gap remains between SELF and C on the benchmarks. The SELF code, however, is doing more useful work, checking arithmetic overflow and array bounds. Also, the pure object-oriented source code lends itself to reuse, whereas the C source employs nonreusable specific types and functions.

Because SELF's optimizations occur at runtime, compilation speed is quite important. Fortunately, even though it performs extensive optimizations, SELF's compile times are in the same ballpark as optimized C's.

Recent work

Although the optimization techniques described here are very successful for the Stanford integer benchmarks, not every SELF program runs at half the speed of optimized C. For example, the Richards

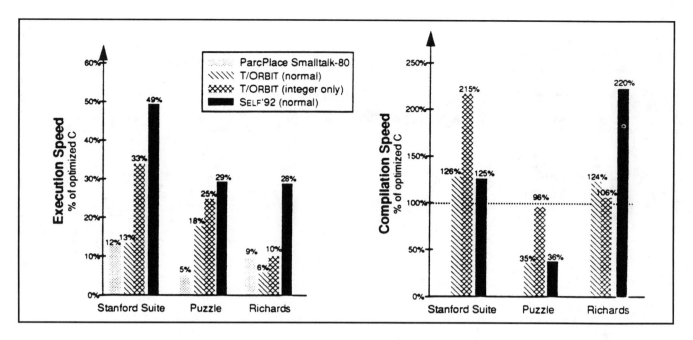

Figure 11.

benchmark (an operating-system simulation) runs 3.5 times slower than C, principally because the compiler's type analysis cannot infer as many types as it can in the other programs. Furthermore, even though the SELF-91 compiler's compilation speed is comparable to the speed of C compilers, it is still too slow for pleasant interactive use. The newest system (SELF-93) addresses both problems with the help of two new techniques:

- *Dynamic recompilation.* When performed at runtime, the advanced optimizations, as well as the more conventional optimizations such as register allocation and code scheduling, can result in compile pauses that distract and disturb users. This problem can be alleviated by adding a fast and simple compiler to the system. Rather than always optimizing all code, SELF-93 uses the simple compiler when a method is first invoked, thus minimizing pauses in runtime compilation. The result of the simple compilation is unoptimized machine code that includes a counter to tally its invocations. If any of the unoptimized code proves to be a bottleneck (as ascertained by checking the counters) the optimizing compiler is called in to *recompile* and optimize the hot spot. Dynamic recompilation dramatically reduces compilation times: on a fast workstation, compilation pauses are often unnoticeable and

rarely exceed one second (18, 33).

- *Type feedback.* When recompiling a method to optimize it, the SELF-93 optimizing compiler uses runtime-receiver type information rather than rely on static type analysis to inline message sends (17, 18). Using this runtime type information, the compiler can inline almost any send (if it wants to), even where type analysis does not work well. As a result, the new compiler outperforms SELF-91 by a factor of 1.5 on a suite of large SELF applications (17, 33).

Related work

Others have tackled the challenge of inferring type information for programs without explicit type declarations. Although these approaches can help the programmer write programs, they usually compute high-level abstract types that describe an object's interface, not its representation. Therefore, they cannot supply the information on low-level representation that the compiler needs to generate good code. A recently proposed algorithm (27) may partly solve this problem, computing representation-level type information for programs written in a Smalltalk-like language. It is too early to judge, though, if this approach is practical for large real-world programs.

A different approach to achieving ob-

ject-oriented performance came out of work by the Typed Smalltalk (TS) project (14, 16) . In TS, programmers can annotate programs with type declarations. Such annotations can help make the code more readable, can lead to fewer runtime errors, and can help the TS optimizing compiler produce better code by performing runtime type casing and message inlining. Unfortunately, the type annotations needed by the optimizing compiler use representation-level types and thus turn reusable methods into more restricted versions that cannot be safely reused with other types. Although performance data for the TS system are very scarce, the few published numbers appear to indicate that TS reaches only about half the speed of the current SELF system.

An early APL compiler (20) used techniques similar to customization to generate more efficient code. If an expression was first executed with two-dimensional integer arrays, the compiler would generate "hard" code specialized for this case. If the type of the variables changed in later executions, the compiler would produce less specialized "soft" fallback code. Unlike the SELF compiler, the APL system did not generate multiple specialized copies of code to save compile time and code space. Some compilers designed to optimize scientific FORTRAN programs can also duplicate procedures to improve the effect of some optimizations (7). Similarly, the partial-evaluation *polyvariant*

Conclusions

Object-oriented programming promises to make it easier to write programs. Dynamically bound messages allow methods to transcend the representation of the objects they manipulate, and inheritance allows different objects to share the same methods without copying them. SELF offers a particularly simple and pure version of object-oriented programming in which every action is performed by sending a message. SELF's utter uniformity allows code to be reused and refactored even more easily than in other object-oriented languages.

Dynamically bound messages, however, cannot be optimized by conventional compilers. For example, a conventional implementation of SELF would probably run at least forty times slower than optimized C. Fortunately, this performance barrier can be overcome with new compilation techniques. *Customizing* creates multiple copies of the same source method, each specialized for a receiver type. In every copy, many messages can subsequently be *inlined,* often completely eliminating overhead for message passing. Splitting carries this idea one step further by generating specialized versions for parts of methods. Combined with other techniques such as type prediction, these new methods of compilation can dramatically reduce the high frequency of dynamically dispatched message sends. Subsequent conventional optimizations such as global- register allocation and code scheduling can be used to speed up the code even further.

The new compilation techniques help make pure object-oriented languages practical. The benchmarks we measured run three to six times faster in SELF than they run in the next fastest pure object-oriented language implementation. For the Stanford integer benchmarks, our compilation techniques have even narrowed the performance gap between SELF and optimized C to a factor of two, despite the vastly different execution models of these two languages. Today, even a radically pure language such as SELF can be implemented efficiently, combining the benefits of ubiquitous objects with good performance.

specialization technique (1) involves replicating nodes based on unique values or types of variables.

Acknowledgments

Many people have done much to make this work possible. The other members of the SELF group, Bay-Wei Chang, Ole Agesen, John Maloney, Lars Bak, and Mario Wolczko, have put their hearts and souls into other aspects of this project. Elgin Lee was part of the group for a time in the beginning and helped bring the first implementation of SELF to life. Peter Deutsch has been a constant source of interesting ideas and inspiration. Since 1991, the SELF project has found a congenial home in Sun Microsystems Laboratories, thanks to Wayne Rosing, Bill Joy, Jim Mitchell, Bert Sutherland, and Alberto Savoia. The first author also thanks David Patterson for teaching him how to think about optimizing and analyzing the performance of computer systems. Finally, we express our gratitude for our families' constant support.

References

1. Bulyonkov, M. A. Polyvariant mixed computation for analyzer programs. *Acta Informatica,* vol. 21 (1984), pp. 473–484.

2. Chambers, Craig. The Design and Implementation of the SELF Compiler, an Optimizing Compiler for Object Oriented Programming Languages. Ph.D. Thesis, Computer Science Department, Stanford University, April 1992.

3. Chambers, Craig, David Ungar, and Elgin Lee. An efficient implementation of SELF, a dynamically-typed object-oriented language based on prototypes. In OOPSLA '89 Conference Proceedings, pp. 49–70, New Orleans, La., 1989. Published as *SIGPLAN Notices,* vol. 24, no. 10 (October 1989).

4. Chambers, Craig, and David Ungar. Iterative type analysis and extended message splitting: Optimizing dynamically-typed object-oriented programs. In *Proceedings of the SIGPLAN '90 Conference on Programming Language Design and Implementation,* White Plains, N.Y., June 1990. Published as *SIGPLAN Notices,* vol. 25, no. 6 (June 1990).

5. Chambers, Craig, and David Ungar. Making pure object-oriented languages practical. In OOPSLA '91 Conference Proceedings, pp. 1–15, Phoenix, Ariz., October 1991.

6. Conroy, Thomas J., and Eduardo Pelegri-Llopart. An assessment of method-lookup caches for Smalltalk-80 implementations. In Glenn Krasner, ed., *Smalltalk-80: Bits of History and Words of Advice.* Reading, Mass.: Addison-Wesley, 1983.

7. Cooper, Keith D., Mary W. Hall, and Ken Kennedy. Procedure cloning. In *Proceedings of the IEEE International Conference on Computer Languages,* pp. 96–105, Oakland, Calif., April 1992.

8. Deutsch, L. Peter. The Dorado Smalltalk-80 implementation: Hardware architecture's impact on software architecture. In Glenn Krasner, ed., *Smalltalk-80: Bits of History and Words of Advice.* Reading, Mass.: Addison-Wesley, 1983.

9. Deutsch, L. Peter, and Alan Schiffman. Efficient implementation of the Smalltalk-80 system. *Proceedings of the 11th Symposium on the Principles of Programming Languages,* Salt Lake City, Utah, 1984.

10. Dixon, R., T. McKee, P. Schweitzer, and M. Vaughan. A fast method dispatcher for compiled languages with multiple inheritance. In *OOPSLA 89 Conference Proceedings,* pp. 211–214, New Orleans, La., October 1989. Published as *SIGPLAN Notices,* vol. 24, no. 10, October 1989.

11. Ellis, Margaret A., and Bjarne Stroustrup. *The Annotated C++ Reference Manual.* Reading, Mass.: Addison-Wesley, 1990.

12. Falcone, .Joseph, and James Stinger. The Smalltalk-80 implementation at Hewlett-Packard. In Glenn Krasner, ed., *Smalltalk-80: Bits of History and Words of Advice. Reading, Mass.: Addison-Wesley, 1983.*

13. Goldberg, Adele, and David Robson. *Smalltalk-80: The Language and Its Implementation.* Reading, Mass.: Addison-Wesley, 1983.

14. Graver, Justin O., and Ralph E. Johnson. A type system for Smalltalk. In *Conference Record of the 17th Annual ACM Symposium on Principles of Programming Languages,* pp. 136–150, San Francisco, Calif., January 1990.

15. Hölzle, Urs, Craig Chambers, and David Ungar. Optimizing dynamically-typed object-oriented programs using polymorphic inline caches. In *ECOOP '91 Conference Proceedings,* pp. 21–38, Geneva, Switzerland, July 1991.

16. Hölzle, Urs, Craig Chambers, and David Ungar. Debugging optimized code with dynamic deoptimization. In *Proceedings of the SIGPLAN 92 Conference on Programming Language Design and Implementation,* pp. 32–43, San Francisco, Calif., June 1992.

17. Hölzle, Urs, and David Ungar. Optimizing dynamically-dispatched calls with runtime type feedback. In *Proceedings of the SIGPLAN 94 Conference on Programming Language Design and Implementation,* Orlando, Fla., June 1994.

18. Hölzle, Urs. Adaptive Optimization for SELF: Reconciling High Performance with Exploratory Programming. Ph.D. Thesis, Stanford University, Computer Science Department, 1994.

19. Johnson, Ralph E., Justin O. Graver, and Lawrence W. Zurawski. TS: An optimizing compiler for Smalltalk. In *OOPSLA '88 Conference Proceedings,* pp. 18–26,

San Diego, Calif., October 1988. Published as *SIGPLAN Notices*, vol. 23, no. 11, November 1988.

20. Johnston, Ronald E. The dynamic incremental compiler of APL\3000. *ACM APL Quote Quad*, vol. 9, no. 4, June 1979, pp. 82–87.

21. Kiczales, Gregor, and Luis Rodriguez. Efficient Method Dispatch in PCL. Technical Report SSL-89-95, Xerox PARC, 1989.

22. Bobrow, D. G., L. G. DeMichiel, R. P. Gabriel, S. E. Keene, G. Kiczales, and D. A. Moon. Common Lisp Object System Specification X3J13. In *SIGPLAN Notices*, vol. 23 (Special Issue), September 1988.

23. Kranz, David Andrew. ORBIT: An Optimizing Compiler for Scheme. Ph.D. thesis, Yale University, 1988.

24. Krasner, Glenn, ed. *Smalltalk-80: Bits of History and Words of Advice.* Reading, Mass.: Addison-Wesley, 1983.

25. Lea, Douglas. Customization in C++. In *Proceedings of the 1990 Usenix C++ Conference*, pp. 301–314, San Francisco, Calif., April 1990.

26. Meyer, Bertrand. *Eiffel: The Language.* Englewood Cliffs, N.J.: Prentice- Hall, 1992.

27. Oxhoj, Nicholas, Jens Palsberg, and Michael I. Schwartzbach. Making type inference practical. In *ECOOP '92 Conference Proceedings*, Utrecht, The Netherlands, June 1992.

28. Pugh, William, and Grant Weddell. Two-directional record layout for multiple inheritance. In *Proceedings of the SIGPLAN '90 Conference on Programming Language Design and Implementation*, pp. 85–91, White Plains, N.Y., June 1990. Published as *SIGPLAN Notices*, vol. 25, no. 6, June 1990.

29. Rose, John R. Fast dispatch mechanisms for stock hardware. In *OOPSLA 88 Conference Proceedings*, pp. 27–35, San Diego, Calif., October 1988. Published as *SIGPLAN Notices*, vol. 23, no. 11, November 1988.

30. Schaffert, Craig, Topher Cooper, Bruce Bullis, Mike Kilian, and Carrie Wilpolt. An introduction to Trellis/Owl. In *OOPSLA '86 Conference Proceedings*, pp. 9–16, Portland, Ore., September 1986. Published as *SIGPLAN Notices*, vol. 21, no. 11, November 1986.

31. David Ungar. *The Design and Evaluation of a High Performance Smalltalk System.* Cambridge: MIT Press, 1987.

32. Ungar, David, and Randall B. Smith. SELF: The power of simplicity. In *OOPSLA '87 Conference Proceedings*, pp. 227–241, Orlando, Fla., October 1987. Published as *SIGPLAN Notices*, vol. 22, no. 12, December 1987. Also published in *Lisp and Symbolic Computation*, vol. 4, no. 3, Kluwer Academic Publishers, June 1991.

33. Hölzle, Urs, and David Ungar. A Third Generation Self-Implementation: Reconciling Responsiveness and Performance. In *OOPSLA Oct. 94 Conference Proceedings*.

David Ungar
Sun Microsystems Laboratories, Inc.,
2550 Garcia Ave., MTV 29-116, Mountain View, CA 94043
david.ungar@sun.com
(415)336-2618

Randall B. Smith
Sun Microsystems Laboratories, Inc.,
2550 Garcia Ave., MTV 29-116, Mountain View, CA 94043
randall.smith@sun.com
(415)336-2620

Craig Chambers
Department of Computer Science and Engineering , Sieg Hall, FR-35
University of Washington, Seattle, WA 98195
chambers@
cs.washington.edu
(206)685-2094

Urs Hölzle
University of California at Santa Barbara
Dept. of CS, CA 93106
urs@cs.ucsb.edu

Appendix A: Per-benchmark raw data

Compile times are not available for Smalltalk-80. All times were measured on a lightly loaded SPARCstation-2.

Run Times (milliseconds)	Smalltalk	T (normal)	T (Int only)	SELF'92	C (opt)
bubble	1020	440	140	95	67
matrix multiply	640	1230	500	300	110
perm	540	460	110	96	44
queens	330	250	95	55	35
quicksort	470	700	340	105	41
towers	380	300	130	120	63
treesort	750	670	460	500	220
puzzle	6790	1830	1320	1170	335
richards	3250	4520	2860	1040	290

Compile Times (sec)	SELF'92	T (normal)	T (Int only)	C (opt)
bubble	1.4	1.4	0.7	1.4
matrix multiply	1.5	1.5	0.7	2.3
perm	1.6	1.0	0.5	2.4
queens	2.8	1.7	0.8	1 4
quicksort	2.0	1.6	0.9	1.8
towers	0.8	1.7	1.8	2.6
treesort	1.1	1.7	1.2	1.6
puzzle	12.6	12.7	4.7	4.5
richards	3.1	5.5	6.4	6.8

To Probe Further. More detailed information on the SELF language and the compilation techniques mentioned here (including references 2-5, 15, 16, and 33) are available electronically in PostScript form. To obtain a copy, ftp to self.stanford.edu and read the README file in /pub/papers. The current SELF implementation is also available without charge from the same host; see the file /pub/README for details. On the worldwide Web, SELF can be found at http://www.Sun.com/smli, or http://SELF.stanford.edu.

Easy-to-Use Object-Oriented Parallel Processing with Mentat

Andrew S. Grimshaw, University of Virginia

Reprinted from *Computer*, May 1993, pp. 39–51.
Copyright © 1993 by The Institute of Electrical and
Electronics Engineers, Inc. All rights reserved.

Two problems plague programming for parallel multiple-instruction, multiple-data (MIMD) architectures. First, writing parallel programs by hand is very difficult. The programmer must manage communication, synchronization, and scheduling of tens to thousands of independent processes. Correctly managing the environment requires considerable time and energy and often overwhelms the programmer. Second, code implemented on a particular architecture is seldom usable on other MIMD architectures, since the tools, techniques, and library facilities to parallelize the application are platform specific. Thus, porting the application to a new architecture requires considerable effort. Given the plethora of new architectures and the rapid obsolescence of existing architectures, this represents a continuing time investment.

Mentat, an object-oriented parallel processing system that I developed with my students at the University of Virginia, directly addresses the difficulty of programming MIMD architectures and the portability of applications. Its three primary design objectives are to provide (1) easy-to-use parallelism, (2) high performance via parallel execution, and (3) application portability across a wide range of platforms. The underlying premise is that writing programs for parallel machines does not have to be difficult. Instead, it's the lack of appropriate abstractions that has made parallel architectures difficult to program and kept them inaccessible to mainstream production-system programmers.

The Mentat philosophy on parallel computing is guided by two observations. The first is that the programmer understands the application domain and can make better data and computation partitioning decisions than the compiler. The truth of this is evidenced by the fact that most successful production parallel applications have been hand-coded using low-level primitives. In these applications the programmer has decomposed and distributed both the data and the computation.

The second observation is that management of tens to thousands of asynchronous tasks, where timing-dependent errors are easy to make, is beyond the capacity of most programmers. Compilers, on the other hand, are very good at ensuring that events happen in the right order and can more readily and correctly manage communication and synchronization, particularly in highly asynchronous, non-SPMD (single program, multiple data) environments.

Lack of appropriate abstractions makes programming for parallel architectures more difficult than writing sequential software. Mentat addresses this problem by extending C++ to include parallelism encapsulation.

91

These two observations lead to our underlying philosophy of exploiting the comparative advantages of both humans and compilers. Therefore, in Mentat, the programmer tells the compiler, using a few key words, what computations are worth doing in parallel and what data are associated with the computations. The compiler then takes over and does what it does best, manage parallelism.

What makes Mentat different from the dozens of other concurrent and distributed object-oriented systems is its emphasis on parallelism and high performance. Mentat is not yet-another-RPC-based system. Unlike RPC (remote procedure call) systems, it uses parallel-processing compiler and runtime support technology in conjunction with the object-oriented paradigm to produce an easy-to-use high-performance system that facilitates hierarchies of parallelism.

Mentat accomplishes these objectives through two primary components. The Mentat programming language,[1] an object-oriented programming language based on C++, masks the complexity of the parallel environment from the programmer. The underlying Mentat runtime system[2] provides a virtual machine abstraction for easy portability to new architectures. The language and runtime system are introduced below, followed by performance figures for two applications on different platforms, a network of Sun workstations and the Intel iPSC/2. (For more detailed performance figures, see our companion article in the May 1993 issue of *IEEE Parallel & Distributed Technology*.)

Mentat programming language

The Mentat programming language (MPL) is a C++ extension designed to simplify the writing of high-performance parallel applications by supporting both intra- and interobject parallelism encapsulation. This high-level ease-of-use objective is realized via four specific design features.

First, MPL is object-oriented. The object-oriented paradigm is ideal for parallel and distributed systems because users of an object interact with the object via the object's interface. The ob-

---

Emphasis on parallelism and high performance distinguishes Mentat from many of other object-oriented systems.

---

ject's data hiding, or encapsulation, properties prevent direct access of private object data. This simplifies concurrency control on object data structures, since objects can be treated as monitors. MPL extends the notions of data and method encapsulation to include parallelism encapsulation (see sidebar on encapsulation).

Second, MPL extends an existing language, C++, with minimal changes. The syntax and semantics of the extensions follow the pattern set by the base language, maintaining its basic structure and philosophy whenever possible.

Third, the language constructs have a natural mapping to the macro dataflow model, the computation model underlying Mentat. It is a medium-grain datadriven model in which programs are directed graphs. The vertices of the program graphs are computation elements (called actors) that perform some function. The edges model data dependencies between the actors.

Fourth, since the extensions are based on concepts applicable to a broad class of languages, the Mentat approach is easily used in other contexts.

These goals have been met in MPL by extending C++ in three ways: the specification of Mentat classes, the *rtf()* value return mechanism, and the select/accept statement. The basic idea is to let the programmer specify which C++ classes are of sufficient computational complexity to warrant parallel execution and let the compiler manage communication and synchronization between instances of these classes.

Instances of Mentat classes are called Mentat objects. The programmer uses Mentat objects just as any other C++ object. The compiler generates code to construct and execute data dependency graphs in which the nodes are Mentat-object member-function invocations and the arcs are the data dependencies found in the program. Thus, interobject parallelism encapsulation is largely transpar-

ent to the programmer. To obtain intraobject parallelism encapsulation, a graph node (member function) can be transparently implemented by a subgraph; the caller sees only the member function invocation.

(The examples that follow assume familiarity with C++ terms. See the sidebar on p. 42 for a short primer on C++.)

Mentat class definition. C++ objects are defined by their class. Each class has an interface section that defines member variables and functions. Not all objects should be Mentat objects. In particular, objects not having a sufficiently high computation ratio (that is, whose object operations are not sufficiently computationally complex) should not be Mentat objects. The required complexity depends on the architecture, but in general, the minimum size is several hundred instructions. At smaller sizes, the communication and runtime overhead takes longer than the member function, resulting in a slowdown rather than a speedup.

Mentat's object model distinguishes between two types of objects: contained objects and independent objects — a not unusual distinction driven by efficiency considerations. Contained objects are objects contained in another object's address space, including instances of C++ classes, integers, structs, and so on. Independent objects possess a distinct address space, a systemwide unique name, and a thread of control. Communication between independent objects is accomplished via member function invocation. Independent objects are analogous to Unix processes. Mentat objects are independent objects.

Because Mentat objects are address-space disjoint, member function calls are by value. Results of member functions are also returned by value. Pointers to objects, particularly variable-size objects, can be used as both parameters and return types. To provide programmer control of the degree of parallelism, Mentat allows both standard C++ classes and Mentat classes. By default, a standard C++ class definition defines a standard C++ object.

The programmer defines a Mentat class by using the keyword "mentat" in the class definition. The programmer can further specify whether the class is persistent or regular. The syntax for Mentat class definitions is

```
new_class_def ::
   mentat_definition class_definition |
   class_definition
mentat_definition ::
   persistent mentat |
   regular mentat |
class_definition ::
   class class_name {class_interface};
```

Persistent objects maintain state infor-mation between member function invo-cations, while regular objects do not. Thus, regular-object member functions are pure functions, which frees the system to instantiate new instances of regular classes at will. Regular classes can have local variables, much as procedures do, and can maintain state information for the duration of a function invocation.

A class should be a Mentat class when its member functions are computationally expensive, when its member functions exhibit high latency (for example, I/O), or when it holds state information that needs to be shared by many other objects (for example, shared queues, databases, physical devices). Classes whose member functions have a high computation cost or high latency should

---

Intraobject and interobject parallelism encapsulation

A key feature of Mentat is the transparent encapsulation of parallelism within and between Mentat-object member-function invocations. Consider for example an instance *matrix_op* of a *matrix_operators* Mentat class with the member function *mpy()* that multiplies two matrices together and returns a matrix. As a user, when I invoke *mpy()* in *x = matrix_op.mpy(B,C);*, it is irrelevant whether *mpy()* is implemented sequentially or in parallel; all I care about is whether the correct answer is computed. We call the hiding of whether a member function implementation is sequential or parallel "intraobject parallelism encapsulation."

Similarly, we make the exploitation of parallelism opportunities between Mentat-object member-function invocations transparent to the programmer. We call this "interobject parallelism encapsulation." It is the responsibility of the compiler to ensure that data dependencies between invocations are satisfied, and that communication and synchronization are handled correctly.

Intraobject parallelism encapsulation and interobject parallelism encapsulation can be combined. Indeed, interobject parallelism encapsulation within a member function implementation is intraobject parallelism encapsulation as far as the caller of that member function is concerned. Thus, multiple levels of parallelism encapsulation are possible, each level hidden from the level above.

To illustrate parallelism encapsulation, suppose X, A, B, C, D, and E are matrix pointers. Consider the sequence of statements

```
X = matrix_op.mpy(B,C);
A = matrix_op.mpy(X,matrix_op.mpy(D,E));
```

On a sequential machine, the matrices B and C are multiplied first, with the result stored in X, followed by the multiplication of D and E. The final step is to multiply X by the result of D∗E. If we assume that each multiplication takes one time unit, then three time units are required to complete the computation.

In Mentat, the compiler and runtime system detect that the first two multiplies, B∗C and D∗E, are not data dependent on one another and can be safely executed in parallel. The two matrix multiplications will be executed in parallel, with the result automatically forwarded to the final multiplication. That result will be forwarded to the caller, and associated with A. The execution graph is shown at the left in the figure.

The difference between the programmer's sequential model, and the parallel execution of the two multiplies afforded by Mentat, is an example of interobject parallelism encapsulation. In the absence of other parallelism, or overhead, the speedup for this example is a modest 1.5.

$$\text{Speedup} = \frac{T_{\text{Sequential}}}{T_{\text{Parallel}}} = \frac{3}{2} = 1.5$$

However, that is not the end of the story. Additional, intraobject, parallelism can be realized within the matrix multiply. Suppose the matrix multiplies are themselves executed in parallel (with the parallelism detected in a manner similar to the above). Further, suppose that each multiply is executed in eight pieces (shown on the right-hand side in the figure). Then, assuming zero overhead, the total execution time is 0.125 + 0.125 = 0.25 time units, resulting in a speedup of 3/0.25 = 12. As matrix multiply is implemented using more pieces, even larger speedups result. The key point is that the programmer need not be concerned with data dependence detection, communication, synchronization, or scheduling; the compiler does it.

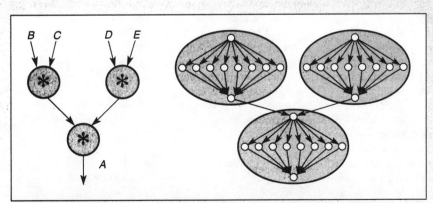

Parallel execution of matrix multiply operations: (left) interobject parallelism encapsulation; (right) intraobject parallelism encapsulation where the multiplies have been transparently expanded into parallel subgraphs.

be Mentat classes to permit overlapping with other computations and latencies, that is, executing them in parallel with other functions. Shared state objects should be Mentat classes for two reasons. First, since there is no shared memory in the model, shared state can be realized only by using a Mentat object with which other objects can communicate. Second, because Mentat objects service a single member function at a time, they provide a monitor-like synchronization, providing synchronized access to their state.

> **All Mentat objects have a separate address space, a thread of control, and a systemwide unique name.**

To illustrate the difference between regular and persistent Mentat classes,

suppose we wish to perform matrix operations in parallel, for example, a matrix-matrix multiply. Recall that a matrix-matrix multiply forms a new matrix. Each element in the result is found by performing a dot product on the appropriate rows and columns of the input matrices (Figure 1a). Because matrix-matrix multiply is a pure function, we could define a regular Mentat class *matrix_operators* (Figure 1b). In this case, every invocation of an *mpy()* creates a new Mentat object to perform the multiplication, and the arguments are

Introduction to C++

C++, an object-oriented extension of C developed by Bjarne Stroustrup of AT&T Bell Labs, avoids the performance penalty usually associated with object-oriented languages. C++ supports object-oriented concepts such as objects, classes, encapsulation, inheritance, polymorphism, and function and operator overloading. The most important extensions revolve around classes. Classes are structurally similar to C structs.

Classes support the concept of encapsulation via the provision of private and protected member variables and member functions. Private members (for example, *top*) can be accessed only by member functions of the class (for example, *push()*). Protected members can be accessed only by members of the class and by members of derived classes. Nonaccessible members can still be indirectly manipulated via public member functions. By limiting access to members, the language supports encapsulation.

Inheritance means that classes can be defined in terms of other classes, inheriting their behavior (public, private, and protected members). When a class can have at most one super (parent) class, we say a language supports single inheritance, and a tree-like class structure results. When there can be multiple super classes, we say the language supports multiple inheritance. C++ supports multiple inheritance.

A limited form of polymorphism is supported in C++ via virtual functions. Multiple classes, all derived from the same base class, may all define different implementations of a virtual function. When the function is invoked on a pointer or reference to an instance of the base class, the appropriate function is bound and called. The function binding is done at runtime and depends on the class of the object to which the pointer points. This can be contrasted with compile-time binding where the compiler decides at compile-time which function to use. The canonical example is a base class *shape* and a virtual function *draw()*. The classes *square* and *triangle* are derived from *shape*. Suppose *x* is defined as *shape *x;*. At runtime, *x* may point to a *shape*, a *square*, or a *triangle*. When *x->draw()* is executed, the correct draw (*square* or *triangle*) will be bound and invoked.

Function and operator overloading permits the programmer to redefine, or overload, the meaning of both the standard binary and unary operators, as well as user-defined functions. The compiler determines which function to use, based on the number and type of the arguments.

Classes in C++ are defined in a manner similar to structs in C. The class *int_stack*

```
class int_stack {
protected:
    int max_elems, top;
    int *data;
public:
    int_stack(int size = 50);
    void push(int);
    int pop();
};
```

has three protected member variables defined: *max_elems*, *top*, and *data*. They cannot be directly manipulated by users of instances of *int_stack*, but they can be used by derived classes. The constructor for *int_stack*, *int_stack(int size)*, is called whenever a new instance is created. Constructors usually initialize private data structures and allocate space. Instances are created when a variable comes into scope (for example, *{int_stack x(40);}*) or when instances are allocated on the heap (for example, *int_stack *x = new int_stack(30);*). The member functions *push(int)* and *int pop()* operate on the stack and are the sole mechanism to manipulate private data.

To illustrate member function invocation, suppose that *x* is an instance of *int_stack*. Member functions are invoked using either the dot notation, *x.push(5);*, or if *x* is a pointer, the arrow notation, *x->push(5);*.

References

1. B. Stroustrup, "What is Object-Oriented Programming?" *IEEE Software*, Vol. 5, No. 3, May 1988, pp. 10-20.

2. B. Stroustrup, *C++ Programming Language*, 2nd ed., Addison-Wesley, Reading, Mass., 1991.

transported to the new instance. Successive calls create new objects and transport the arguments to them.

Alternatively, we could define a persistent Mentat class *p_matrix* (Figure 1c). To use a *p_matrix*, an instance must first be created and initialized with a *matrix**. Matrix-matrix multiplication can then be accomplished by calling *mpy()*. When *mpy()* is used, the argument matrix is transported to the existing object. On successive calls, argument matrices are transported to the same object. In both the persistent and the regular case, the implementation of the class may hierarchically decompose the object into subobjects and operations into parallel suboperations.

Mentat object instantiation and destruction. An instance of a Mentat class is a Mentat object. All Mentat objects have a separate address space, a thread of control, and a systemwide unique name. Instantiation of Mentat objects differs slightly from standard C++ object instantiation semantics. First, consider the C++ fragment

```
{// A new scope
    int x;
    p_matrix mat1;
    matrix_operators m_ops;
} // end of scope
```

In C++, when the scope in which *x* is declared is entered, a new integer is created on the stack. In MPL, because *p_matrix* is a Mentat class, *mat1* is a name of a Mentat object of type *p_matrix*. It is not the instance itself. Thus, *mat1* is analogous to a pointer.

Names (for example, *mat1*) can be in one of two states, bound or unbound. An unbound name refers to any instance of the appropriate Mentat class. A bound name refers to a specific instance with a unique name. When an instance of a Mentat class (a Mentat variable) comes into scope or is allocated on the heap, it is initially an unbound name; it does not refer to any particular instance of the class. Thus, a new *p_matrix* is not instantiated when *mat1* comes into scope. When unbound names are used for regular Mentat classes (for example, *m_ops*), the underlying system logically creates a new instance for each invocation of a member function. This can lead to high levels of parallelism, as we'll see later.

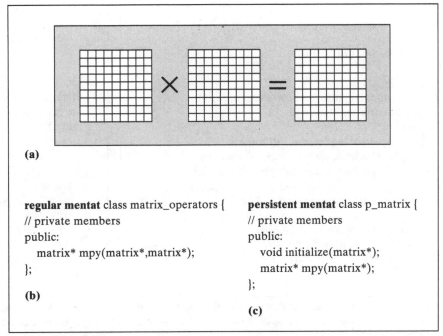

(a)

regular mentat class matrix_operators {
// private members
public:
    matrix* mpy(matrix*,matrix*);
};

(b)

persistent mentat class p_matrix {
// private members
public:
    void initialize(matrix*);
    matrix* mpy(matrix*);
};

(c)

Figure 1. Matrix-matrix multiplication (a) performed by regular (b) and persistent (c) Mentat class definitions.

Binding and instantiation. A Mentat variable (for example, *mat1*) can become bound in one of three ways: It can be explicitly created using *create()*, it can be bound by the system to an existing instance using *bind()*, or the name can be assigned to a bound name by an assignment.

The *create()* call tells the system to instantiate a new instance of the appropriate class. There are five flavors of *create()*, as shown below (assuming the definition *p_matrix mat1;*):

(a) mat1.create();
(b) mat1.create(COLOCATE another_object);
(c) mat1.create(DISJOINT object1, object2);
(d) mat1.create(HIGH_COMPU-TATION_RATIO);
(e) mat1.create(int on_host);
(f) mat1 = expression;
(g) mat1.bind(THIS_HOST);

When *create()* is used as in (a), the system chooses the processor to instantiate the object.[2] The programmer can also use location hints, as in (b), (c), (d), and (e), to specify where he or she wants the new object to be instantiated. In (b), the programmer specified placing the new Mentat object on the same processor as the object *another_object*. In (c), the programmer specified that the new object should not be placed on the same processor as any of the listed Mentat objects. In (d), the programmer specified that the new object will have a high computation-to-communication ratio and can be placed on a processor with high communication expense. In (e), the programmer specified placing the new object on a specific processor. Names can also be bound as the result of assignment to an expression, as in (f).

Mentat variables can also be bound to an existing instance, using the *bind(scope)* member function, as shown in (g). The parameter scope can take any one of three values, BIND_LOCAL, BIND_CLUSTER, and BIND_GLO-BAL, to restrict the search for an instance to the local host (the host can be a multiprocessor), to the cluster (subnet), and to the entire system, respectively.

Mentat-object member-function invocation. Member-function invocation on Mentat objects is syntactically the same as for C++ objects. Semantically, there are two important differences. Mentat member functions are always call-by-value, and Mentat member-function invocation is nonblocking. The nonblocking nature of Mentat-object member functions provides for the parallel execution of member functions whenever data dependencies permit. This is

```
class string {
public:
    int size-of ();
};

int string::size_of() {return(strlen(this)+1);}
persistent mentat class m_file {
public:
    int open(string* name, int mode);
    data_block* read(int offset, int num_bytes);
    void write(int offset, data_block* data);}
{
    // A code fragment using m_file
    m_file f;
    f.create(); // No location hints.
    int x = f.open((string*) "my_file",1);
    if (x < 0) {/* error code */}
}
```

Figure 2. Class m_file declaration and use. Note that execution does not block on the open() call until the result _x_ is used.

```
regular mentat class data_processor {
public:
    data_block* filter_one(data_block*);
    data_block* filter_two(data_block*);
};

    m_file in_file,out_file;
    data_processor dp;
    in_file.create();
    out_file.create();
    int i,x;
    x = in_file.open((string*)"input_file",1);
    x = out_file.open((string*)"output_file",3);
    data_block *res;
    for (i=0;i<MAX_BLOCKS,i++) {
        res = in_file.read_block(i);
        res = dp.filter_one(res);
        res = dp.filter_two(res);
        out_file.write_block((i*BLK_SIZE,res);
    }
```

Figure 3. A pipelined data processor. The main loop reads MAX_BLOCKS data_blocks, passes them through filter_one() and filter_two(), and then writes them to the output file. The loop is unrolled at runtime and a pipeline (Figure 4) is formed.

transparent to the user and is called interobject parallelism encapsulation.

Because Mentat objects are address-space disjoint, Mentat-class member functions always use call-by-value semantics. When pointers are used as arguments, the designated object (or structure) is sent to the callee. If the object size is variable, the class of the object must provide a member function _int size_of()_ that returns the size of the object in bytes. If a structure or class has contained pointers, they are not "chased." Call-by-value semantics is common in systems that provide an RPC-like service. The alternative is to allow pointer passing between address spaces.

Example 1. Consider the code fragment shown in Figure 2. The member function _open()_ takes two parameters and returns an integer. The first parameter is of type _string*_. Because strings are of variable length, we provided the function _int size_of()_. _Size_of_ is called

at runtime to determine the size of the first parameter, and _size_of()_ bytes will be sent to the Mentat object _f_. The second argument is an integer. Fixed-size arguments such as integers and structs do not require a _size_of()_ function. The compiler ensures that the correct amount of data is transferred.

The example in Figure 2 illustrates the creation of a persistent object and a simple RPC to a member function of that object. The difference between Mentat and a traditional RPC is what happens when an RPC call is encountered. In traditional RPC, the arguments are marshalled (packaged into a message), sent to the callee, and the caller blocks waiting for the result. The callee accepts the call, performs the desired service, and returns the results to the caller. The caller then unblocks and proceeds.

In Mentat, when a Mentat-object member function is encountered, the arguments are marshalled and sent to the callee, but the caller does not block

waiting for the result (_x_ in Figure 2). Instead, the runtime system monitors (with compiler-provided code) where _x_ is used. If _x_ is later used as an argument to a second or third Mentat object invocation, then arrangements are made to send _x_ directly to the second and third member-function invocations. If _x_ is used locally in a strict operation, for example, $y = x + 1$, or _if (x<0)_, then the runtime system will automatically block the caller and wait for the value of _x_ to be computed and returned. This is the case in Example 1. Note, though, that if _x_ is not used locally (except as an argument to a Mentat-object member function), then the caller never blocks and waits for _x_. Indeed, _x_ might never be sent to the caller, it might only be sent to the Mentat-object member functions for which it is a parameter. This is illustrated in the next example.

Example 2. This example illustrates construction of a simple pipeline process. We define the regular Mentat class _data_processor_. The member functions _filter_one()_ and _filter_two()_ are filters that process blocks of data. Consider the code fragment in Figure 3. After some initialization, creating and opening input and output files, the loop in the code fragment sequentially reads MAX_BLOCKS data blocks from

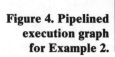

Figure 4. Pipelined execution graph for Example 2.

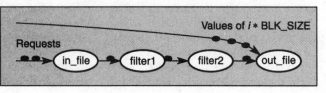

input_file, processes them through filters one and two, and writes them to *output_file*. Note that the variable *res* is used as a temporary variable and as a conduit for passing information between the filters. This fragment is written in a manner that is natural to C programmers.

In a traditional RPC system, this fragment would execute sequentially. Suppose each member-function execution takes 10 time units and each communication takes 5 time units. Then the time required to execute an iteration of the loop in a sequential RPC system is the sum of four times the member-function execution time, plus seven times the communication time (because all parameters and results must be communicated from/to the caller). Thus, the total time required is 75 time units.

The average time per iteration for the Mentat version is considerably less, just over 10 time units. First, observe that the time for a single iteration is four times the communication time, 20 time units, plus four times the execution time, 40 time units, for a total of 60 time units. There are only four communications because intermediate results are not returned to the caller; rather, they are passed directly where needed. Next, consider that the reads, the two filter operations, and the writes can be executed in a pipelined fashion with each operation executing on a separate processor (see Figure 4).

Under these circumstances, each of the four member-function invocations, and all of the communication, can be performed concurrently. The communication for the *i*th iteration can be overlapped with the computation of the *i*th + 1 iteration. (We assume that communication is asynchronous and that sufficient computation and communication resources exist.)

Using a standard pipe equation

T_{All} = time for all iterations
T_{Stage} = time for longest stage
= 10 time units
T_1 = time for first iteration
= 60 time units
T_{Avg} = average time per iteration
T_{All} = $T_1 + T_{Stage} * (\text{MAX\_BLOCKS} - 1)$
T_{All} = $60 + 10*(\text{MAX\_BLOCKS} - 1)$
T_{Avg} = $\dfrac{(60 + 10*(\text{MAX\_BLOCKS}-1))}{\text{MAX\_BLOCKS}}$

When MAX_BLOCKS is one, the time to complete is 60 time units, with

---

an average of 60 time units. This is marginally faster than a pure RPC (75 time units) because intermediate results are not sent to the caller. When MAX_BLOCKS is greater than one, the time required for the first iteration is 60 time units, and successive results are available every 10 time units. Thus, as MAX_BLOCKS increases, the average time per iteration drops and approaches 10 time units.

Now consider the effect of quadrupling the time to execute *filter_one()* from 10 to 40 time units. The time to execute the traditional RPC version goes from 75 to 105 time units. Using the standard pipe equation, the first result is available at time 90, and successive values every 24 time units. The standard pipe equation assumes that there is just one functional unit for each stage. This assumption is invalid in Mentat in this example, and the time per iteration for the Mentat version remains unchanged at 10 time units, if there are sufficient computation resources. To see why, consider that the *data_processor* class is a regular Mentat class. This means that the system can instantiate new instances at will to meet demand. A new instance of *data_processor* to service *filter_one()* requests is created whenever a result is generated by the read. There would be five instances of the *data_processor* class active at a time, four performing *filter_one()* and one performing *filter_two()*.

There are four items to note from this example. First, the main loop may have executed to completion (all MAX_BLOCKS iterations) before the first write has completed. Second, suppose our "caller" (the main loop) was itself a server servicing requests for clients. Once the main loop is complete, the caller can begin servicing other requests while the first request is still being completed. Third, the order of execution of the different stages of the

different iterations can vary from a straight sequential ordering (for example, the last iteration may "complete" before earlier iterations). This can happen, for example, if the different iterations require different amounts of filter processing. This additional asynchrony is possible because the runtime system guarantees that all parameters for all invocations are correctly matched and that member functions receive the correct arguments. The additional asynchrony permits additional concurrency in those cases where execution in strict order would prevent later iterations from executing even when all of their synchronization and data criteria have been met. Finally, in addition to the automatic detection of interobject parallelism opportunities, we may also have intraobject parallelism encapsulation, where each of the invoked member functions may be internally parallel. Thus, we obtain even more parallelism.

Return-to-future mechanism. The return-to-future function, *rtf()*, is Mentat's analog to C's *return*. It allows Mentat member functions to return a value to the successor nodes in the macro dataflow graph in which the member function appears. Mentat member functions use *rtf()* as the mechanism for returning values. The returned value is forwarded to all member functions that are data dependent on the result and to the caller if necessary. In general, copies can be sent to several recipients.

While there are many similarities, *rtf()* differs from *return* in three significant ways. First, in C, before a function can return a value, the value must be available. This is not the case with *rtf()*. Recall that when a Mentat-object member function is invoked, the caller does not block, and results are forwarded wherever they are needed. Thus, a member function may *rtf()* a "value" that is the result of another Mentat-object member function that has not completed, or perhaps even begun, execution. Indeed, the result can be computed by a parallel subgraph obtained by detecting interobject parallelism.

Second, a C *return* signifies the end of the computation in a function, while an *rtf()* does not. An *rtf()* indicates only that the result is available. Since each Mentat object has its own thread of control, additional computation can be performed after the *rtf()*, for example, to update state information or to communicate with other objects. By making the result available as soon as possible, we permit data-dependent computations to proceed concurrently with the local computation that follows the *rtf()*.

Third, a *return* returns data to the caller. *Rtf()* may or may not return data to the caller, depending on the program's data dependencies. If the caller does not use the result locally, then the caller does not receive a copy. This saves on communication overhead. The next two examples illustrate these features.

Example 3. Consider a *persistent class sblock* used in Gaussian elimination with partial pivoting. In this problem, illustrated in Figure 5a, we are trying to solve for x in $Ax = b$. The *sblocks* contain portions of the total system to be solved. The *sblock* member function

    vector* sblock ::
        reduce(vector*);

performs row reduction operations on a submatrix and returns a candidate row. Pseudocode for the reduce operation is given in Figure 5b. The return value can be quickly computed and returned via *rtf()*. The remaining updates to the *sblock* can then occur in parallel with the communication of the result (Figure 5c). In general, best performance is realized when the *rtf()* is used as soon as possible.

Example 4. Consider a transaction manager (TM) that receives requests

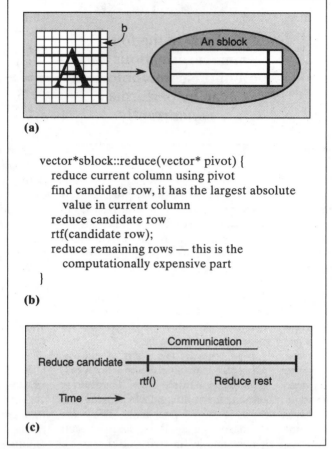

(a)

```
vector*sblock::reduce(vector* pivot) {
    reduce current column using pivot
    find candidate row, it has the largest absolute
        value in current column
    reduce candidate row
    rtf(candidate row);
    reduce remaining rows — this is the
        computationally expensive part
}
```

(b)

(c)

Figure 5. Gaussian elimination with partial pivoting illustrating the use of rtf() to overlap communication and computation: (a) decomposition into sblocks; (b) sblock::reduce() pseudocode; (c) overlap of communication and computation with rtf().

for reads and writes, and checks to see if the operation is permitted. If it is, the TM performs the operation via the data manager (DM) and returns the result. Figure 6a illustrates how the read operation might be implemented. In an RPC system, the record *read* would first be returned to the TM and then to the user. In MPL, the result is returned directly to the user, bypassing the TM (Figure

6b). Further, the TM can immediately begin servicing the next request instead of waiting for the result. This can be viewed as a form of distributed tail recursion or simple continuation passing.

MPL compiler. The MPL compiler (MPLC) is responsible for mapping MPL programs to the macro dataflow model. It accomplishes this by translating MPL programs to C++ programs with embedded calls to the Mentat runtime system. These C++ programs are, in turn, compiled by the host C++ compiler (see Figure 7). This approach is similar to that used by the AT&T C++ compiler, which translates C++ programs into a portable assembly language, C.

Runtime system

The Mentat runtime system[2] supports Mentat programs via a portable virtual macro-dataflow machine (Figure 8). The virtual machine provides support routines that perform runtime data dependence detection, program graph construction, program graph execution, token matching, scheduling, communication, and synchronization. The compiler generates code that communicates with the runtime system to correctly manage program execution.

The Mentat runtime system is not an operating system. Instead, the runtime system is layered on top of an existing host operating system, using the host operating system's processes, memory,

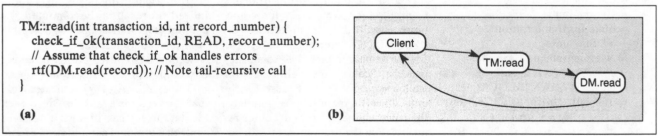

```
TM::read(int transaction_id, int record_number) {
    check_if_ok(transaction_id, READ, record_number);
    // Assume that check_if_ok handles errors
    rtf(DM.read(record)); // Note tail-recursive call
}
```

(a)   **(b)**

Figure 6. Tail recursion in MPL: (a) code fragment for transaction manager read; (b) call graph illustrating communication TM:read() with arcs representing message traffic.

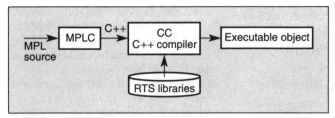

Figure 7. Compilation steps for the Mentat programming language.

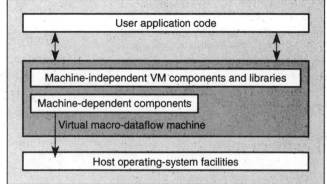

Figure 8. Mentat virtual-machine model.

C library, and interprocess communication services.

The virtual machine model permits the rapid transfer of Mentat to new architectural platforms. Only the machine-specific components need to be modified. Because the compiler uses a virtual machine model, porting applications to a new architecture does not require any user source-level changes.* Once the virtual machine has been ported, user applications are recompiled and can execute immediately.

The Mentat virtual macro-dataflow machine is implemented by the Mentat runtime system (RTS). The RTS is in two sections, runtime libraries that are linked into Mentat objects and runtime objects that provide runtime services such as scheduling, naming, and binding. The runtime libraries are responsible for program graph construction, select/accept execution, and reliable communication.

The logical structure of a Mentat system is that of a collection of hosts communicating through an interconnection network (see Figure 9a). Each host can communicate with any other host via the interconnection network, although not necessarily at uniform cost.

The logical interconnection network is provided by the lowest layer of the runtime system, the modular message-passing system. MMPS provides an extensible point-to-point message service that reliably delivers messages of arbitrary size from one process to another.

Each host has a complete copy of the runtime system server objects (Figure 9b). These include the instantiation manager i_m and the token matching unit (TMU). The instantiation manager is responsible for high-level Mentat-object scheduling (deciding on which host to locate an object) and for instantiating new instances. The high-level scheduling algorithm is distributed, adaptive, and stable. The TMU is responsible for matching tokens for regular objects and instantiating new instances (via the i_m) when needed.

Dynamic data dependence detection and program graph construction are accomplished by the MPLC in conjunction with the runtime system (Figure 9c). The MPLC generates library calls that tell the RTS when certain variables, called potential result variables (PRVs), are used on either the lefthand or righthand side of expressions (for example, X in $X = matrix\_op.mpy(B,C)$; in the sidebar on encapsulation). By carefully observing where PRVs are used at runtime, the RTS can construct data-dependency program graphs and man-age communication and synchronization.

One final note on the runtime system: Because we use a layered approach and mask differences in the underlying operating system and interprocess communication, applications are completely source-code portable between supported architectures. We routinely develop and debug software on Sun workstations and use the sources unchanged on the Intel iPSC/2. In this day of incompatible parallel computers, this is quite useful. The fact that the sources are identical allows us to compare architectures using the same code and to measure the effect of known architectural differences on algorithm performance (for example, to measure algorithm sensitivity to communication latency).

The only real difficulty when porting applications is grain size selection. Each platform has a different optimum grain size. To date, we have overcome this problem either by decomposing the

---

*Application code may benefit from changes but does not require them. For example, on the Sun 3/60, loop unrolling provides no benefit; on the Sparcstation it may.

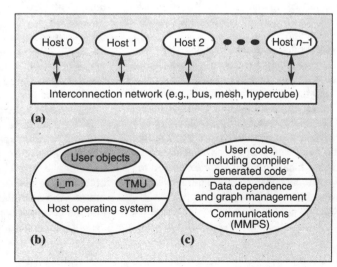

Figure 9. Mentat runtime system structure: (a) logical system structure, a collection of hosts; (b) logical host structure, user objects and system objects; (c) Mentat object structure.

problem with the largest grain size needed for any platform, or by parameterizing the Mentat class to indicate the number of pieces into which the problem should be decomposed. We are currently examining ways to automate this process based on information provided by the programmer.

Performance

Ease of use and programming models aside, the bottom line for parallel processing systems is performance. As of this writing, we have implemented the Mentat runtime system and run benchmarks on a network of Sun 3 and 4 workstations, the Silicon Graphics Iris,

> **Ease of use and programming models aside, the bottom line for parallel processing systems is performance.**

the Intel iPSC/2, and the Intel iPSC/860. Speedups for two benchmarks on the Sun 3 and the iPSC/2 are given below.

In each case the speedup shown is relative to an equivalent C program,

not relative to the Mentat implementation running on one processor. We have been very careful to use the same level of inner-loop hand optimization and compiler optimization for both the C and MPL versions. In both cases the inner loops were optimized in C using standard loop-optimization techniques; no assembly language was used.

The two benchmarks are matrix multiply and Gaussian elimination. Each benchmark was executed for several matrix dimensions (for example, 100×100, 200×200). Single-precision 32-bit values were used. Matrix multiply and Gaussian elimination were chosen because they are de facto parallel processing benchmarks. Execution times were measured from just after the main pro-

Related work

Mentat does not exist in a vacuum. There are many other systems and projects that are similar in some respects to Mentat, and that share many of the same goals. Mentat has much in common with both distributed object-oriented systems and with parallel processing systems. Mentat inherits features from both, ease of use from the object-oriented paradigm, and models and compiler techniques from the parallel processing domain.

What distinguishes Mentat from other distributed object-oriented systems is the combination of its objectives: easy-to-use high performance via parallelism and reliance on compiler and runtime techniques to transparently exploit parallelism. Many other systems[1,2] have fault tolerance (for example, transaction support), the use of functional specialization (for example, file servers), and the support of inherently distributed applications (for example, e-mail), as their primary objectives. For most of these systems, high-performance is simply not an issue, leading the implementations to rely on blocking RPC-like mechanisms, as opposed to the nonblocking invocations of Mentat. Alternatively, many systems permit parallelism but require the programmer to exploit and manage it.

In the object-oriented parallel processing domain, Mentat differs from systems such as Presto[3] and other shared-memory C++ systems[4] in its ability to easily support both shared-memory MIMD and distributed-memory MIMD architectures, as well as hybrids. PC++,[5] on the other hand, is a data-parallel C++. Mentat accommodates both functional and data parallelism, often within the same program. ESP[6] is perhaps the most similar of the parallel object-oriented systems. It too is a high-performance extension to C++ that supports both functional and data parallelism. What distinguishes Mentat is our compiler support. In ESP, remote invocations either return values or futures. If a value is returned, then a blocking RPC is performed. If a

future is returned, it must be treated differently. Futures may not be passed to other remote invocations, limiting the amount of parallelism. Finally, ESP supports only fixed-size arguments (except strings). This makes the construction of general-purpose library classes (for example, matrix operators) difficult.

The parallel processing (as opposed to distributed) domain has many languages for writing parallel applications, from fully explicit manual approaches to implicit compiler-based approaches. In fully explicit approaches, a traditional language such as C or Fortran is extended with communication and synchronization primitives such as send and receive or shared memory and semaphores. The advantages of this approach are that it (1) is relatively easy to implement, (2) reflects the underlying hardware model, and (3) lets the programmer use application domain knowledge to partition and schedule the problem. However, the programmer must also correctly manage communication and synchronization. This can be an overwhelming task, particularly in the presence of Heisenbugs.* Low-level primitives such as send and receive are the assembly language of parallelism. Anything can be done with them, but at the cost of increased burden on the programmer. Therefore, much as high-level languages and compilers were developed to simplify sequential programming, compilers have been built for parallel systems.

In fully automatic compiler-based approaches the compiler is responsible for performing dependence analysis and finding and exploiting opportunities for parallelism.[7] Compiler-based approaches are usually applied to Fortran. Ideally, application of this approach would permit the automatic parallelization of "dusty deck" Fortran programs. The advantage of compiler-based techniques is that the compiler can be trusted to get communication and synchronization right. The problem is that compilers are

gram had been loaded and arguments parsed to just before the program exited. All overhead costs, including loading Mentat object executables, I/O, and data distribution, have been included in the execution times.

Execution environment. The network of Suns consists of eight Sun 3/60s serviced by a Sun 3/280 file server running NFS connected by thin Ethernet. All of the workstations have eight megabytes of memory and an MC68881 floating-point coprocessor.

The Intel iPSC/2 is configured with 32 nodes. Each node has four megabytes of physical memory and an 80387 math coprocessor. The nodes are not equipped with either the VX vector pro-

> **Overhead, including loading Mentat object executables, I/O, and data distribution, is included in the execution times.**

cessor or the SX scalar processor. The NX/2 operating system provided with the iPSC/2 does not support virtual memory. The lack of virtual memory, coupled with the amount of memory consumed by the operating system, lim-

ited the problem sizes we could run on the iPSC/2.

Matrix multiply. The implementation tested is for the regular Mentat class *matrix_operators*. The Mentat times include the time to copy the arguments. The speedups for matrix multiply are shown in Figures 10a and 10b. The algorithm (and application source) is the same for both systems. Suppose the matrices A and B are to be multiplied. If k pieces are to be used, the B matrix is split into sqrt(k) vertical slices, and the A matrix into k/sqrt(k) horizontal slices. Each of the sqrt(k)*(k/sqrt(k)) workers gets an appropriate piece of A and of B to multiply. The results of the invocations are merged together and sent to

best at finding fine-grain and loop-level parallelism, and not good at detecting large-grain parallelism. This is because they lack knowledge of the application, forcing them to "reason" about the program using a fine-grain dependence graph. Message-passing MIMD architectures require medium- to coarse-grain parallelism to operate efficiently. Thus, purely compiler-based approaches are inappropriate for this class of machines because of the mismatch of granularity. Recently, there have been attempts to exploit programmer knowledge to improve data distribution.[8] This approach is best suited to data parallel problems.

Mentat strikes a balance that captures the best aspects of both explicit and compiler-based approaches. The user makes granularity and partitioning decisions using high-level Mentat class definitions, while the compiler and run-time system manage communication, synchronization, and scheduling. We believe that such hybrid approaches offer the best ease-of-use/performance trade-off available today. In the long term, we expect compiler technology to improve, and the need for programmer intervention to decrease.

Several recently introduced mechanisms provide application portability across platforms. Examples include PVM[9] and Linda.[10] They, like Mentat, achieve portability by providing a virtual machine interface to the programmer. The virtual machine can then be ported to new architectures, and if the applications programmer is limited to that interface, the application will port.**

The key difference between Mentat and these systems is the level at which applications must be written. Other systems are low-level, explicit parallel systems, suffering all of the disadvantages, and gaining all of the advantages, of fully explicit systems. Mentat provides a high-level language, eliminating many of the disadvantages.

References

1. H. Bal, J. Steiner, and A. Tanenbaum, "Programming Languages for Distributed Computing Systems," *ACM Computing Surveys*, Vol. 21, Vol. 3, Sept. 1989, pp. 261-322.

2. R. Chin and S. Chanson, "Distributed Object-Based Programming Systems," *ACM Computing Surveys*, Vol. 23, No. 1, Mar. 1991, pp. 91-127.

3. B.N. Bershad, E.D. Lazowska, and H.M. Levy, "Presto: A System for Object-Oriented Parallel Programming," *Software Practice and Experience*, Vol. 18, No. 8, 1988, pp. 713-732.

4. B. Beck, "Shared Memory Parallel Programming in C++," *IEEE Software*, Vol. 7, No. 4, July 1990, pp. 38-48.

5. J.K. Lee and D. Gannon, "Object-Oriented Parallel Programming Experiments and Results," *Proc. Supercomputing 91*, IEEE CS Press, Los Alamitos, Calif., Order No. 2159-02, pp. 273-282.

6. S.K. Smith et al., "Experimental Systems Project at MCC," MCC Tech. Report ACA-ESP-089-89, Austin, Tex., Mar. 1989.

7. C. Polychronopoulos, *Parallel Programming and Compilers*, Kluwer Academic Publishers, 1988.

8. D. Callahan and K. Kennedy, "Compiling Programs for Distributed-Memory Multiprocessors," *J. of Supercomputing*, Kluwer Academic Publishers, No. 2, 1988, pp. 151-169.

9. V.S. Sunderam, "PVM: A Framework for Parallel Distributed Computing," *Concurrency: Practice and Experience*, Vol. 2, No. 4, Dec. 1990, pp. 315-339.

10. N. Carriero and D. Gelernter, "Linda in Context," *Comm. ACM*, Apr. 1989, pp. 444-458.

---

*Heisenbugs are timing-dependent bugs that go away when debugging, or tracing, is turned on. They are among the most frustrating bugs to find.

**Virtual machine abstractions are not new. The concept was carried to its logical extreme in the 1970s in the University of California at San Diego's p-machine. There were p-machine implementations for every major microprocessor of the day. Programs were object-code compatible between supported architectures. Only one executable was ever needed.

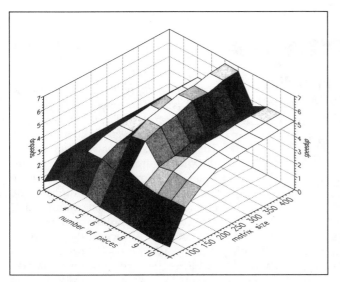
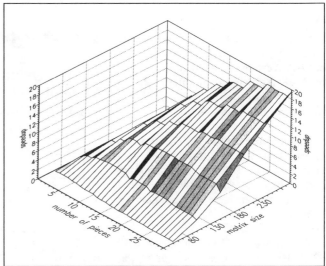

Figure 10. Speedup for matrix multiply: (a) eight-processor Sun 3/60 network; (b) 32-processor Intel iPSC/2.

computations that are dependent on the result of the $A*B$ operation. The effect of the partitioning can be clearly seen in Figure 10a. The speedup for four pieces is the same as five pieces, and the speedup for six pieces is the same as for seven pieces. This is because the underlying object will not split the work into five or seven pieces. The falloff in Figure 10a at eight pieces is due to the fact that there are only eight processors, as a result of which the scheduler must place two objects on one processor.

Gaussian elimination. In our algorithm, the controlling object partitions the matrix into n strips and places each strip into an instance of an *sblock*, a Mentat class. Then, for each row, the reduce operator is called for each sblock using the partial pivot calculated at the end of the last iteration. The reduce operation of the *sblock* reduces the *sblock* by the vector, selects a new candidate partial pivot, and forwards the candidate row to the controlling object for use in the next iteration. This algorithm results in frequent communication and synchronization. The effect of frequent synchronization can be clearly seen when the speed-up results for Gaussian elimination in Figures 11a and 11b are compared to the results for matrix multiply.

Writing software for parallel and distributed systems that effectively uses available CPU resources has proven more difficult than writing software for sequential machines. This is true even though most of the work has been done by programmers who have a good understanding of the machines on which they're working.

Given the current software crisis for sequential machines, it is unlikely that parallel architectures will be widely used until software tools are available that hide the complexity of the parallel environment from the programmer. Mentat is one such tool. With Mentat, we have

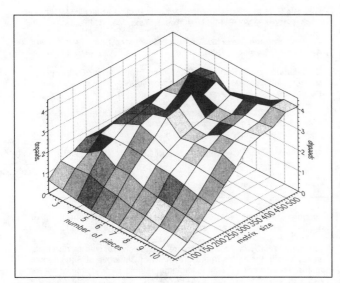
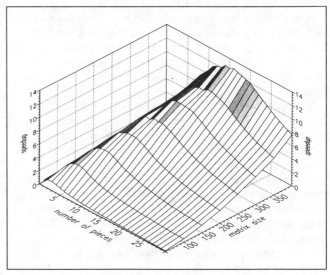

Figure 11. Speedup for Gaussian elimination: (a) eight-processor Sun 3/60 network; (b) 32-processor Intel iPSC/2.

demonstrated that writing object-oriented, high-performance parallel software is possible.

It is possible, indeed probable, that a good programmer could write more efficient concurrent programs using raw send and receive. We believe, though, that send and receive (and semaphores) are the assembly language of parallelism. Just as early high-level language compilers could be beaten by a good programmer writing in assembly language, MPL performance can be beaten by a hand-coded application using send and receive. Extending the analogy, just as high-level languages now have good optimizing compilers that do as well as most programmers, and better than many, we expect MPL compiler technology to improve. Indeed, several optimizations are already planned.

The question that must be answered, for both high-level languages versus assembly languages and for MPL versus raw send and receive, is whether the simplicity and ease of use are worth the performance penalty. We believe they are. ■

Acknowledgment

This work was partially supported by NSF Grants ASC-9201822 and CDA-8922545 and by NASA Grant NAG-1-1181.

References

1. A.S. Grimshaw, E. Loyot Jr., and J. Weissman, "Mentat Programming Language (MPL) Reference Manual," Univ. of Virginia, Computer Science TR 91-32, 1991.

2. A.S. Grimshaw, "The Mentat Runtime System: Support for Medium-Grain Parallel Computation," *Proc. Fifth Distributed Memory Computing Conf.*, IEEE CS Press, Los Alamitos, Calif., Order No. 2113, Vol. II, 1990, pp. 1,064-1,073.

Andrew S. Grimshaw is an assistant professor of computer science at the University of Virginia. His research interests include high-performance parallel processing, compilers for parallel systems, operating systems, and high-performance parallel I/O. He is the chief designer and architect for Mentat.

Grimshaw received his MS and PhD degrees from the University of Illinois at Urbana-Champaign in 1986 and 1988. He is a member of Phi Kappa Phi, Tau Beta Pi, the IEEE Computer Society, and ACM.

Readers may contact Grimshaw at the Department of Computer Science, University of Virginia, Charlottesville, VA, 22903. His e-mail address is grimshaw@virginia.edu. For more information on Mentat, write mentat@virginia.edu.

Chapter 4

Object-Oriented Database Management System Architecture

Architecture of an Open Object-Oriented Database Management System

David L. Wells, José A. Blakeley, and Craig W. Thompson

Texas Instruments

The Zeitgeist object-oriented database management systems, developed by Texas Instruments between 1985 and 1990,[1] supported applications in computer-aided design and manufacturing, software engineering, knowledge representation, and hypermedia systems. From the Zeitgeist project, we learned that these applications have widely varying database management needs. We concluded that such applications would be better served by an open, extensible object-oriented database (OODB) management system, whose functionality could be tailored, rather than by a single monolithic database management system. Our conclusions are consonant with other research and development efforts.[2,3]

The lack of a standard application program interface, de facto or otherwise, to OODBs has slowed acceptance by potential users concerned about application portability. Development of OODBs has been slow because OODB developers and researchers must construct an entire OODB from scratch rather than reuse standardized components. Fortunately, when we examine the OODB system design landscape, we see several areas of near consensus for both interface and internal organization.[4] The Open OODB project is an effort to

- describe the design space of OODBs,
- build an architectural framework that lets developers configure independently useful modules to form an OODB,
- verify the suitability of this open approach by implementing an OODB to these specifications, and
- determine areas where consensus exists or is possible.

This article describes the architecture of the Open OODB system. First we discuss its requirements, then its computational model, which builds database functionality as an extensible collection of transparent extensions to existing programming languages. We also describe how Open OODB's *system architecture* is decomposed into a kernel *meta-architecture* and a collection of modules imple-

An open, incrementally extensible object-oriented database management system lets developers tailor database functionality for applications. It can also serve as a platform for research.

106

menting specific behavioral extensions. Finally, we discuss risks of the approach and report on the project's status.

Requirements

As the sidebar "Open OODB requirements" shows, we grouped the requirements into a set of *functional requirements* describing the capabilities the Open OODB must provide to its users, and a set of *metarequirements* describing the organizational and operational characteristics the OODB must display while satisfying the functional requirements. We based these requirements on previous experience with Zeitgeist applications plus new requirements from automated manufacturing, concurrent engineering, image understanding, software development environments, and simulation.

In this section we address the object data model functional requirement and the metarequirements. We address other functional requirements later in the section headed "Architecture."

Object data model. Although there is general agreement on some features that an object data model should support, there is wide divergence on the precise semantics of individual features. (See the sidebar "Object data model approaches.") For example, it is generally accepted that inheritance must be supported, but there are several notions of inheritance with different semantics. Open OODB is designed to be datamodel independent. We have achieved partial success by building OODBs based on C++ and Common Lisp under the same architectural framework.

Openness (extensibility). A system is *open* if developers or researchers can control, modify, or extend some part(s) of its architecture or implementation. *Extensible* openness appears as a small set of choices for specific system policies (for example, version management can be linear or branching, or there may be no version management). *Programmable* openness lets the developer specify a procedure or function callable for specific purposes (for example, a user-defined abstract data type). *Modular* openness lets developers replace or improve existing modules, add modules, or reconfigure existing modules. The "binding time" for different forms of

---

Open OODB requirements

Functional requirements
Object data model
Persistence, object translation, and name management
Concurrent access
Distribution with location transparency
Data dictionary
Query capability
Change management capability
Class libraries
Security
Access to existing database management systems

Metarequirements
Openness
Seamlessness
Reusability
Performance

---

openness ranges through system design, system configuration, application compilation (type definition), and execution time. Open OODB uses all of the above forms of openness. Extensible database management system projects such as Exodus,[5] Genesis,[2] Postgres,[6] and Starburst[3] have goals similar to those of Open OODB. However, each focuses on a different aspect of extensibility, addresses it at various degrees of breadth and depth, or uses a different approach to achieve it.

Seamlessness. Seamlessness (transparency) is important not only to increase application developers' productivity but also to facilitate and support extensibility. If additional functionality is added seamlessly, applications can optionally ignore it and existing applications will require minimal modifications when the added functionality becomes available. Operating systems, programming languages, and database management systems provide many ex-

---

Object data model approaches

There is currently no single, widely agreed upon object data model in the sense of the relational model. Hence, OODB designers have principally used three approaches.

(1) A programming-language-neutral object model extends relational or semantic data models with object-oriented features (for example, by encapsulating structural and behavioral properties of entities in an extended entity-relationship model). The main objective of this approach is to increase the level of data sharing across applications developed in different programming languages. Data models in this approach (used, for example, in Probe[1]) are usually semantically richer than models in the other two approaches.

(2) With a database programming language, a new programming language (for example, Galileo[2]) is designed from the ground up to support database capabilities.

(3) In the programming-language-specific approach, the object data model is equivalent to the type system of an existing programming language, with the objective of eliminating the impedance mismatch between the programming language and the database. Examples of this approach include PS-Algol[3] and commercial OODB products by Objectivity, Object Design, Ontologic, Servio, and Versant. A challenge in this approach is achieving interoperability of applications written in multiple programming languages, each having a different type system.

References

1. F. Manola and U. Dayal, "PDM: An Object-Oriented Data Model," *Proc. Int'l Workshop Object Oriented Database Systems*, IEEE CS Press, Los Alamitos, Calif., Order No. 734, 1986, pp. 18-25.

2. A. Albano, L. Cardelli, and R. Orsini, "Galileo: A Strongly Typed, Interactive Conceptual Language," *ACM Trans. Database Systems*, Vol. 10, No. 2, June 1985, pp. 230-260.

3. M. Atkinson et al., "An Approach to Persistent Programming," *Computer J.*, Vol. 26, No. 4, Dec. 1983, pp. 360-365.

amples of seamless extensions to help application developers increase their productivity. Virtual memory and garbage collection hide the details of memory management from the programmer. Distributed environments hide the details of communications and distributed computation. Database management systems provide seamless logging of operations within a transaction for recovery purposes, seamless locking protocols to control concurrent access to data, and seamless index maintenance for database updates. Persistent programming languages extend conventional programming languages by seamlessly transferring objects between main memory and permanent storage. Extensible relational database management systems allow user-defined access methods, abstract data types, or operators to be used in the same way as the native database management system facilities. Open OODB provides common mechanisms to support transparent extensions to programming languages.

Reusability. With an open system, researchers can focus on modules of interest without having to build complete systems. This approach reduces duplication by encouraging the reuse of system components, and it increases the quality and depth of the components by letting developers focus on smaller portions of the system. Eventually, it can lead to "best-of-class" modules that can be reused in a larger set of systems. Since the scope of extensibility in the Open OODB project is ambitious, we need a generic framework for extensibility that allows reuse of components developed by different research groups and organizations.

Performance. OODBs must provide the performance needed for demanding applications, including automated design and manufacturing, concurrent engineering, image understanding, software development environments, and simulation. Since many of these applications involve intensive computations on large working sets, performance must approach virtual memory speeds. Open-

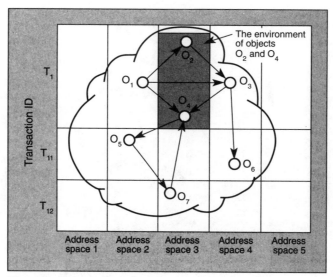

Figure 1. Partitioning the universe of objects.

ness lets us trade portability and speed by changing external representations and object materialization mechanisms. (See the later subsection "Translation.")

Computational model

Open OODB's computational model is based on transparently extending the behavior of normal operations (events) in application programming languages. While we can certainly build database functionality such as persistence, transactions, concurrency control, versioning, distribution, replication, and indexing via explicit function calls, exposing their existence to application programmers causes a seam with respect to the original language. Such seams are a conceptual problem for application programmers interacting with databases, because seams force them to think in two distinct data models. Seams are also an implementation problem, since crossing them may require up to 30 percent of the application code.[7]

In the Open OODB computational model, all objects accessible to a program exist in a *universe of objects*. Within any language, the universe of objects is flat (that is, within the language, a program manipulates all objects in the same way). There are two distinct phases to performing an operation on objects: locating the arguments and applying some function. Locating the arguments may involve resolving a *reference* to an actual object. At least conceptually, a reference is modeled as a

type, because there are many possible representations (subtypes) that may need to coexist (for example, names, object identifiers, pointers, and value-based selections) to provide different size and performance trade-offs or added functionality. Programmers can create, resolve, compare, and assign references; the reference subtype determines the semantics of these operations. An *event* is the application of an operation to a particular set of (argument) objects. An *extension* to a programming language is modeled as enhancements to the behavior of events in the language.

Objects within the universe of objects of a programming language have one or more implicit *environmental attributes* (not the same as object attributes, data members, or slot values) that are not visible to the programmer. Environmental attributes include information about the address space where the object resides (persistent or transient, local or remote), replicas of the object, and lock status and transaction owning the lock. Environmental attributes are implicit because for a given attribute in a programming language, all objects have the same immutable value. For example, in C++ and Common Lisp, the "address space" attribute of any object is the local address space, and there is no facility for moving objects to a different address space or manipulating objects in different address spaces. Because of this, the environmental attributes have no effect on events, and programmers usually do not consider them.

To extend a language, we must define an environmental attribute whose domain has cardinality greater than one. For example, if we need an extension to allow objects to reside in a remote address space, we can define an attribute named "address space" that identifies the location of the object using domain values from the set of address spaces where the object could reside. Similarly, if we need an extension to support transactions, we can define an attribute named "transaction ID" to identify the transaction controlling a given subset of objects.

Consider the universe of objects to be

a Cartesian space whose axes are environmental attributes, each with a domain with cardinality greater than one. The values along the axes, representing a set of environmental attributes under consideration, partition the universe of objects into a collection of computational *environments*. Environments are separated by *boundaries*. An unextended language has only one environment (and hence no boundaries), since all attribute domains have cardinality equal to one. Figure 1 shows a universe of objects partitioned into environments by environmental attributes "address space" and "transaction ID." In the figure, O_2 and O_4 are in the same environment; the reference from O_4 to O_5 crosses a boundary.

There are four generic reasons to extend the behavior of events:

- *Method extension.* Something special about an object may require an operation on it to have a hidden side effect. For example, applying an operation on an indexed object may require automatic index updating.
- *Object access.* Work might be required to get at the object to operate on it. For example, the object might be remote and require fetching.
- *Object selection.* The object may have multiple representations (as in the case of a replicated, versioned, or partitioned object), and the correct representation may need to be transparently selected for applying an operation.
- *Constraint enforcement.* Some constraints (security or concurrency control) may apply to manipulating the object.

We model these general extensions using environment values and boundaries. Method extension and selection among object alternatives are modeled as the object residing in an environment with a distinguished attribute value. Object access and constraint enforcement are modeled as a boundary crossing, since the extension says something about a difference between the environment of the accessor (physical or logical) and the environment of the object being accessed. Modeling an extension by a boundary crossing is useful when we extend the act of touching an object, while extension based on residency is useful when we extend the operations on the objects.

In the original programming language environment, programmers cannot directly operate on objects across boundaries, operate on objects in designated environments, and move objects across boundaries. Each axis partitioning the universe of objects defines a particular extension, so definers of the axes may specify (in principle at least) invariants to be met by any of the above types of operations. For example, if an extension defines the ability to operate on remote objects, an invariant could state that the operator and the operands need to be instantiated in the same physical address space.

An invariant can be satisfied in many ways. For example, operators can move to operands or vice versa. Each way of meeting the invariant is called a *policy*, implemented by a *policy performer*. Under different circumstances, there may be an advantage to one policy or another in terms of space, time, and reliability trade-offs. For example, the sizes of arguments and returned values may dictate local or remote execution. Specific policies can be invoked directly. However, since all policies applicable to a particular extension satisfy the same invariant, applications often do not care which particular policy is actually applied. To hide the choice of policy, or to allow it to be determined dynamically, we introduce a *policy manager* that determines which policy to invoke in particular circumstances.

Seamless extension requires the invoker of an event to see the original behavior and interface, unless the extension requires the invoker to be informed about some exception (for example, an error message returned for lack of access rights). Thus the invocation of the policy performer must be hidden. To extend an event, the event must be detected and its relevant characteristics captured (the operation being performed, the reference being followed). This requires the detection of events involving objects in designated environments or references across boundaries. Event detection is the responsibility of a *sentry*. After detecting the event, the sentry cooperates with a policy manager to extend the event. Sentries and policy managers are realized by the meta-architecture support module described in the next section.

The following examples illustrate how we model and implement extensions. The most common form of extension in OODBs is an *object fault*, that is, the transparent retrieval of an object from a shared persistent object base into an application's workspace when an application attempts to dereference the nonresident object. Sentries monitor references across the boundary between a "workspace" and a "persistent space." The policy available in most OODB systems is to bring the referenced object into memory and continue the operation, placing sentries on any references emanating from the faulted object. Another policy is to prefetch additional objects according to criteria such as physical locality, similar type, or graph closure. An alternative policy would be to determine the operation that caused the fault and ship the operation to some other workspace where it could operate on the object right there.

A second type of extension traps on a method invocation rather than on an object dereference. In the case of *index maintenance* as a transparent extension, the index maintenance policy performer must know which object has been touched and in what way (by which method and with what arguments) to update the proper index. The system must deploy a sentry to detect "interesting" operations that may require index maintenance. When a sentry detects such an event, it traps the operator and arguments and passes them to a policy manager specializing in index maintenance.

Most policy managers need one additional capability: that of suspending or delaying execution of a policy subject to reawakening by a sentry. When fetching objects, locking objects, maintaining indexes, creating versions, and performing many other OODB activities, it is often impractical or impossible for a policy performer to execute the entire operation at one time. Because the extent of object graphs is often unknown and potentially very large, incremental retrieval makes better use of resources and, unlike eager retrieval, does not unnecessarily block other users from parts of the graph that may not be traversed. With an extension such as automatic index maintenance, whenever a member of an indexed collection is updated, a policy performer cannot perform all maintenance activities at the time the extension is declared because the object updates that force index maintenance will not have occurred yet.

Extensible relational database management systems like Starburst use concepts equivalent to event, sentry, and policy manager, although under different names. In Starburst, the equivalent of an event occurs before and after invocations of relational insert, delete, and update operations. Sentries are routines that trap these events; a new sentry is deployed when a new kind of attachment is added to the system. Policies are the different attachment implementations invoked as a result of an event on a relation and may be suspended. However, in Starburst, operations in the application workspace are not extensible as in Open OODB.

Architecture

The Open OODB system architecture has two parts:

(1) A meta-architecture consisting of a collection of kernel modules and definitions providing the infrastructure for creating environments and boundaries, specifying and implementing event extensions, and regularizing interfaces among modules.

(2) An extensible collection of extender modules implementing the policies providing OODB functionality via behavioral extensions.

The subset of functional requirements addressed determines the set of extender modules in any system instantiation. Since the model supports different extensions, systems other than OODBs could be configured in this way. Figure

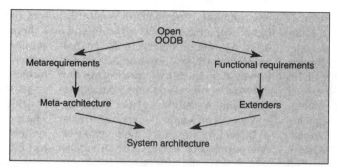

Figure 2. The Open OODB requirements and architecture.

2 shows this partitioning of the system architecture to satisfy the metarequirements and functional requirements. The sidebar "Open OODB partitioning philosophy" offers further insight.

Meta-architecture. The computational model requires one or more address spaces in which objects reside, at least one of which must allow event execution. If more than one address space exists, there must be a communications mechanism and translation routines to effect transfer between them. A data dictionary serves as a globally known repository of system, object, and type information. A meta-architecture support module provides the extension mechanism and defines interface conventions to which other modules must adhere.

Address space managers. The various existing address spaces (virtual memories, file systems, object servers, and so on) use a variety of representations and

Open OODB partitioning philosophy

Five major arguments justify Open OODB's functional partitioning.

Common service used by several modules. Functional capabilities are factored into separate modules if they can be reused in different system configurations as a common service. Examples in the Open OODB architecture include the data dictionary, communications, address space manager, and translation modules.

Optional functionality. It is useful to tailor a system to include only the functionality required by the applications that use it. We achieve this by decomposing the architecture of a database management system into a collection of functional modules independent of the other modules. Then we can implement different Open OODB system configurations that do or do not support persistence, queries, change management, remote communications, or various notions of transactions.

Extensibility of a functional aspect. Several Open OODB modules have potentially rich semantics. It is essential to design these modules for functional extension without affecting other modules of the Open OODB. For example, the ability to configure the object query module in different ways permits experimentation with different query languages and different optimization and execution strategies.

Research team expertise and interests. Factoring the Open OODB into modules encourages separate experimentation within a particular area of functionality, potentially leading to a best-of-class design in which different research and development teams compete to develop improved OODB components. This divide-and-conquer approach to building an OODB accelerates progress in each area of the architecture.

Complexity and degree of maturity of a specific field. The maturity of different Open OODB modules varies. In some cases — for example, change management — a "grand unification" may be possible[1] and work on standards is already under way. In other areas — such as extended transactions, which include cooperative, nested, optimistic, distributed, and several other kinds of transaction schemes — much experimentation lies ahead.

Reference

1. R.H. Katz, "Toward a Unified Framework for Version Modeling in Engineering Databases," *ACM Computing Surveys*, Vol. 22, No. 4, Dec. 1990, pp. 375-408.

addressing schemes. To allow uniform access to objects from outside an address space, Open OODB defines an abstraction called an address space manager, which supports global identifiers and mappings between the global identifier and addressing conventions local to an individual address space. Open OODB recognizes several subtypes of address space managers: computational or noncomputational, recoverable or nonrecoverable, and persistent or transient. To support the computational model of event extension, an address space manager must host an instance of the meta-architecture support module.

Communications. Open OODB's communications module is a veneer that normalizes the interfaces to one or more underlying communications mechanisms. The communications module supports the movement of objects, the invocation of remote operations, error detection, recovery, and a broadcast capability.

Translation. The translation module translates objects between the computational, storage, and exchange formats required by the various address spaces, programming languages, programming language implementations, operating systems, communications systems, and hardware platforms present in a particular Open OODB instantiation. Translation allows Open OODB to provide a form of physical data independence. It is open to new translation routines added as the system architecture changes. While the Open OODB is object oriented, the translation module deals with the basic units of transfer in the system, whether they are objects or pages.

Data dictionary. The data dictionary is a globally known repository of data model and type information, instance information, name mappings (of application-specific names to instances), and possibly system configuration and resource utilization information.

Meta-architecture support. The meta-architecture support module implements the mechanisms to extend events uniformly and defines interface conventions used by other Open OODB modules. The module contains one or more sentry implementations to detect and trap events. A variety of sentry imple-

Table 1. Mapping extended behavior to policy managers.

Extension	Module
Object persistence and naming	Persistence policy manager
Transactions and controlled sharing	Transaction policy manager
Distributed (remote) access to objects	Distribution policy manager
Indexed sets of objects	Index policy manager
Object queries	Object query processor
Versions, configurations, and dependencies	Change policy manager

mentations with different coverage and selectivity, different deployment times, and abilities to detect different kinds of events optimizes sentry mechanism costs. To hide this variety of sentry types, the meta-architecture support module contains a *sentry manager* that is used for declaring event extensions. To allow any sentry to invoke any policy manager, the module defines a common interface presented by all policy managers. Other interface conventions include

- a system of pragmas allowing application programmers to provide performance hints about policies without making the system "brittle,"
- a public interface for all reference types,
- a definition of global object identifiers to be used by all modules,
- a common exception mechanism, and
- mechanisms for setting and determining the environment attributes within which the system is operating.

Extenders. Table 1 summarizes Open OODB's initial extender modules. Other extenders for object replication, security control, access to foreign databases, and interlanguage sharing are possible in the future. A given instantiation of Open OODB does not need all these extensions. For example, a concurrency control policy manager may not be included in an instantiation for single-user applications. An embedded system may not need version or configuration management support. A less obvious OODB instantiation would provide all database functionality in a transient environment by eliminating the persistence policy manager and using only transient address space managers.

Each extender module can support many different policies within the same policy family. We now describe several extenders and sketch some policy variations in each.

Persistence. Persistence is the ability of objects to exist beyond the lifetime of the program that created them. The persistence policy manager gives applications an interface through which they can create, access, and manipulate persistent objects. Many OODBs are best characterized as a persistent extension of a programming language. There are many different models of persistent programming, varying in

- the types of objects that can be made persistent,
- the times when and manner in which objects become persistent,
- the ways in which persistent objects are bound to programming language constructs,
- the way object transfer between address spaces is initiated, and
- the relationship (if any) between persistence and other modules.

The system achieves persistence using the distribution policy manager, the translation module, the communications module, the data dictionary, various kinds of address space managers, and sentries, which allow graceful bindings between application structures and the persistent space. Optionally, system developers can extend persistence with a transaction policy manager and a change policy manager. Open OODB provides a separate persistence policy manager because, in our experience, it is nontrivial to construct a consistent model of persistence, given the wide variety of persistence models and interfaces already found.

Transactions. The transaction policy manager enables concurrent access to persistent and transient data and supports recovery of changes on these data when the system fails. A transaction is a sequence of operations on objects grouped together and treated as an indivisible logical unit of work. Traditionally, transactions satisfy the atomicity, consistency, isolation, and durability properties. Atomicity means that either all operations in the unit of work are performed or none is performed. Consistency means that transactions provide transitions between consistent states. Isolation means that no information flows between active transactions. Durability means that the effect of a committed transaction is permanent in the database. Because we want Open OODB to support a wide range of transaction models, we leave it to the transaction policy manager to define its atomicity, consistency, isolation, and durability procedures. The initial transaction policy manager supports transactions but does not preclude more general models such as lightweight, nested, long-duration, and cooperative transactions.

Distribution. The distribution policy manager supports the behavioral extension of distributed event execution by hiding the distinction between address spaces, thus giving the illusion of a large, flat address space. To do this, the distribution policy manager defines distribution references that, when resolved, cause it to either move the object to the current execution space or execute the event remotely. At the same time, the distribution policy manager decides what objects accompany the object(s) being moved, perhaps depending on resource utilization such as load balancing or memory availability. In any case, the event execution will behave as though it occurred in the local address space. The system itself can use the distribution policy manager to reach Open OODB modules at remote locations.

Query processing. The object query module gives end users, application programmers, and other modules efficient access to large bulk objects on the basis of their structural and behavioral properties. Queries are often used explicitly to provide a functionality most programming languages lack. Therefore, instead of seamlessness, we aim at good integration between the programming language and the query language extension, using the following criteria:

- Equivalence between the programming language type system and the object data model, including support for strong typing and encapsulation.
- Uniform treatment of object queries regardless of such object extensions as persistence, versioning, and distribution.
- Support of queries in programming language expressions, and programming language expressions in queries.
- Uniform syntax and semantics of query and programming language statements.
- Support for queries on query results.

According to these criteria, a different syntactic binding is required for each programming language extended. For example, we can bind C++ with an SQL-like extension called OQL[C++].[8] The object query module architecture is open with respect to extensions to the query language, optimization, and execution.[3,9]

Change management. The change policy manager provides a consistent set of techniques to aid programmers in evolving the design and implementation of an abstraction. Cooperating users can apply these techniques to record history, reconstruct or efficiently store different system configurations, explore design alternatives, navigate through hierarchical designs, and manage multiple representations of changing information. The change policy manager includes three orthogonal subcomponents:

- a version management submodule to manage linear or branching derivation histories,
- a configuration management submodule to govern object composition, and
- a dependency management submodule to manage relationships between associated representations.

Also, *metadata evolution* is an important application: The change policy manager tracks and controls the change of data dictionary information.

Risks

The Open OODB architecture poses potential risks:

- *Degraded performance.* The requirements of openness and performance may conflict with each other. If there are too many interfaces between modules in a system and no good way to "compile them away," then performance might suffer. However, many systems, including object class libraries, are modular and contain many interfaces. Developers instantiating an open OODB with iteratively replaceable modules can select best-of-class module implementations. Seamlessness provides opportunities to hide performance enhancements.
- *Lack of foresight.* Any partitioning of a system is only as good as its basis for modularity. Changing requirements for openness may demand a different partitioning of the system to satisfy the new requirements, but repartitioning may not be possible. Of course, this risk is also present in any monolithic system. During the architecture design phase, we tried to alleviate this problem by considering foreseeable future requirements for OODBs (for example, security, parallelism, and distribution) in several application domains. The sidebar "Similarity to Object Management Group architecture" compares our approach with that of another group.
- *Going too far.* There is a risk in considering too many future requirements. Should a fully open system be developed as a whole? Would such a system be usable? An open architecture actually reduces such risks because we can develop the system modularly and incrementally, testing critical paths before completing the whole design.
- *Premature standards.* For monolithic OODBs, there is a reasonable probability that any suggested standard will be premature. In a modular system, we can approach standardization in a divide-and-conquer manner: We can strive for consensus separately for different interfaces, potentially accelerating the standardization process.

The current Open OODB system contains implementations of several policy performers, including atomic transactions, query processing, version and configuration management, concurrency control based on two-phase locking, and several persistence policies for Common Lisp and C++ objects. When better modules become available, we can replace the current modules for communications, persistence application programming interface, persistent address space management, query language, and configuration management. Furthermore, we have coupled our query language extension to C++ with a commercial C++-based OODB. We have developed persistent address space managers based on a file system, a relational database management system, and the Exodus storage manager. We have also developed translation modules for Common Lisp and C++ objects, and Common Lisp implementations of sentries and policy managers. We are currently experimenting with implementations of the sentry and policy managers in C++.

These experiences give initial evidence that the Open OODB architectural framework lets us enhance an OODB by importing modules developed independently. The modular design also lets us export our modules to other systems. ∎

Acknowledgment

This research is sponsored by the Defense Advanced Research Projects Agency under DARPA Order No. 7558 and managed by the US Army CECOM, under contract DAAB07-90-C-B920. The views and conclusions contained in this document are those of the authors and should not be interpreted as necessarily representing the official policies, either expressed or implied, of the Defense Advanced Research Projects Agency or the US government.

References

1. S. Ford et al., "Zeitgeist: Database Support for Object-Oriented Programming," in *Advances in Object-Oriented Database Systems, Proc. Second Int'l Workshop Object-Oriented Database Systems*, Springer-Verlag, Berlin, 1988, pp. 23-42.

2. D.S. Batory et al., "Genesis: An Extensible Database Management System," *IEEE Trans. Software Eng.*, Vol. 14, No. 11, Nov. 1988, pp. 1,711-1,730.

3. L. Haas et al., "Starburst Midflight: As the Dust Clears," *IEEE Trans. Knowledge and Data Eng.*, Vol. 2, No. 1, Mar. 1990, pp. 143-160.

4. E. Fong et al., "X3-Sparc-DBBSG-OODBTG Final Report," tech. report, National Institute of Standards and Technology, Gaithersburg, Md., 1991. Available from Elizabeth Fong, (301) 975-3250, e-mail fong@ise.ncsl.nist.gov.

5. M.J. Carey, D.J. Dewitt, and S.L. Vandenburg, "A Data Model and Query Language for Exodus," *Proc. ACM SIGMOD 1988 Int'l Conf. Management of Data*, ACM, New York, 1988, pp. 413-423.

6. M. Stonebraker and L.A. Rowe, "The Design of Postgres," *Proc. ACM SIGMOD 1986 Int'l Conf. Management of Data*, ACM, New York, 1986, pp. 340-355.

7. M. Atkinson et al., "An Approach to Persistent Programming," *Computer J.*, Vol. 26, No. 4, Dec. 1983, pp. 360-365.

8. J.A. Blakeley, C.W. Thompson, and A. Alashqur, "A Strawman Reference Model for Object Query Languages," *Computer Standards and Interfaces*, Vol. 13, Nos. 1-3, Oct. 1991, pp. 185-199.

9. G. Graefe and D.J. Dewitt, "The Exodus Optimizer Generator," *Proc. ACM SIGMOD 1987 Int'l Conf. Management of Data*, ACM, New York, 1987, pp. 160-172.

Similarity to Object Management Group architecture

Is the decomposition of the Open OODB system into modules arbitrary, or will other efforts to build a system with similar functionality result in a similar factoring? It is too early to report that such experiments necessarily result in similar factorings, but the Open OODB's factoring into modules is very similar to the application integration framework being developed by the industrial consortium Object Management Group.

OMG was founded in 1989 and now has over 200 member companies. Its objective is to put in place a software architecture that provides interoperating object-oriented tools and services. Application builders benefit because they can use common services provided by the framework without having to build them from scratch (for example, a common help system). Or they can replace and improve services to satisfy specialized requirements. End users benefit because the system presents a common semantic "look and feel" across different applications.

The overall architecture consists of a software bus or backplane and a collection of "plug-in" object services. OMG's backplane is called the "common object request broker" and provides object distribution. The group has adopted an object model called IDL (Interface Description Language), which is close to C++. Members are currently working on the specification of basic object services. These include interchange (equivalent to Open OODB's object translation), persistence, concurrency control and transactions, object naming, implementation and interface repository (data dictionary), versioning and configuration management, queries, relationships, events, and security. The OMG list of services is a superset of the Open OODB. Furthermore, the OMG object services architecture guide lists as goals and principles that the OMG services should be independent and modular, and support interoperability when there are dependencies between modules.

Thus, the OMG and the Open OODB architectures are almost isomorphic. It is interesting that one is viewed as an application integration framework architecture and the other as an OODB architecture.

David L. Wells is a member of the technical staff at Texas Instruments' Computer Science Laboratory, where he is coprincipal investigator of the Open OODB project. Before joining TI, he was on the faculty at Southern Methodist University, where, in addition to databases, his research interests included computer security, and computer graphics and architectures using fractals.

Wells received his doctor of engineering from the University of Wisconsin–Milwaukee in 1980.

José A. Blakeley has been a member of the technical staff at Texas Instruments' Computer Science Laboratory since 1989. His research interests include database query processing, extensible and object-oriented database systems, distributed and heterogeneous databases, and query processing support for spatial and real-time databases. Before joining TI, he was an assistant professor of computer science at Indiana University, where he conducted research on query optimization for relational and nested relational database systems.

Blakeley received his BSc in computer systems engineering from the Instituto Tecnológico y de Estudios Superiores, Monterrey, Mexico, in 1978. He received his MMath and PhD in computer science from the University of Waterloo, Canada, in 1983 and 1987, respectively.

Craig W. Thompson manages the DARPA Open OODB project at Texas Instruments' Computer Science Laboratory. His research centers on engineering databases, hypermedia systems, and natural-language interfaces. Before joining TI in 1981, he taught at the University of Tennessee at Knoxville. Thompson was a coeditor of the final report of the ANSI X3-Sparc-DBBSG-OODB Task Group. He holds two US patents and has three patents pending.

Thompson received his BA in mathematics from Stanford University in 1971 and his MA and PhD in computer science from the University of Texas at Austin in 1977 and 1984, respectively. He is a senior member of IEEE, a member of the IEEE Computer Society, and an active member of the ANSI X3H7 Object Information Management Technical Committee, the Object Management Group, and the ACM.

The authors can be reached at Texas Instruments Inc., PO Box 655474, MS 238, Dallas, TX 75265, e-mail {wells, blakeley, thompson}@csc.ti.com.

Object-Oriented Database Management Systems:
Evolution and Performance Issues

A.R. Hurson and Simin H. Pakzad, Pennsylvania State University

Jia-bing Cheng, IBM-Research Triangle Park

Reprinted from *Computer*, February 1993, pp. 48–60.

Database management systems have been widely used in the data processing environment since their introduction in the late 1960s. The success of DBMSs is due to their inherent support of data sharing, independence, consistency, and integrity. Traditional file management systems do not inherently support these characteristics.

To provide a formal framework for the representation and manipulation of data, a database system is usually organized according to a data model. In past years, the three most popular models have been hierarchic, network, and relational. All three of these models are record-based, although they differ in the way they organize records. They were designed mainly for applications that process large amounts of relatively simple and fixed-format data. DBMSs based on these models along with sophisticated indexing and query-optimization techniques have served business-oriented database applications especially well.

During the 1980s, the simplicity and mathematical foundation of the relational data model brought the relational DBMS to predominance. Today, almost every business DBMS on the market supports the relational model and structured query language (SQL). This trend will very likely continue through the 1990s.

Changing database environment

Relational DBMSs were originally designed for mainframe computers and business data processing applications. Moreover, relational systems were optimized for environments with large numbers of users who issue short queries.

Many of today's applications are workstation-based and serve relatively few users. These applications include design databases, multimedia systems, and knowledge bases. They involve complex data and operations. For example, a design database requires the support of composite objects and different versions of the same object. A multimedia database may contain variable-length text, graphics, images, and audio and video data. Finally, a knowledge-base system requires data rich in semantics.

Using a relational DBMS in any one of these applications leads to an awkward

---

Applications that involve complex data and operations are not served well by conventional data models and DBMSs. This article surveys current research and development in object-oriented DBMSs.

0-8186-6222-0/95 $4.00 © 1993 IEEE

decomposition of data and thus poor performance. Therefore, many existing systems exclude the use of DBMSs and are built instead on top of raw file systems; hence, they require extra programming effort and suffer from problems of data incompatibility and inconsistency.

Research to model and process complex data has gone in two directions: (a) extending the functionalities of relational DBMSs (for example, Postgres,[1] Exodus,[2] and Starburst[3]) and (b) developing and implementing object-oriented DBMSs that follow the research on semantic data modeling and the increasing popularity of object-oriented programming languages.

Limitations of the relational model. The relational model, although simple and powerful, imposes some restrictions on the representation of data. By organizing data into relations (tables), it presumes horizontal and vertical homogeneity in the data. Horizontally, each tuple of a given relation has the same definition for attributes; vertically, a given attribute contains the same kind of information in each tuple. Relations must be at least in *first normal form*, which inhibits the direct representation of multivalued or set-valued attributes.

Furthermore, the relational model does not explicitly include semantics as part of the data representation. Instead, the application programs interpret data semantics. Moreover, when a real-world entity cannot fit into the relational model directly, an artificial decomposition becomes necessary. This decomposition not only decreases efficiency but also raises the possibility of losing the semantics associated with data.

New database applications. Some applications that require the manipulation of large amounts of data can benefit from using a DBMS. However, the nature of the data in these applications does not fit well into the relational framework[4]:

(1) *Design databases.* Engineering design databases are useful in computer-aided design/manufacturing/software engineering (CAD/CAM/CASE) systems. In such systems, complex objects can be recursively partitioned into smaller objects. Furthermore, an object can have different representations at differ-

ent levels of abstraction (equivalent objects). Moreover, a record of an object's evolution (object versions) should be maintained. Traditional database technology does not support the notions of complex objects, equivalent objects, or object versions.

(2) *Multimedia databases.* In a modern office information or other multimedia system, data include not only text and numbers but also images, graphics, and digital audio and video. Such multimedia data are typically stored as sequences of bytes with variable lengths, and segments of data are linked together for easy reference. The variable-length data structure cannot fit well into the relational framework, which mainly deals with fixed-format records. Furthermore, applications may require access to multimedia data on the basis of the structure of a graphical item or by following logical links. Conventional query languages were not designed for such applications.

(3) *Knowledge bases.* Artificial intelligence and expert systems represent information as facts and rules that can be collectively viewed as a knowledge base. In typical AI applications, knowledge representation requires data structures with rich semantics that go beyond the simple structure of the relational model. Artificial decomposition and mapping would be necessary if a relational DBMS were used. Furthermore, operations in a knowledge base are more complex than those in a traditional database. When a rule is added, the system must check for contradiction and redundancy. Such operations cannot be represented directly by relational operations, and the complexity of checking increases rapidly as the size of the knowledge base grows.

In general, these applications require the representation of complex data elements as well as complex relationships among them. Users in these environments have found relational technology inadequate in terms of flexibility, modeling power, and efficiency.

Mapping problems. Among the issues raised by these new database applications, we concentrate here on data mapping in design databases that demand high performance. In fact, DBMSs were excluded from this area mainly because of inadequate performance. Many CAD tools were built on top of raw file systems to gain efficiency. One study showed that implementing a CAD application on a relational DBMS increased the time for data retrieval by a factor of five compared to a nondatabase (file-based) implementation.[5] Similar arguments can be presented for other applications as well.

Designers have used CAD systems to construct very large scale integrated (VLSI) circuits, high-performance computer systems, and large software systems, as well as mechanical and architectural designs. A design database stores and manipulates complete information about design objects. Typical design objects are large and have complex internal structures. Users who access the database are designing object components or modifying existing designs. They can access directly through query languages or indirectly through CAD design tools (such as a graphic editor or a circuit simulator). In such an environment, mapping design objects to a relational DBMS or other conventional DBMSs (hierarchic and network) leads to several difficulties:

(1) *Nonhomogeneous data.* Engineering design data contains a heterogeneous collection of design objects. These design objects are characterized by a large number of types, each with a small number of instances. Conventional data models deal with homogeneous collections of simple entities that are characterized by a small number of types, each with a large number of instances.

(2) *Variable-length and long strings.* Digitized designs contain long strings; they have variable-length records of textual information. Furthermore, the spatial relations are important in designs for layout, placement, and assembly operations. Conventional DBMSs are mainly suited for formatted numbers, short strings, and fixed-length records. They provide no support for spatial relationships.

(3) *Complex objects.* A complex object has a hierarchical data structure. It will not fit into a single flat record representation. As a result, a complex object must be decomposed and stored as records scattered over different relations. Nevertheless, the user should be able to manipulate the object as if it were a single unit. Conventional models do not provide this kind of abstraction; a record is always the basic element for any operation.

For many applications, DBMSs based on conventional data models are simply too slow.

---

(4) *Version control.* In a design system, it is necessary to keep old versions or alternatives for an object. These design histories are maintained for backtracking and recovery purposes. A conventional database represents data at the present time; old versions of data do not exist or at least are not automatically available to the user.

(5) *Schema evolution.* Schemas change constantly in design databases because designs usually go through a long period of evolution. However, in conventional DBMSs, schemas are rather static entities that change little. Conventional DBMSs do not support schema changes efficiently enough for the design environment.

(6) *Equivalent objects.* There are several possible views of a design object. For example, a VLSI chip may be represented at the gate level for logic verification, at the transistor level for timing analysis, or at the layout level for design-rule checking. Although the representations differ, they stand for the same design object. If a portion of the design is changed in one representation, the system should be able to mark the same portion in other representations as out-of-date. Conventional DBMSs do not provide mechanisms to model semantics of equivalent representations.

(7) *Long transactions.* Transactions are sequences of database read and write actions that leave the database consistent. Conventional transactions were developed for short durations, such as those found in airline reservation systems. Typically, transactions are atomic; all changes become visible at once, or none become visible. Transactions are also convenient units for recovery; if a crash occurs before a transaction is committed, the system simply rolls back to the state before the transaction was initiated. Transactions in design databases are different. They are of long duration; a designer may "check out" a design object and work on it for several weeks before "checking in" its modified form. If the system crashes, the conventional strategy could result in the loss of hours or days of work. The DBMS should allow the database to return to the most recent state possible — not just to the state at the last committed transaction.

DBMSs based on conventional data models will still be useful in areas where they are efficient, but for many new applications, they are simply too slow. Clearly, a next-generation DBMS is needed to provide adequate modeling power and, more importantly, performance.

Object-oriented data model

Object-oriented database management systems show promise for meeting the new database application requirements. Figure 1 shows what concepts are drawn from different areas toward the development of an object-oriented data model (ODM).

Origins. We can trace the concept of *object* to Simula, a simulation language designed in the early 1970s. However, it was not until the announcement of Smalltalk-80 (Xerox Corp., 1980) that researchers started to show interest in object-oriented programming languages. Since then, the literature has addressed many such languages. A recent survey reviewed 88 object-oriented languages.[6] These include Lisp-based languages such as Object Lisp (LMI Corp., 1985) and CommonLoops (Xerox, 1985); C-based languages such as Objective-C (StepStone Corp., 1983) and C++ (AT&T Bell Labs, 1986); and Ada-like languages such as Eiffel (Interactive Software Engineering Inc., 1987). Moreover, Apple Computer has implemented Object Assembler and Object Pascal. These languages are widely available on popular personal computers and workstations.

Concepts in object-oriented programming languages can be best described in Smalltalk terms (see Figure 2). An *object* is a package of information (data) and descriptions of its manipulation (procedures). A *class* is a description of one or more similar objects. A *message* is a specification for an object's manipulations. A *method* is a procedure-like entity that describes a sequence of actions to be performed upon receiving a message. An *instance* is an object described by a particular class.

Objects have the characteristic of *encapsulation*, that is, data inside an object is protected from the outside world. The only way to access an object's data is by sending a message to that object. Upon receiving a message, the object activates the corresponding method and returns the result to the sender. Objects also have the characteristic of *inheritance*. A class may have several subclasses; a subclass inherits all or part of the properties from its superclass. Inherited properties need not be redefined in the subclasses; however, new properties can be added to the subclasses as necessary.

Interest in the application of object-oriented programming in software engineering is based on its reliability and reusability.[6] With its popularity, researchers have attempted to add the feature of *persistent data* to the programming environment such that data elements can exist after programs terminate. The result is a system with the power of object-oriented programming and the features of databases — that is, an object-oriented DBMS.

Another area affecting the development of object-oriented databases is semantic data modeling. Examples of semantic data models include the entity-relationship model, the functional data model, and the semantic database model. Semantic data models were introduced as schema design tools. They provide more powerful abstractions for specifying database schemas than the relational, hierarchic, and network models can support. A database schema could first be designed using a high-level semantic model and then translated into one of the traditional models for implementation. Semantic data models have two powerful constructs:

(1) *Aggregation*. Aggregates are abstract entities that contain heterogeneous components. Using relational terms, an aggregated tuple has attributes that are themselves tuples of different relations. This relationship can be nested to any depth. Aggregation is one way of representing hierarchical structure among tuples of different relations.

(2) *Generalization*. Elements of a class can be specialized and grouped into sub-

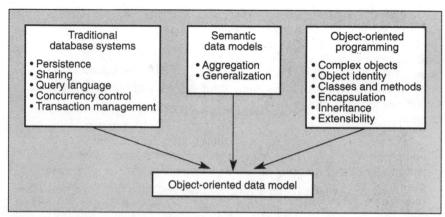

Figure 1. Origins of object-oriented database concepts.

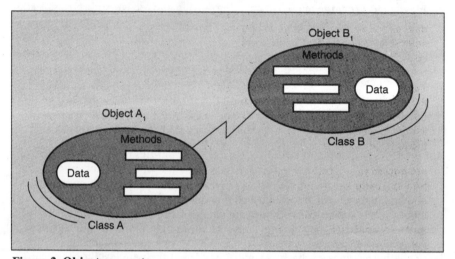

Figure 2. Object concepts.

classes. A subclass inherits all the properties of its parent class. Elements of a subclass also belong to their parent class. This subclass mechanism is called generalization.

Model. The object-oriented data model was developed differently from the relational model. Rather than having a simple definition and a strong mathematical foundation, the ODM originates from the tradition of semantic data modeling. But it takes a view of data that is closely aligned with object-oriented programming languages. Since the mid-1980s, the literature has reported many object-oriented database systems. (These include Orion, Iris, Encore, GemStone, Versant, Ontos, and ObjectStore, which are discussed in the next section. For a summary of the ways they represent physical objects, see the sidebar on page 52.)

Recently, there has been an effort to unify the definition of the ODM.[7] Al-

though different proposed and developed systems support their own particular notions of objects, they do share several common features that are essential for any DBMS to be object-oriented:

(1) *Objects and instance variables*. All conceptual data entities are modeled as objects. An object consists of private memory that holds its state. A primitive object has only a value, such as an integer or a string of characters. A more complex object consists of a collection of instance variables (that is, attributes). Instance variables can be primitive objects, or they can be references to other objects that contain instance variables. Each object has an object identifier to identify itself uniquely so that other objects can reference it.

(2) *Methods and messages*. Methods define the operations to manipulate or return the state of an object. Objects communicate with one another by send-

Physical object representation

Orion — implements each complex object as a collection of records. One of those records is designated as the *root* record, while other records are *component* records. All complex objects of the same type (class) are stored in two files: one for all the root records and the other for all the component records.

Orion's two-file approach is more flexible and efficient than a single-file approach for selective object retrieval and update. However, when entire objects must be retrieved, the two-file approach creates a 40 to 100 percent overhead over a single-file approach that retrieves data incrementally at the record level. Nevertheless, if a complex object could be accessed as a single unit, this overhead could be reduced to 4 to 7 percent (see Table 1, Reference 2).

Iris — stores long fields (typically used for text, voice, and images) in a data structure similar to that used by Exodus[2] — that is, a long field is represented on disk as a B^+-tree indexed on byte position within the field plus a collection of leaf (data) blocks.

The Iris Storage Manager assigns a unique identifier to each long field. Tuples may use this identifier to reference the entire long field or a subset of it by a list of offsets and lengths. The Storage Manager allows retrieval or update of a long field by reference or by value. Each long field also keeps a list of tuples that reference it. This list is needed to maintain integrity when the long field is updated.

GemStone — breaks large objects into pieces and organizes them as a tree spanning several pages. The tree structure makes it possible to access and update pieces of an object without bringing the whole object into main memory. It is similar to the B^+-tree structure used to store long fields in Iris and Exodus. Intelligent staging of objects between disk and memory might improve GemStone performance.

Encore — introduces the notion of the *segment* data structure to improve performance. A segment contains objects that the DBMS expects a client to access during a transaction. It is also the unit of transfer between client and server.

Encore ensures that a segment is contiguously stored on disk, thus eliminating frequent disk head motion and single object transfers. Upon requesting one object, the whole segment containing the object is moved into the client's memory. This provides a way of preloading and yields better performance. Encore also allows clients to define larger working sets as *segment groups*. SGs contain several related segments. After a segment is transferred to the client's memory, the object server synchronously returns other segments in the same SG. This provides another level of preloading that can occur in the background.

Ontos — allows object clustering via either system default or application control. The storage manager performs application-specific clustering by specifying the location of an object relative to another object; then it stores the new object in the same segment as the target object. The servers use segments as units of transfer from/to the secondary storage, thus providing segment-based prefetching and buffering.

Versant — lets users cluster objects frequently accessed as a group. The object servers also try to cluster composite objects when subobjects are not shared. The object manager maintains an object cache for each user session. Objects are automatically cached in memory when used in a program.

ObjectStore — caches the entire composite object upon the first reference to one of its components; subsequent references to related components can be processed at memory speed.

ing messages. For each message understood by an object, there is a corresponding method that executes the message. An object reacts to a message by executing the corresponding method and returning an object. The attributes and methods are collectively called *properties*, which are invisible from outside the object. Only the acceptable messages are visible by other objects. This phenomenon in called *encapsulation*.

(3) *Classes and instances.* For conceptual simplicity and implementation efficiency, similar objects are grouped into classes. Objects in the same class are called instances of that class. Instances share the same definition for attributes and methods, and they respond to the same set of messages. In addition to records, the basic building blocks for classes include sets and arrays.

(4) *Class hierarchy and inheritance.* A class hierarchy specifies the is_a relationship among classes. If A is_a B, then all properties (including attributes and methods) defined on B will also be defined on A. A is called a *subclass* of B and B a *superclass* of A. The inheritance concept says that the properties specified for a class are inherited by all of its subclasses in the hierarchy. This is similar to the generalization construct in semantic data modeling.

(5) *Class lattice and multiple inheritance.* If a class can have only one superclass, the class hierarchy forms a tree. Sometimes it is useful for a class to have multiple superclasses; this generalizes the class hierarchy tree to a directed acyclic graph (DAG), simply called a lattice. In a class lattice, a class can inherit properties from multiple superclasses. This feature is called multiple inheritance.

In addition to these basic concepts, the ODM can easily support some advanced features:

(1) *Composite object.* In addition to an is_a relationship, many applications find it useful to provide an is_part_of relation between an object and the objects it references. This is similar to the aggregation concept in semantic data modeling. A composite object can be defined as an object with a hierarchy of exclusive component objects that form a tree structure. However, it can also form a DAG structure if component objects can be shared. Composite ob-

jects are often treated as units in data storage, retrieval, and integrity enforcement.

(2) *Version control.* Version control captures the record of evolution for data objects. This is particularly important in CAD/CAM and office information systems with compound documents. Users in such environments often need to experiment with multiple versions of an object before selecting one that satisfies their requirements. Two properties, *previous-version* and *next-version*, may be used to express the appropriate temporal relationships among object versions. An object version can have only one previous version. However, the next-version property can be multivalued, thereby allowing a given version object to have multiple successors. Any one of the multiple successors is called an *alternative*. In general, the version history forms a tree structure.

(3) *Equivalence object.* In applications such as design databases, an object can have different representations that are equivalent. The real purpose of equivalent objects is to impose constraints on the database. For example, the functional and layout representations of an IC design should be consistent with each other. When one is updated, the other must be updated as well. This relation between objects can also be modeled using semantic links in the ODM.

Strengths. The object-oriented data model provides capabilities to represent object identity, abstract data, and object relationships. It gives users flexibility and extensibility in handling complex data. Now we will show how ODM can remove the shortcomings of the relational data model in design database applications.

(1) *Nonhomogeneous data.* The relational data model puts homogeneous tuples in a relation; analogously, ODM groups similar objects as a class. However, the data structure of a class is not flat. It can contain multivalued attributes that break the first-normal-form limitation of the relational model. Common features of classes can be extracted to form a superclass. The class hierarchy (or lattice) provides an organized way of managing data types.

(2) *Variable-length and long strings.* In ODM, variable-length strings can be defined as a new data type (class). Accordingly, a string is no more than an

---

The object data model can represent object identity, abstract data, and object relationships.

---

object with a unique identifier. A string can be accessed through its object identifier or its contents. Special string-search operations can be defined as the methods of this class. Very long strings can be indexed using schemes such as the B^+-tree. To save memory space, the system could allow retrieval of parts of a long string rather than retrieval of the whole object.

(3) *Complex objects.* ODM represents complex data entities as complex objects, possibly composite objects. A complex object can be retrieved as a single unit. Therefore, users do not have to collect tuples from different relations to reconstruct the complete object.

(4) *Version control.* ODM can model versions by using the previous-version and next-version attributes described earlier. Similar techniques can be used to model other relations between objects.

(5) *Schema evolution.* Conventional DBMSs do not support efficient mechanisms for schema evolution mainly because business database applications do not require frequent schema changes. While it is hard to add such mechanisms to a traditional DBMS, ODM allows user-defined operations, making the addition easier. Schema evolution includes changes to the definition inside a class and changes to the structure of the class lattice. A set of invariants and rules can be defined so that the schema will remain consistent as it evolves.

(6) *Equivalent objects.* ODM uses generic objects to represent the semantics of equivalent objects explicitly. A generic object contains attributes that identify different representations of the same object. Constraints can be added to the definition of the generic object so that modifications in one representation are reflected in others.

(7) *Long transactions.* Design transactions are not atomic in the conven-

---

tional sense. They are of long duration, so partial results of a transaction should be visible. During a transaction period, the system can issue one check-out for modification so that only one designer can update the data, but it can issue many check-outs for browsing. The system can also implement savepoints for crash recovery. In addition, ODM's support for versions can be integrated with transaction management to simplify concurrent access and recovery.

ODM concepts are obviously promising for new database applications. We turn now to the implementation of its features, which is far from a trivial task.

Object-oriented DBMSs

Developers have taken two general approaches to implementing object-oriented databases — namely, extending a relational system to support the object concept or extending an object-oriented programming language to include persistent storage. Although many object-oriented DBMSs have been proposed within these approaches, they differ in their interpretation of the object-oriented data model. In general, the proposed/developed object-oriented DBMSs, in spite of their differences, support the concepts of complex objects and object encapsulation at different levels. They can be categorized based on the level of object orientation[8]:

(1) *Structurally object-oriented.* The data model allows defining data structures for entities of any complexity (that is, it supports complex objects). As an example, the x and y coordinates represent a point, and two diagonal points represent a rectangle. More complex objects — say, the layout mask for an integrated circuit — can be represented by a collection of rectangles.

(2) *Operationally object-oriented.* The data model includes operators to deal with complex objects in their entirety. Since it does not make much sense otherwise, operational object-orientation usually implies structural object-orientation. For example, with regard to a rectangle, users should be able to issue a query such as "Find all rectangles overlapping within a specified area," instead of specifying the relative amplitudes of x and y values.

(3) *Behaviorally object-oriented*. The data model also incorporates features for users to define object types and operators associated with the types. In this case, instances can be used only by calling these operators (that is, objects are encapsulated). Following the same example, if a rectangle is an encapsulated object, the user cannot modify its coordinates without going through predefined operators.

Structurally object-oriented models are similar to the concept of *nested relations* for representing complex entities. In this case, operations on data are not defined as part of the database; each application program defines its own operations. Most proposed object-oriented databases are either operationally or behaviorally object-oriented. In this section, we survey several developed/proposed object-oriented DBMSs, although our selection is by no means comprehensive. Our goal is to demonstrate the architectural features and efficiency issues of complex objects in some object-oriented database systems.

Orion. Orion started as a single-user, multitask database system running in a workstation environment. Orion is intended for applications in CAD/CAM, artificial intelligence, and office information system domains. It implements all the common ODM features. In addition, it supports advanced functions of composite objects, version control, schema evolution, query management, transaction management, and multimedia information management.

The first implementation of Orion, Orion-1, has been extended to a client/server architecture (Orion-1SX), which was designed to run on a local area network of computers. Orion's developer, Microelectronics and Computer Technology Corp. (MCC), has also proposed a fully distributed system (Orion-2) in which all computers can be used as servers.

Orion defines a complex object as a complex attribute where a complex attribute consists of a combination of simple attributes and other complex attributes. In the absence of complex attributes, a complex object reduces to a relational tuple. As such, we can view a complex object hierarchy as a nested relation. Classes are modeled as relations, instances of objects as tuples, and

---

Most proposed object-oriented databases are either operationally or behaviorally object-oriented.

---

attributes as columns of relations. Each relation is augmented with a system-defined unique identifier (UID) column to identify the tuples. In this way, object-oriented queries are transformed into corresponding SQL-like relational queries. Queries with simple predicates are easily transformed into selection operations. Queries with complex attributes are transformed into join operations where the domains of the complex attributes are the UID columns of the referenced relations.

The Orion storage subsystem was built on top of Wisconsin Storage System (WiSS), a prototype relational storage subsystem. WiSS allows data pages to contain records of different types (relations). It also allows specification of a storage location when a new record is inserted. Using these two features, all records belonging to the same complex object can be clustered on the disk. Furthermore, WiSS supports variable-length records for implementing variable-length and set-valued attributes. It also provides B^+-tree and hash indices to speed up the associative search of complex objects.

Iris. The Iris database management system is a series of increasingly capable prototypes developed at Hewlett-Packard Laboratories. It was implemented using a combination of C and Lisp on HP-9000 Unix workstations. Most constructs are implemented as C functions, while the query language (Object-SQL) is implemented in Lisp. The application areas intended for Iris include office information systems, knowledge-base systems, engineering test and measurement, and computer-aided hardware and software designs.

The Iris architecture consists of three parts. The Interface Modules facilitate users' access to persistent objects both interactively and through embedded languages. The Object Manager imple-

ments the Iris data model, which supports object-oriented constructs such as classification, generalization/specialization, and aggregation. The Storage Manager is (currently) a conventional relational storage subsystem that provides associative access and update capabilities to a single relation at a time. Object-oriented queries are translated into an extended relational algebra.

The Iris Storage Manager is built on top of HP-SQL, which is very similar to System R's Research Storage System. The Storage Manager was extended to support the generation of unique object identifiers and was augmented with parent-child links to support both relational and network query processing. In general, it operates over a single table per request; joins and aggregate operations are done outside it. The Storage Manager supports database functions such as transactions with savepoints, concurrency control, logging, and recovery.

Two extensions on top of HP-SQL — support for foreign operators and for long fields — manage the diverse set of intended applications. Foreign operators are needed to support complex operations typically found in object-oriented database applications. Users define them and can use them to specify operations in new data types. The Storage Manager can invoke the body of foreign functions in the same way it evaluates any predefined operators in a predicate.

GemStone. The GemStone database system is the result of a development project at Servio Logic Corporation. The targeted applications include CAD, hypermedia, knowledge bases, and office information systems. GemStone merges the object-oriented concepts of Smalltalk with those of database systems. Since Smalltalk was implemented as a single-user, memory-based, single-processor system, several enhancements were required to meet the requirements for a database system. These included support for (a) a multi-user, disk-based environment, (b) recovery from program failures and consistency among multiple users, (c) large objects even when they do not fit into main memory, and (d) physical placement of objects on persistent disk. Based on the syntax and semantics of Smalltalk, GemStone provides a database language called Opal for data definition, data manipulation, and general computation. It is a step toward the unification of query and programming languages.

A GemStone prototype was implemented using a VAX as the host and IBM PCs as workstations connected to the host through a local area network. Stone and Gem are actually different processes implemented on the host computer under the VMS operating system. Stone serves as the storage manager and Gem supports the object data model. Gem also provides the capabilities of compiling Opal methods and session control. A separate Gem process is maintained for each active user.

Stone is built on the VAX file system, and provides secondary storage management and support for associative access. It uses unique surrogates called object-oriented pointers (that is, OIDs) to refer to objects. An object table is maintained to map an OID to a physical location. Since OIDs are logical rather than physical addresses of objects, this approach gives the flexibility of moving objects around in secondary storage. In Stone, subobjects belonging to the same complex object can be stored separately, but their OIDs are always kept together.

Encore. Encore (Extensible and Natural Common Object Resource) is the result of research efforts at Brown University. It provides a set of special facilities that are useful for design database applications. They include version control, transaction mechanism, and composite object. Encore supports a high-level object view of data and relies on an underlying storage manager called Ob-Server (Object Server). The overall system architecture consists of a network of workstations with the server and the data residing on a single node. The system was implemented under the Unix 4.3 BSD operating system. Clients at different workstations can access the ObServer concurrently through the Unix remote procedure call.

The ObServer is a typeless backend: It simply reads and writes chunks of memory from secondary storage. Ob-Server allocates disk space and generates a UID for each chunk of data. Encore uses chunks of memory to implement objects. All objects are instances of some type that describes the behavior of its instances. Related objects from different types can be aggregated to form complex objects. Chunks

of memory belonging to a complex object can be allocated contiguously or noncontiguously depending on access patterns.

Other commercial systems. Among the systems already described, Gem-Stone is commercially available, Orion is available only on a limited basis, while Iris and Encore are research prototypes. Recently, some commercial object-oriented DBMSs appeared on the market:

(1) *Ontos*. This successor to Vbase can be installed as a multiple-client/multiple-server configuration on a variety of platforms, including Sun, DEC, and HP Apollo workstations. The targeted applications are CAD/CAM, CASE, documentation, hypermedia, and office automation. Its approach toward object orientation is to add persistent storage to the C++ programming environment. In other words, users write their application with standard C++ codes and Ontos takes care of the underlying file manipulation. Furthermore, Ontos supports SQL with extension to support objects.

(2) *Versant*. Also a client/server object-oriented DBMS, Versant aims for CAD/CAM, CASE, computer-aided publishing, and integrated office automation applications. The core modules of a typical Versant architecture are the object manager, object servers, and user interfaces. The object manager is a database kernel that manages object definition and access. An object server is a storage system that handles data in the form of objects and performs I/O functions. The user interface to the database is through C or C++ programs.

(3) *ObjectStore*. This DBMS targets developers of highly interactive, design-oriented applications such as CAD, CASE, computer-aided publishing, and image- and multimedia-based office in-

formation applications. ObjectStore was designed to run under a Unix-based system, and it can be accessed by C and C++ programs, as well as by SQL queries. To provide fast access to persistent data, ObjectStore focuses on object mapping, caching, and clustering techniques. The user can allocate objects either to a specified segment of the database or as close as possible to a specified object.

Table 1 summarizes the systems surveyed here. Their targeted applications overlap in CAD/CAM, CASE, and office information systems. This overlap indicates user demand for a more efficient DBMS than the relational systems. The table shows that most commercial object-oriented DBMSs use C++ as the user interface. This is an interesting trend that may affect the direction of future development.

Issues and future research directions

The powerful modeling capabilities of the object-oriented data model provide a rich set of topics for database researchers. Despite previous efforts, there are still many interesting topics that deserve special consideration. We investigate some of them in this section. In particular, we emphasize performance-related issues because they are the key to successful object-oriented database management systems in applications such as design databases where speed is critical.

Fundamental issues. The research of object-oriented DBMSs is still in an early stage compared to relational systems. Several fundamental issues must still be resolved:

(1) *Unified data model*. Unlike the well-defined relational model, object-oriented DBMSs lack a coherent data model and a standard query language. As a result, different proposed systems use different object models that have different notation and expressive power. Research should be directed toward the definition of a universal ODM with a standard query language like SQL in relational DBMSs.

(2) *Integration*. To access relational databases through embedded SQL, us-

Table 1. Overview of surveyed object-oriented DBMSs.

Categories/ Systems	Developer	Experimental/ Commercial	Relational (R)/ Language Ext. (L)	Targeted Applications
Orion[1-3]	MCC	Experimental	R, WiSS	CAD/CAM, AI, office information systems (OIS)
Iris[1,4]	HP	Experimental	R, HP-SQL	OIS, AI, CAD, CASE
GemStone[5]	Servio Logic	Commerical	L, Smalltalk	CAD, AI, OIS, hypermedia, aerospace
Encore[6]	Brown Univ.	Experimental	—	CAD, OIS, programming environments
Ontos/Vbase[7]	Ontologic	Commercial	L, C++	CAD/CAM, CASE, OIS, hypermedia, document processing
Versant[8]	Versant Object	Commercial	L, C++	CAD/CAM, OA, CASE, computer-aided publishng (CAP)
ObjectStore[9]	Object Design	Commercial	L, C++	CAD, CASE, CAP, OIS

References

1. W. Kim and F.H. Lochovsky, *Object-Oriented Concepts, Databases, and Applications*, Addison-Wesley, Reading, Mass., 1989.

2. W. Kim, H.-T. Chou, and J. Banerjee, "Operations and Implementation of Complex Objects," *Proc. Third Int'l Conf. Data Eng.*, IEEE CS Press, Los Alamitos, Calif., Order No. 762, 1987, pp. 626-633.

3. W. Kim et al., "Architecture of the Orion Next-Generation Database System," *IEEE Trans. Knowledge and Data Eng.*, Vol. 2, No. 1, Mar. 1990, pp. 109-124.

4. D.H. Fishman et al., "An Object-Oriented Database Management System," *ACM Trans. Office Information Systems*, Vol. 5, No. 1, 1987, pp. 48-69.

5. D. Maier and J. Stein, *Research Directions in Object-Oriented Programming*, MIT Press, Cambridge, Mass., 1987, pp. 355-392.

6. M.F. Hornick and S.B. Zdonik, "A Shared Segmented Memory System for Object-Oriented Databases," *ACM Trans. Office Information Systems*, Vol. 5, No. 1, 1987, pp. 70-95.

7. *Ontos Release 2.0 Data Sheet*, Ontologic Inc., Burlington, Mass., 1990.

8. *Versant Product Profile*, Versant Object Technology, Menlo Park, Calif., 1990.

9. *An Introduction to ObjectStore, Release 1.0*, Object Design Inc., Burlington, Mass., 1989.

ers must know the query language as well as the host language (for example, PL/1, Cobol). Since the object concept is similar in object-oriented programming languages and object-oriented databases, a new possibility is to use the host language itself as the data definition and manipulation language. Researchers have tried to merge database features with object-oriented languages such as Smalltalk and C++. The ultimate goal is to combine a database with data processing languages to form an integrated software engineering environment.

(3) *Implementation*. Implementation of complex objects and their operations is critical to the performance of an object-oriented database. The object-oriented database environment may require specialized access paths, specialized storage structures, and specialized main-memory buffering.[8]

(4) *Other issues*. Object versions, object identity, protection and locking mechanisms, long-duration transactions, and recovery and consistency control also require further research. Some of these issues are not unique to object-oriented databases; however, the characteristics of object-oriented databases make it necessary to develop new schemes for their proper implementation.

Among these issues, efforts to define a unified data model are underway.[7,9] Efforts regarding language integration are stalled on the choice between compatibility with the SQL standard and a highly integrated system using only C++ or Smalltalk. Currently, some commercial systems based on C++ support an extension of SQL, Object-SQL, as an embedded language. This may be a good compromise for the near future, but a long-term solution will depend on user needs. Regarding implementation issues, most proposed/developed systems use ad hoc schemes to improve the performance. A systematic study is still lacking.

The rest of this section concentrates on the efficient management of complex objects in object-oriented database systems.

Efficient management of complex objects. Object-oriented DBMSs were proposed to increase the modeling power of conventional data models. However, the notions of complex object and object identity complicate the requirements

123

for the DBMS storage manager. Due to the nature of the underlying applications, retrieving complex objects and navigating among related objects are the two most frequent operations performed in an object-oriented database system.

In many applications, efficient traversal of graphs representing the structure of complex objects is important. Traditional performance-improvement schemes were mainly designed to speed up associative queries where attribute matching is the most frequent operation; they do not provide direct support for graph traversal. Researchers have suggested several mechanisms including indexing, clustering, buffering, and query optimization to improve database performance.[9]

In relational databases, the relationships among different relations are not explicitly represented; they are implicitly defined via attribute values. To reveal a relationship, the system must perform a join operation on attributes of the same domain. Searching by the attribute values is the key requirement for a join.

In object-oriented databases, objects can be accessed by content or logical links. Accessing by content is similar to relational selections, but accessing by logical links is not directly supported by relational systems. The logical links are used to represent relationships among objects; they are in the form of object identifiers that are controlled by the system. Given a relational record, the system cannot determine directly which record in another relation is related to this one; but given an object, the system knows exactly what other objects are linked to it. Thus, an object-oriented database system can define a scope and ensure that the next object accessed by logical links is within this scope. This supports improved performance by clustering and/or buffering the objects within the scope.

Object clustering. The goal of object clustering is to reduce the number of disk I/Os for object retrieval. Typically, the unit of data transferred from disk is a page instead of an individual object. If two objects are clustered on the same page, it will take only one disk I/O to access both objects successively. The buffer manager actually prefetches the second object when the first one is accessed. If the page size is larger, more

---

Object-oriented DBMSs can use special "structured objects" to organize regular data objects.

---

objects can be clustered on a page, and one disk I/O can access them all.

In object-oriented databases, complex objects are the basic units of data manipulation. The subobjects of a complex object may come from different classes. Traditional storage systems tend to group records of the same type physically close to each other on disks. This results in tedious and expensive reconstruction procedures (such as join operations) to retrieve complex objects. Therefore, it sounds logical to cluster related objects of different classes together to achieve acceptable performance.

One of the major advantages of object-oriented DBMSs is their ability to explicitly represent relationships among data elements as part of the data definition by using object identifiers. The DBMS can use special "structural objects" to organize regular data objects, much as directories are used to organize files in a file system. For example, one structural object may record the version history of the same logical object, while another structural object may record the configuration structure of a composite object.[10] Since the DBMS has knowledge about interobject relationships, the system can use this knowledge to cluster related objects and thus improve performance.

To support object clustering, a storage manager must be capable of accepting commands such as "Store object XX near object YY," and then trying to put the two objects on the same or adjacent pages. Such commands are low-level, object-by-object hints. If the user gives such detailed hints for each object, the DBMS's job for clustering is straightforward. However, this means the user is totally responsible for controlling the clustering structure, which directly violates the data-independence criterion for any DBMS (namely, users should be unaware of the data's physical repre-

sentation). Thus, a system should adopt a clustering scheme that accepts higher level hints (for example, clustering objects based on their configuration relationship) and generates low-level clustering commands automatically.

In many practical applications, object relationships (for example, configuration links) are not totally random. They can be expressed as a hierarchy or a directed acyclic graph (DAG). Typical operations performed on a hierarchy/DAG include navigation through links and retrieval of the ancestors/descendants of a given node.

A good strategy for clustering objects is to arrange the hierarchy/DAG nodes into a linear clustering sequence to allow efficient performance of these operations. To cluster a hierarchy, one can store the nodes of a hierarchy in depth-first order such that any node p in the hierarchy will have all its descendant nodes stored immediately after p. This is very effective when an object and all its descendants must be retrieved together.

The clustering process for a DAG is more complicated. First, a DAG is augmented with a virtual root node, and then transformed into an equivalent hierarchy to be the subject of a depth-first clustering sequence. For each node with multiple parents, a particular parent is chosen such that all descendants of a DAG node can be fetched in a single forward scan. The result is a spanning tree starting from the virtual root node.

It has been shown that clustering can improve the I/O cost by a factor of two to 15, depending on object size. As expected intuitively, clustering is more effective when object size is small compared to page size (Table 1, Reference 2).

Several characteristics are common to existing studies of clustering schemes:

(1) The schemes are static (that is, objects are clustered when they are created, and once allocated, they are not reclustered at runtime).
(2) The schemes use disk pages as clustering units (that is, they assume an average access time for each page and do not take into consideration the physical adjacency of individual pages).
(3) The schemes cluster objects on the basis of a unique type of relationship among the data elements; other relationships are ignored for clustering purposes.

Two potential problems arise from these characteristics:

(1) A static clustering scheme initially offers a good placement policy for complex objects but does not take into account the dynamic evolution of objects. In applications such as design databases, objects are constantly updated early in the design cycle. Frequent updates may destroy the initially clustered structure. It might be necessary to reorganize the object structure for efficient future accesses.

(2) Objects may be connected by several relationships that form independent hierarchies/DAGs. For example, in a design database, a design evolves through several phases — creation, design-rule checking, correction, extraction, and simulation. At each phase, the design tool requires its own access pattern, which may or may not be the same as the one supported by the initial static clustering. It might be preferable to use different clustering structures in different phases. Moreover, several users may access the same set of objects concurrently through different access patterns. Clustering objects on the basis of one application's needs may sacrifice those of others. A good clustering scheme must take multiple relationships into consideration. If related objects cannot be tightly clustered on the same page, they should be clustered on the same track or cylinder. Furthermore, as access patterns change or updates occur, reclustering may be necessary. The choice of the optimum reorganization point is a function of parameters such as read/write ratio, physical characteristics of objects, and I/O devices.

Cheng and Hurson[5] have shown that, in general, reclustering should be performed whenever possible to keep the related objects physically clustered. Moreover, for applications in which the read/write ratio is high, a fully dynamic reclustering strategy is justifiable. Furthermore, when the read/write ratio is not high enough, frequent reorganization degrades the overall performance. The system can always perform off-line reclustering during off-peak hours to gain the clustering benefit.

A scheme similar to the leveled clustering algorithm[5] can be used to cluster objects with multiple connectivity. (Tightly connected objects are physically clustered closer than loosely connected objects.) The effectiveness of such an algorithm has been studied for a weighted digraph (that is, objects with multiple relationships). In applications with three levels of connectivity among objects, this approach has drastically improved the average access time for tightly connected objects (for example,

> **The buffer manager can use the object-oriented DBMS's explicit representation of relationships.**

by approximately 10 times), while significant improvement has also been observed for the loosely connected objects.

Object buffering. The disk buffer concept is similar to the memory cache design found in high-performance computer architectures. Designing a cache involves choices for block size, replacement policy, and mapping algorithm. Similarly, a disk buffer manager determines the buffer *prefetching* and *replacement* policies using a software approach. When the object-hit ratio is high and object faults are rare, the response time should be faster.

For prefetching, the simplest strategy is no prefetching at all. However, since objects are usually clustered based on their semantic meanings, it is logical to adopt a prefetching policy that brings all objects of a disk page or adjacent pages into the buffer pool on every object fault (for example, Orion and Encore operate this way). This strategy assumes that the relationship used for clustering objects is exactly the one needed for retrieval. However, in many practical applications, multiple relationships exist among objects, and the clients' access patterns do not always follow a single relationship. This scheme is not very effective when some of the requested objects are not tightly clustered.[11] Since object-oriented DBMSs allow the representation of object relationships through explicit semantic links, the buffer manager can use this knowledge for effective prefetching and replacement of data objects. The user can give hints (for example, "my primary access pattern is via configuration relationships"). When an application program requests an object X, the storage manager brings into the buffer pool all the pages containing objects connected to X by configuration links.

For buffer replacement, designers usually recognize LRU (least recently used) as a good policy because it is simple and effective. Several alternatives are possible, including LFU (least frequently used), Clock (also known as second chance), GClock (Generalized Clock), and LRD (least reference density). These policies presume locality of references; however, they do not take advantage of knowledge about object relationships. As a result, some likely-to-be-used objects may be swapped out because the buffer manager does not consider that these objects are structurally related to the one currently in use.

To take advantage of this knowledge, Chang and Katz[10] suggested a context-sensitive replacement policy that uses hints about access patterns and interobject relationships to set relevant priorities. In this approach, when an object is touched, its related pages in the buffer will increase their priorities so that they will not be replaced in the near future.

It has been shown that aggressive prefetching and priority-based replacement policies together outperform LRU-without-prefetching by 150 percent in response time. This approach is promising. However, it does not address the issue of buffer space utilization, nor does it consider the impacts of multiple relationships on physical access time. A page-based buffering scheme based on user's hints is not space efficient because many of the prefetched pages may contain unneeded objects. Therefore, a more space-efficient and sophisticated buffering scheme — that is, an object-based buffering scheme — with multiple prefetching hints is required to cache objects connected by multiple relationships in memory.

A dual object-based buffering scheme has been proposed and analyzed.[11] This analysis showed that an object-based buffering policy at the second level provides better space utilization than the traditional page-based buffering scheme. Furthermore, balancing the overhead of physical disk I/Os requires adapting a "smart" prefetching and replacement policy that treats the loosely and tightly connected objects differently.

Our review of research prototypes and commercial object-oriented DBMSs emphasizes the representation and manipulation of complex objects. We believe that clustering and buffering schemes tailored to typical complex object operations offer the best near-term means of improving the performance of object-oriented databases. Future research in clustering and buffering should address recent advances in disk technology — optical and parallel disks.

Such research, together with research addressing issues relative to the object-oriented data model, may open the way to object-oriented DBMSs that efficiently manage the complex objects and operations in applications such as engineering design, multimedia, and knowledge-base systems. ∎

References

1. L.A. Rowe and M. Stonebraker, "The Postgres Data Model," *Proc. 13th Int'l Conf. VLDB*, Morgan Kaufman Publications, Palo Alto, Calif., 1987, pp. 83-96.

2. M. Carey et al., "Storage Management for Objects in the Exodus," *Object-Oriented Concepts, Databases, and Applications*, W. Kim and F.H. Lochovsky, eds., Addison-Wesley, Reading, Mass., 1989, pp. 341-369.

3. J. McPherson and H. Pirahesh, "An Overview of Extensibility in Starburst," *Database Engineering*, Vol. 6, 1987, pp. 92-99.

4. H.F. Korth and A. Silberschatz, "New Database Applications," *Database System Concepts*, McGraw-Hill, New York, 1986, pp. 465-473.

5. J.-b. Cheng and A.R. Hurson, "Effective Clustering of Complex Objects in Object-Oriented Databases," *Proc. ACM SIGMOD Int'l Conf. Management of Data*, ACM, New York, 1991, pp. 22-31.

6. J.H. Saunders, "A Survey of Object-Oriented Programming Languages," *J. Object-Oriented Programming*, Mar./Apr. 1989, pp. 5-10.

7. E. Fong et al., "Object-Oriented Database Task Group: Final Report," Nat'l Institute of Technology, US Dept. of Commerce, 1991, Gaithersburg, Md.

8. K.R. Dittrich, "Object-Oriented Database Systems: The Notion and the Issues," *Proc. Int'l Workshop Object-Oriented Database Systems*, IEEE CS Press, Los Alamitos, Calif., Order No. 734, 1986, pp. 2-6.

9. M. Atkinson et al., "The Object-Oriented Database System Manifesto," *Proc. First Conf. Deductive and Object-Oriented Databases*, Kyoto, Japan, 1989, pp. 40-57.

10. E.E. Chang and R.H. Katz, "Exploiting Inheritance and Structure Semantics for Effective Clustering and Buffering in an Object-Oriented DBMS," *Proc. ACM SIGMOD Int'l Conf. Management of Data*, ACM, New York, 1989, pp. 348-357.

11. J.-b. Cheng and A.R. Hurson, "On the Performance Issues of Object-Based Buffering," *Proc. Parallel and Distributed Information Systems*, IEEE CS Press, Los Alamitos, Calif., Order No. 2295, 1991, pp. 30-37.

A.R. Hurson is on the computer engineering faculty at Pennsylvania State University. For the past 12 years, his research has been directed toward the design and analysis of general- and special-purpose computer architectures.

Hurson has published more than 110 technical papers. He is the coauthor of *IEEE Tutorial on Parallel Architectures for Database Systems* and the cofounder of the IEEE Symposium on Parallel and Distributed Processing. He is a member of the Computer Society Press editorial board and the IEEE Distinguished Visitors Program.

Simin H. Pakzad is assistant professor of computer engineering at Pennsylvania State University. Her research interests include parallel processing, interconnection networks, database systems, neural networks, and fault-tolerant interconnection networks.

Pakzad received her MS in computer science from the University of Iowa and her PhD in computer science from the University of Oklahoma.

Jia-bing Cheng is a member of the development staff at IBM-Research Triangle Park. His research interests include database machines, information retrieval systems, object-oriented systems, and network management architectures.

Cheng received his BS in electrical engineering from the National Taiwan University in 1983, and his MS and PhD in computer engineering from Pennsylvania State University in 1988 and 1991, respectively. He is a member of IEEE, the Computer Society, and ACM.

Readers can contact A.R. Hurson at Pennsylvania State University, Department of Electrical and Computer Engineering, University Park, PA 16802; e-mail A2H@ecl.psu.edu.

Chapter 5

Object-Oriented Distributed Systems

Object Orientation in Heterogeneous Distributed Computing Systems

John R. Nicol, C. Thomas Wilkes, and Frank A. Manola

GTE Laboratories Inc.

Reprinted from *Computer*, June 1993, pp. 57–67.
Copyright © 1993 by The Institute of Electrical and
Electronics Engineers, Inc. All rights reserved.

A least-common-denominator approach to object orientation is emerging as a key strategy for flexibly coordinating and integrating networked information processing resources.

Computer usage is spreading into all functions of large organizations, as can be seen in the widespread appearance of powerful PCs for desktop use and powerful workstations for more specialized uses. Because computers are becoming commonplace in routine business functions, future information-processing environments will likely consist of vast networks of heterogeneous, autonomous, and distributed computing resources, including computers (from mainframe to personal), information-intensive applications, and data (files and databases). The telecommunications infrastructure provides a clear example of such an environment.

There is a growing need for technology to flexibly coordinate computing resources to create networkwide integrated distributed systems that address challenging new information processing requirements. In some cases, these systems might combine resources belonging to different individuals or organizations (for example, connections between customer inventory systems and supplier order-entry systems).

The first phase in creating integrated, large-scale, distributed information systems is interconnectivity. Until recently, most computers were stand-alone systems unable to communicate with other systems. Two or more computing resources are *interconnected* if they can exchange messages. However, interconnectivity guarantees only communication, not cooperation.

For interconnectivity, the client-server model is the most pervasive. This model organizes a distributed system as a number of distributed server processes that offer various services to client processes across the network. Via interprocess-communication mechanisms such as remote procedure calls, servers typically provide clients with access to general system-defined services such as file-storage, printing, processing, authentication, and name services, as well as user-defined services.

The second phase is the more ambitious goal of *interoperability*. Two or more resources are interoperable if they can interact to execute tasks jointly. Simple tools for achieving interoperability are provided by programming capabilities such as an RPC mechanism extended with a data-translation facility. More advanced forms of interoperability require mutual understanding not only at the level of complete systems or programs, but also at the data-type level. Interoperability at this level supports the integration of heterogeneous information in, for example, advanced multimedia applications, and supports information storage in integrated repositories.

Although client-server distributed systems do support a level of interoperability, experience with such systems has been predominantly with local networks. To achieve interoperability in a more global context, systems issues of scale, heterogeneity, configuration management, accounting, and network monitoring are critical. The basic client-server model will not provide the total solution because the complexity of migrating from locally distributed to more global systems demands new tools and techniques.

The object-oriented approach to computing shows promise in addressing this complexity explosion. Object-oriented concepts originated in the programming-language domain, where they have reduced the cost and complexity of software specification, development, and maintenance. Since then, however, computing disciplines such as databases, office information systems, artificial intelligence, and distributed systems have adopted the concepts. Several research projects at GTE Laboratories, including the Distributed Computing Systems and Distributed Object Management projects, are investigating these issues and related standards efforts for telecommunications.[1,2]

In this article, we examine the basic properties of object orientation and their application to heterogeneous, autonomous, and distributed systems to increase interoperability. We argue that object-oriented distributed computing is a natural step forward from the client-server systems of today. To support this claim, we examine the differing levels of object-oriented support already found in commercially available distributed systems — in particular, the Distributed Computing Environment of the Open Software Foundation and the Cronus system of Bolt Beranek and Newman (BBN). We investigate emerging object-oriented systems and standards, focusing on the current convergence toward a least-common-denominator approach to object-oriented distributed computing embodied by the Object Management Group's Common Object Request Broker Architecture. We also examine OSF's Distributed Management Environment and the ISO/CCITT Open Distributed Processing standardization effort.

Controlling complexity through objects

The construction of large-scale, heterogeneous information systems introduces new technical problems not found in conventional systems, including[3]

- naming, protection, sharing, and translation issues resulting from component heterogeneity;
- accounting and resource management issues created by component autonomy; and
- synchronization, consistency, error recovery, and other control problems resulting from component distribution.

The additional complexity of these systems makes structuring mechanisms important. The ISO Open Systems Interconnection Reference Model identified as key structuring concepts the use of layers containing services with well-defined interfaces, with the services being further divided into (possibly distributed) modules.

The emphasis on interfaces and modules has brought many experts to agree that modeling a distributed system as a distributed collection of interacting *objects* is appropriate for integrating distributed information processing resources, in both distributed computing and telecommunications environments.[4] Committees working on communications, distribution, database, programming-language, and repository standards are moving toward adopting, or have already adopted, an object-oriented approach. This trend is evident not only in official standards bodies, such as ISO and CCITT, but also in industry consortia, such as OSF and the Object Management Group in the US, and Architecture Projects Management in the UK. The recent formation of X3H7, an X3 technical committee to coordinate object-development activities, further reflects the increasing popularity of standards involving object-oriented approaches.

The object concept has been applied to the phases of software development: analysis, design, and implementation. Object orientation has also been applied in different areas of software systems, for example, in

- programming languages, for software reuse and modularity;
- databases, for composition of attributes, modeling behavior of real-world objects, and persistence; and
- distributed systems, for encapsulation and interoperability.

Because of these different emphases, a particular area might not require the full power of object orientation. For

Glossary

ANSI: American National Standards Institute

CCITT: Consultative Committee on International Telephony and Telegraphy

CORBA: Common Object Request Broker Architecture

DCE: Distributed Computing Environment

DME: Distributed Management Environment

DOMS: Distributed Object Management System

IDL: Interface definition language

ISO: International Standards Organization

ODP: Open Distributed Processing

ORB: Object request broker

OSF: Open Software Foundation

OSI: Open Systems Interconnection

RM-ODP: Reference Model for Open Distributed Processing

RPC: Remote procedure call

example, the benefits of inheritance — which facilitate software reuse — are not a major factor in distributed systems and can significantly degrade their performance.[5] The sidebar presents a general definition of object orientation suitable for distributed systems.

Objects form a natural model for a distributed system because distributed components can communicate with each other only using messages addressed to well-defined interfaces. Components are assumed to have their own locally defined procedures, enabling them to respond to messages. We can effectively apply the object concept to various levels of a computing architecture. For example, many distributed processing infrastructures use the object abstraction to present applications with an encapsulated view of printing, processor, and file services. Likewise, object-oriented programming languages use objects to model individual application abstractions or even individual data items. Although object granularity typically varies at different levels of a system architecture, the same basic object abstraction can be applied.

This use of objects also naturally accommodates the heterogeneity and autonomy of large-scale, distributed systems: heterogeneity because messages sent to distributed components depend only on the components' interfaces, not on their internals; and autonomy because components can change independently and transparently, provided they maintain their interfaces.

It is becoming increasingly difficult to avoid object technology in one form or another. An organization need not decide to adopt such technology as a matter of policy or conscious decision making — object technology might already be present in currently used systems, either explicitly or implicitly. For example, the OSF Motif windowing toolkit is both structured in an object-oriented fashion and presents an object model to the Motif programmer, even though it is written in C, a non-object-oriented language.

Thus, regardless of whether organizations adopt object-oriented tools and methodologies, object-oriented approaches to programming or system architectures are becoming common. Also, traditional technologies are evolving in an object-oriented direction, as recent developments in Cobol and SQL demonstrate. Organizations will have to use

Object orientation in distributed systems

Wegner developed a classic definition of object orientation[1]:

object oriented = objects + classes + inheritance

This definition suits the domain for which it was developed — programming-language design. However, it does not apply directly to other domains, including distributed systems.[2]

We suggest a working definition of object orientation better suited for distributed systems[2]:

object oriented = encapsulation + abstraction + polymorphism

Elements of this definition are as follows:

• *Encapsulation.* A combination of two aspects: the *grouping* of object state and operations, and *data hiding*; that is, the restriction of access to the object state via a well-defined interface (the operations).
• *Abstraction.* The ability to group associated entities according to common properties; for example, the set of instances belonging to a given class.
• *Polymorphism.* The ability of abstractions to overlap and intersect. A popular form of polymorphism is *inclusion polymorphism*, in which operations on a given type are also applicable to its subtypes.[3] Inclusion polymorphism is often implemented via an inheritance mechanism, as in Smalltalk and C++.

This definition of object orientation is essentially a generalization of Wegner's definition. It corresponds precisely to Wegner's definition when the mechanisms for encapsulation, abstraction, and polymorphism are objects, classes, and inheritance, respectively.

References

1. P. Wegner, "Dimensions of Object-Based Language Design," *SIGPlan Notices*, Vol. 22, No. 12, Dec. 1987, pp. 168-182.

2. G.S. Blair et al., "A Synthesis of Object-Oriented and Functional Ideas in the Design of a Distributed Software Engineering Environment," *Software Eng. J.*, Vol. 5, No. 3, May 1990, pp. 193-204.

3. D. Watt, *Programming Language Concepts and Paradigms*, Prentice Hall, Englewood Cliffs, N.J., 1991.

products conforming to new object standards, or they will have to explicitly refrain from using the important features of new products.

To varying degrees, contemporary client-server distributed systems also possess features of object-oriented computing. RPC mechanisms such as those provided by the OSF Distributed Computing Environment and BBN Cronus permit encapsulation of server functionality: The server's data is accessible only via a defined set of operations (the server's *interface*). Thus, a server can be considered an object. Cronus goes further in providing mechanisms supporting object classes and a form of inheritance. In this sense, the object-oriented

approach in distributed systems is an evolution of the client-server approach.

At the far end of the spectrum lies the *distributed object management* approach. This approach is based on current trends in object-oriented distributed-systems models, application-integration environments, and object-oriented databases. These trends are evolving so that the complete set of resources available on a distributed network — including computers, network facilities, data, and programs — can be treated as a commonly accessible collection of objects. A distributed object system will combine these objects in arbitrary ways to provide new information processing capabilities. Intelligent interoperability in such a distributed object system would let it treat network resources much like the objects in an advanced object-database system. A client would not only have access to the system's available objects via interfaces defined in a common object model. The client could also express requests at a very high level — and potentially involving large numbers of objects — to the system as a whole, and have it (or the objects, acting together) determine an optimum means of satisfying the request.

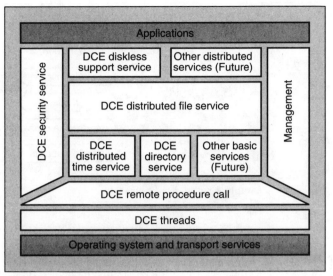

Figure 1. DCE architecture.[6]

Object support in commercial systems

We now examine object-model support in commercial distributed-systems technology. We discuss OSF's Distributed Computing Environment, a recently released system that appears on its way to becoming a de facto standard, and BBN's Cronus system, a mature distributed system with relatively rich support for object-oriented development. Later, we examine emerging standards and implementation efforts in object technology.

Distributed Computing Environment. The OSF DCE[6] facilitates application construction and maintenance in a heterogeneous computing environment. It provides tools and an integrated, comprehensive set of services to support distributed applications. OSF released version 1.0 of DCE in January 1992.

Figure 1 shows DCE's architecture. Elements in shaded boxes (for example, operating system and transport services) are not provided by DCE itself, but rather by the host system (such as Unix or VMS) or the application. We limit our attention to two elements of the DCE architecture: the remote procedure call and the directory service.

DCE provides a traditional RPC mechanism — derived from the RPC mechanism in HP-Apollo's Network Computing System[7] — that programmers can use for structuring client-server systems or other systems using point-to-point communication. This mechanism is used widely in the con-

struction of the services provided by DCE itself.

The RPC mechanism provided in DCE supports *encapsulation* (see the "Object orientation in distributed systems" sidebar) at the granularity of an individual server: A server accepts only the operations its interface defines. Thus, clients can manipulate a server's resources only by invoking operations provided by this interface. A DCE server is thus sometimes called an RPC object. The server interface is defined by a C-like interface definition language.

Although DCE's RPC supports encapsulation, it does not support *abstraction* or *polymorphism*. Thus, DCE does not give users the object model's full power. However, several DCE components — for example, the cell directory service and the global directory service — are designed or implemented (or both) using object-oriented technology. Internally, these directories represent the entities they store as objects created, accessed, and deleted via the X/Open Object Management application programming interface. This interface provides many of the facilities specified by the Common Object Request Broker Architecture (which we describe later), but DCE does not make it available to the user.

Cronus. BBN's Cronus[8] has been under development since 1981. The system has been used both in the field (for example, to integrate elements of a knowledge-based decision-support application[9]) and in the laboratory (to support an experimental, emergency-

response telephony application[1]).

Cronus provides services and communication layers directly on top of the host systems, primarily to transmit operation invocations from clients to object managers in a host-independent way. The Cronus kernel also implements the basic abstractions for processes and objects, and monitors and controls other Cronus activity on the host. The kernel is implemented as a host-system process executing in the user space of each host forming part of a Cronus cluster. Above the Cronus kernel reside *object managers*, which implement services, and *clients*, which use the services provided by the managers. To use another manager's services, a manager can take on the role of a client.

Cronus includes a number of base object managers, including a name service, a type-definition service, a file service, and a database-access service. It also includes a rich programming toolkit for developing new object managers (potentially building on existing managers via inheritance). New object managers are *first class* in the sense that Cronus does not distinguish them from the base managers. This lets users adapt Cronus to fulfill new application requirements, such as those in telecommunications.[1]

Unlike DCE, Cronus supports object technology with

• inclusion polymorphism via inheritance (although currently it does not support an aspect often associated with polymorphism — late binding of operations, as with C++ virtual functions), and

• a rich toolkit for defining, implementing, and debugging object managers.

Figure 2 shows a partial type hierarchy as an example of Cronus' use of inheritance. All Cronus object types derive from the base type Object. The type SQLDefs defines common behavior for a set of derived classes that provide access to various database engines supporting SQL queries, including Informix and Oracle. By using the operations of the SQLDefs object type, a programmer can write queries that apply to any supported database engine.

More fully object-oriented systems

Currently available distributed systems exhibit a degree of object orientation — minimal in DCE but somewhat more sophisticated in Cronus. The Distributed Object Management System approach to the design of fully object-oriented heterogeneous computing sys-

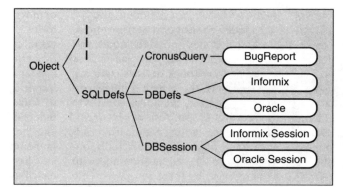

Figure 2. A sample Cronus type hierarchy.

tems is becoming increasingly popular. Following discussion of the generic aspects of DOMS, we describe an actual specification: the Object Management

Group's CORBA, which takes a minimalist approach to the interoperability problem.

Two important efforts relate to the DOMS approach. The sidebar below presents aspects of OSF's Distributed Management Environment project, which has as a basic component an implementation of CORBA. In the sidebar on pp. 62-63, we give an overview of the Open Distributed Processing standardization effort. While it is synergistic with CORBA and shares similar goals, it adopts a more holistic approach to interoperability.

OSF Distributed Management Environment

The Open Software Foundation's goal for the Distributed Management Environment is to unify systems management in heterogeneous environments, including functions such as software installation, performance monitoring, and configuration changes.[1] DME addresses three major shortcomings in current management technology:

• the lack of *consistency* in management-system user interfaces, via a common management graphics user interface based on OSF's Motif;
• the lack of *interoperability* between different management systems, via support for several common management protocol standards; and
• the lack of *scalability* to large heterogeneous environments, via a three-tiered hierarchical approach (node, cell, enterprise) adapted from the OSF DCE.

DME's overall architecture consists of

• a set of basic *management protocols*, including the Simple Network Management Protocol (SNMP), ISO's Common Management Information Protocol (CMIP), and an OSF protocol developed for management of DCE RPC (support for specialized telecommunications protocols can be added later);
• a foundation layer of *object services*, including management request brokers (for object registration and location), plus authentication and authorization services for object-access control;
• a set of customizable management *services* implementing management domains and policies;
• several *application services*, including license management, software installation and management, printing, and host management services; and
• a Motif-based *management user interface*, providing a model reflecting the underlying object-services layer and a set of tools for generating interfaces to new management applications.

These facilities are based on DCE RPC and use of the corresponding DCE services (for example, the directory and authentication services). DME will also provide a toolkit with compilers for generating object definitions and other tools.

The intent of DME is to provide a framework for construction of third-party management applications. DME's application services are by no means a complete solution to the distributed management problem; rather, they are common services needed by all applications, and models for the design of third-party management services.

OSF issued a request for technology in July 1990 to solicit component technologies for DME based on the architecture described above. An OSF document[2] describes the rationale for the final selection of technologies and reproduces the original request for technology in an appendix. OSF is currently integrating the component technologies, with an initial release of the framework targeted for the second half of 1993.

DME's object-services layer is explicitly based on the CORBA specification. In particular, its management request broker is an implementation of CORBA's object-request broker, extended and optimized to support management applications. In a sense, DME is a "value-added" CORBA.

DME supports several management protocols (notably SNMP and CMIP). Several of these protocols' naming schemes are not yet fully specified or are for internal use only. DME uses an *adapter object* mechanism (similar to the CORBA concept of *object adapter*) to translate from these various naming schemes to a common model.

References

1. *OSF Distributed Management Environment Architecture*, Open Software Foundation, Cambridge, Mass., May 1992 (member review version).

2. *Distributed Management Environment — Rationale*, Open Software Foundation, Cambridge, Mass., Sept. 1991.

Distributed Object Management Systems. Elements of object orientation are found in various mature and emerging distributed-systems technologies. The movement toward full object orientation in distributed systems is best seen in ongoing work on standards specification for DOMS. Besides placing greater emphasis on object orientation, DOMS will be key to achieving application portability and interoperability in large-scale, heterogeneous environments such as in telecommunications.

A DOMS consists of an arbitrary number of distributed (physical) nodes and clients.[2] Each node supports one or more application programs, database systems, and objects (if the system is object oriented). Together, the nodes constitute the system's computing *resources*. DOMS *clients* (which might also be application programs, software tools, objects, and so on) request operations to be performed by these resources. One or more *distributed object managers* act as intermediaries between clients and resources. Distributed object managers make the system's computing resources appear as *objects* (whether they are object oriented or not). They allow clients to make requests involving resources that reside anywhere in the system. Clients need not know the location and implementation details of the resources. Clients and resources connect to the distributed object managers through

Open Distributed Processing

To develop standards for services across multiple systems and their components, ISO and CCITT are working on a joint standardization effort known as *Open Distributed Processing*. ODP's initial goal is a reference model to integrate a wide range of future ODP standards for distributed systems and to maintain consistency across such systems, despite heterogeneity in hardware, operating systems, networks, programming languages, databases, and management authorities. An ODP system must support mechanisms that hide the underlying system's heterogeneity from users and applications. These mechanisms will address such fundamental issues as access, location, migration, concurrency, failure, and replication transparency.

Development of the basic Reference Model for Open Distributed Processing has been under way since 1987. RM-ODP provides a conceptual framework to integrate distribution, interoperability, and portability. It identifies the infrastructure and architectural functions for open distributed processing. RM-ODP's precise concepts derive from current distributed processing developments and, as far as possible, use formal description techniques for specification of the architecture.

The model will be published in four parts:

Part 1: *Overview and Guide to Use of Reference Model* provides a motivational overview of ODP — giving scope, justification, and explanations of key concepts — and outlines the ODP architecture.

Part 2: *Descriptive Model* defines the concepts and analytical framework, and notation for normalized description of (arbitrary) distributed processing systems.

Part 3: *Prescriptive Model* specifies the characteristics that qualify distributed processing systems as open. These are the constraints to which ODP standards must conform.

Part 4: *Architectural Semantics* formalizes ODP's basic modeling and specifications concepts defined in the *Descriptive Model*, provides requirements for specification techniques, and evaluates the standardized formal description techniques against these requirements.

RM-ODP contains both descriptive and prescriptive elements. The *descriptive* elements provide a common vocabulary and a consistent way of looking at the construction of a generalized distributed system. The *prescriptive* elements constrain what can be built in support of distributed systems to just what is required for an open distributed system.[1]

Descriptive framework. In recognition of the growing complexity of large-scale distributed systems, RM-ODP considers such a system from different viewpoints, each an abstraction of a given distributed system placing special emphasis on a particular set of concerns. RM-ODP provides a framework to verify the completeness and consistency of viewpoint descriptions.

RM-ODP presently recognizes five viewpoints. The *enterprise viewpoint* is concerned with the social, managerial, financial, and legal policy issues that constrain the human and machine roles of a distributed system and its environment. The *information viewpoint* concentrates on information modeling and flow, plus structure and information-manipulation constraints. The *computational viewpoint* focuses on the structure of application components and the exchange of data and control among them. The *engineering viewpoint* concerns the mechanisms that provide the distribution transparencies to the application components. The *technology viewpoint* focuses on the constraints imposed by technology and the components from which the distributed system is constructed.

The models of a distributed system constructed from each viewpoint will be object based. The RM-ODP object model establishes common terms for object-oriented concepts, and their definitions can be used across all five viewpoints.

Prescriptive framework. The prescriptive model has two major parts: (1) the definition of a set of viewpoint languages required in an ODP system, and (2) the definition of architectural functions required in an ODP system.

Viewpoint languages. The viewpoint languages are prescriptive constraints on the use of the viewpoints by writers of ODP standards.[1] In this context, we use the term language in its broadest sense: a set of terms and the rules for the construction of statements from terms. Each language draws its most primitive terms from the basic object-model-

software *interfaces* that translate requests and results passing through them to the forms required by the various components.

At a minimum, a DOMS architecture includes

• a collection of *object implementations* (DOMS resources), that is, entities having both state (data) and a set of operations that they can perform;

• *client interfaces* that let clients request objects (or the distributed object managers) to perform operations, provide the arguments to the operations, and receive results;

• *messaging facilities* (provided by the distributed object managers) that forward client requests to the specified objects;

• *object interfaces* that let the distributed object managers invoke the implementations of objects in support of client requests; and

• a distributed collection of (physical) *computer systems* that provide the environments in which the above components run, and *communication facilities* connecting them.

Figure 3 shows this generic architecture. In addition to the DOMS that routes requests among components and uses attached components to perform the actual requested operations, the architecture has a *common object model* to

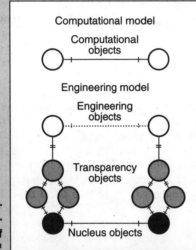

Figure A. Computational and engineering models of object interaction.[1]

ing concepts in the RM-ODP descriptive model. The viewpoint languages are specializations of the basic object model contained in the RM-ODP descriptive model and will be used to specify ODP systems. The following languages are presently defined:

• *Enterprise language* concentrates on the roles played by various enterprise objects (agents); the behaviors that are permitted, forbidden, or required of an agent (deontic state); and the performative acts that alter the deontic state of an enterprise object.

• *Information language* focuses on the structure of concept classes in which information objects might have membership, the relations among classes, and the conditions under which an object changes its class membership.

• *Computational language* is concerned with the specification of interface types, the computational semantics of interactions between interfaces, and rules for the composition of computational activities.

• *Engineering language* focuses on the types of objects that make up an ODP system's infrastructure and their architectural relationships.

• *Technology language* expresses how to implement ODP specifications and conformance relationships.

Architecture. The relationship between the computational and engineering viewpoint models (see Figure A) illustrates an ODP system's general architecture.

The computational viewpoint emphasizes specification of computational structures and statements of properties for interactions between objects. The engineering viewpoint focuses on the engineering mechanisms to ensure these properties. Through a particular distribution mechanism, computational viewpoint object specifications can call on a number of transparency objects, each representing a system property, to realize distribution transparencies. Transparency objects at each node require the services of a nucleus object, an abstraction of the local host environment, and the communications services necessary for internucleus interactions.

ODP status. RM-ODP development is an ongoing effort. Part 2 of the reference model has already undergone the first balloting at the committee draft level. Part 3 reached committee draft status in November 1992, and efforts are under way to align parts 2 and 3. Development of parts 1 and 4 is also in progress. A further ODP work item now in progress concerns the ODP *trader*, a specific architectural function requiring standardization to support dynamic matching of typed object interfaces. With the recent maturation of RM-ODP, we anticipate the commencement of new work items in the near future.

ODP and CORBA. The ODP community and the Object Management Group share the goal of achieving interoperability of heterogeneous, distributed systems. In the near term, the emergence of CORBA-compliant software will likely be a critical factor in reaching this goal. In the longer term, compliance with emerging ODP standards will help achieve this goal. Therefore, we predict convergence of the CORBA and ODP efforts.

Reference

1. C.J. Taylor, "A Status Report on Open Distributed Processing," *First-Class* (Object Management Group newsletter), Vol. 2, No. 2, June/July 1992, pp. 11-13.

provide a set of abstractions understood and supported by all the distributed object managers. General acceptance (or standardization) of the object model and interfaces to such an architecture would facilitate independent development of objects and supporting software to function in a DOMS environment. This is the Object Management Group's goal in specifying CORBA, as we describe later.

The object implementations must support the object interface expected by the DOMS. Developers can create such implementations by developing arbitrary modules that conform to published specifications for this interface, through adapters that tailor existing software or automatically through DOMS-provided object-construction facilities. Thus, the DOMS itself need not fully provide object-definition facilities. The facilities might simply be mechanisms to link independently implemented objects to the system.

Common Object Request Broker Architecture. The Object Management Group is an industry consortium dedicated to producing specifications for commercially available object-oriented environments. The consortium has several hundred member organizations. The CORBA specification is an initial attempt by the OMG to satisfy these goals. We first present an overview of CORBA, condensed from the CORBA specification.[10] We then consider the current specification's possible impact and limitations.

In its current form, CORBA specifies a bare-bones architecture for distributed object management. It includes five interfaces dependent on the object-request broker, offering applications and objects access to the architecture's functions. Figure 4 shows these interfaces, plus the architecture's eight major components.

A *client* is an entity that wishes to invoke an operation on a target object via the ORB. The *object implementation* comprises the code and data that realize the target object's behavior. The ORB locates an object implementation for a request, ensures that the object implementation is ready to receive the

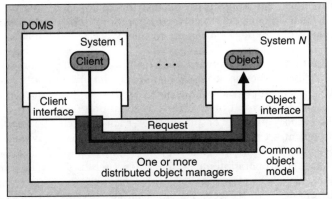

Figure 3. Distributed object management.[2]

request, and transmits the request data and results between the client and the target object.

We now present the major elements of the CORBA framework.

Object model. The CORBA object model provides facilities for defining the objects from which applications can be constructed and how these objects might interact. The Object Management Group has kept the model simple to facilitate its mapping onto the variety of vendor-specific object models that will ultimately support concrete implementations. The model has several key features:

• *Objects* are identifiable, encapsulated entities providing one or more services that clients can request. Objects are created and destroyed as a result of executing object requests. A client identifies an object via an object reference, which always uniquely denotes the same object.

• *Requests* are the mechanism through which clients request other objects' services. Associated with each request are several pieces of information: an operation, a target object, zero or more actual parameters, and an optional request context. The client uses the request context to pass additional information to the target object — for example, to indicate client preferences or to describe the client's execution environment. The target object returns an exception if an abnormal condition occurs during request processing.

• *Types* classify objects according to shared characteristics. Developers use types in operation signatures to restrict parameters included in message requests or to characterize request results. The object model defines a set of primitive

and compound types typical of those found in many high-level programming languages.

• *Interfaces* describe to the rest of the system the operations a client can request of objects. An interface is satisfied by any object capable of responding to each operation defined in the interface. An object can support multiple interfaces through interface inheritance.

• *Operations* are named entities denoting services that can be requested. Every operation has a signature that specifies the arguments required to invoke the operation, the results a client should receive in response to invoking the operation, and the exceptions that might be returned in the case of abnormal processing of the operation.

Presently outside the CORBA object model's scope are richer modeling features, including version and configuration management, hot links, and transactions.

The ORB core. The ORB core brokers requests between clients and object implementations. Brokering involves (target) object location, message delivery, and method binding. Since the ORB core must support a variety of object mechanisms, CORBA is structured so that ORB components above the ORB core provide interfaces that mask differences between the mechanisms found across different ORB cores.

Object implementations. An object implementation comprises the data and code required to realize an object's behavior (as specified by its interface). An object implementation generally defines the code (method) implementing each operation but might also include code to activate and deactivate objects. In addition, an object implementation often uses other objects or additional software.

Although CORBA permits flexible object implementation, it does establish the interface to the CORBA services for all implementations. As a result, implementers can implement an object's behavior by writing a single program for each method or by writing a single program to implement each object interface. However, all object implementations access CORBA services via an interface called the *object adapter* (presented below).

Although object-implementation styles can vary widely, an implementation will engage in the same general process following an invocation — that is, a call to the appropriate method of an implementation. One method argument identifies the object invoked. Using this, the method can locate the data for the object. The method execution, on completion, returns output parameters or exception results to the client.

Interface definition language. The CORBA interface definition language describes the operations and associated attributes of an object interface in terms the rest of the system can understand. IDL makes it possible to translate the functionality offered by resources such as network devices, databases, and applications into object-oriented interface specifications required by a distributed object-management system. In this way, IDL lets a particular object implementation inform potential clients about the operations it offers and how these should be invoked.

IDL provides clients with a uniform set of semantics for all client interfaces in CORBA. A client can invoke operations via either the static or the dynamic client interfaces (presented later). In the former case, IDL specifications are compiled into client stubs and target-object skeletons. In the latter case, they are stored in an interface repository accessible through the dynamic invocation interface (see Figure 5).

IDL is independent of any general-purpose programming language but is intended to support different programming languages through convenient language mappings to CORBA objects. For example, from an object-oriented language such as C++ or Smalltalk, it might be desirable to view CORBA objects as programming-level objects rather than rely on a separate application

programming interface for access to CORBA objects. At present, CORBA defines a mapping only for C.

Static invocation interface. The stub routines compiled from IDL interface specifications support CORBA's static invocation interface. A client program uses a set of stub routines, each of which corresponds to a particular operation on a particular object. To invoke an operation on an object, the client calls the corresponding stub routine for the target object. The stub routine marshals the information required to execute the operation before calling on a transport mechanism (usually RPC) to deliver the request to the target object for execution.

Dynamic invocation interface. Using the dynamic invocation interface, a client names the request's target object and calls on the ORB core services to add the required arguments to the request. Once it constructs the request, the ORB core delivers it to an object adapter that parses the request before arranging for its execution. The dynamic invocation interface supports both synchronous and asynchronous requests.

Interface repository. Supporting the dynamic invocation interface is the interface repository (see Figure 5). The interface repository stores objects representing IDL information in a form used at runtime. On receipt of an application's request, a client typically interrogates the interface repository to determine the interfaces capable of satisfying the request — some of which might not have been available at the time the client code was compiled. On the basis of the information, the client might be able to use the dynamic invocation interface primitives to construct the argument list of a request to the selected target object.

In addition, both the static and dynamic invocation interfaces can use information stored in the interface repository to facilitate type checking of objects at runtime. The interface repository also provides a convenient place in the ORB for developers to stash additional information associated with interfaces to objects, including debugging information, stub and skeleton libraries, or routines facilitating convenient examination of objects.

The role of the CORBA interface repository suggests that it will be key to interoperability between different ORB implementations.

Object adapter. CORBA object adapters serve a dual purpose. First, they provide the main interface through which object implementations invoke the ORB core services. Second, they augment the basic CORBA object model by implementing support for richer object-modeling features. Thus, an object adapter provides a mapping from the various object models on which object implementations are

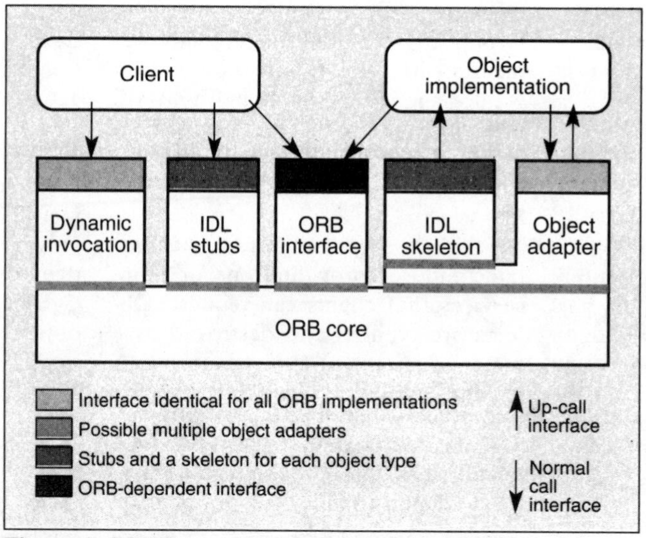

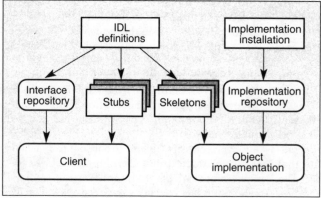

Figure 4. CORBA components and interfaces.[10]

Figure 5. CORBA interface and implementation repositories.[10]

based to the basic ORB core object model.

CORBA defines the *basic object adapter*, which is intended to be widely available and support a wide variety of common object implementations. The basic object adapter provides convenient interfaces to the following functions necessary to satisfy requests:

- activation and deactivation of object implementations when no implementation is available in memory to satisfy a request,
- generation and interpretation of object references,
- object-implementation storage and access control,
- authentication of client requests,
- registration of object implementations, and
- method invocation (via *skeletons* — interface-specific ORB components used by object adapters to pass requests to particular methods).

Because the ORB implementation might be required to accommodate a diverse range of object features — such as lifetimes, policies, and granularities — it might be necessary to provide multiple object adapters, each with interfaces to support objects with similar characteristics.

An object adapter can maintain its own state to accomplish its tasks. Furthermore, depending on a given ORB implementation's functionality, an object adapter might delegate some of its responsibilities to the underlying ORB core or to an object implementation (for example, in an object-oriented database-management system).

CORBA analysis. Despite the promise of the Object Management Group's initial effort to produce an industry standard for distributed object management systems, the CORBA specification is presently limited in a number of areas.[11]

Interoperability. The success of the ORB approach to distributed object management systems will depend greatly on the ease with which objects across different ORB implementations can call on one another's services. (Naming lies at the heart of the interoperability issue. CORBA does not specify how one ORB implementation should reveal its naming scheme to others for cross-ORB object interactions.)

Rymer[11] observes that the CORBA specification offers mere suggestions for ORB developers to follow to help achieve interoperability. However, suggestions fall short of specifications: Different vendor implementations will probably have proprietary communications and naming conventions. Initially, ORB users can become bound to a given vendor's ORB implementation. This is quite a significant limitation. If CORBA is to be effective for users trying to integrate diverse systems, ORB implementations must interoperate across a wide range of platforms.

Portability. A major challenge to the CORBA standards effort is to enable construction of distributed applications through the synthesis of existing objects. By supporting a mix of portable, vendor-independent object implementations across a number of ORB servers, CORBA would let developers take a plug-and-play approach to the implementation of new applications. The object adapter provides the CORBA interface for portable object implementations, but CORBA does not yet go far enough. The main players in CORBA development have agreed on the basic object adapter, a generic interface for all conventional object implementations. However, even they acknowledge its inadequacy for certain object implementations. CORBA clearly needs multiple object-adapter specifications, an issue that raises a couple of further concerns.

First, how many object-adapter definitions are required? In addition to the basic object-adapter specification, the CORBA specification suggests two further possible object adapters: a library object adapter (mainly used for objects having library implementations) and an object-oriented database adapter (which yields access to objects through an object-oriented database). Given that Object Management Group members want to stimulate rapid growth in the development of distributed object applications, it would be a hindrance to allow too many object-adapter specifications. Third-party vendors might hold back from developing their own ORB-compliant products while they determine which adapters win general marketplace acceptance. Furthermore, third-party application-development costs would grow as a result of having to port products across multiple interfaces.

Second, assuming that a small number

of object adapters is preferable, who should define them? Rymer[11] suggests that, rather than waiting for market forces to stimulate the production of object-adapter specifications (which could result in long delays), the Object Management Group members should take chief responsibility.

Dynamic applications. Although CORBA's dynamic invocation interface offers applications flexibility in discovering interfaces and invoking operations on objects supporting them, the specification describes the interface repository as a read-only service. Thus, additional interfaces cannot be included in the repository at runtime. Without this capability, the advantage of CORBA's dynamic invocation interface is significantly reduced.

Three stages. Although these issues will doubtlessly be addressed in due course, CORBA must overcome them to achieve marketplace acceptance. Rymer[11] has predicted three stages in the development of fully CORBA-compliant products:

(1) Proprietary ORB products that support much CORBA functionality but do not comply with the CORBA specification.
(2) ORB products that comply with either the static or dynamic invocation interfaces (but not both).
(3) CORBA-compliant products that implement both the static and dynamic invocation interfaces.

As witnessed by the abundance of emerging distributed systems standards and technology efforts, there is clear evidence of the evolution of today's client-server systems along the road to full object orientation. Hence, a major issue in distributed systems is identification of the minimal set of object technology required for interoperability in the growing universe of object-oriented systems.

While the evolution of object-oriented technology has not been entirely smooth, recently we have seen significant progress. An indicator of this progress is the convergence of views concerning the best approach to stimulate growth of object-oriented software products. Major computer vendors agree about the general architectural approach for distributed object-oriented software environments. Identification of a least common denominator or base set of object services has been a major factor.

Convergence on this approach has been no accident. Many organizations expert in object-oriented systems have closely cooperated. These include hardware and software vendors; industrial consortia including the Object Management Group, OSF, and the UK's Architecture Project Management; numerous academic institutions; and standards-related bodies, such as ISO, CCITT, and ANSI.

This least-common-denominator approach is evident in the development of CORBA, which appears well poised to become a de facto standard for emerging distributed object technologies. For example, a major component of the OSF Distributed Management Environment — the object services layer — is an enhanced implementation of CORBA. Furthermore, several major computer vendors are developing CORBA-compliant software. Also, the Harness consortium (which includes Architecture Project Management) plans to produce a CORBA-compliant implementation of ANSAware — the most significant embodiment to date of Open Distributed Processing technology. ∎

Acknowledgments

We thank Calvin Taylor of US West Advanced Technologies for his assistance in writing this article, and Joseph Boykin and Steven Gutfreund for their comments on an earlier version. Finally, we acknowledge the contributions of our late colleague Joseph Fitzgerald Jr.

References

1. J.R. Nicol et al., "Experiences with Accommodating Heterogeneity in a Large-Scale Telecommunications Infrastructure," *Proc. Third Symp. Experiences with Distributed and Multiprocessor Systems*, Usenix Assoc., Berkeley, Calif., 1992, pp. 233-247.

2. F. Manola et al., "Distributed Object Management," *Int'l J. Intelligent and Cooperative Information Systems*, Vol. 1, No. 1, Mar. 1992, pp. 5-42.

3. *Distributed Systems — Architecture and Implementation*, B.W. Lampson, M. Paul, and H.J. Siegert, eds., Springer-Verlag, Berlin, 1981.

4. G.I. Williamson and M. Azmoodeh, "The Application of Information Modeling in the Telecommunications Management Network," *British Telecom Technology J.*, Vol. 9, No. 3, July 1991, pp. 18-26.

5. J.K. Bennett, "Experiences with Distributed Smalltalk," *Software Practice and Experience*, Vol. 20, No. 2, Feb. 1990, pp. 157-180.

6. Open Software Foundation, *Introduction to OSF DCE*, Prentice Hall, Englewood Cliffs, N.J., 1992.

7. T. Lyons, *Network Computing System Tutorial*, Prentice Hall, Englewood Cliffs, N.J., 1991.

8. R.E. Schantz, R.H. Thomas, and G. Bono, "The Architecture of the Cronus Distributed Operating System," *Proc. IEEE Int'l Conf. Distributed Computing Systems*, IEEE CS Press, Los Alamitos, Calif., Order No. 697 (microfiche only), 1986, pp. 486-493.

9. B.M. Anderson and J.P. Flynn, "CASES: A System for Assessing Naval Warfighting Capability," *Proc. 1990 Symp. Command and Control Research*, Science Applications Int'l Corp., Report No. SAIC-90/1508, 1990.

10. Object Management Group and X/Open, "The Common Object Request Broker: Architecture and Specification," OMG Document No. 91.12.1 (Revision 1.1), OMG, Framingham, Mass., 1991.

11. J.R. Rymer, "Common Object Request Broker — OMG's New Standard for Distributed Object Management," *Network Monitor*, Vol. 6, No. 9, Sept. 1991, pp. 3-27.

C. Thomas Wilkes is a senior member of technical staff at GTE Laboratories, where he participates in the Distributed Computing Systems Project. His research involves the application of advanced distributed-systems technology to next-generation telecommunications networks. From 1987 to 1991, Wilkes was an assistant professor of computer science at the University of Massachusetts at Lowell. At the Georgia Institute of Technology, he participated in the Clouds Distributed Object-Based Operating System Project, for which he designed and implemented the Aeolus language for distributed, fault-tolerant programming.

Wilkes received his BS in physics in 1979 and his MS and PhD in information and computer science from the Georgia Institute of Technology in 1982 and 1987. He is a member of IEEE, IEEE Computer Society, and ACM, and is treasurer of the IEEE Computer Society Technical Activities Board.

Frank A. Manola is a principal member of technical staff at GTE Laboratories and is the principal investigator of the Distributed Object Management Project. His research interests include distributed and multimedia object technology, object-database technology, and data security. Manola is a member of the X3 Technical Subcommittee X3H7 on Object Information Management. From 1978 to 1987, Manola was a senior computer scientist at Computer Corporation of America. He has also worked at the Naval Research Laboratory in Washington, D.C.

Manola received his BS in civil engineering from Duke University in 1966 and his MSE in computer science from the University of Pennsylvania in 1971. He is a member of IEEE, IEEE Computer Society, and ACM.

John R. Nicol is a senior member of technical staff at GTE Laboratories and is the principal investigator of the Distributed Multimedia Applications Project. His research interests include distributed systems, operating systems, multimedia, and computer-supported collaborative work. Nicol is also vice chair of the X3 Technical Subcommittee X3T3 on Open Distributed Processing. From 1986 to 1990, Nicol was a lecturer of computer science at Lancaster University in the UK. While at Lancaster, he codesigned the Cosmos Distributed Software Engineering Environment and later managed the Zenith Distributed Object Management Project.

Nicol received a BSc from the University of Strathclyde in 1983 and a PhD from Lancaster University in 1986, both in computer science. He is a member of IEEE, IEEE Computer Society, and ACM.

Readers can reach the authors at GTE Laboratories Inc., Computer and Intelligent Systems Laboratory, 40 Sylvan Road, Waltham, MA 02254. Their Internet addresses are {nicol, ctwilkes, fmanola}@gte.com.

Chapter 6

Object-Oriented Software Engineering System Architecture

Design and Construction of a Software Engineering Environment: Experiences with Eiffel

Chris Bosch, Hassan Gomaa, and Larry Kerschberg

Introduction

While performing research in domain modeling and reuse at George Mason University's Center for Software Systems Engineering, we have embarked on designing and constructing a software engineering environment to support our domain-modeling method (8, 9, 10). This environment consists of a suite of tools ranging from graphical editors to knowledge-based systems as well as an underlying object repository that serves as the common information store for these tools.

Object-oriented technology is generally viewed as a key technology enabling the integration of tools in such an environment. In this chapter we describe our use of a specific object-oriented technology —the development environment and reuse libraries provided by Interactive Software Engineering Inc. for the Eiffel object-oriented language — to design and construct our environment.[1] By describing our experiences with Eiffel, we hope to illustrate the utility of features of the Eiffel language such as genericity, multiple inheritance, encapsulation of foreignlanguage procedures, and assertions which form invariants on the state of an object as well as pre- and post-conditions on the execution of routines. Further, we will comment on tools supporting the development of object-oriented systems with the goal of identifying profitable avenues of research. With these goals in mind, let us sketch the subject covered here.

First we present the architecture of an integrated software engineering environment which guided our design and construction efforts, following which we explain why we chose to develop this environment in Eiffel. Next, we describe our work creating a pivotal element of the environment — the object repository — which serves as the common store for information produced by the environment's tools. We then describe our first steps towards constructing tools, using Eiffel to encapsulate a user interface management system as well as an expert system shell. In a final section we summarize our development experiences and itemize the lessons we learned.

Architecture of an integrated CASE environment

Among the greatest challenges facing the CASE community, Forte and Norman write, is the "need for tighter integration among tools" (6). Figure 1 depicts the architecture for an integrated software engineering environment that guided our work in design and construction. This architecture provides for integrating tools on two levels. At the presentation level this architecture integrates the tools by bringing each of their interfaces to rely upon one set of user-interface services. At the data level the tools are integrated by having each of them access and manipulate one set of objects stored persistently in an object repository.

We can consider this architecture to be a simplified version of the reference

---

[1]Specifically, we discuss our experiences with Release 2.3 of Interactive Software Engineering's development environment and reuse libraries for Eiffel (14, 16, 17). As described in (15), Release 3 is now the official version.

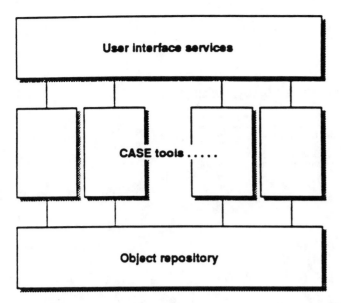

Figure 1. Architecture of an integrated CASE environment

model for integrated software engineering environments being developed by the National Institute for Standards and Technology (NIST) and the European Computer Manufacturers Association (ECMA). Ours shares that model's integration at the data and presentation levels but lacks that model's process-management and messaging services, which provide for integration at the control level. For a brief description of the NIST/ECMA reference model, see (5), and for full specification of that model, see (18).

At both of these levels, object-oriented technology can make it possible to integrate the CASE tools. Object-oriented technology has long been recognized as a way to facilitate rapid development of graphical user interfaces (21), and today a great number of interface-management systems are commercially available. More recently, object-oriented database-management systems have been proposed as a way of satisfying the complex data-management needs of environments supporting computer-aided design, computer-aided software engineering, distributed cooperative computing, and other applications (1, 12). For these reasons we chose to employ object-oriented technology in designing and constructing our software engineering environment.

Choosing Eiffel

Our primary goals in developing this environment were to explore and then demonstrate our domain-modeling method. Having decided to employ ob-

ject-oriented technology, we were faced with choosing between two object-oriented development environments then available at George Mason University's Center for Software Systems Engineering:

One was the GemStone object-oriented database management system and associated development tools provided by the Servio-Logic Corporation (4).

The second choice was the development environment and reuse libraries provided by Interactive Software Engineering, Inc. for the Eiffel object-oriented language (14, 16, 17). Ultimately, we chose to pursue development with Eiffel because we believed features in that language such as genericity, multiple inheritance, and assertions would allow us to model our domain-modeling method more closely than we could with GemStone's language for defining and manipulating data and formulating queries (OPAL). That language, a Smalltalk derivative, supports only single inheritance and provides for neither assertions nor specifying generic classes.

In choosing to pursue development with Eiffel, though, we had to forgo GemStone's data-management services, such as transaction management and concurrency, security, recovery, and an interpreted query language—a tradeoff we found acceptable because our work was exploratory.

Developing the object repository

In the earliest stages of our research on domain modeling, we knew that our

method would rely upon multiple graphical views to specify a domain model. Generally, graphical specification techniques such as inheritance graphs, state-transition diagrams, object-communication diagrams, and aggregation hierarchies are modeled as directed graphs or trees. To persistently store objects representing graphical specifications in our environment's object repository, that repository's schema should include classes representing directed graphs and trees.

Examining the Eiffel library of reusable classes to see what fundamental data structures it provided, we learned that although this library does provide generic classes representing lists, sets, stacks, queues, and trees (17), classes representing directed graphs are absent. With these classes we began developing the object repository's schema; we next illustrate how we used genericity and assertions in specifying these classes.

Generic graphs. A directed graph is simply a collection of nodes and arcs. Associated with each node are two sets of arcs, the *arc set in* and the *arc set out*. Likewise, each arc has a *source node* and a *sink node*. As directed graphs are applied in modeling techniques, a node typically includes something (a reference to a real-world entity or the state associated with some object) and arcs typically have a label (a reference to a data structure, a message, a transition between states). Without knowing precisely which type of object each node will include and which type of label each arc will have, it was still possible to write classes defining nodes and arcs using formal generic parameters for those classes, as provided by Eiffel.

Figure 2 is a partial interface for the class we wrote defining nodes, and Figure 3 is a complete interface for the class we wrote defining arcs.[2]

Each of these classes has two formal generic parameters: *TN*, which represents the type of the node's contents, and; *TA*, which represents the type of an arc's label. Classes which inherit from these classes or which make use of their services as clients may instantiate these two formal generic parameters to specify the type of objects a node will include and the type of

---

[2] The class interfaces in this chapter were generated from Eiffel source code with the "short" documentation tool provided with the Interactive Software Engineering (ISE), Inc. development environment for Eiffel.

objects with which arcs will be labeled.

Class *NODE* exports to its clients three attributes, two procedures, and nine functions. Of the three attributes, two reference the sets of arcs coming in to and going out from the node. The third attribute references the node's contents. The two procedures exported by class *NODE* allow clients of this class to create new nodes and to update the contents of a node. Of the functions exported by class *NODE*, two return integers representing the number of arcs coming in to and going out from the node. Three boolean-valued functions can be used to determine whether the node is connected to other nodes, is a source node, or is a sink node. The remaining functions can be used to determine the sets of nodes preceding or succeeding a node in a directed graph.

Notice in the interface to class *NODE* (Figure 2) that assertions are used to establish invariants on the state of objects belonging to this class as well as postconditions on the execution of routines applied to such objects. The invariant assertions for class *NODE*, included in a clause beginning with the keyword **invariant**, state that its *arc_set_in* and *arc_set_out* attributes will never include a void reference; they will always refer to a set of arcs. The postcondition to the *Create* procedure, included in a clause beginning with the keyword **ensure**, states that the sets of arcs coming in to and going out from a newly created node will be empty.

Class *ARC* exports to its clients three attributes and two procedures. Of the three attributes, two reference the arc's source and sink nodes, and the third references the arc's label. The two procedures exported by class *ARC* allow its clients to create new arcs and to update an arc's label. The interface to class *ARC* (Figure 3) includes an example of using assertions to establish preconditions on the execution of routines applied to objects in this class. Its *Create* procedure has a precondition, included in the clause beginning with the keyword **require**, which prevents its execution if either of its input arguments includes a void reference.

We found Eiffel's provision for using assertions in **require**, **ensure**, and **invariant** clauses as described above to be quite useful during our design efforts. It was a simple, declarative way of specifying the data semantics for classes of objects to be stored in the object repository. When we began implementing tools for accessing and manipulating information stored in

---

class interface *NODE* [*TN, TA*] **exported features**

> *arc_set_in, contents, arc_set_out, update_contents,*
> *in_degree, out_degree, is_connected, is_source, is_sink,*
> *immediate_predecessors, immediate_successors, all_predecessors,*
> *all_successors*

feature specification

> *arc_set_in: INDEXED_SET* [*ARC* [*TN, TA*]]
> > — The set of all arcs entering the node.
>
> *contents: TN*
> > — Contents of the node.
>
> *arc_set_out:* **like** *arc_set_in*
> > — The set of all arcs leaving the node.
>
> *Create*
> > — Create a node with no arcs.
> >
> > **ensure**
> > > *arc_set_in.empty;*
> > > *arc_set_out.empty*
>
> *update_contents* (*c:* **like** *contents*)
> > — Update contents of node with c.
> >
> > **ensure**
> > > *contents = c*
>
> *in_degree: INTEGER*
> > — Number of arcs coming in to the node.
> >
> > **ensure**
> > > Result = arc_set_in.count
> >
> > $\vdots$

invariant

> **not** *arc_set_in.Void;*
> **not** *arc_set_out.Void*

end interface — class *NODE*

Figure 2. Partial interface for class NODE

---

class interface *ARC* [*TN, TA*] **exported features**

> *source, label, sink, update_label*

feature specification
> *source: NODE* [*TN, TA*]
> > — Node that is the source of the arc.
>
> *label: TA*
> > — Label of the arc.
>
> *sink:* **like** *source*
> > — Node that is the sink of the arc.
>
> *Create* (*src:* **like** *source, snk:* **like** *sink*)
> > — Create an arc and assign values to its
> > — source and sink attributes.
> >
> > **require**
> > > **not** *src.Void;*
> > > **not** *snk.Void*
> >
> > **ensure**
> > > *source = src;*
> > > *sink = snk*
>
> *update_label* (*l:* **like** *label*)
> > — Update the value of the arcs label attribute.
> >
> > **ensure**
> > > *label = l*

invariant

> **not** *source.Void;*
> **not** *sink.Void*

Figure 3. Interface for class ARC

Figure 4. Partial interface for class DAG

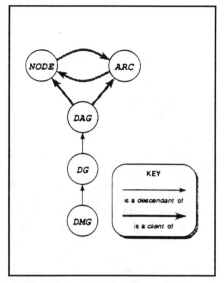

Figure 5. Structural relationships among classes defining directed graphs

the object repository, we again found Eiffel's provision for using assertions useful as a way of ensuring that information's semantic integrity.

Once we had written classes defining nodes and arcs, we set about writing classes defining directed graphs. A *directed multigraph* is a set of nodes with no restrictions on the number of arcs connecting any two nodes and no restrictions on the presence of cycles in the graph. A *directed graph* still has no restrictions on the presence of cycles in the graph, but no node can have more than one arc going to any other node. A *directed acyclic graph* is additionally restricted in that the graph may have no cycles.

To model these three types of directed graphs, we began by writing a class *DAG* representing directed acyclic graphs. Figure 4 depicts a partial interface for this class, which exports to its clients three attributes, five procedures, and eight functions. The attributes exported by class *DAG* include references to the set of nodes defining the graph, the last node added to the graph, and the last arc added to the graph. The procedures exported by class *DAG* allow clients to create new graphs as well as to add and remove nodes and arcs. Its exported functions tell clients the number of nodes in the graph, which node includes a specific item, which of its nodes are sources and which are sinks, whether it is strongly or weakly connected, and whether an arc or a path lies between two specified nodes.

The other two types of directed graphs differ from the directed acyclic graph only in that arcs can be added to them under conditions in which it would not be possible to add arcs to a directed acyclic graph. For example, we can add an arc to a regular directed graph that will introduce a cycle, but it is not possible to add such an arc to a directed acyclic graph. Otherwise, regular directed graphs and directed multigraphs have the same structure and require the same functions and procedures as those we defined for class *DAG*.

To express the similarity in structure and behavior between directed acyclic graphs and regular directed graphs, we defined a class *DG* (representing directed graphs) that inherits from class *DAG*. So that we could add arcs introducing cycles to the graph, we redefined the *add_arc* procedure and weakened the precondition to it, as shown here.

```
add_arc (f, t: NODE [TN, TA])
        --Add an arc from node f to node t
        --and update the last_added_arc
        --attribute with the new arc.
    require
        not arc_exists(f,t)
    ensure
        f.out_degree = old f. out_degree + 1
        t.in_degree = old f.in_degree + 1
```

To express the similarity in structure and behavior between directed graphs and directed multigraphs, we defined a class *DMG* (representing directed multigraphs), which inherits from class *DG*. To add arcs between a source and a sink that are already connected by an arc, we again redefined the *add_arc* procedure and weakened the pre-condition to it, as shown here.

add_arc (f, t: NODE [TN, TA])
    — Add an arc from node *f* to node *t*
    — and update the *last_added_arc*
    — attribute with the new arc.
  ensure
    f.out_degree = **old** *f.out_degree* + 1;
    t.in_degree = **old** *t.in_degree* + 1

Figure 5 depicts overall the structural relationships among the five classes we first wrote for our object repository. In this and subsequent diagrams, thin black arrows represent *inheritance* relationships between classes (pointing from a descendant class to a parent class) and thick gray arrows represent *client* relationships between classes (pointing from a client class to its supplier class). A client relationship connects class *NODE* and class *ARC* because each node has an arc set in and an arc set out. A client relationship connects class *ARC* and class *NODE* because each arc has a source node and a sink node. Class DAG is a client of both class *NODE* and class *ARC* because of its procedures for adding and deleting nodes and arcs, and other connections. As we have seen, class *DMG* inherits from class *DG*, which itself inherits from class *DAG* .

It may seem counterintuitive to say that the class of directed acyclic graphs is a superclass of the class defining regular directed graphs and that the class defining regular directed graphs is a superclass of the class defining directed multigraphs. In fact, our initial conceptualization of these classes led us to specify class *DMG* as the parent class to class *DG*, which in turn would be the parent class for class *DAG*. We found, however, that with this inheritance structure it was not possible to specify the semantics for the *add_arc* procedure in a manner consistent with Eiffel's rule for redefining assertions, as formulated by Meyer and shown here (13).

Rule for redefining assertions:

Let *r* be a routine in a class *A*, and *s* a redefinition of *r* in a descendant of *A*, or an effective definition of *r* if *r* was deferred. Then pre_s must be weaker than or equal to pre_r, and $post_s$ must be stronger than or equal to $post_r$.

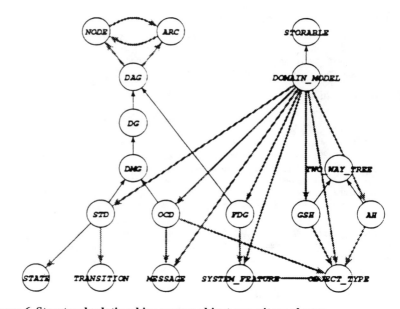

Figure 6. Structural relationships among object-repository classes

The rule for redefining assertions guarantees that any operation that may be applied to an instance of some class may also be applied to instances of any subclasses of that class. The definitions of classes *DAG*, *DG*, and *DMG* presented in this chapter are in accordance with this rule. While we were developing these classes we recognized how useful features of the Eiffel language were, such as assertions and formal generic parameters, and, encouraged by this initial development, we proceeded with design and construction of our object repository.

Specific graphic formalisms

We have said that early in our research on domain modeling we knew our method would rely upon multiple graphical views as a way to specify a domain model. As the research progressed, we identified a number of graphic formalisms, each of which would provide a different view into our overall domain model. An *aggregation hierarchy* captures the IS_PART_OF relationship that may connect object types within the application domain. A *generalization/specialization hierarchy* similarly describes the IS_A relationship between object types. An *object-communication diagram* portrays possible paths for communication among object types, and *state-transition diagrams* describe the valid states and transitions between states associated with an object type. A *feature-dependency graph* represents dependencies among the features (functional capabilities) of target systems within the application domain.

To represent these five specific graphic formalisms in the object repository's schema, we defined five new classes, each of which inherits most of its structure and behavior from an appropriate generic class selected from among those we wrote defining directed graphs or from those in the Eiffel library defining trees. For example, class *OCD* (representing object-communication diagrams) and class *STD* (representing state-transition diagrams) both inherit from class *DMG* because the two types of diagram are simply specialized forms of directed multigraphs. Similarly, class *FDG* (representing feature-dependency graphs) inherits from class *DAG* because our domain-modeling method does not permit cycles in a feature-dependency graph Class *AH* (representing aggregation hierarchies) and class *GSH* (representing generalization/specialization hierarchies) inherit from class *TWO_WAY_TREE*, which is part of the Eiffel library of reusable classes (17).

When inheriting from these generic classes, we instantiated their formal generic parameters so that the resulting classes would no longer be generic. For example, nodes in an object-communication diagram will include instances of class *OBJECT_TYPE* and arcs will be labeled with instances of class *MESSAGE*. Nodes in a state-transition diagram will include instances of class

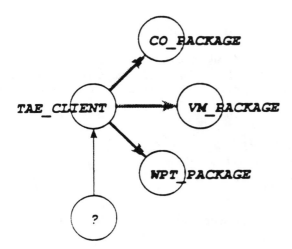

STATE and arcs will be labeled with instances of class *TRANSITION*. Nodes in a feature-dependency graph will include instances of class *SYSTEM_FEATURE* but its arcs will be unlabeled, and nodes in the aggregation and generalization/specialization hierarchies will include instances of class *OBJECT_TYPE*. Figure 6 presents the structural relationships among these classes. Again in this diagram, thin black arrows represent inheritance relationships and thick gray arrows represent client relationships.

At first, the classes *OBJECT_TYPE, MESSAGE, STATE, TRANSITION,* and *SYSTEM_FEATURE* shown in Figure 6 existed in name only. We identified the need for these classes while defining the specific graphic formalisms used in our domain-modeling method, but did not specify any operations, properties, or constraints for them. As we have continued to develop our domain-modeling method, we have elaborated the definition of these classes, and in doing so, identified yet more classes of objects to be included in the schema of our object repository.

Eventually we defined a class *DO-MAIN_MODEL* that either directly or indirectly aggregates all other classes forming the schema of our object repository (also shown in Figure 6). So that we could persistently store objects representing domain models, this class inherits from class *STORABLE*, which is defined as part of the Eiffel library of reusable classes (17). Having reached the stage at which we could create and persistently store objects representing domain models, we began to design and construct tools for accessing and manipulating information stored in the object repository.

Laying the foundation for constructing tools

Among the first steps we took in designing and constructing tools for accessing and manipulating information stored in the object repository was to encapsulate a user-interface management system (UIMS) as well as an expert system tool. The UIMS we have encapsulated is the Transportable Applications Environment (TAE) Plus tool developed by NASA's Goddard Space Flight Center (22). The expert system tool we have encapsulated is the C Language Integrated Production System (CLIPS) developed by the Artificial Intelligence Section at NASA/Johnson Space Center (2). Both of these software products are distributed through NASA's distribution center, COSMIC. In subsequent sections we discuss how we have used Eiffel's mechanism for referencing external routines to encapsulate the functionality of these two software products.

Encapsulating TAE Plus

NASA's Goddard Space Flight Center developed the Transportable Applications Environment (TAE) Plus system for user interface development and management in response to the need for "an integrated software environment that allows interactive prototyping and development of user interfaces, as well as management of the user interface within the operational domain" (22).

The target platform for an application with an interface developed with TAE Plus is one of the many current graphics workstations capable of running X-Windows. We envisioned that tools for accessing and manipulating information stored in our object repository would require sophisticated graphical user interfaces like those possible in the X-Windows environment. Although ISE's development environment for Eiffel did provide a reuse library of classes for creating scrollable windows, pop-up menus, and the like that will operate in an X-Windows environment, it did not provide the separation between specifying the user interface and developing the application that allows for rapid prototyping. As a result, changing the interface of an application developed with the Eiffel library of graphics classes would require changing source code and potentially lengthy recompilations. For that and other reasons we chose to encapsulate the functions provided by TAE Plus within Eiffel classes and to develop user interfaces for our tools with the TAE Plus WorkBench.

TAE Plus provides three packages of C routines that may be called from any application that is to have an interface developed with the TAE WorkBench.

1. The Collection (Co) package
2. The Variable Manipulation (Vm) Package
3. The Window Programming Tools (Wpt) package

We encapsulated each of these packages in its own Eiffel class and exported their features to the class *TAE_CLIENT*. Any class in an application program that is to interact with the user through an interface developed with TAE's WorkBench can access the services provided by TAE's three packages of C routines by inheriting from class *TAE_CLIENT*, as shown in Figure 7. It is easy enough to say that these classes encapsulate the services provided by TAE Plus, but it is worth examining in detail just one of these classes to see how to do so and to discuss the problems that may arise while encapsulating external routines.

Figure 8 shows a partial interface for class *WPT_PACKAGE*. This class exports sixteen routines to its clients—we show how three of these routines are packaged. Ideally, one encapsulates a package of C routines by defining an Eiffel class corresponding to that package, writing one Eiffel routine for each C routine, listing the C routine as **external** within implementation of the Eiffel routine, and then calling the C routine as appropriate within the body of the Eiffel routine. An example of this ideal appears when we implement the *begin_wait* procedure, as shown here.

```
begin_wait(panelId: INTEGER) is
— Puts up a visual indication to the
— user that the program is busy.

    external
      Wpt_BeginWait
          name "Wpt_BeginWait"
          language "C"
    do
      Wpt_BeginWait(panelId);
    end; — begin_wait
```

In our experience with TAE Plus, however, we found that encapsulating a package of C routines within an Eiffel class is not necessarily straightforward.

One minor problem that we had to be aware of while encapsulating these routines was that the physical representation of strings in C differs from that in Eiffel. We can solve this problem with two routines associated with class *STRING*, as defined in the Eiffel library of reusable classes (17, pp. 31-33). The *from_c* procedure defined for class *STRING* takes an integer argument representing a C string, and, when applied to an Eiffel string, converts that string to the C string's equivalent. The *to_c* function defined for class STRING, when applied to an Eiffel string, returns an integer representing the equivalent C string. An example of using the *to_c* function appears in the implementation of the *display _message* procedure shown here.

```
display_message(panelId: INTEGER,
              message: STRING) is
— Displays 'message' for panel with
— Id 'panelId' and waits for the
— user to acknowledge the message.

    external
      Wpt_PanelMessage
        name "Wpt_PanelMessage"
        language "C"
    do
      Wpt_PanelMessage(panelId,
                  message.to_c);
    end; — display_message
```

Another minor problem we struck while encapsulating these routines was that some of the C routines in the three TAE Plus packages required input arguments for which Eiffel had no equivalent.

---

class interface *WPT_PACKAGE* exported features

> *begin_wait, close_items, end_wait, initialize, new_panel, next_event, erase_panel, display_message, reset_panel, reject_parameter, update_parameter, update_view, set_integer, set_real, set_string, set_no_value*

feature specification

> *begin_wait (panelId: INTEGER)*
> — Puts up a visual indication to the user
> — that the program is busy.
>   ⋮
> *initialize*
> — Initializes the window system for
> — application use.
>
>   ⋮
>
> *display_message (panelId: INTEGER, message: STRING)*
> — Displays *message* for panel with Id panelId and
> — waits for the user to acknowledge the message.

end interface — class *WPT_PACKAGE*

Figure 8. Partial interface for class WPT_PACKAGE

For example, TAE Plus' Wpt__Init routine required a null pointer as an input argument, which could not be generated by Eiffel. To get around this complication we wrote a C routine that returned a null pointer and then referred to that external routine when required. Here is an example in the implementation of the initialize procedure:

```
initialize is
— Initializes the window system
— for application use.

    external
      NullPointer: INTEGER
          name "NullPointer"
          language "C";
      Wpt_Init
          name "Wpt_Init"
          language "C"
    do
      Wpt_Init(NullPointer);
    end; — initialize
```

A third problem we ran into while encapsulating these routines was that some of the C routines in the three TAE Plus packages passed relevant output back out through their argument lists instead of returning them as conventional function

values. To get around this problem, we again had to write C routines that would extract the relevant results from the argument list and then return them as conventional function values.

A final problem were the multiply defined symbolic names between the TAE Plus packages of routines and the routines forming the Eiffel runtime system. These multiply defined names initially prevented the Eiffel system-assembly tool from assembling an executable program when that program was to make use of the services provided by the classes encapsulating TAE Plus. After consulting with Interactive Software Engineering (ISE), Inc., we got around this block by modifying and rebuilding the Eiffel runtime system.

Although encapsulating the three packages of C routines provided by TAE Plus was not entirely straightforward, it has certainly proved to be worth the effort as we have further developed tools within our software engineering environment. Using the TAE Plus Work-Bench to create interfaces to our tools has saved much effort that we expect would have been required to directly apply the Eiffel library of graphics classes provided by ISE.

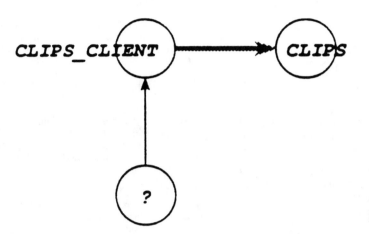

Figure 9. Accessing services provided by CLIPS

Encapsulating CLIPS

Having encapsulated the TAE Plus user-interface management system, we used Eiffel to encapsulate the expert system tool known as CLIPS. The Artificial Intelligence Section at NASA/Johnson Space Center developed the C Language Integrated Production System (CLIPS) to provide a highly portable, low-cost expert system tool easy to integrate with external systems (2). The Eiffel language provides no rule-based processing of information, but does have a way of referencing external routines written in C, as we have shown. Thus, when we sought knowledge-based tools that could access and manipulate information stored in our object repository, an obvious solution was to encapsulate the functions provided by CLIPS within an Eiffel class.

Encapsulating the CLIPS C routines presented no problems that we had not already encountered in encapsulating TAE Plus. We have defined a class *CLIPS* that encapsulates these routines and exports its features to class *CLIPS_CLIENT*. Any class in an application program requiring rule-based processing of information can access the services provided by CLIPS by inheriting from class *CLIPS_CLIENT*, as shown in Figure 9.

Lessons learned

Once we had laid the foundation for constructing tools by encapsulating the TAE Plus user-interface management system and the CLIPS expert system tool, we went on to create tools for our software engineering environment. As we continue work on this environment we find we have learned many lessons about constructing object-oriented systems in Eiffel.

Designing and constructing the object repository continues to be highly iterative. The class definitions forming the object repository's schema continually evolve as we refine our domain-modeling method. Gibbs et al. (7) detail issues in such class evolution in object-oriented systems and describe approaches for improving a collection of classes, such as *class tailoring, class surgery, class versioning*, and *class reorganization*. We next discuss what we have learned about constructing object-oriented systems in Eiffel, applying these four approaches to improve a collection of classes.

Class tailoring, as described by Gibbs et al., involves specializing existing classes —specialization that may require redefining inherited properties and operations (7). Here we learned that Eiffel provides a disciplined approach to class tailoring with its rule for redefining *assertions*, ensuring that the semantics of redefined operations are not changed in a manner inconsistent with the principle of dynamic binding. Its *type-redefinition rule* states that "an attribute, a function result, or a formal routine argument declared in a class may be redeclared with a new type in a descendant class, provided the new type conforms to the original one" (13). Our redefinition of the

add_arc procedure for classes *DG* and *DMG* is just one example of how we used class tailoring while we developed the object repository. Other examples include specializing generic classes that represent graphs and trees into classes representing specific graphic formalisms.

Class surgery, as described by Gibbs et al., involves more extensive changes than simply specializing classes (7). Changes possible under class surgery may involve adding, deleting, or modifying operations, properties, or constraints to classes as well as adding classes to, deleting classes from, or otherwise modifying the inheritance structure. Here we learned that ISE's development environment for Eiffel provides a systematic approach to class surgery by applying its *system-assembly tool*, which analyzes a collection of classes and determines where changes have been made and whether inconsistencies have been introduced into the collection. While we were developing the object repository, applying this tool gave us confidence that the definition for each constituent class in the object repository's schema was consistent with the definition of other classes in the schema.

Class versioning, as presented by Gibbs et al., is a technique for managing class development and evolution that "enables programmers to try different paths when modeling complex application domains and to record the history of class modifications during the design process" (7). We found that ISE's development environment for Eiffel provides no support for class versioning—something that we could have used extensively while developing the object repository. Because our design and construction of that repository proceeded concurrently with efforts to define our domain-modeling method, we often found that we wanted to test new concepts but retain previous implementations in case our new ideas didn't work out. Without tool support for class versioning, such backtracking could not be easily accomplished. Research directed at the problem of schema evolution in object-oriented databases has touched on the problem of class versioning (3, 11, 19, 20); but this subject is one in which research may still be profitably pursued.

The Gibbs et al. discussion of class reorganization deals mainly with "tools that automatically restructure a class collection and suggest alternative designs" (7, p. 101). Again, ISE's development environment for Eiffel provides no automatic tools for reorganizing classes. In our work on the object repository we manually reorganized the collection of classes more than once. For example, during its development we found that we had many classes with an attribute named *identifier* and a corresponding procedure named *update_identifier*. Similarly, we had many classes with an attribute named *annotation* and a corresponding procedure named *update_annotation*. To avoid replicating these features among many classes, we created two new classes of objects, one called *IDENTIFIED_OBJECT* and another called *ANNOTATED_OBJECT*. The classes in our object repository's schema that previously had features named *identifier*, *annotation*, *update_identifier*, and/or *update_annotation* now inherit from one or both of these classes. Because Eiffel supports multiple inheritance, this class reorganization was possible and we have been able to more closely model the abstractions in our domain- modeling method.

We learned another vital lesson about constructing object-oriented systems in Eiffel while developing the object repository and laying the foundation for constructing tools. Encapsulating external C routines in Eiffel is not necessarily a straightforward proposition. We found it necessary to perform data conversion on the input to and output from routines, to write additional C routines as a way of solving other input and output problems, and eventually to modify and rebuild the Eiffel runtime system. Even though the act of encapsulating external C routines in Eiffel was not entirely straightforward, we feel that the problems were to be expected and that the results have proved to be well worth the effort as we pursue further development of tools in our software engineering environment.

Acknowledgments

The authors acknowledge the support provided for this work by NASA/Goddard Space Flight Center's Automated Technology Section (Code 522.3) under the Code R research program as well as by the Virginia Center for Innovative Technology. Thanks to Bertrand Meyer of Interactive Software Engineering (ISE), Inc. for reminding us of the significance of Eiffel's rule for redefining assertions during a visit to GMU in Fall 1990. Thanks also to Vince Kraemer of ISE for technical support provided during our development efforts. Finally, we acknowledge the contributions of Liz O'Hara-Schettino, Vijayan Sugumaran, Iraj Tavakoli, and Fatma Dandashi in other aspects of our domain-modeling research.

References

1. Ahmed, S., et al. Object-oriented database management systems for engineering: A comparison. *Journal of Object-Oriented Programming*, 5(3) (June 1992), pp. 27-43.

2. Artificial Intelligence Section, Lyndon B. Johnson Space Center, *CLIPS Reference Manual*. May 1989.

3. Björnerstedt, A., and C. Hulten. Version control in an object-oriented architecture. In W. Kim and F. H. Lochovsky, eds., *Object-Oriented Concepts, Databases, and Applications*. New York: ACM Press, 1989, pp. 451-485.

4. Bretl, Robert, et al. The GemStone data management system. In W. Kim and F. H. Lochovsky, eds., *Object-Oriented Concepts, Databases, and Applications*. New York: ACM Press, 1989, pp. 83-308.

5. Chen, M., and R. J. Norman. *A framework for integrated CASE*. IEEE Software, vol. 9, no. 2 (March 1992), pp. 18-22.

6. Forte, G., and R. J. Norman. A self-assessment by the software engineering community. *Communications of the ACM*, vol. 5, no. 4 (April 1992), pp. 28-32.

7. Gibbs, S., et al. Class management for software communities. *Communications of the ACM*, vol. 33, no. 9 (September 1990), pp. 90-103.

8. Gomaa, H. An object-oriented domain analysis and modeling method for software reuse. In *Proceedings of the Hawaii International Conference on Systems Sciences* (January 1992).

9. Gomaa, H., and L. Kerschberg. An evolutionary domain life cycle model for domain modeling and target system generation. In *Proceedings of the Workshop on Domain Modeling for Software Engineering*, ICSE '91 (May 1991).

10. Gomaa, H., L. Kerschberg, and R. Fairley. Towards an evolutionary domain life cycle model. In *Proceedings of the Workshop on Domain Modeling for Software Engineering*, OOPSLA '89 (October 1989).

11. Kim, W., and H. T. Chou. Versions of schema for object-oriented databases. In *VLDB '88* (1988), pp. 148-159.

12. Loomis, M. E. S. Object databaseæintegrator for PCTE. *Journal of Object-Oriented Programming*, vol. 5, no. 2 (May 1992), pp. 53-57.

13. Meyer, Bertrand. *Object-Oriented Software Construction*. Englewood Cliffs, N.J.: Prentice-Hall, 1988.

14. Meyer, B. Eiffel: The language. *Technical Report TR-EI-17/RM, Interactive Software Engineering*, Inc., 270 Storke Road, Suite 7, Goleta, CA 93117, December 1989.

15. Meyer, B. Eiffel: *The Language*. Englewood Cliffs, N.J.: Prentice-Hall, 1992.

16. Meyer, B., et al. Eiffel: The environment. *Technical Report R-EI5/UM*, Interactive Software Engineering, Inc., 270 Storke Road, Suite 7, Goleta, CA 93117, October 1990.

17. Meyer, B., and J.-M. Nerson. Eiffel: The libraries. *Technical Report TR-EI-7/LI*, Interactive Software Engineering, Inc., 270 Storke Road, Suite 7, Goleta, CA 93117, October 1990.

18. National Institute of Standards and Technology, Gaithersburg, MD. *Reference Model for Frameworks of Software Engineering Environments*, Draft Version 1.5, 1991.

19. Skarra, A., and S. Zdonik. *The management of changing types in an object-oriented database*. In OOPSLA '86, 1986.

20. Skarra, A. H., and S. B. Zdonik. Type evolution in an object-oriented database. In B. Shriver and P. Wegner, eds., *Research Directions in Object-Oriented Programming*. Cambridge, Mass.: MIT Press, 1987, pp. 393-415.

21. Smith, R., P. Barth, and R. Young. A substrate for object-oriented interface design. In B. Shriver and P. Wegner, eds., *Research Directions in Object-Oriented Programming*. Cambridge: MIT Press, 1987, pp. 253-315.

22. Szczur, Martha R. A user interface development tool for space science systems. *Paper presented at the AIAA/NASA Symposium on Space Information Systems*, September 1990.

Part 3

Object-Oriented Applications

Chapter 7

Real-Time System Applications

An Object-Oriented Real-Time Programming Language

Yutaka Ishikawa, MITI Electrotechnical Laboratory

Hideyuki Tokuda and Clifford W. Mercer, Carnegie Mellon University

Reprinted from *Computer*, October 1992, pp. 66–73.
Copyright © 1992 by The Institute of Electrical and
Electronics Engineers, Inc. All rights reserved.

The demand for real-time systems increases with the demand for time-critical applications such as multimedia, robotics, factory automation, telecommunication, and air traffic control. Traditional programming languages do not support real-time systems development. They have neither the analytical techniques for modeling systems accurately nor the explicit specifications for timing constraints.

By providing high-level abstractions of program modules, the object-oriented paradigm makes it easier to design and develop applications. However, the object-oriented model and its implementing languages typically offer no more support for real-time programming than traditional languages do.

We have developed an extended object-oriented model — the real-time object model. It encapsulates rigid timing constraints in an object. We have also designed and implemented RTC++, a programming language that extends C++ on the basis of the real-time object model.

Basic issues

Schedulability analysis. A system is said to be *schedulable* if it meets all deadlines of a task set. One major difficulty in building a real-time system is the lack of good techniques for analyzing schedulability.

Schedulability analysis lets a program designer predict (under certain conditions) whether given real-time tasks can meet their timing constraints. It requires a bound on the execution time of each task. To meet this requirement, the system must avoid priority inversion problems that occur when a higher priority task must wait while a lower priority task executes.[1] For example, under priority-based scheduling, a low-priority task that holds a computational resource, such as a shared lock, blocks a higher priority task from this resource until the low-priority task completes. If several tasks of intermediate priority lie between the lower and higher priority tasks, the blocked high-priority task must wait for a period bounded only by the number of medium-priority tasks. This problem makes it very difficult to put an accurate bound on task execution times.

Specifying rigid timing constraints. Conventional real-time programs do not explicitly describe timing constraints in the program text. Instead, they describe

The real-time object model is a methodology for describing real-time systems. RTC++ is a programming language that extends C++ based on this model.

them in a separate timing chart or document. This makes it difficult to enforce timing constraints or detect timing errors during compile time or runtime.

Moreover, current systems pose difficulties in specifying the timing characteristics of a periodic task. Languages or operating systems often use the duration of a delay statement to implement a periodic task. However, this can lead to an inaccurate value for the waiting time. For example, consider the following program written in Ada:

```
1  loop
2    — . . . body of cyclic activity . . .
3    dtime := nexttime – currenttime;
4    delay dtime;
5  end loop
```

The execution of the statement at line 3 is not an atomic action, so the dtime variable may have a wrong value. For example, if the program's execution is suspended after currenttime is evaluated and resumed later, dtime is calculated with the incorrect value of currenttime. So the program might be delayed too long in the delay statement.

This delay problem and other issues related to real-time programming in Ada are addressed in a proposal for the coming Ada standard, Ada 9X.[2]

Scheduling approach

Many developers use the cyclic executive to predict timing correctness for real-time systems with periodic tasks[3] (see the sidebar on scheduling). This approach offers a framework for scheduling periodic tasks, but it has some problems. First, a programmer must use tools for deterministic scheduling. These tools require much insight into timing requirements and program structure. Sometimes, a task's structure must be changed to satisfy the timing constraints; for example, a single logical task might be split into two parts that fit better into the timing structure.

Second, programs built with the cyclic executive are very difficult to extend or modify. Changes tend to violate timing structure and constraints that were tuned to specific characteristics of the original problem.

Instead of the cyclic executive, our approach employs the rate monotonic scheduling analysis.[4] Rate monotonic

Scheduling

Two major approaches to developing schedulable real-time systems dominate the current state of the art.

The cyclic executive. This approach performs a sequence of actions during fixed periods of time. The execution is divided into two parts. The major cycle schedules computations to be repeated indefinitely. The major cycle is composed of minor cycles. A programmer divides each task into subcomponents so that the execution of each subcomponent fits into the minor cycles in a way that satisfies the timing constraints. In other words, this programming style forces a programmer to schedule programs using static analysis tools with some manual scheduling or reprogramming to ensure predictable execution timing.

Rate monotonic scheduling. This approach uses a preemptive fixed-priority scheduling algorithm that assigns higher priority to tasks with shorter periods. The CPU utilization of a task i, $U(i)$, is calculated by $U(i) = C(i) / T(i)$, where $C(i)$ and $T(i)$ are the execution time and period of task i, respectively.

Assume a task's deadline is the same as its period. Its CPU utilization is schedulable up to 100 percent in the case of a harmonic task set where all periodic tasks start at the same time and all periods are harmonic. In the general case, n independent periodic processes can meet their deadlines if the following formula holds:

$$\sum_{i=1}^{n} \frac{C(i)}{T(i)} \le n\left(2^{1/n} - 1\right)$$

This formula is very simple but pessimistic: A task set that does not satisfy this condition may or may not be schedulable. There is a more precise schedulability analysis of the rate monotonic algorithm (see references 1 and 5 in the main article). However, in this article, we use this pessimistic formula for simplicity.

scheduling uses a preemptive fixed-priority scheduling algorithm that assigns higher priority to the tasks with shorter periods. With this algorithm, the schedulability of a given task set is analyzed by applying a closed formula (see the sidebar on scheduling).

Rate monotonic scheduling does not require programmers to split tasks by hand as the cyclic executive does, but the tasks must be preemptive and there is some penalty for context-switch overhead. Critical regions that require mutual exclusion interfere with the preemptability constraint of rate monotonic analysis, and the resulting potential for priority inversion must be accounted for.

Therefore, our approach employs the priority inheritance protocol[1] to bound the duration of priority inversion. In the priority inheritance protocol, if a task has to wait for the completion of a lower priority task's execution, the low-priority task's priority is temporarily changed to the priority of the higher task. Thus, tasks of intermediate priority cannot disturb the execution of the lower priority task. This lets us bound a task's blocking time (that is, the time a task spends waiting for a resource, such as a mutual exclusion lock, to become available). Note that the term inheritance as used in priority inheritance protocol has no relation to the inheritance of objects in the object-oriented methodology.

Using the priority inheritance protocol under rate monotonic scheduling, all periodic tasks meet their deadline if the following formula holds[1,5]:

$$\frac{C(1)}{T(1)} + \cdots + \frac{C(n)}{T(n)} + \max\left\{\frac{B(1)}{T(1)}, \cdots, \frac{B(n-1)}{T(n-1)}\right\} \le n\left(2^{1/n} - 1\right) \quad (1)$$

where $C(i)$, $T(i)$, and $B(i)$ are the execu-

153

tion time, period, and blocking time, respectively, of the task i and n is the number of tasks. In this formula, a task whose subscript is smaller has a shorter period and a higher priority. To use these methods effectively for scheduling analysis, we need a good methodology to specify the execution and blocking times (due to both synchronization and communication) in the program text.

Real-time object model

Timing encapsulation. The real-time object model extends the object-oriented model to describe real-time properties in programs. In the real-time object model, active objects with timing constraints describe a system, together with their interaction through message passing. Such an active object is called a *real-time object*.

An active object, as described here, has one or more threads that can be executing when a message arrives. Various message-passing schemes have been introduced to describe concurrency among objects in object-oriented concurrent programming.[6] Figure 1 illustrates the typical execution flow between active objects. The sender object at (1) sends a message to the receiver at (2) and waits for the reply message. After the execution of (3) in the receiver, the receiver sends a reply message at (4). Then both the sender and receiver objects execute concurrently at (5) and (6).

Nonpreemptive object. A nonpreemptive real-time object consists of internal data, operations called *methods* with timing properties, and a thread. We call the object nonpreemptive because the object performs the senders' requests sequentially and cannot interleave the execution of various requests. The following notation describes the timing properties of objects in the real-time object model:

- $Sm(o)$ is the set of methods in an object o.
- $C(m, o)$ is the worst case execution time (not including blocking time) of method m of object o.
- $Ms(m, o)$ is the multiset of other objects' methods called by method m of object o.

Figure 2 shows an example of real-time objects. Object O_1 has method M_1, whose worst-case execution time is 55 milliseconds. Object O_2 has method M_2, whose worst-case execution time is 30 milliseconds. Object O_3 has three methods, M_{31}, M_{32}, M_{33}, whose worst-case execution times are 30, 20, and 30 milliseconds, respectively. An arrow indicates an object's invocation sequence. Method M_1 in object O_1 invokes methods M_{31} and M_{32} in object O_3, while method M_2 in object O_2 invokes method M_{32} in object O_3.

By using the information about timing and execution dependency, we can analyze the timing constraints of the program as follows: Because M_1 of O_1 calls two methods (M_{31} and M_{32}) in O_3, the worst case execution time of M_1 must be greater than the summation of the worst-case execution times of M_{31} and M_{32}. Moreover, the worst-case execution of M_2 must be greater than the worst case execution of M_{32}. That is,

$$C(M_1, O_1) > C(M_{31}, O_3) + C(M_{32}, O_3) \rightarrow 55 > 30 + 20$$
$$C(M_2, O_2) > C(M_{32}, O_3) \rightarrow 30 > 20$$

One advantage of this model is that the schedulability of a task set is easily analyzed under the rate monotonic scheduling as described in the sidebar

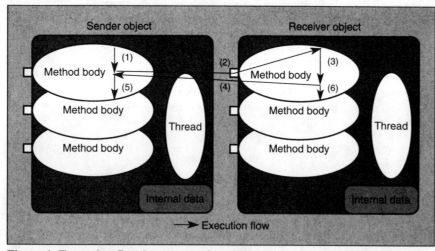

Figure 1. Execution flow between active objects.

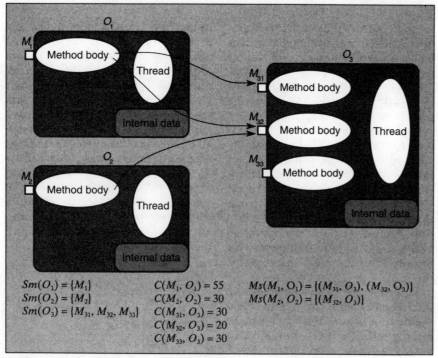

$Sm(O_1) = \{M_1\}$

$Sm(O_2) = \{M_2\}$

$Sm(O_3) = \{M_{31}, M_{32}, M_{33}\}$

$C(M_1, O_1) = 55$

$C(M_2, O_2) = 30$

$C(M_{31}, O_3) = 30$

$C(M_{32}, O_3) = 20$

$C(M_{33}, O_3) = 30$

$Ms(M_1, O_1) = \{(M_{31}, O_3), (M_{32}, O_3)\}$

$Ms(M_2, O_2) = \{(M_{32}, O_3)\}$

Figure 2. An example of real-time objects.

on scheduling. Another advantage is that a reusable object is easily built for real-time applications. For example, we can provide a real-time object library such that several objects have the same functionality with the same interface but with different timing constraints, arising from their internal algorithms. Programmers can choose an object from the real-time library that fits their timing constraints.

Preemptive object. Nonpreemptive real-time objects can suffer from priority inversion due to blocking at an object invocation (see the sidebar on priority inversion in an active object). Two ways to reduce the blocking time are *concurrent execution* in the object or the abort-and-restart methodology.[7]

An object can execute requests concurrently if it has multiple threads, each of which is responsible for some methods. However, this doesn't eliminate blocking time due to the synchronization of internal data in an object. In the abort-and-restart methodology, if a process is going to be blocked at the request of an object, the current execution of the object is aborted. When the execution is aborted, the object is responsible for maintaining the consistency of the data. This methodology should be applied if the abort, recovery, and requeueing cost is less than the blocking cost. For simplicity, we do not consider the abort-and-restart methodology here.

The real-time object model can describe objects with multiple threads.[8] Each thread is responsible for performing one or more methods. A collection of threads may be responsible for the same set of methods, in which case the threads constitute a thread group.[9] Real-time objects with multiple threads are called *preemptive objects*. A preemptive object is described using the following notation in addition to the notation of the nonpreemptive object:

- $G(i)$ is thread group i (that is, the set of thread numbers), where $\forall i,j, i \neq j, G(i) \cap G(j) = \phi$.
- $Gm(m, o)$ is a thread group that executes the method.
- $Mr(m, o)$ is the multiset of pairs of critical region and its worst-case execution time in the method.

Let us say O_3 is a preemptive object instead of a nonpreemptive object. As shown in Figure 3, threads Th_1 and Th_2 are responsible for executing methods

Priority inversion in an active object

Figure A shows an example of priority inversion in an active object. Suppose we have a server object S and client objects L and H where L's priority is lower than H's. If the server is executing for L as a result of a request received from client L and client H sends a message to S, client H's request is postponed until the server's execution for client L finishes. Because H's priority is higher than L's but processing for L precedes processing for H, we have a case of priority inversion in the server.

Moreover, if we assume that another object M is running independently with a medium priority, effectively bounding the execution time of H requires S to run with no interference from M whenever H is waiting for S's reply. Thus, the priority of S has to change based on the highest priority of the requests waiting for service. This scheme for dynamically adjusting the priorities is called the priority inheritance protocol.

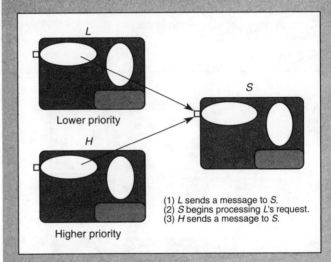

(1) L sends a message to S.
(2) S begins processing L's request.
(3) H sends a message to S.

Figure A. Priority inversion in an object.

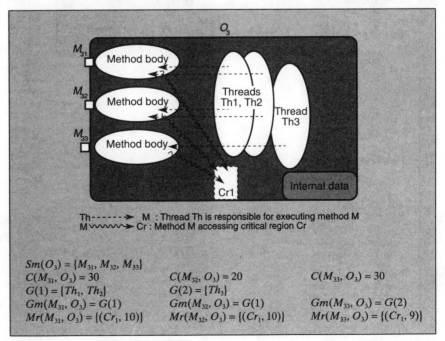

Th ------> M : Thread Th is responsible for executing method M
M ∿∿∿> Cr : Method M accessing critical region Cr

$Sm(O_3) = \{M_{31}, M_{32}, M_{33}\}$
$C(M_{31}, O_3) = 30$ $C(M_{32}, O_3) = 20$ $C(M_{33}, O_3) = 30$
$G(1) = \{Th_1, Th_2\}$ $G(2) = \{Th_3\}$
$Gm(M_{31}, O_3) = G(1)$ $Gm(M_{32}, O_3) = G(1)$ $Gm(M_{33}, O_3) = G(2)$
$Mr(M_{31}, O_3) = \{(Cr_1, 10)\}$ $Mr(M_{32}, O_3) = \{(Cr_1, 10)\}$ $Mr(M_{33}, O_3) = \{(Cr_1, 9)\}$

Figure 3. Preemptive object O_3.

Active object scheduling analysis

Suppose we have a real-time system composed of periodic tasks, active objects called by those tasks, and other independent active objects — all executing on a single CPU machine. We also assume that all method-calling sequences to other objects can be determined statically and that there are no recursive calls or unbounded iterations.

A periodic task has its period and deadline specified as timing properties. The task set is described by several objects and the interaction among those objects. Thus, a periodic task is defined as follows:

- $T(n)$ is the period of task n.
- $D(n)$ is the deadline of task n.
- $Ms(n)$ is the multiset of other objects' methods called by periodic task n.

Nonpreemptive object. Figure B shows an example where periodic tasks send messages to the objects defined in Figure 2 of the main text. The system task Timer is defined to handle task scheduling. The context-switch overhead is accumulated in the execution of the Timer. To analyze the schedulability of this example under rate monotonic scheduling, we prioritize the tasks Timer, P_1, P_2, and P_3 as highest, high, middle, and low, respectively. This priority corresponds to the shortest to longest task periods.

We analyze the worst-case execution time of each task first. This is easy to do because each of an object's methods has timing constraints. The worst-case execution of P_1 is 85 milliseconds because it calls two methods, M_1 of O_1 and M_2 of O_2, whose worst-case execution times are 55 and 30 milliseconds, respectively. In the same way, we determine that the worst-case execution times for P_2 and P_3 are 30 milliseconds each.

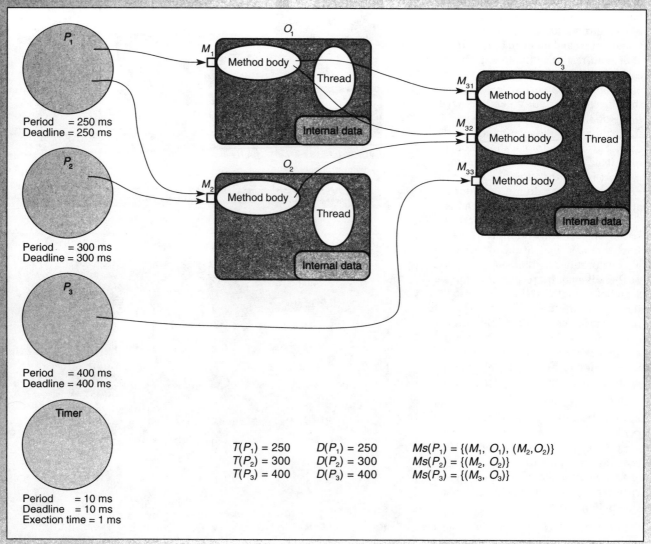

$$T(P_1) = 250 \quad D(P_1) = 250 \quad Ms(P_1) = \{(M_1, O_1), (M_2, O_2)\}$$
$$T(P_2) = 300 \quad D(P_2) = 300 \quad Ms(P_2) = \{(M_2, O_2)\}$$
$$T(P_3) = 400 \quad D(P_3) = 400 \quad Ms(P_3) = \{(M_3, O_3)\}$$

Figure B. A task set.

156

Second, we analyze the blocking time of all tasks except for the lowest priority task. In other words, we determine the time each task must wait for synchronization or communication with other activities. There are two cases where the execution of P_1 is blocked due to P_2. One case is when P_2 has called method M_2 of O_2 and then P_1 tries to call the same method. In this case, the worst-case blocking time of P_1 is 30 milliseconds because the request can be postponed until the execution of M_2 is finished.

The second case is when M_{32} of O_3 has been called by M_2 under P_2's request and later O_1 calls M_{31} or M_{32} under P_1's request. The execution of M_{31} and M_{32} cannot both be blocked by P_2 during one period of P_1. However, under the priority inheritance protocol, one of them can be blocked because the execution of P_2 is temporarily given the highest priority until the completion of O_3's M_{32}. After P_2 executes, it cannot disturb P_1. Thus, the blocking time at O_3 is 20 milliseconds.

P_2 can block the execution of P_1 at O_2 for 30 milliseconds and at O_3 for 20 milliseconds. However, if P_2 blocks P_1's execution at M_{32}, then P_2 also blocks the execution of M_2 for P_1 during one period of P_1. Thus, we estimate that 30 milliseconds is the worst-case blocking time of P_1 due to P_2.

Let us consider the relation between P_1 and P_3 in terms of blocking time. P_1 can be blocked by P_3 when P_1 calls M_{31} or M_{32} of O_3 during the execution of M_{33} under P_3's request. Here, the worst-case blocking time of P_1 is 30 milliseconds because the execution time of O_3's M_{33} is 30 milliseconds.

To summarize this analysis of P_1, the blocking time of P_1 is 60 milliseconds — 30 milliseconds due to P_2 and 30 milliseconds due to P_3. In this way, we can estimate other blocking times. The execution of P_2 can be disturbed by P_3 at M_{33} of O_3. The worst-case blocking time of P_2 is 30 milliseconds.

Table A summarizes the timing analysis. Using the table we can analyze the schedulability of the task set under rate monotonic scheduling by applying formula (1) from the main text:

$$\frac{C(Timer)}{T(Timer)} + \frac{C(1)}{T(1)} + \frac{C(2)}{T(2)} + \frac{C(3)}{T(3)} + \max\left(\frac{B(1)}{T(1)}, \frac{B(2)}{T(2)}\right)$$

$$= 0.1 + 0.34 + 0.1 + 0.075 + \max(0.24, 0.1)$$
$$= 0.855 > 3(2^{1/3} - 1) = 0.780$$

Thus, using this simple (pessimistic) test, we cannot guarantee the schedulability of this task set under rate monotonic scheduling.

Preemptive object. Suppose we replace object O_3 described above with another implementation that is preemptive (as defined in Figure 3 of the main text). To ana-

Table A. Timing information for Figure B (in milliseconds)

Task	Period (T)	Deadline	Execution (C)	C/T	Blocking (B)	B/T
Timer	10	10	1	0.100	0	0
1	250	250	85	0.340	60	0.24
2	300	300	30	0.100	30	0.10
3	400	400	30	0.075	0	0

Table B. Timing information for Figure B with preemptive object (in milliseconds)

Process	Period (T)	Deadline	Execution (C)	C/T	Blocking (B)	B/T
Timer	10	10	1	0.100	0	0
1	250	250	85	0.340	39	0.156
2	300	300	30	0.100	9	0.030
3	400	400	30	0.075	0	0

lyze the schedulability of a task set with this object, we modify the implementation of object O_3 without changing the execution time. The execution times of all tasks are the same as in the previous example.

Now we estimate the blocking time of P_1 and P_2. P_1's blocking time due to P_2 does not change, because P_1 calls M_2 of O_2, which calls O_3. So the blocking time of P_1 by P_2 is still 30 milliseconds. The blocking time of P_1 due to P_3, however, changes to 9 milliseconds because the method M_{32} blocks only for the duration of the critical region shared in O_3. Thus, the blocking time of P_1 is 39 milliseconds — 30 milliseconds for P_2 and 9 milliseconds for P_3. P_2's blocking time is also reestimated as 9 milliseconds.

Table B shows the results of this analysis. Using the table we can analyze the schedulability of the task set under rate monotonic scheduling as follows:

$$\frac{C(Timer)}{T(Timer)} + \frac{C(1)}{T(1)} + \frac{C(2)}{T(2)} + \frac{C(3)}{T(3)} + \max\left(\frac{B(1)}{T(1)}, \frac{B(2)}{T(2)}\right)$$

$$= 0.1 + 0.34 + 0.1 + 0.075 + \max(0.156, 0.03)$$
$$= 0.771 < 3(2^{1/3} - 1) = 0.780$$

The result shows that the task set is guaranteed schedulable.

```
1  active class O3 {
2      private:
3          // private data definition
4      public
5          int       m31(char* data, int size) bound(0t30m);
6          int       m32(char* data, int size) bound(0t20m) timeout(m32_abort);
7          int       m33(float f) bound(0t30m);
8      activity:
9          slave[2]  m31(char*, int), m32(char*, int);
10         slave     m33(float f);
11 };
```

Figure 4. A real-time object in RTC++.

```
1  active class P1 {
2      private:
3          // private date definition
4          void      main();
5      activity:
6          master    main() cycle(0; 0; 0t200; 0t200);
7  };
```

Figure 5. A periodic task in RTC++.

M_{31} and M_{32}, while thread Th_3 is in charge of performing the method M_{33}. Suppose there is one critical region inside the object. During the execution of method M_{31}, it accesses the critical region for 10 milliseconds. The time of the critical region accessed by M_{32} is 10 milliseconds while the time of the region accessed by M_{33} is 9 milliseconds. All execution times of methods in O_3 are the same as they were in the nonpreemptive case.

The sidebar on the previous two-page spread analyzes the schedulability of a nonpreemptive active object and compares it to a preemptive active object. The results show that a system built using preemptive active objects provides better schedulability.

RTC++

RTC++[9] is an extension to C++. Its design is based on the real-time object model. In addition to C++ objects, RTC++ provides active objects. If an active object is defined with timing constraints, it is called a real-time object. Figure 4 shows the declaration of the active object O_3. An active object decla-

ration is almost the same as the original C++ object declaration, except for the addition of the keyword Active before the keyword Class and the addition of a part for Activity.

Activity part. An active object has a single thread by default. A user can specify multiple threads, which we call *member threads* in the active object. Member threads are declared in the activity part of the class declaration. There are two types: slave and master.

A *slave thread* is an execution unit related to a method or a group of methods. Line 10 of Figure 4 declares that one slave thread is dedicated to handling the M_{33} requests. Line 9 specifies that two threads are responsible for executing methods M_{31} and M_{32}. That is, at most two requests of either M_{31} or M_{32} can be interleaved. These threads are called a *slave thread group*.

We employ the priority inheritance protocol in object invocation. That is, a slave thread inherits the priority from the sender. If there is a queue of waiting messages, the messages are ordered according to priority, and the priority of the slave thread is set to the highest priority of the invocations in the queue.

When a new message for those methods arrives and the sender's priority is higher than the current thread's priority, the thread's priority is changed to the higher priority, and the message is enqueued at the head of the priority queue.

Figure 5 shows an example of a periodic task in RTC++. The *master thread* in line 6 is declared to specify the periodic task within an active object. The syntax of the cycle clause is as follows:

cycle(<start-time>; <end-time>; <period>; <deadline>);

In Figure 5, <start-time> and <end-time> are unspecified, so those constraints are free, and 0t200 indicates a time duration of 200 milliseconds. Therefore, the period is 200 milliseconds and the deadline coincides with the period.

Timing specification. Two types of timing information must be specified in RTC++: execution time and deadline time. RTC++ allows us to specify this timing information by using the Bound and Within constructs. The Bound construct asserts the worst-case execution time, while the Within construct asserts the deadline time.

As shown in Figure 4, all methods are declared with the worst-case execution time constraint. For example, the CPU usage in the execution of method M_{31} must be completed within 30 milliseconds. Line 6 shows that method M_{32} has a worst-case execution time of 20 milliseconds and that if this constraint is violated at runtime, the exception handler, m32_abort, is called.

Communication. RTC++ supports synchronous communication. The syntax of communication among active objects is the same as C++ syntax. For example:

```
1  O3 *v;
2  // . . .
3  n = v->m31(buf, size);
4  // . . .
```

RTC++ provides two means of sending a reply message: return and reply statements. In a return statement, a reply message is sent to the sender and the execution of the method is finished. In a reply statement, a reply message is sent and the subsequent statements are executed instead of finishing the execution of a method.

In addition to the features described in this article, RTC++ provides sophisticated facilities for programming applications: statement-level timing constraints, guard expressions, critical regions with timing constraints, and exception handling. Moreover, RTC++ provides facilities for programming distributed applications.

We think the constructs we proposed can be adapted to many other object-oriented languages besides C++. We have compared RTC++ with other real-time programming languages in a previous paper,[9] and the Ada 9X proposal[2] describes the impact of these issues on Ada.

RTC++ is currently running under the ARTS Kernel[10] on Motorola MC68030-based machines such as Sun3, Force Board, and Sony News. The RTC++ compiler generates C++ source programs and uses additional runtime support routines. ∎

References

1. L. Sha, R. Rajkumar, and J.P. Lehoczky, "Priority Inheritance Protocols: An Approach to Real-Time Synchronization," *IEEE Trans. Computers*, Vol. 39, No. 9, Sept. 1990, pp. 1,175-1,185.

2. T. Baker and O. Pazy, "Real-Time Features for Ada 9X," *Proc. 12th IEEE Real-Time Systems Symp.*, IEEE CS Press, Los Alamitos, Calif., Order No. 2450, 1991, pp. 172-180.

3. T.P. Baker and A. Shaw, "The Cyclic Executive Model and Ada," *Proc. Ninth IEEE Real-Time Systems Symp.*, IEEE CS Press, Los Alamitos, Calif., Order No. 894 (microfiche only), 1988, pp. 120-129.

4. C.L. Liu and J.W. Layland, "Scheduling Algorithms for Multiprogramming in a Hard Real Time Environment," *J. ACM*, Vol. 20, No. 1, 1973, pp. 46-61.

5. L. Sha and J.B. Goodenough, "Real-Time Scheduling Theory and Ada," *Computer*, Vol. 23, No. 4, Apr. 1990, pp. 53-62.

6. *Object-Oriented Concurrent Programming*, A. Yonezawa and M. Tokoro, eds., MIT Press, Cambridge, Mass., 1987.

7. H. Tokuda and T. Nakajima, "Evaluation of Real-Time Synchronization in Real-Time Mach," *Proc. Second Mach Symp.*, Usenix, Berkeley, Calif., 1991, pp. 213-221.

8. C.W. Mercer and H. Tokuda, "The ARTS Real-Time Object Model," *Proc. 11th IEEE Real-Time Systems Symp.*, IEEE CS Press, Los Alamitos, Calif., Order No. 2112, 1990, pp. 2-10.

9. Y. Ishikawa, H. Tokuda, and C.W. Mercer, "Object-Oriented Real-Time Language Design: Constructs for Timing Constraints," *Proc. Object-Oriented Programming Systems, Languages, and Applications*, ACM Press, New York, 1990, pp. 289-298.

10. H. Tokuda and C.W. Mercer, "ARTS: A Distributed Real-Time Kernel," *Operating Systems Rev.*, Vol. 23, No. 3, July 1989, pp. 29-53.

Yutaka Ishikawa is a senior researcher at Electrotechnical Laboratory, MITI, Japan. His research interests include real-time systems, distributed/parallel systems, and object-oriented programming languages.

Ishikawa received the BS, MS, and PhD degrees in electrical engineering from Keio University. He is a member of the IEEE Computer Society, ACM, and Japan Society for Software Science and Technology.

Hideyuki Tokuda is a senior research computer scientist in the School of Computer Science at Carnegie Mellon University and an associate professor of environmental information at Keio University. His research interests include distributed real-time systems, multimedia systems, communciation protocols, and massively parallel distributed systems.

Tokuda received BS and MS degrees in engineering from Keio University and a PhD degree in computer science from the University of Waterloo. He is a member of the IEEE, ACM, Information Processing Society of Japan, and Japan Society for Software Science and Technology.

Clifford W. Mercer is a PhD candidate in the School of Computer Science at Carnegie Mellon University. His research interests are in operating systems support for audio and video applications and distributed real-time systems.

Mercer graduated with university honors from Carnegie Mellon University with a BS in applied mathematics and computer science in 1988. He is a member of Sigma Xi and a student member of IEEE and ACM.

Readers can contact Hideyuki Tokuda at Carnegie Mellow University, School of Computer Science, 5000 Forbes Avenue, Pittsburgh, PA 15213; e-mail hxt@cs.cmu.edu.

Object-Oriented Real-Time Systems: Concepts and Examples

Thomas E. Bihari, Adaptive Machine Technologies

Prabha Gopinath, Honeywell

Reprinted from *Computer*, December 1992, pp. 25–32.
Copyright © 1992 by The Institute of Electrical and
Electronics Engineers, Inc. All rights reserved.

I n a real-time system, the specification of correct system states and behaviors includes constraints related to time in the real world. Real-time software usually interacts with entities in the real world. Such software can be embedded in a single mechanical device or distributed over hardware across thousands of miles. Aircraft avionics, factory robotics, chemical- and nuclear-plant control, air-traffic control, and battlefield management are all examples of real-time applications.

In many such applications, the real world is extremely dynamic. Aircraft enter and leave airspaces; products move through factories; manipulators grasp unknown payloads. Real-time software must be capable of adapting to these changes. During initial system design, it might be impossible to specify all the possible influences the real world can have on software. Nevertheless, software must behave in a predictable manner. Those developing real-time software must therefore strive to ensure predictable real-time behavior, under both normal and abnormal operating conditions.[1]

Building large real-time systems

Five or 10 years ago, a typical large real-time software system might have contained 100,000 lines of high-level source code; that amount wasn't large by the general software standards of the day. Today, 1 million-line real-time software systems — large by any standard — are becoming commonplace. For example, approximately 1.5 million lines of code are expected to be written in the US Advanced Tactical Fighter project.[2] A large real-time software system is therefore subject to all the problems (such as maintainability) of any large software system, in addition to the problems associated with real-time operation. Furthermore, in many real-time applications, tight real-time constraints might affect only part of the software system. For example, an estimated 10 to 30 percent of a typical vehicle-control software system is directly related to the vehicle's actual real-time control. Real-time software engineering methodologies that address only real-

Large, dynamic real-time systems require complex embedded software. This article examines Chaos, an object-based language and programming/execution paradigm designed for dynamic real-time applications.

0-8186-6222-0/95 $4.00 © 1992 IEEE

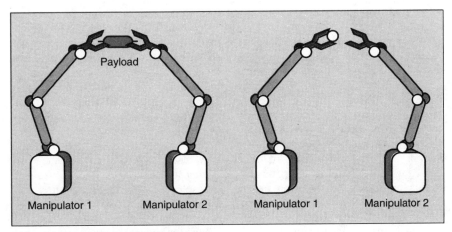

Figure 1. Cooperating manipulators.

time constraints at the expense of good overall software engineering are therefore unacceptable.

Real-time constraints must nonetheless be taken seriously. Timely execution of the control software of a fly-by-wire aircraft (one activated entirely by electronic controls) is essential for safety. In such applications, anything less than guaranteed timeliness is insufficient and unacceptable. Software engineering methodologies that offer only haphazard or partial support for real-time constraints are therefore also unacceptable.

Managing temporal complexity. Large software systems are generally difficult to understand, maintain, and modify. Real-time systems exacerbate this situation by introducing the additional complexity of time-dependent behavior. A real-time system's temporal characteristics fall into two main categories:

- states and behaviors *required* of the system (for example, constraints on process deadlines and execution precedence) and
- states and behaviors *exhibited* by the system (for example, process execution times).

As modern real-time systems become larger and more dynamic, understanding their temporal characteristics becomes more difficult. While it might be possible to amass large amounts of data concerning the temporal behavior of a particular software system, understanding and correlating this data to the complete system's overall behavior can be difficult.

Making it easier to understand, main-

tain, and modify large, dynamic, real-time software systems requires advances in operating systems, languages, programming environments, and other disciplines. However, the most important component is the development of the underlying models used to represent the systems. Such a model should ideally possess formal semantics that allow the system's correctness to be verified. At the same time, it should represent the software and real-world entities in a way that feels natural to system designers.

For general-purpose applications, object-oriented programming has been shown to be an improvement over traditional procedural programming, particularly in the areas of understandability, adaptability, and code reusability. While most of the concepts underlying object-oriented programming have been around for nearly two decades, its broad popularity in recent years can be traced to the availability of Smalltalk-80, C++, and other object-oriented languages on inexpensive personal computers and workstations. New languages and tools for object-oriented programming appear frequently. In real-time systems, however, object-oriented programming has caught on more slowly. There seem to be two reasons for this:

(1) Implementations of most existing object-oriented languages and runtime systems can have unpredictable temporal characteristics. Equally important, perhaps, is the perception that object-oriented systems are inherently inefficient. Neither "problem" is an intrinsic shortcoming of the object-oriented model, however, as we discuss in this article.

(2) The object-oriented model runs counter to the traditional process-oriented model often applied to real-time systems: as a collection of processes with constraints on their execution times.

Processes versus objects. In the process-oriented model of real-time systems, the problem decomposition results in a collection of processes, each responsible for a specific portion of the overall task. The processes operate on data flowing through the system.

The process-oriented model's primary building blocks represent the functional or, borrowing from medicine, "physiological" aspects of a system. The mapping from software modules to real-world entities is often not apparent from the code's structure. Much of the information about the structure or the system's "anatomy" is distributed globally throughout the system architecture.[3] This can make it difficult to understand, maintain, and reuse such code.

Furthermore, treating real-time systems as groups of time-constrained processes prejudices software design toward an "event-action" view: Events are generated by real-world entities or software processes; actions must be performed by software processes in timely response to these events.

Unfortunately, in many real-time systems, the discrete events are approximations of what are really continuous activities. In these systems, temporal constraints are more naturally viewed as time-based information consistency constraints, much like those arising in temporal databases.

For example, in many robotic systems, the software interface to a physical manipulator periodically polls the physical manipulator to read its state and to send actuator commands. The software in such a system contains an image of the physical manipulator. This image must be kept consistent with the physical manipulator's actual state or the motion-planning software might generate inappropriate motions.

In implementation, this consistency constraint is translated into a temporal constraint of N time units on the polling period. When reasoning about the behavior of such a system, however, the broader concept that "the software must contain an accurate image of the hardware" might be more understandable than the more specific implementation requirement that "the period must be N time units."

In contrast to the process-oriented model, the primary building blocks of the object-oriented model directly represent the structural or anatomical aspects of a system. The system's functional aspects are represented by intraobject computations and interobject communications — natural reflections of those of the physical system.

Structuring dynamic real-time applications. In a dynamic environment, real-world entities appear and disappear, combine and separate. Software entities and their temporal constraints correspondingly appear, disappear, and change. Consider, as Figure 1 shows, the case of two manipulators operating in a factory environment. In such an application, the manipulators might be able to interact in a variety of ways.

For example, when the two manipulators work as a team to move payloads, the team's physical characteristics can be quite different from those of individual manipulators. The control software must change to reflect the creation of this new dual-arm manipulator, which might be capable of operating in different modes. It might be able to use both arms to grasp a large payload that neither individual arm could grasp within its single gripper, thus trading increased payload capacity for a restricted range of motion. Or it might operate in a "bucket brigade" mode where the two arms pass payloads back and forth, increasing the range of motion with no increase in payload capacity.

Managing the computing resources to satisfy temporal constraints can be difficult. In some applications, it might be possible to enumerate the potential interaction modes and choose fixed resource allocation strategies for each mode. However, when managing resources for software that must deal with unpredictable worlds, the flexibility to negotiate the temporal constraints dynamically, and guarantee their satisfaction, is essential. A common tenet of recent work in "intelligent" real-time systems is that there is never enough processing power to optimally reason about all the information available in the environment in real time.[4] Therefore, the software must always focus its attention on important matters and flexibly assign the available resources to achieve the most good.

In the case of temporal constraints on software associated with the servo control of machinery, negotiability can be limited, since the machine's physical characteristics — its mass, for example — cannot be changed and can dictate the temporal constraints. On the other hand, the temporal constraints that often arise from specific missions chosen for the system might be negotiable. For example, a temporal constraint on a robot's motion-planning algorithm can be relaxed through negotiation among the affected software entities if the robot is allowed to move more slowly without jeopardizing its mission. This ability to negotiate requires

(1) a complete understanding of the temporal constraints' sources and the relationship between the temporal constraints and other constraints on the system, such as accuracy and reliability (This provides a basis for trade-offs among constraints);

(2) a system model that encapsulates or partitions the temporal constraints into understandable, manageable groups and provides a structure for temporal constraint negotiation (This, we believe, is a strength of the object-oriented model); and

(3) an implementation of the model that provides predictable temporal characteristics, allowing objects to guarantee that the temporal constraints, once negotiated, will be met. We address this later in this article.

Object-oriented model

In the object-oriented model, the entire world is made up of two types of entities: *objects* and *messages*. Both physical entities and software entities are represented as objects. For simplicity, we use the term *physical object* to mean objects that exist in the real world (for example, a manipulator), *software object* for software, and the term *object* to be synonymous with either or both types when there is no ambiguity.

Software objects encapsulate data and provide units of code called *methods* for accessing the data. Each object has a unique name, which other objects use to address it. Objects communicate by sending and receiving messages. A message is addressed to the receiving object and contains the name of a specific method of the receiving object that is to be executed, along with parameters such as the names of other objects. Sending a message to an object with the name of a specific method is the only mechanism by which an object can manipulate another object's encapsulated data. The object-oriented model thus provides data and program abstraction, hiding details of an object's implementation from other objects.

A *class* represents all objects with some set of similar characteristics (for example, all electrically actuated manipulators). Classes can have subclasses. A subclass represents all objects that belong to the same (super)class and that possess some additional common characteristics (for example, all electrically actuated manipulators that, in addition, possess six degrees of freedom). A class can have more than one superclass (for example, all six-degree-of-freedom manipulators and all electrically actuated manipulators).

A class can have one or more specific *instances* (for example, the manipulator with serial number 12345, which is one instance of the class of electrically actuated, six-degree-of-freedom manipulators). A class is analogous to a template from which instances are "stamped out." An object instance is an instance of only one class.

An object class *inherits* characteristics from its superclasses. Inheritance is a powerful concept that can greatly simplify the design and implementation of a system. In particular, a class inherits all the methods of its superclass by default, unless the class chooses to provide new methods that override the defaults. This allows new classes to be created easily from old classes.

The object-oriented model's features and benefits are well documented; Booch[3] is particularly readable. Properly used, object-oriented techniques can produce real-time software that is understandable and reusable, provides functional and temporal independence among software entities, and facilitates dynamic changes to software structures.

Object-oriented real-time languages

A number of research teams have been exploring real-time object-oriented languages, usually as extensions to existing object-oriented languages. C++

is a particularly popular base language in this regard, in part because it is readily available and compatible with C. Flex,[5] RTC++,[6] and Robot-Independent Programming Environment[7] are all real-time extensions to C++. Furthermore, despite its lack of built-in support for real-time applications, standard C++ is already being used in some embedded systems.

Ada does not support inheritance and is therefore considered an *object-based* language rather than an object-oriented language. However, its support for data and program abstraction, generic types, and operator overloading make it attractive for large applications with moderate real-time constraints. Furthermore, the 9X revision to the Ada standard is expected to correct some of the current Ada standard's real-time deficiencies.

Our work has included the development of the Concurrent Hierarchical Adaptable Object System (Chaos),[8] an object-based language and programming/execution system designed for dynamic real-time applications. Chaos was designed to study real-time method and message issues, so we decided it need not support inheritance. Chaos objects and messages have both functional and temporal attributes.

Chaos consists of three major components:

(1) a C-based runtime library for the real-time kernel,
(2) a programming environment centered around an entity-relationship database, and
(3) a specification language.

The specification language and programming environment together allow an application programmer to structure a real-time application as a collection of objects interacting via messages. A programmer specifies the mapping between real-world entities and corresponding software objects via the programming environment. The environment then generates a set of configuration files, which are compiled into executable code to create object classes and instances. The environment is used to analyze the application's temporal behavior and monitor its execution at runtime. All

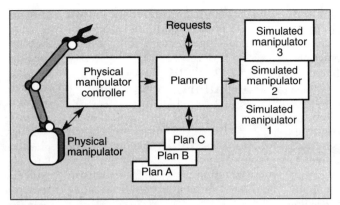

Figure 2. A manipulator system.

the application's major functional and temporal attributes are stored in the database and can be accessed both during and between program executions.

Chaos supports the construction of adaptable software that can change its behavior statically and/or dynamically to accommodate changes in the operating environment. Adaptability is often designed into systems that are meant to be highly survivable. For example, the F-22 fighter's avionics system is designed around four or five common modules. Should a failure occur in a critical module at runtime, then another less important module is dynamically reconfigured to take over the failed module's tasks.[2] This is in contrast to earlier generation aircraft that had 25 or more distinct avionics modules, each specialized for a particular function.

Real-time object-oriented model

The requirements for a real-time object-oriented model differ from those of a nonreal-time object-oriented model in two important ways:

(1) The object model should support the encapsulation, abstraction, and understanding of the object's functional and the temporal characteristics.
(2) Implementation of the object model (classes, instances, methods, and messages) and the associated runtime mechanisms should have predictable temporal characteristics.

In the past, object-oriented models were avoided in real-time applications, in part because of the perception that

object-oriented runtime systems perform duties such as dynamic memory management that can require long, unpredictable amounts of time. This is a valid criticism of many object-oriented implementations (in some nonreal-time object-oriented applications, garbage collection accounts for more than half of processor time). But it is not an intrinsic object-model weakness. Any real-time software system that interacts with a dynamic real world must deal with dynamic resource management because a computer's resources are bounded. If the underlying model does not support "forgetting" old information and reusing its storage area, this function must be handled explicitly by the application programmer, as is the case in many existing systems.

One of the object-oriented model's most attractive aspects is its uniformity: Everything in the world is represented as objects and messages. In a manipulator control software system, for example, software objects can be used to represent the manipulator itself, individual actuators and links, and conceptual entities like plans.

Figure 2 shows a manipulator system that includes a physical manipulator, a software interface to the physical manipulator, a planner, several plans, and several simulated manipulators. Using a planning technique called *super real-time simulation*, the planner repeatedly examines the physical manipulator's state, generates one or more manipulator motion plans, tries the plans on the simulated manipulators, and chooses the best one to command the physical manipulator to perform. This sequence must be completed before the physical manipulator reaches the end of its previous plan, or the manipulator can be damaged.

In a nonreal-time object-oriented environment, elegant implementation can succeed over timely implementation. In a real-time environment, the predictable temporal behavior of objects and messages is important. This can require different implementations of objects and messages in different situations.

Real-time object-oriented systems should, from the application programmer's perspective, support a uniform model of computation. The underlying implementation, however, should use every known technique to support the model. This is beyond the capabilities of existing technology. Most existing real-time object-oriented systems provide language constructs that allow the programmer to tailor the implementations of specific objects and messages to gain acceptable efficiency and predictability. This is a subversion of the pure object-oriented model, but it can be successful if the programmer can make a smooth mental transition between the pure model and the subverted implementation model.

Methods. The real world is full of concurrency. Unless they are constrained to operate in sequence, many physical objects — from atoms to automobiles — naturally operate in parallel. Object-oriented software is naturally parallel as well. Explicit synchronization can be used where necessary, but the default is concurrent operation.

In most real-time systems, this concurrency must be approximated by the execution of many objects' methods on shared processors. Scheduling of method executions requires predictable method execution times. Temporal analysis for method execution is often based on worst-case execution times obtained either through profiling runs or by other estimation techniques. Temporal predictability of method execution can be enhanced by using intelligent compiler techniques,[9] which perform statistical code analysis, instruction-level code reordering, and monitoring-code insertion. Information obtained at runtime from the monitoring code can then be used to refine method execution schedules.

As mentioned earlier, an object class in the Chaos system[8] can be statically selected to have a particular degree of internal concurrency. This is achieved by creating objects that *own* operating system processes. Processes are not statically bound to methods. Instead, such binding occurs dynamically as messages arrive for methods. This allows considerable runtime flexibility. Other classes of objects might have no internal processes. Sending a message to such an object is equivalent to executing the desired method as a procedure call.

Because Chaos objects can be con-

Information obtained at runtime from the monitoring code can be used to refine method execution schedules.

---

current (that is, they can have more than one active process within them), an object can respond to several messages simultaneously. To deal with the resulting problem of object data structure consistency, concurrent objects provide a specialized coordinator object that is responsible for checking the sanity of all accesses to shared structures.

Chaos objects can be adapted at runtime. Such adaptations range from switching in different versions of object methods, to changing the number of internal server processes within an object, to changing the relative priorities of object methods by modifying the behavior of the object's coordinator.

Messages. As with method execution, highly concurrent interobject communication in the real world is usually implemented by scheduling messages on predominantly sequential communication media. Therefore, the message-passing mechanism's underlying implementation must also have predictable temporal behavior. As with method execution, temporal analysis for message transmission is often based on worst-case execution times obtained either through profiling runs or by other estimation techniques.

Interactions via messages involves two main actions: (1) binding the message to a particular method and (2) transferring the message. Because objects can inherit methods from superclasses, the inheritance mechanism must track down the appropriate piece of code to execute. In the pure object-oriented model, late or dynamic binding occurs every time a message is sent. This allows easy object reusability, since the client objects need not contain "wired-in" information about the types of objects to which they send messages. Dynamic binding can cause predictability prob-

lems, however, since the binding can take different amounts of time for different objects.

Most real-time systems resort to early or static binding when the software is compiled or linked, trading improved predictability for lower reusability. Some object-oriented systems, such as C++, allow the application programmer to choose between early and late binding on a case-by-case basis. Other systems, such as Chaos, automatically cache each method address the first time an object uses it. However, this technique limits the degree to which an object's defining class and superclasses can be modified at runtime since these modifications can invalidate the cached method addresses.

There are three phases to message transfer. In the first phase, software at the sender's end resolves the object and method name, packs parameters into some standard format, and introduces the message into the transmission medium. In the second phase, the message propagates over the medium. In the third phase, the message is received at the target and unpacked. Predictability depends on the nature of the underlying communication medium and the traffic across the medium. Predictable communication media (like Futurebus+) are gradually becoming available, and on simple, uniprocessor systems the communication medium is just the processor's common, shared-memory space.

Just as objects in Chaos can have various "flavors" and temporal attributes to suit the real-time domain, messages in Chaos can have temporal attributes and can be specialized and parameterized to suit the application. In pure object-oriented systems, messages come in a single flavor. The problem with this approach is that methods in real-time objects are often of different sizes with different execution costs. For an object representing a manipulator, an *update-plan* method could require thousands of bytes of parameters for execution. The same object could also have a *close/grip* method that requires no parameters. In the face of such variations in method and message size, some application programmers attempt to subvert the object-message model — for example, by caching the method address and then directly calling the method as a procedure. Chaos addresses this problem by providing a variety of message flavors, each of which offers a certain combina-

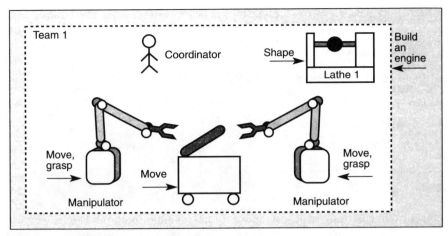

Figure 3. A team in an automated factory.

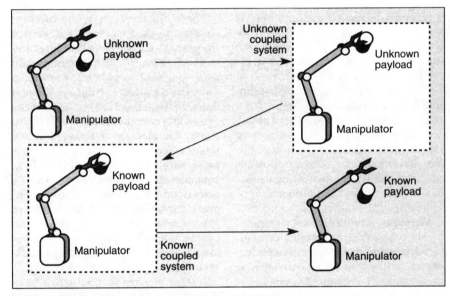

Figure 4. Dynamic class creation and destruction.

tion of functionality and execution overhead.

Since a fixed library of message primitives might not match the requirements of specific applications, the Chaos programming environment provides techniques by which an application programmer can specify and synthesize application-specific message primitives. Thus, varieties of fast messages, data-streaming messages, or messages of other flavors can be generated statically.

While such specializations of objects and messages are extremely useful, there is an attendant cost. Specializations, such as those we have incorporated into Chaos, require that the clients have some knowledge of the characteristics of the methods and messages they require and select the appropriate message flavor to

use. Therefore, specializations, to a certain extent, do subvert the object model's uniformity.

Dynamic instance creation and destruction. A uniform object-oriented model supports the creation of objects as needed by the application and the destruction of objects when no longer needed. In a dynamic environment, physical objects "appear" and "disappear" continually. These can include workpieces in a factory or aircraft in an airspace. In the object-oriented model, the physical objects correspond to software objects that must also be created and destroyed in real time. Even in situations with a fixed number of physical objects, the objects can frequently be rearranged and regrouped. In an auto-

mated factory, for example, a team of machine tools, automated guided vehicles (AGVs), and manipulators can be assigned to a particular task (see Figure 3). The individual components (both the physical hardware and the corresponding software) already exist. However, the team itself is a new object offering new methods. For example, a team can build an engine, something no single machine tool, AGV, or manipulator can do.

Predictable, dynamic creation and destruction of objects is necessary for real-time systems. At runtime, object classes are personified by *class managers*, objects that create, destroy, and otherwise manage class instances. The application programmer should not be burdened with learning the tricks necessary for predictability. However, the class manager can handle dynamic instance creation by maintaining a pool of precreated server instances (as in Chaos), or even by dynamic compile-link-load sequences, if it can be accomplished predictably.

For each class in the application, a pool of object instances is created at class-creation time. Unfortunately, for any reasonable-sized application, the storage overhead of creating these pools can be quite high. We have addressed this problem to a certain extent by associating a *pool/size* attribute with each class. This attribute can be set by the programmer at class-creation time. At runtime, when the application software issues an instance creation call, the class manager selects a precreated instance from the pool, the parameters from the call are copied into it, and its name is registered with a systemwide name server object. This technique makes dynamic instance management relatively predictable. When the application software issues a call to destroy an instance, the class manager merely returns it to the pool. A more intelligent class manager could manage an unbounded pool by creating new instances whenever the pool becomes too low and destroying instances when the pool becomes too large.

Dynamic class creation and destruction. In the preceding discussion, we tacitly assumed that the team's class is designed off line. In some circumstances, dynamic creation and destruction of instances of a statically created class is not enough. Classes must also be created and destroyed dynamically.

Figure 4 shows a manipulator and a cylindrical payload of similar mass. The manipulator is already well-defined and associated with a software object. The payload is unknown and can be associated with an instance of some unknown payload class. At the instant the manipulator grasps the payload, a new combined manipulator/payload object is formed, with new characteristics derived from both of its components plus the relationship between them.

As the payload is manipulated, its characteristics can gradually become known. Thus, the payload object can "mutate" over time from unknown to cylindrical. Eventually, the payload can be recognized as an instance of an existing class of payloads or become the first instance of a new class.

The dynamic creation, mutation, and destruction of object classes is an open research area. Because dynamic class modification deals with the application's semantics, support must be provided so that application programmers can specify how the new class is to be formed. In fact, much of the work in model-based robotics can be cast as algorithms for creating new classes of objects.

Although some preliminary work has been done in the dynamic creation and linking of new classes,[10] we are not aware of any attempts to do so in real time. Despite the practical difficulties with creating new classes "from scratch," the more limited goal of real-time creation of subclasses within existing classes can be tackled, at least in part, by using parameterized generic classes. For example, the inverse kinematics of a general six-degree-of-freedom manipulator can be parameterized, allowing it to be matched to the dimensions of different classes of manipulators.

The dynamic modification of class hierarchies can enable real-time software to remain consistent with the changing real world. However, this flexibility can cause efficiency and predictability problems. For example, since methods can potentially be changed at runtime, each time a method is activated through a message, it is necessary to chain back through the class hierarchy to the superclass that defines the method. This can be inefficient and unpredictable since the depth of a class hierarchy, and hence the cost of traversing it, cannot be known statically.

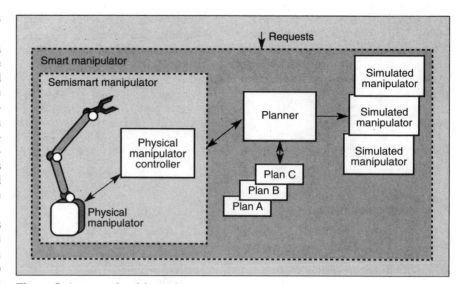

Figure 5. Aggregation hierarchy.

Chaos supports a limited form of dynamic parameterization of generic classes to allow easy development of different implementations of an object. For example, one of the parameterized attributes is the concurrency of an object, which is implemented by creating a number of internal server processes for the object. From a generic class, a number of classes can be created dynamically by changing the concurrency attribute. Another parameterized attribute of a Chaos object allows optimizing concurrent objects to execute on parallel machines. Such objects can be "sliced" so that each slice of an object executes on a different node of the parallel machine. No other form of parameterized classes is supported by Chaos.

Aggregation. Aggregation or composition of objects into part-of hierarchies is essential for managing the complexity of large real-time systems. In a hierarchical model, composite objects are made up of other composite objects or bottom-level basic objects.

A composite object is essentially a group of objects, and management of a composite object includes management of all of its components. For example, dynamic creation of a smart manipulator includes recursive dynamic creation of its components.

Figure 5 shows the system in Figure 2 as an aggregation hierarchy of objects. The scopes of the internal objects' names are limited to the surrounding object. External clients of the smart manipulator object cannot see the object's internal composition. Clients send messages to the smart manipulator, which must pass the messages to the appropriate internal objects.

The hierarchy's representation at runtime depends on the trade-offs between dynamic modifiability and efficiency. Information regarding the hierarchical structure of a software system is part of the system's semantics. If object hierarchies are maintained at runtime, then efficiency and predictability can suffer since a hierarchy of arbitrary depth will have to be traversed to resolve a method reference. This is similar to the problem with inheritance in class hierarchies described earlier. One implementation solution, the approach adopted by the Chaos system, is to flatten out aggregation hierarchies at runtime. This reduces the cost of traversing the hierarchies, but makes changes to the application structure expensive at runtime.

Future work. When we designed Chaos, we intentionally ignored the problems of dynamic class creation and inheritance. However, many of the Chaos tools and mechanisms for supporting concurrency, adaptability, and real-time execution could be applied to a true object-oriented language like C++. We are in the process of making the transition from C to C++ in our robotics applications and will apply the lessons we learned from Chaos as we do so.

In the long term, we believe that one promising method of building real-time software is to construct the software as a set of smart objects or agents.[11] These agents are sentient or have knowledge about themselves (for example, they know what they know and what they don't know). They actively manage themselves and negotiate with each other.

Each agent must have access to temporal information, since it is responsible for managing its own timeliness. It can then negotiate with other agents to guarantee timeliness. For example:

> Client agent: Can you guarantee execution of method X by time T?
> Server agent: No, but I can guarantee it by time $T + 1$.
> Client agent: OK. I'll take it.
> Server agent: You have a deal.

This type of negotiation is within the range of current research.

Similarly, dynamic instance management requires smart class managers that can negotiate with the client agents and offer guarantees on the timeliness of the creation and destruction operations. The class manager need not fully understand the application's semantics, only the temporal characteristics of creation and destruction mechanisms, the protocol for negotiating with its clients, and possibly some programmer-specified or statistical information about frequency of requests for creations and destructions.

As with the creation and destruction of instances, creation and destruction of classes requires a language for negotiating with clients. In this case, however, the class (and class manager) is itself created by an application-specific algorithm. This is a long-term research problem.

Even perfect real-time object-oriented models and support mechanisms are of little value if they are not used correctly. The proper design of real-time object-oriented application software is an active area of research.[3,12] We are optimistic that valuable analysis, design, and implementation techniques borrowed from the process-oriented model can be combined and used under the object-oriented model's umbrella.

Predictable object-oriented constructs depend on predictable operating systems, processors, and communication links for underlying support. Without them, no real-time software can be truly predictable. Representatives of each of these technologies are, or soon will be, commercially available, but more work remains.

As the number of large, dynamic real-time systems continues to grow, we believe that the object-oriented model's intrinsic benefits will make it the model of choice for many real-time systems. ∎

References

1. J.A. Stankovic, "Misconceptions About Real-Time Computing: A Serious Problem for Next-Generation Systems," *Computer*, Vol. 21, No. 10, Oct. 1988, pp. 10-19.

2. B.W. Henderson, "Design and Planning Make High-Tech F-22 Easy to Maintain and Support," *Aviation Week and Space Technology*, July 1991, pp. 50-51.

3. G. Booch, *Object-Oriented Design With Applications*, Benjamin/Cummings, Redwood City, Calif., 1991.

4. B. Hayes-Roth, "Research on Intelligent Agents," *Proc. Workshop Intelligent Real-Time Problem Solving*, Cimflex Teknowledge, Palo Alto, Calif., 1990, pp. VII-1 to VII-12.

5. K.B. Kenny and K.-J. Lin, "Building Flexible Real-Time Systems Using the Flex Language," *Computer*, Vol. 24, No. 5, May 1991, pp. 70-78.

6. Y. Ishikawa, H. Tokuda, and C.W. Mercer, "An Object-Oriented Real-Time Programming Language," *Computer*, Vol. 25, No. 10, Oct. 1992, pp. 66-73.

7. D.J. Miller and R.C. Lennox, "RIPE: An Object-Oriented Robot-Independent Programming Environment," *Proc. 1990 Usenix C++ Conf.*, Usenix, Berkeley, Calif., 1988, pp. 115-124.

8. K. Schwan, P. Gopinath, and W. Bo, "Chaos: Kernel Support for Objects in the Real-Time Domain," *IEEE Trans. Computers*, Vol. C-36, No. 8, Aug. 1987, pp. 904-916.

9. P. Gopinath and R. Gupta, "Applying Compiler Techniques to Scheduling in Real-Time Systems," *Proc. 11th Real-Time Systems Symp.*, IEEE CS Press, Los Alamitos, Calif., Order No. 2112, 1990, pp. 247-256.

10. D. Jordan, "Implementation Benefits of C++ Programming Language," *Comm. ACM*, Vol. 33, No. 9, Sept. 1990, pp. 61-64.

11. Y. Shoham, "Agent-Oriented Programming," Tech. Report Stan-CS-90-1335, Computer Science Dept., Stanford Univ., Stanford, Calif., Feb. 1990.

12. T. Bihari, P. Gopinath, and K. Schwan, "Object-Oriented Design of Real-Time Software," *Proc. 10th Real-Time Systems Symp.*, IEEE CS Press, Los Alamitos, Calif., Order No. 2004, 1989, pp. 194-201.

Thomas E. Bihari is chief scientist at Adaptive Machine Technologies, Columbus, Ohio. His research interests include software engineering, real-time systems, robotics, human-computer interfaces, and artificial intelligence.

Bihari received a BS in mathematics from Kent State University in 1978, and an MS in mathematics, and MS and PhD degrees in computer science from Ohio State University in 1982, 1983, and 1987, respectively. He is a member of the IEEE, the IEEE Computer Society, and ACM.

Prabha Gopinath is a principal research scientist at Honeywell's Sensor and System Development Center, Minneapolis, Minnesota. He previously served on the faculty of the University of Central Florida and the Florida Institute of Technology, and was a senior member of the research staff at Philips Research Laboratories. His research interests are in real-time systems, object-oriented techniques for high-performance systems, timing specification methodologies, and compilers for real-time applications.

Gopinath received his MS in 1984 and his PhD in 1988, both from Ohio State University. He is a member of the IEEE Computer Society and ACM.

Readers can contact Bihari at Adaptive Machine Technologies, 1218 Kinnear Rd., Columbus, OH 43212. His e-mail address is 72170.2655@compuserve.com. Gopinath can be reached at the Sensor and System Development Center, Honeywell, MN 65-2350, 3660 Technology Dr., Minneapolis, MN 55418. His e-mail address is gopinath_prabha@ssdc.honeywell.com.

Chapter 8

Graphics System Applications

Application Graphics Modeling Support Through Object Orientation

Parris K. Egbert* and William J. Kubitz

University of Illinois at Urbana-Champaign

Reprinted from *Computer*, October 1992, 84–91. Copyright © 1992 by The Institute of Electrical and Electronics Engineers, Inc. All rights reserved.

I n an application with computer graphics, the user assembles, transforms, and manipulates data by interpreting portions of it as logically connected and interdependent. Thus, the user naturally encapsulates individual data groups as separate *objects*. Whether or not the data represents real-world phenomena, the user thinks of each data group as a distinct object. For example, a biologist doing molecular modeling thinks in terms of atoms and molecules, each as a separate object. The same is true for almost all other applications. Thus, object orientation is a natural vehicle for performing computer graphics, at least from the user's perspective.

This article presents our work in developing a graphics system specifically designed to capitalize on the object-oriented paradigm. In particular, our system lets the programmer work at a higher level of abstraction, encapsulate object data and interfaces, and extend the system through inheritance, subclassing, and code reuse. It also reduces the user's learning time for the application.

Computer graphics technology has improved dramatically over the past 15 years. New algorithms produce near-photorealistic images, and new hardware accelerators lower the time required to run them. Much work has been devoted to improving image quality and reducing rendering time, but less work to making graphics easy to use in a broad set of applications. Addressing this "ease of use" issue was one of our principal motivations in developing the system we call Grams, which stands for Graphical Application Modeling Support system.

Many people have anticipated the benefits of marrying graphics with object orientation, and a few researchers have designed systems toward this end. Wisskirchen[1] implemented the functionality of GKS and PHIGS in an object-oriented fashion using Smalltalk. His work showed not only that combining graphics with object orientation is feasible, but also that the result has many desirable characteristics. However, the system he designed is not problem free. PHIGS has many archaic attributes, such as support for vector displays and carryovers from the ACM Core System work. Since Wisskirchen's system is designed around PHIGS, it perpetuates many PHIGS attributes.

HOOPS[2] is another graphics system touted as object oriented. It is not imple-

> **This object-oriented system raises the level of abstraction at which the user performs modeling and provides a simple interface between the application and the graphics system.**

---

*Egbert recently joined the faculty at Brigham Young University.

mented in an object-oriented language but derives benefits of the object-oriented paradigm by allowing application programmers to group primitives and attributes as objects. Once an object has been defined in this manner, it can then be used to form other objects. However, because HOOPS lacks classing and inheritance, today's standard definitions[3] would more appropriately designate it as *object based* rather than object oriented.

Dore[4] is another object-based graphics system. Because Dore is independent of any graphics standard, the application programmer can easily extend it. Although it is an improvement over the previously cited systems, Dore is still too low level for application users; it is not at the level of abstraction at which users prefer to work.

The Application Visualization System[5] is an object-oriented system for the visualization of scientific data. Users link modules via a visual interface that performs various functions on their data. By connecting appropriate modules, users can visualize the data in a variety of ways. The system's goal was to provide an easily understood interface for visualization, and it does this well. However, it was not designed as a general graphics system, and extending it to accommodate other graphics applications would be difficult.

Zeleznik et al. have created an object-based graphics system designed for producing animation.[6] This system uses delegation as opposed to the classical approach of inheritance and classing. Thus, it does not fully utilize some features of object orientation.

Drawbacks of current systems

Taken together, current graphics systems have several problems. Most apparent is disregard for applications for purposes of system efficiency. The result is that applications must work at the renderers' level rather than at their natural level.

Another problem is that system components are too tightly coupled. This is done for efficiency and to lower cost and storage requirements. The problem is that this approach discourages experimentation with new algorithms and ideas. With the rate at which computer

graphics is expanding and improving, it is not desirable or feasible to alter an entire system to upgrade a single component.

Grams overview

Grams is a three-dimensional graphics system that raises the abstraction level at which the application programmer and the end user interact with the system in the image-generation process. Rather than build the system around an existing standard or system, we built Grams from scratch. This let us emphasize the needs of application users and design the system so that people other than graphics specialists can use it. At the same time, Grams does not preclude high-quality graphics techniques or the addition of new application functionality. For example, after we built the system, we added a PEX renderer in a very straightforward fashion, even though PHIGS is not the basis of the system design. Other functionality is likewise easily incorporated.

Figure 1 shows a logical division of the overall system into three components: the application, graphics, and rendering layers. Grams defines the

graphics layer and the interfaces between it and the other two layers. It does not formally define the application and rendering layers, but because of the interaction between these layers and Grams, we discuss them briefly. Then we overview the graphics layer and present its object-oriented aspects. A more detailed discussion of the three layers is available elsewhere.[7,8]

Application layer. At the application layer the application user interacts with the system. Objects at this level are *application objects*. An application object contains all data deemed appropriate by the application: geometry information, material type or properties, cost information, supplier information, or any other data the application must store. The information is organized in an object-oriented fashion and stored in the application database.

The application uses the other two layers, the graphics and rendering layers, to produce a graphical image of the application objects. As such, these layers are simply tools used by the application: They use application-provided information but do not alter it.

Rendering layer. Actual image generation takes place at the rendering layer. The graphics layer sends data to the rendering layer in a form understandable by the renderers. For easy system extensibility, all renderers must accept a small number of low-level graphics primitives. In addition, all graphic objects must be able to transform themselves into one of these primitives. The primitives in this set of common objects are points, lines, and polygons. With these two requirements, we instituted a method for easily adding new renderers or graphics primitives without having to simultaneously alter other portions of the system.

The main problem with requiring the

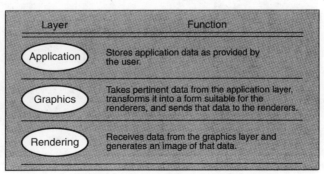

Layer	Function
Application	Stores application data as provided by the user.
Graphics	Takes pertinent data from the application layer, transforms it into a form suitable for the renderers, and sends that data to the renderers.
Rendering	Receives data from the graphics layer and generates an image of that data.

Figure 1. The system layers.

renderability of this set of common objects is that renderers may be able to render other objects more efficiently. Allowing them to render only these low-level primitives may decrease their performance dramatically. We overcame this problem by letting renderers communicate with the graphics system. If a renderer can render a graphic object other than those specified in the minimal set, it sends a message to the graphics layer. The renderer also provides an efficiency measurement so that the graphics system can prioritize the graphic objects renderable by a particular renderer and send the objects that are most efficiently rendered by that renderer. Thus, renderers use their built-in capabilities to improve rendering.

The system can use any style of renderer that accepts the set of common graphics primitives. Different applications will use different renderers, depending on their requirements. In addition, one application will often use a fast, low-quality renderer to set up a scene, and then switch to a high-quality renderer to produce the final image.

We have experimented with three renderers. The first was UIPEX, the University of Illinois implementation of PEX.[9] We next extended the system to include a renderer based on the Silicon Graphics GL library.[10] This provided more hardware support for the graphics and decreased image-generation time. The third renderer we used is a Monte Carlo renderer written by Peter Shirley.[11] This is a hybrid ray-tracing and radiosity renderer that produces very high quality images.

The application associates a renderer with each application object in the scene. To render the object using a different renderer, the application simply associates the new renderer with the object. No other changes are necessary.

Graphics layer. The graphics layer mediates between the application and rendering layers. It gleans pertinent information from the application, interprets that information in a semantically correct manner, and transforms the information into a form understood by the renderers. Objects at this level are known as *graphic objects*. To visualize an application object, the user must associate an appropriate graphic object with the application object. Once that association is established, the application need not be concerned further about the graphics process. It simply instructs the graphic object to render itself. The graphic object must then extract the pertinent application data, transform it into a suitable form, and send that data to the renderers.

The graphics system needs only a small amount of application data: the object's geometry, the material the object is to be made of, coordinate transformations pertaining to the object, and the graphic object associated with the application object. For each of these quantities, each application object contains an instance variable, which is a pointer to an abstract class. As the application specifies the data it will store in these instance variables, the system creates instances of appropriate subclasses that encapsulate the application data. Subclassing in this fashion permits unified and consistent interfacing from the graphics layer to the application layer.

Class hierarchies in Grams

An important decision in an object-oriented design is the organization of the class hierarchies. Designers should group object classes according to similar characteristics among the objects. The problem is identifying the appropriate characteristics to determine the grouping. As system design progresses

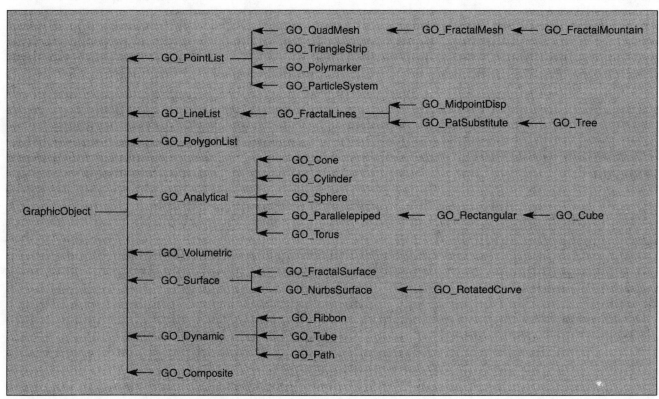

Figure 2. Upper layers of the graphic object class hierarchy.

and the designers understand more about the objects and their characteristics, they often need to revise the class hierarchies. Booch[12] says it usually takes three or four definitions of a class hierarchy to find the correct one.

With Grams, the application must be familiar with two distinct class hierarchies: the application class hierarchy and the graphic object class hierarchy.

The application completely defines and owns the application class hierarchy, which is probably relevant only to that particular application. The application defines the attributes used to determine the classing structure. A different application using the same types of objects will probably structure the classes much differently.

The graphic object class hierarchy is defined by Grams and contains all graphic objects in the system. These objects are subsequently used by the application to visually represent an application object.

Figure 2 shows the top layers of the graphic object class hierarchy. We defined these levels to provide a broad base so that all graphic objects an application may eventually use will fit neatly into one of the classes. The class GraphicObject is defined at the root level. All other graphic objects are subclasses of this abstract class.

The criterion we used to group objects as subclasses of the same class is a commonality in the internal representations of the objects; that is, objects defined and stored in a similar fashion share a common superclass. For example, a quadrilateral mesh is most easily defined as a list of points interpreted as a two-dimensional grid. Likewise, a triangle strip is generally defined as a list of points, with the understanding that each set of three consecutive points in the list represents a triangle. Because of the similarities in the ways these two objects are stored, we defined them as subclasses of the same class — the GO_PointList class.

The root class GraphicObject defines the data and methods common to all graphic objects. It defines storage locations for references to the application object's geometry, material, and transformations, as well as methods that set those values appropriately. In addition, it provides methods to handle the rendering of the graphic objects.

Eight classes are direct subclasses of GraphicObject. GO_PointList is the superclass of objects naturally defined as a list of points. The class GO_LineList contains the necessary data for storing and manipulating a list of lines. The GO_PolygonList class provides similar functionality for lists of polygons. Objects that can be defined analytically fall under class GO_Analytical. Included here are objects such as cones, spheres, and tori. The class GO_Volumetric stores and provides interfaces to volumetric data. Specific applications subclass this class to handle various types of volume data. Objects defined as surfaces have as their superclass the class GO_Surface. These are currently divided into fractal surfaces and NURBS surfaces. Further subclassing produces specific object types. The class GO_Dynamic is the superclass of objects that move over time and has the notion of time built in. Subclasses specify particular time parameters as well as the actual objects to be traced. The GO_Dynamic class calculates time-variant positions of the objects associated with it. The final subclass of GraphicObject is GO_Composite. This class is the superclass of graphic objects built as simple combinations of other graphic objects. From the user's perspective, these composite objects are atomic in their aggregate form.

We defined the above classes to have one superclass. However, the system provides multiple inheritance — that is, multiple superclasses — for applications that require them. For example, if an application performs animation on a sphere, it could create a new class that has both GO_Sphere and GO_Dynamic as superclasses.

Figure 3 shows how the system uses subclassing. Each of the five objects in this scene is defined as a subclass of the class GO_RotatedCurve. GO_RotatedCurve is defined by the system as a subclass of GO_NurbsSurface, which is a subclass of GO_Surface. GO_RotatedCurve takes

Figure 3. Objects that are subclasses of class GO_RotatedCurve.

a list of control points defining a curve, rotates them about the y axis to produce control points for a surface, and then generates a NURBS surface from the resulting surface control points. Subclasses of GO_RotatedCurve simply provide the list of curve points; the superclasses do all other computations automatically.

We defined the objects GO_Vase, GO_FlowerVase, GO_Goblet, GO_Candlestick, and GO_Bowl in this fashion. With the functionality built into the superclasses, defining these new classes required minimal coding. The GO_Bowl class required four lines of C++ code for the class definition and 16 lines of code for the actual coding of the class methods. GO_Candlestick required four lines of code for the definition and 30 for the implementation of the methods.

Once these objects are defined, the user-supplied code is minimal. The objects in this scene required about five lines of C++ code each. Figure 4 shows the code to create the goblet.

The first line creates the application object goblet, which is an instance of

```
ApplicationObject goblet = new ApplicationObject();
goblet.setGraphicObject(new GO_Goblet());
goblet.setGeometry(Point(0.6, –1.3, –1.5), 0.5);
goblet.setMaterial(MAT_GOLD);
world_object.addApplicationObject(goblet, monte_carlo_renderer);
world_object.render();
```

Figure 4. Code to create the goblet in Figure 3.

the class ApplicationObject and is the object the application owns and uses. The second line of code establishes the graphic object to visualize this application object. In this case, the graphic object chosen was GO_Goblet. The third line sets up the geometry information for this application object. The application object is located at the point (0.6, −1.3, −1.5) and has a height of 0.5 unit.

Grams uses this information later to create the image of the goblet. The next line specifies the material the goblet is to be made of — in this case, gold. At rendering time, the system uses this material specification to communicate the appropriate material properties to the renderer. The fifth line associates the Monte Carlo renderer with this application object. The world object keeps

track of which application objects are to be rendered and the renderer to be associated with each object. The last line in the code segment shown in Figure 4 initiates the rendering process. At that point, the graphics system passes the pertinent information to the rendering level, which produces the image (see the sidebar "The image-generation process").

We designed the graphic object class

The image-generation process

The actual image-generation process is initiated when the user sends a render message to the world object. Figure A shows the message flow that results. The world object is a mechanism for keeping track of the application objects to be visualized and the actual viewing parameters to be used in generating the images of these objects. On receipt of the render message, the world object sends the viewing parameters to the renderers used in the scene. Following this, the world object sends a render message to each application object present in it. Also, it sends as a parameter the renderer associated with each application object. The application objects then inform their associated graphic objects that a visualization of the application data has been requested, and send their current transformation and material attributes. Next, the application objects send the graphic objects a render message.

The graphic object must interpret the application data so that the semantics of the application are represented appropriately. It must also transform the application data into a form the renderer can use. The graphic object determines the correct form for sending the data by consulting the renderer capability table. This table is maintained by the system and keeps track of each renderer's capabilities. Capabilities are added to the table as the renderers inform the system of their functionality. By consulting this table, the graphic object determines the types of data the renderer can understand. It then performs the appropriate data transformation and sends the data to the renderer, which generates the image.

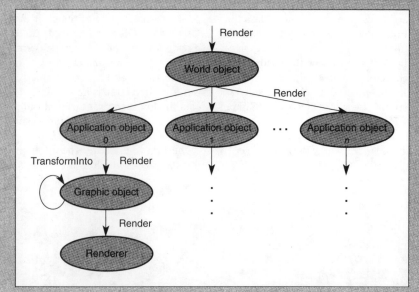

Figure A. Message flow in the image-generation process.

A typical application graphic object

Application graphic objects are designed to interface with the graphics system in a way that shields system details from the application and makes the graphic object very natural for the application to use. Here we present an example that shows the creation of the application graphic object GO_Candlestick. Figure B shows the class hierarchy for the definition of GO_Candlestick. Figure C shows the actual method definitions for the classes involved. The GO_Candlestick graphic object can be defined easily with a list of control points rotated about an axis. The system provides the class GO_RotatedCurve that performs this functionality, and GO_Candlestick fits very nicely as a subclass of this class.

GO_RotatedCurve has defined in it most of the functionality needed by GO_Candlestick. These methods need not be redefined as part of the new graphic object; they can simply be inherited from the superclass. The only new methods the application programmer needs to define are a constructor method and a method that communicates geometry information to GO_Candlestick.

GO_RotatedCurve generates a NURBS surface from the data contained in it. Thus, it is declared as a subclass of the graphic object GO_NurbsSurface. The method generateData() defined as a member function of this class generates the NURBS surface from current data stored in the instance variables of the class.

GO_NurbsSurface is defined as a subclass of GO_Surface. When an object of this type is rendered, this

hierarchy to be easily extensible by the application programmer. It is impossible to provide a system that includes the graphic objects required by all applications. Thus, our aim in Grams is to provide a broad set of general graphic objects and then provide a simple mechanism for extending the system. Thus, the application programmer can include application-specific graphic objects with minimal effort (see the sidebar "A typical application graphic object").

Implementation

We wrote Grams in C++ on an IBM RS6000. It currently consists of about 18,000 lines of code. A problem with object-oriented languages is their inherent overhead. To determine the efficiency penalty for using an object-oriented language in Grams, we ran performance measurements on various parts of the image-generation process. Table 1 shows the timing results for Figures 3 and 5.

The table shows that rendering consumes the most time when the high-

class must generate a NURBS surface. Subclasses of GO_NurbsSurface must set the GO_NurbsSurface instance variables appropriately before image generation. The GO_NurbsSurface methods then perform the actual NURBS surface computations.

The class GO_Surface is a subclass of GraphicObject and contains generic information and methods common to all types of surfaces. Functionality unique to specific surface types must be provided by the subclasses.

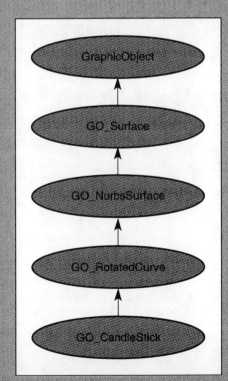

Figure B. The classing structure for GO_Candlestick.

Figure C. The class definitions in the GO_Candlestick class hierarchy.

```
class GraphicObject {
protected:
        Geometry    **geometry;    /* the Geometry of the GO        */
        Matrix4     trans;         /* transformation matrix         */
        Material    *material;     /* the material of the AO that   */
                                   /* this GO is representing        */

public:
        GraphicObject();
        void setGeometry(Geometry*);
        virtual void setMaterial(Material*);
        virtual void setTransformation(Matrix4 &mat);
        virtual GraphicObject* transformInto(int);
};

class NurbsSurface : public GraphicObject {
protected:
        int u_order, v_order, num_u_knots, num_v_knots;
        float *u_knots, *v_knots;
        PointList4 control_pts;

public:
        NurbsSurface();
        void set(int, int, int, int, float*, float*, PointList4&);
        void updateGeometry(Geom_NurbsData*);
        GraphicObject* transformInto(int);
        void transform(Matrix4&);
};

class RotatedCurve : public NurbsSurface {
protected:
        Point    origin;
        int      num_points;
        Point    *points;

public:
        RotatedCurve();
        void set(Point&, int, Point*);
        void generateData();
        Point getCenter();
        void render(Renderer*);
        void transform(Matrix4&);
};

class Candlestick: public RotatedCurve {
public:
        Candlestick();
        void updateGeometry(Geom_PointFloat*);
}
```

175

Table 1. Grams performance measurements.

Characteristic	Figure 3	Figure 5
Image size	512 × 512	512 × 512
Number of application objects in scene	10	13
Transform data to Silicon Graphics GL form	1:25*	2:13
Render using GL renderer	:01**	:01
Transform data to Monte Carlo form	1:38	2:34
Render using Monte Carlo renderer	12:51:20***	8:37:41

* Minutes and seconds
** Seconds
*** Hours, minutes, and seconds

Figure 5. A sample scene using Grams.

quality renderer is used. However, with the lower quality renderer, the time required to transform the data from application specification to renderable form is the bottleneck. Further refinement of the timing measurements showed that approximately 95 percent of this transformation time was spent in the NURBS surface calculations. Thus, the object-oriented overhead is minimal in comparison with other computation times. Our experience shows that the time saved in learning and using the system, as well as the ease in extending it, more than compensates for the overhead incurred by object orientation.

Grams assists the application user in the image-generation process. The graphics layer lets the application provide modeling objects close to the level of abstraction at which the user thinks. Users are freed from low-level graphics details and can focus on their application data.

Figure 5 is composed of 12 modeling primitives. The application performed modeling here using objects such as chairs, goblets, and candlesticks. Contemporary graphics systems would have forced the user to model these objects using polygons. Thus, our system greatly reduced the code and complexity involved in doing the modeling. This scene also shows other system capabilities, including transparency and texture mapping.

In addition to providing an easy-to-use graphics system, Grams is extensible at all levels. The well-defined interface between the three layers lets programmers add new functionality to any level without altering the other levels — a capability other systems lack.

Treating entities as distinct objects in a computer graphics system is a very natural way of thinking. Thus, designing a computer graphics system around the object-oriented paradigm makes intuitive sense. By combining graphics with object orientation we have been able to overcome many of the problems in today's graphics systems. ∎

References

1. P. Wisskirchen, *Object-Oriented Graphics*, Springer-Verlag, Berlin, 1990.

2. B.D. Kliewer, "HOOPS: Powerful Portable 3D Graphics," *Byte*, Vol. 14, No. 7, July 1989, pp. 193-194.

3. P. Wegner, "Dimensions of Object-Based Language Design," *Proc. OOPSLA 87*, ACM, New York, 1987, pp. 168-182.

4. *Dore Reference Manual*, Kubota Pacific Computer Inc., Santa Clara, Calif., 1991.

5. C. Upson et al., "The Application Visualization System: A Computational Environment for Scientific Visualization," *IEEE Computer Graphics and Applications*, Vol. 9, No. 4, July 1989, pp. 30-42.

6. R.C. Zeleznik et al., "An Object-Oriented Framework for the Integration of Interactive Animation Techniques," *Computer Graphics* (Proc. Siggraph), Vol. 25, No. 4, July 1991, pp. 105-112.

7. P.K. Egbert, *An Object-Oriented Approach to Graphical Application Support*, doctoral dissertation, Univ. of Illinois at Urbana-Champaign, 1992.

8. P.K. Egbert and W.J. Kubitz, "The Graphical Application Support System," in *Computer Graphics Using Object-Oriented Programming*, Steve Cunningham et al., eds., John Wiley and Sons, New York, 1992, pp. 137-164.

9. P.K. Egbert, *UIPEX: Design of the Application Programmer Interface*, master's thesis, Report No. UIUCDCS-R-90-1592, Dept. of Computer Science, Univ. of Illinois at Urbana-Champaign, 1990.

10. *Graphics Library Reference Manual, C Edition*, Document No. 007-1203-020, Silicon Graphics Inc., Mountain View, Calif., 1988.

11. P. Shirley, *Physically Based Lighting Calculations for Computer Graphics*, doctoral dissertation, University of Illinois at Urbana-Champaign, 1990.

12. G. Booch, *Object-Oriented Design with Applications*, Benjamin Cummings, Redwood City, Calif., 1991.

William J. Kubitz is a professor and associate head of computer science at the University of Illinois at Urbana-Champaign. He and his students conduct research in VLSI design automation in the areas of automatic timing-driven placement, module generation, and routing, and in object-oriented graphics systems to support scientific and engineering design and visualization.

Kubitz holds a BS in engineering physics, an MS in physics, and a PhD in electrical engineering from the University of Illinois. He is a senior member of IEEE, and a member of AAAS, ACM (Siggraph, SIGDA), and Sigma Xi.

Parris K. Egbert is an assistant professor of computer science at Brigham Young University. His research interests include object-oriented graphics, modeling, and the visualization of scientific data.

Egbert received his BS in computer science and mathematics from Utah State University in 1986, and his MS and PhD in computer science from the University of Illinois at Urbana-Champaign in 1990 and 1992, respectively. He is a member of ACM, Phi Kappa Phi, and Tau Beta Pi.

Egbert's address is Brigham Young University, Department of Computer Science, 3361 TMCB, Provo, UT 84602; e-mail egbert@cs.byu.edu. Kubitz is at the University of Illinois at Urbana-Champaign, Department of Computer Science, 1304 W. Springfield Ave., Urbana, IL 61801.

Chapter 9

Data Systems Applications

ERC+: An Object+Relation-Ship Paradigm for Database Applications

Stefano Spaccapietra, Ecole Polytechnique Fédérale, Lausanne, Switzerland

Christine Parent, Marcos Sunye, Kokou Yetongnon, Université de Bourgogne, France

Antonio Di Leva, Universita degli Studi di Torino, Italy

O bject-oriented data models are designed to model application objects that are close to the user's view. Developers of applications relying on object-oriented database-management systems, though, face difficulties because object-oriented data models are limited in their capacity to describe the full range of possible associations between objects and between processes.

In this paper we focus on the conceptual data-modeling needs of object- oriented database applications, and propose an object+relationship model, ERC+, which meets database application requirements by merging features of traditional semantic data models with object-oriented capabilities such as structural object orientation, inheritance, and object identity. It is an extended entity-relationship model specifically designed to support description of complex objects and to allow multiple perceptions of objects. The ERC+ model provides the foundation for an integrated environment of tools called SUPER, created to help develop database applications. The significant features of the SUPER environment include a graphical schema editor for describing complex objects, a data browser, and a graphical editor for formulating ERC+ queries.

Introduction

Object orientation has rapidly become very popular. It has, indeed, proved to be a powerful and practical programming paradigm, bringing many benefits such as modularity, reusability, flexibility, and extendibility to those who design and develop software systems. Implementors of large and complex systems have found the object-oriented (OO) modeling paradigm particularly appealing for these reasons:

- It uses few but powerful concepts, including abstract data types, an inheritance mechanism, and object identity; the result is a clean, abstract paradigm and methodology on a sound foundation consisting of programming languages.
- It stresses modularity in design of complex systems by transforming them into a collection of interoperable objects, thus allowing developers to react quickly and easily to evolving specifications.
- It provides the inheritance mechanism to enforce reusability of both data-structure descriptions and operational def-

initions, ultimately decreasing time and cost spent in developing software.

Taking advantage of these features, software producers have built complex systems such as: software-engineering environments, CASE tools, OO languages, OO interface systems, and OO database-management systems (DBMS). The benefits of the OO approach have found good acceptance in the database markets.

This success story raises a question: Can domains other than large software-system design get the same benefits by adopting the OO modeling approach? Can database applications benefit from it? Modern applications in such data-intensive fields as computer-aided design and computer-aided manufacturing (CAD/CAM), office automation, computer-integrated manufacturing (CIM), robotics, and geographic systems must deal with highly structured and interrelated information objects. Because these applications are just as complex as large software systems, OO technology has naturally been advocated as a key to their efficient design and implementation. Hopes are high that OO DBMS will be a significant improvement over traditional database technologies in meeting the requirements of these applications. Specifically, systems supporting data structures that allow database objects to look like those users deal with in the real world will make user–DBMS interaction much easier. It will avoid the problem that is presently experienced as impedance mismatch (i.e., having two interacting agents reasoning with different paradigms).

Unfortunately, OO technology applied to information systems has not yet completely fulfilled these expectations. Indeed, when moving a technology from one domain to another, concepts most often have to be reshaped to cope with the new environment, and new ones must be added to achieve full power to meet the new goals. Here is an example of the former. As users change from system programmers to application designers and end users, some OO features may place an additional burden on end users. Data encapsulation of objects, for instance, is highly desirable for efficiently managing design at the implementation level. With it, design can be broken down into parts, allowing each designer to independently develop his or her part. Database practice, though, is based on keeping access to information open to everyone. Encapsulation thus needs to be partly traded for

easy access to attributes, so that general-purpose query languages (SQL and others) may be implemented.

On the other hand, the OO paradigm needs more power to provide conceptual representation of associations among objects, as discussed in detail in the next section. Indeed, the data model's descriptive power is vital in the database field. The system programmer's primary aim is efficiency, but the database designer's is accurate representation. Describing reality in adequate detail, revealing the semantics in the data, but keeping implementation a separate issue—all must be achieved staying as close as possible to the user's perception. This activity is called *conceptual design*. Elaborating an implementation-oriented representation of data and of performance-related specifications is called *physical design,* and is dealt with in a separate design step following conceptual design.

We set out in this paper to bridge the gap between the OO paradigm and its successful use in developing database applications. We begin by contrasting the features of object orientation with the requirements of developers of database applications and offer a proposal on issues in which a deficiency has been identified. These deficiencies are: inadequate representation of associations, lack of support for generic data manipulations, and absence of a concept for describing the application's global behavior. By extending the OO data model, we achieve the approach nowadays known as object+relationship (OR) modeling. Such OR models are meant to combine the advantages of OO models with those provided by semantic-data models. To describe an information system's behavior, traditional research in database modeling offers Petri netlike approaches can be used in conjunction with an OO or OR data model.

We first deal with the issue of conceptual modeling of data structures (objects and associations) by proposing a structural-data model called ERC+. This is an extended entity-relationship (ER) model (11), specifically designed to support objects with complex structure. It is somewhat similar to recently proposed OR models (31), (3), providing full support for explicit conceptual description of generic relationships among objects.

Second, we discuss data-manipulation languages (DML), which complement the data model to provide for full and consistent capabilities for user–DBMS interac-

tion. The ERC+ algebraic-query language is presented here. Together with an equivalent calculus (25), these languages form the theoretical background for developing user-oriented languages. For instance, an ERC+ SQL-like DML has been developed (33).

Third, we present the graphical query language that has been implemented as part of a graphical environment, called SUPER, to help in designing and developing database applications. Based on the ERC+ approach, SUPER presently includes tools for graphically describing database schemas and for manipulating data graphically, either by schema or data browsing or by formulating queries. SUPER ensures user interaction with both OO DBMSs and traditional relational DBMSs, thus providing for DBMS independence. We then demonstrate how ERC+ may be coupled with a Petri-net–based process model to express the global dynamic behavior of the information system. Although OO methods allow us to describe local behavior of objects, the process model takes into account problems in concurrency and synchronization of object messages to represent the sequence in which operations are performed .

We then briefly examine the requirements of database applications and analyze the OO approach from the data-modeling perspective. To meet application requirements, we introduce the characteristics of an enhanced model. Next, we describe in detail and formally the proposed ERC+ model, followed by the issues in using algebra-based data-manipulation languages for defining, accessing, and managing complex-objects databases according to the ERC+ paradigm. We describe the SUPER environment, presenting its graphical schema editor, and discuss its graphical query editor. We consider the requirements for describing the dynamics of database applications and show how a process model of dynamics can be integrated with the structural description capability of ERC+.

Modeling database applications

In database design, the major aim in conceptually modeling application objects is to create representations that are close to reality and independent from implementation issues. Because users can

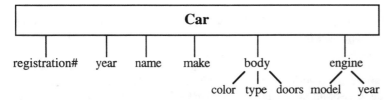

Figure 1. The receptionist's view: one object type, Car (boxes represent object types)

understand conceptual modeling (they need not know about peculiarities of DBM systems), it is easier to check that the resulting database schema meets users' requirements. Thus, chances of a correct design are improved by separating representational from implementation issues. We can change the implementation without having to modify the conceptual schema.

We next discuss requirements of both static (data-structures) and dynamic (behavioral) aspects of database applications for conceptual modeling. We briefly survey the extent to which traditional data models fulfill these requirements. A similar evaluation for OO models is the next subject. And finally we introduce the characteristics of an OR model intended to fully support application requirements.

Applications modeling requirements. Database applications are characterized by their need to represent, relate, and manipulate objects with complex information structures. Typically, objects having the same properties are collected into classes that are described by object types. Attributes are used to represent the properties of the objects in a class. The attribute structure of an object can be described by a tree whose root is the object, whose branches are of variable and unrestricted length, and whose nodes represent the object's components. Such objects are usually called *complex objects,* to contrast them with the simple flat objects supported by the relational approach (the tuples). Each object has a unique object identity (oid), and a composite value. The object value is composed from the atomic values attached to the leaves of the tree, according to the structure of the set of attributes attached to its object type. The object identity is system defined (not visible to users) and allows objects to be denoted independently from their value. From the manipulation point of view, it is essential that objects be manipulable as a whole logical unit, regardless of their complexity, and accessible through any of their components. Examples of complex-object

types are given in Figures 1 and 4.

When objects are shared by different applications, they may be perceived by these applications in different ways. Facilities for allowing multiple perceptions of objects are therefore essential. It must be possible for each application to attach its specific set of properties to an object, while the database keeps the knowledge that the object is unique despite its different representations. Most important is the ability to define different classification schemes—that is, different types of objects and the associations that lie between them. Let us consider a database for managing an automotive-repair garage. From the receptionist's point of view, cars may be perceived as individual objects, grouped in a class described by the Car object type, with properties including description of the car's engine and body (see Figure 1). From the mechanic's point of view, engines and bodies may be perceived as independent objects and described as such in Engine and Body object types. Despite their differences, both points of view model the same reality. The extent to which a modeling approach supports multiple points of view defines the degree of freedom an application has for defining its own perception of the database without having to comply with the perceptions of other applications sharing that database.

Supporting multiple perceptions on complex objects is but the first step in representational power. Objects do not live in isolation; they are related to, and interact with, other objects. If the garage-management application is to deal also with car owners as customers, the database will include a Customer object type, whose objects will be associated to Car objects to express the ownership association. Research on semantic data models shows that several kinds of associations are candidates for inclusion in a data model. They range from generic associations, whose semantics are known only to the application but not to the DBMS, to associations having specific predefined semantics: the component

(part-of) association, the generalization (is-a) association, and so on (8). The car-ownership association is an example of the generic type. Data models differ in support for association types, as they differ in support for complex objects.

Objects, properties, and associations characterize a data model's ability to describe data structures. In dynamic modeling, application requirements command capabilities to describe rules governing the behavior of objects as well as applications. The former express how an object may evolve with time and what operations may be performed on it. Each object type bears such a description. The latter allows us to describe interactions among objects and is typically based on the concepts of event, condition, and action: for each event to which the database should react, a rule describes the pre- and postconditions attached to the event and the corresponding actions to be performed. Object-specific operations too are influential in supporting data-manipulation requirements. They need to be complemented with generic query and update languages, however, to support generic and ad hoc manipulations.

Traditional data models

Current relational DBMSs respond poorly to the requirements listed above. They support only flat data structures—relations, whose components are restricted to atomic value attributes (this restriction is known as the *first normal form* rule). An object in a relation (a tuple) is a list of atomic values. Composite attributes are not allowed: for instance, it is not possible to specify a date attribute as composed of day, month, and year attributes. Multivalued attributes are not allowed: it is not possible to associate several values to a phone# attribute. The description of an object cannot be expressed as a self-contained block of information; it is instead spread over several relations. A major hindrance in such a solution is that the resulting representations do not parallel the structure of the objects being modeled, as perceived by users. Hence the problems users have in understanding a relational representation and in manipulating a relational database.

Moreover, relational DBMSs ignore associations, which have to be represented and managed by applications. Only the most recent versions of some major relational DBMSs include limited support for associations, in the form of ability to specify constraints on referential integrity and to have them checked by the system. For dynamic aspects, relational DBMS provides no specification mechanism. Dynamics is entirely within application programs. Inversely, relational DBMS supports a variety of data-manipulation languages: the relational algebra and calculus, as theoretical basis, SQL and QUEL as textual user-oriented DML, and QBE as graphical language. Using DML functionalities, users may define their own view over the relations in the database schema. Multiple perceptions of the same objects are thus easily defined.

Many extensions or alternatives to the traditional relational data model have been proposed to better capture real-world semantics and allow complex and/or composite objects to be represented. Most notable are nested relational models (also known as NF2: *non-first normal form*), and semantic-data models. Nested relational models (1), partially meet applications requirements by admitting relation-valued attributes: the value of an attribute in a tuple may be a set of tuples. This tactic in essence relaxes the relational first normal form restriction. Relation-valued attributes can be accessed and/or retrieved in the same manner as relations. In complex-object management, however, NF2 models still have a major restriction in that an object's structure is purely hierarchic: sharing of components is not supported and no cycles are allowed in an object's structure (a component cannot be of the same type as the composed object). Furthermore, facilities for restructuring a nested relation to define a different point of view are limited. Thus, NF2 models are not fully appropriate for representing complex objects and multiple perceptions. They also ignore dynamic aspects.

Semantic-data models are designed to represent real-world semantics as closely as possible. The emphasis on data description has not, however, found an equivalent in data manipulation. Semantic models are therefore mainly used in the initial phase of database design to produce a conceptual representation of the future database. This initial representation is then translated into a lower-level target model (e.g., relational or OO) to be implemented onto a DBMS. Extended-ER models, an example of the semantic-data model, use entity, relationship, attribute, generalization, and

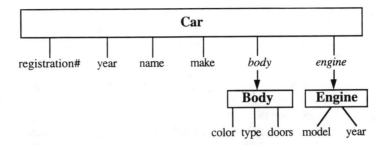

Figure 2. The global OO conceptual schema of the garage database example (arrows with italic labels represent reference attributes)

constraint to closely represent the properties of real-world objects and associations in between. An *entity* is the database representation of an object, with all its information attached: a complex object can be represented as a single entity. *Relationships* are generic associations among two or more objects. *Generalization* is a specific type of association used to specify that entities in one class (the subclass) are also represented in another class (the superclass). For instance, a generalization link (also called an is-a link) associating a Sportscar entity type to a Car entity type specifies that each object in the former class also belongs to the latter (i.e., each sportscar is a car).

The ER approach has not developed concepts for describing behavioral aspects. Dynamic rules may be expressed with associated constraint-specification languages (usually based on first-order logic), but no provision is made for specifying object-specific operations. From the data-manipulation perspective, a few languages have been proposed but none has been implemented in a commercial DBMS. Support for multiple perceptions is achieved to a great extent (32), but work remains to be done, as with NF2, on restructuring operations.

Object-oriented modeling. In databases, the OO approach, the first significant attempt to define a data model, simultaneously takes into account both structural and behavioral specifications. The model decidedly improves the state of the art in database modeling. We examine here how it matches application requirements.

From the data-modeling perspective, the leading features of the OO approach are: object identity, complex data structures, abstract data types, and inheritance. *Object identity* (oid) is used to associate each object with a unique identity. This oid distinguishes the object from others without having to rely on user-defined values. Applications decidedly need this feature as a denotational mechanism. User-defined identifiers (the "unique-key" attributes) cannot safely be used as oids because they confuse identity with data values (19). Updating an attribute that is (part of) a key is not allowed even though it is a value attribute with a specific meaning like those of other value attributes.

Objects may be as complex as needed in an OO schema. Object-oriented models allow unrestricted iterative decomposition of an object into components. Moreover, they allow a component of an object to be an object itself (i.e., with its own identity) rather than a value attribute. Component objects may be of the same type as the object they are part of. Objects whose composition includes other objects are hereinafter named *composite objects*. Conversely, *atomic object* denotes an object whose components are all value attributes. This naming introduces a clear difference between OO models, supporting complex and composite objects, and extended ER models, which support complex objects but do not support composite objects. Allowing composite objects is the OO mechanism to support multiple perceptions of the same object. Every object can at the same time be an object on its own and serve as a component within other objects. This composition association is materialized by a reference attribute that points from the composed object to the component object. The domain of a reference attribute is the set of oids representing the objects that the attribute refers to. *References* are directed one-way links from a composite object to its components. For example, if the composition of a Car includes a Body and an Engine, where Car, Body, and Engine are three object types, then this fact can be expressed by two ref-

183

erence attributes, body and engine, in the Car object type (see Figure 2.).

Composite objects offer limited flexibility in supporting multiple perceptions. It would not always be straightforward to add to the Engine object type a reference to Car to describe the cars that possess this engine, while ensuring that this reference holds a value consistent with those in the (inverse) references from Car to Engine.

Besides composition, OO models' ability to express associations include only the inheritance link. An *inheritance link* between two object classes describes a subclass/superclass relationship, which means that all objects of the subclass are also objects of the superclass. It corresponds to the generalization association. Most often, the link is intended for reuse of structural (attributes) as well as definitions of behavioral (methods). The subtype inherits these definitions from the supertype (downward inheritance). Thus, inheritance may be used as a mechanism for top-down design of a hierarchy of object types, where each design level refines the definitions (superclass) of the upper level into a set of subclass definitions. The description of a car can easily become established by refining the more general definition of a vehicle class. Refinement can be achieved either by adding new attributes or methods that are specific to cars and not valid for vehicles in general, or by redefining attributes and/or methods attached to vehicle to make them more specific to cars.

Abstract data types convey the idea that the structural description of a set of objects (showing the properties they share) has to be complemented with the definition of the operations that can manipulate the objects. Thus both static and dynamic aspects of objects can be captured. The definitions of the allowed operations (the *methods,* in OO terminology) represent the interface of the abstract- data type. Essentially, this interface provides users with information on how to use the objects but not on how the objects are implemented. Furthermore, abstract- data types use data encapsulation to separate implementation details from usage of an object and to ensure that the only operations that can be performed on the objects are those specified in the interface.

These capabilities meet some but not all application requirements. As the name says, the main goal of object orientation is describing objects. From this point of view OO models do provide the function that is needed. On the contrary, their description of associations is far too restricted. Only two kinds of specific associations are available: composition and generalization. Object-oriented programming systems are meant more to reuse the code segments that are used to implement properties and methods than to achieve accurate description of real-world objects. Composition and inheritance links are used mostly to avoid redundant specifications of data structures and operations. The concept of attribute is used as a unifying abstraction both for describing object properties (value attributes) and for embodying associations between objects (reference attributes). Albano et al. (3) point out that the main advantage of this unification is to simplify system implementation by using the same access mechanism to manipulate both attributes and associations. This trade-off between implementation efficiency and conceptual capability reduces the model's expressive power and penalizes designers of database systems.

In database design, a major intent is to create representations that are close to reality and independent from implementation. This goal cannot be achieved using only the composition and inheritance associations. Consider the ownership association between the object types Car and Person, mentioned above. Using reference attributes (composition) to express this generic association may yield many possible representations, including these:

(1) a reference from Person to Car.
(2) a reference from Car to Person.
(3) cross-references between Person and Car.
(4) a new Ownership object is created to include a reference to Person and another to Car.
(5) a new Ownership object is created that is linked by cross-references to both Person and Car.

Composition is a directed association. It cannot properly describe, at the conceptual level, a generic association that is nondirected by definition. A car is not a component of a person, and vice versa. On the other hand, composition may be used to implement the generic association. It is, indeed, when implementation aspects are considered that a choice among the solutions above can be made on the basis of performance criteria and the available information on the access paths most frequently used.

Inadequate representation is not the only drawback in using reference attributes to express generic associations. It also does not allow us to declaratively express semantic information attached to the different roles in an association. Cardinality constraints (How many cars may a person own? How many owners may a car have?) are an example of information that , in the OO approach, has to be coded in implementing the methods used to manipulate the objects, and is therefore hidden from the data-description point of view. Second, representation of the association is spread over the definitions of the objects participating in it. In some of the solutions above, the definition of the Ownership association is partially specified in each of the objects Person and Car. This specification does not promote independent and incremental definition of application objects: establishing a new association among objects may require modifying the definition of these objects. Finally, reference attributes are not appropriate for expressing *n*-ary associations or associations that have attributes.

We have pointed out that, besides the major hindrances of using reference attributes to express associations, the OO approach fails to meet applications requirements on two more issues. The first is providing for generic data- manipulation languages. To this extent, the encapsulation principle has been softened to allow development of OO SQL-like languages. The second weakness is in describing global application dynamics: how application events are monitored by the system and how they have to be taken care of with respect to the evolution of the database. A new stream of research on so-called active databases is developing OO solutions to this problem. A more traditional approach is to combine the OO paradigm with some well-known mechanism (Petri nets, for instance) that has been proved to satisfy these requirements.

Enhancements to overcome these limitations are examined in the next section. Corresponding proposals are suggested in later sections.

Object+relationship models

Recently, researchers have attempted to make up for the above-mentioned structural limitations of object orientation in database applications by including constructs for representing associations and integrity constraints in OO models (31, 3). Rumbaugh et al. (31) present an extended OO modeling technique that they have used to support conceptual design and implementation of software systems. Beyond the usual features of OO models, their model supports three types of relationships that have the same meaning as their semantic data-model counterparts: generalization, aggregation, and generic association. The model, however, limits all relationships to binary links between object classes. Another notion that is included in their model is the cardinality concept, which is used to indicate the number of objects of one class that can be related to an object of the other class. Albano et al. have also proposed mechanisms for including relationships and integrity constraints in a strongly typed, object-oriented database programming language. Their extensions to the OO model are more comprehensive than the proposal in (31). They offer capabilities for expressing *n*-ary relationships and relationships that have their own attributes. Their model also incorporates mechanisms for expressing many types of integrity constraints. For example, inclusion and disjointedness constraints can be defined between object classes. Referential constraints can be specified on a class to ensure that whenever an object is inserted into a class, all the objects used as components are elements of the corresponding classes.

Extended OO models that include the concept of generic relationships are called *object relationship* (OR) models. In this chapter we propose another approach for defining an OR model. Unlike the Albano et al. (3) proposal, which aims to embed relationship capabilities in a strongly typed OO programming language, we start with the ER approach, well known and favored by many database designers, which has specific capabilities for representing the semantics of relationships; we extend that idea to permit description of complex and composite objects. The ER paradigm has succeeded for many reasons: it is powerful but still simple (few concepts), its concepts are easily understood by users, its database entities correspond to real-world objects, and its database schemas may be illustrated with easy-to-read diagrams. By combining the ER paradigm

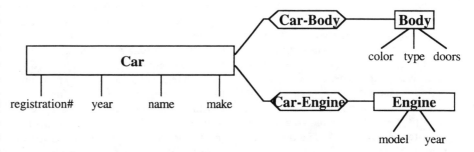

Figure 3. The garage conceptual schema described with objects and relationships (diamond-shaped boxes represent relationship types)

with the OO behavioral- modeling concept (i.e., attaching methods to entity and relationship types), we complement a tool designed for conceptual modeling with features it still lacks. This might be the most profitable way to achieve the best conceptual-model database that designers are looking for.

Extended-ER approaches (13, 25) model real-world objects with entity types. They use relationship types to model generic associations between two or more entities (objects). Like OO models, they provide an object identity for each entity and structural capabilities for describing complex objects. In fact, for object modeling, the fundamental difference between extended-ER approaches and the OO approach is that the ER paradigm restricts an object's components to being attributes and the OO paradigm allows components to be objects. If objects of type *B* are part of objects of type *A*, then the ER representation will show two entity types, *A* and *B*, linked by a relationship *R*, whose semantics will be known to the application as "*B* is component of *A*." This result also holds for recursively composite objects, where a component of an object of type *A* is an object of the same type *A*. In other words, the composition association is not supported in ER and is replaced by a generic association (but OO, as stated above, does exactly the inverse).

The ER separation between objects and attributes relies on the assumption that, when a designer designates something in the real world as an object, any information he or she wants to keep on this object has to be considered a property of the object, hence represented as an attribute. That another designer classifies the same reality in some other way should not inhibit the first perception.

Instead of using composite objects, the OR model we propose uses a more flexible mechanism to support multiple perceptions: derived-entity types (also called *virtual classes,* or *views*). Like views in relational systems, a derived-entity type represents objects that, by some derivation rule expressed in the OR data-manipulation language, are built from other objects and relationships of the database. Derived-entity types model virtual objects in the sense that they do not add new objects to the database, but define a new point of view over existing information.

To illustrate how this mechanism supports multiple perceptions, let us again consider the garage example. The goal is to support both the receptionist's point of view (one object class, Car, with attributes including body and engine) and the mechanic's (where Car, Body, and Engine are object classes). The modeling process first represents by an entity type whatever is seen as an object class by at least one user. Next, relationships are defined among these entity types to represent generic and composition associations. The OR schema for the garage database will show three entity types—Car, Body, Engine—related by two relationships, Car-Body and Car-Engine. The attributes attached to each entity type are those defined by designers, except for the attributes that have been attached to a related "component" entity type. The Car entity type does not include information about the car's engine and body (see Figure 3). This information is available in the Engine and Body entity types, and may be accessed from the car entities via the relationships. The resulting structure forms the basic schema, the conceptual description of database objects. Derived-entity types are added to the basic schema to represent objects that are perceived by designers differently from the structure in the basic schema. This description applies to cars as seen by the receptionist. A derived-entity type, say RecepCar, is defined to merge in a single virtual entity type the information from the three basic entity types. Its schema is the one represented in Figure 2.1. The derivation rule in this case specifies a relationship-join operation. The receptionist will use the derived- entity type for his or her interactions with the database.

Relationships and the derivation mechanism offer more flexibility than OO composite objects. If A and B are two related object types, it is easy to define a view in which A has B as component attribute and a view wherein B has A as component attribute. For instance, if the ownership relationship links Person and Car, relationship-join operations may build both Person-with-cars (each person with the cars he or she owns) or Car-with-persons (each car with its owners), depending on the order of the operands. This result is harder to achieve relying on composite objects because of the inherent direction of the composition link.

The generalization association is also supported by OR models. The model we propose, ERC+, uses it to express subclass–superclass relationships. The model does not, however, associate it with an implicit inheritance mechanism. Inheritance has to be asked for explicitly as part of the database manipulation. Again, this method allows for more flexibility by letting the user specify which inheritance (downward, upward), if any, he or she wants. Moreover, ERC+ supports another association type, called the *may-be-a link,* to express the idea that objects may belong to two classes (which is called *conjunction*), without one class being a subclass of the other. These enhancements to the OO inheritance link are discussed in detail in the next section.

ERC+: An object+relationship data model

ERC+ is an extended entity-relationship model, specifically designed to support complex objects. Its goal is to closely represent real-world objects. It uses the concept of entity type to describe objects

and the concept of relationship type to represent relationships among objects. An object identity (oid) is associated with each entity. A real-world object, regardless of its complexity, may be modeled as an occurrence of a single-entity type: entity types may comprise any number of attributes that may in turn, iteratively, consist of other attributes. The structure of an entity type can be regarded as a tree whose root and inner nodes are respectively represented by the entity type and its composing attributes, as shown in Figure 3.1(a). Attributes, entities, and relationships may be valued in multisets (i.e., allowing duplicates).

ERC+ fully supports the concept of relationship type. Several (two or more) entity types may be linked by a relationship type. Like entity types, a relationship type may have attributes. Relationship types may be cyclic (a relationship type may bind twice—or several times—the same entity type, each time with a different role).

Here is a problem: Do relationships have oids? Relationship types are not full objects like entities; therefore one could say that a relationship does not deserve an oid. Moreover, unlike entity types, relationship types do not form a generalization hierarchy. But we have two reasons for describing relationships with oids:

(1) Duplicate relationships can coexist, linking the same entities. For example, in the vineyard database of Figure 3.1(b), if a wine grower harvests the same vineyard twice in a year, picking the same quantity each time, two duplicate relationships *harvest* will coexist. (In some very sunny years, a few grapes mature later and are harvested one month after the main harvest.)

(2) Updating a relationship type requires that we be able to select its occurrences that are to be modified or deleted. Oids are then useful as handles for designating those occurrences.

In ERC+, relationships have oids that are different from those of entities.

Furthermore, ERC+ supports two other kinds of links between entity types: the "is-a" link and the "may-be-a" link. Both are used to relate two entity types that to some extent represent the same real-world objects, each with a different point of view. Entities representing the

same real-world object share the same oid, which is associated with the real-world object.

- The classical "is-a" link (or generalization link) specifies that the population of an entity type ES is a subclass (specialization) of another entity type EG (generalization). Thus, every oid contained in ES is also an oid of EG. This link is depicted in ERC+ diagrams by an arrow: $ES \rightarrow EG$. An entity type may be a subclass (superclass) of several generic (respectively, specific) entity types. In a faculty database, one may want to describe the group of postdoctoral students who give courses as a subclass of both the Faculty and the Student entity types. No cycle is allowed in the generalization graph. It is a lattice.

- The "may-be-a" link (or conjunction link) between two entity types E_1 and E_2 is used to specify that some (possibly all) entities of E_1 describe the same real- world objects as entities of E_2 do, and vice versa (26, 29); i.e., the populations of E_1 and E_2 may share oids. The may-be-a link is graphically represented by a dashed line between E_1 and E_2: $E_1 - - - E_2$.

The is-a and may-be-a links allow us to model these three situations that may arise between the sets of oids of two entity types E_1 and E_2:

- the sets of oids are disjoint: there is no link between E_1 and E_2.

Venn diagram

ERC+ diagram

- the set of oids of one entity type (E_2)

is included in the other set: this is an *is-a* link.

- the set of oids of one entity type (E_2)

Venn diagram

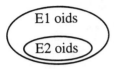

ERC+ diagram

- E_1 and E_2 share some oids: this is a may-be-a link.

Venn diagram

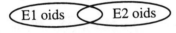

ERC+ diagram

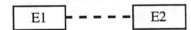

Both is-a and may-be-a links allow inheritance of properties from one entity type to another. The inheritance mechanism represents the means by which users can gather the information scattered over entity types that represent different points of view of the same real-world object (i.e., entity types bound by is-a or may-be-a links). Inheritance can apply to all the properties attached to an entity: attributes, relationships, and is-a and may-be-a links. The algebraic operation (*i*-join) used to implement the inheritance mechanism is presented later in the paper.

An example: the vineyard database. Figure 4 depicts an example that will be used to highlight the important points in the formal description of the ERC+ model presented. It represents a vineyard database that comprises these entity types:

- Vineyard: the Vineyard entity type (Figure 4) includes a set of attributes to describe its label, the location of the vineyard, and the size of the area planted. It also includes a multivalued attribute "best years" to record good harvest years for each vineyard. Whenever a vineyard is planted, as a whole or in part, the data-base records the year of the planting, the percentage of the vineyard that is planted, and the plants (the plant brand identification and the number of plants planted). These facts together form a complex multivalued attribute "planting." This attribute is multivalued, because the same vineyard may undergo different partial plantings over different years.
- Red Vineyard: this entity type is a subclass of Vineyard. In addition to the attributes that it can inherit from Vineyard, it has a specific attribute

to describe the exposure of each red vineyard to sunlight.
- White Vineyard: in addition to the heritable attributes, White Vineyard includes a specific attribute "heating" to describe if there is any device in the vineyard to prevent spring frosts.
- Owner: an entity type used to represent the vineyards' owners. For each owner, its name is recorded.
- Wine Grower: for each wine grower the database stores its lastname, firstname, and address. A wine grower may also be an owner and vice versa. Thus, a may-be-a link is drawn between entity types Owner and Wine Grower in the diagram.

The vineyard database also includes three relationship types: "Owns," which links the entity types Vineyard and Owner, "Harvest," which connects the entity type Wine Grower to Vineyard, and a cyclic relationship "Family" on the entity type Wine Grower. Notice that the relationship type "Harvest" has two simple attributes to describe the year of a harvest and the quantity harvested.

The diagrams in Figure 4 and 5 use these graphical notations: a single straight line denotes a monovalued attribute or role; a double line (one straight, one dotted) denotes a multivalued mandatory attribute or role; a double dotted line denotes a multivalued optional attribute or role. V, O, W, child-of, and parent-of are role names.

Formal definition of the ERC+ model

Domains. Domains define the set of all possible values for an attribute, an entity,

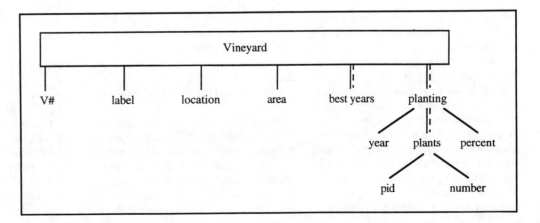

Fig. 4. The vineyard entity type

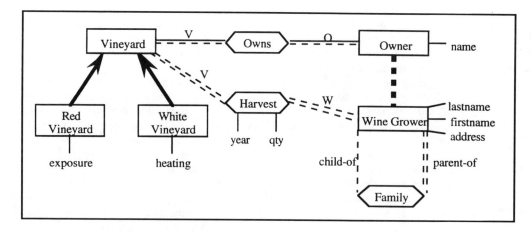

Fig. 5 The ERC+ schema of the vineyard database example

or a relationship type. Values may be either atomic, like Mary or 1991, or complex—i.e., composed of other values. A complex value is a set of pairs <attribute name , ν> where ν is either a value or a multiset of values. For example, a complex value for a Vineyard entity may be:

{ (*V#*, 1335),
(*label*, Côte de Beaune),
(*location*, Bourgogne),
(*area*, 1000),
(*best_years*, {1986, 1988, 1989}),
(*planting*, { < (*year*, 1980),
(*plants*, { < (*pid*, pinot111), (*number*,
1000) >,
< (*pid*, pinot113) (*number*, 5000))> },
(*percent*, 100) } >) }

Let *ED* be the set of domains of atomic values, called *elementary domains*. These are defined:

Elementary domain: *ed*
$ed \in ED \Leftrightarrow ed = (name, V, R)$

- name(*ed*) $\in$ NAMES (where name(*ed*) is the name of the domain and NAMES is the set of all names)
- $V(ed)$ is the set of elementary (atomic) values in the domain
- $R(ed)$ is the set of relational operators defined on $(V(ed))^2$.

Example: an elementary domain to be used for the attribute *label* above could be defined as:

(label_domain, {Pommard, Côte de Beaune, Macon, ...}, {=,≠}) .

Let *CD* be the set of complex domains. A complex domain is a set of complex values all of which have the same format. There is also a special complex domain whose purpose is to represent the lack of value of relationships and entities that have no attribute. Complex domains are defined:

Complex domain: *cd*
$cd \in CD \Leftrightarrow cd = (name, V)$ such that:

name(*cd*) $\in$ NAMES is the name of the complex domain
$V(cd) = \{\emptyset\}$ (the empty domain of entities and relationships without attributes)
or

Nonempty complex domains are sets of complex values all of which adhere to the same format. This format specifies, for each component of the complex value, its name, its domain, and its cardinalities:

$\exists I = \{1,2,....,n\}, n \in \mathbb{N}^* \exists F = \{$
$(A_i, d_i, min_i, max_i) / i \in I\}$, such that :

$\forall i \in I, A_i \in$ NAMES $\wedge d_i \in (ED \cup CD)$
$\wedge min_i \in \mathbb{N} \wedge max_i \in \mathbb{N}^* \wedge min_i \le max_i$

$\wedge \quad \forall (k,j) \in \mathbb{N}^2 \quad A_k = A_j \Rightarrow$
$(A_k, d_k, min_k, max_k) = (A_j, d_j, min_j, max_j)$

and $V(cd) = \{ \{(A_{i,i})/i \in I\} / \forall i \in ,$
$\exists (A_i, d_i, min_i, max_i) \in F \wedge _i \in$
$P^{min_i:max_i}(V(d_i)) \wedge$

$\forall (k,j) \in \mathbb{N}^2 A_k = A_j \Rightarrow (A_{k,k}) = (A_{j,j}) \}$

where $P(V)$ means the powerset of V, extended to multisets, called power-multiset of V;
and $P^{m:n}(V)$ means the power-multiset of V, generating multisets containing at least m elements and at most n elements (including duplicates).

Example: a complex domain to be used for a complex attribute *plants* (with two atomic components: *pid* and number) could be defined as:

(plants_domain , {{ (*pid*, $_1$), (*number*, $_2$)} / $_1 \in V$(pid_domain)
$\wedge_2 \in V$(number_domain) }) .

A complex value in the domain above may be:

< (*pid*, pinot111), (*number*, 1000) >.

Structures. The concept of structure bears the recursiveness necessary for describing complex objects. This concept conveys the characteristics of an attribute (its name and cardinalities, its composition and domain) independently from its association to the object it describes. This

arrangement allows different attributes (representing similar properties for different object types) to share the same structure, which simplifies the formal definition of the algebraic operators, whose action often includes creating a new attribute with the same structure as the attribute it is derived from.

Let S be the set of structures. These are defined:

$S \in S \Leftrightarrow S = ($ name,min,max,comp,$d)$
such that:

- name(S) $\in$ NAMES is the name of the structure (the attributes associated to the structure will have this name)
- min(S) $\in \mathbb{N}$, max(S) $\in \mathbb{N}^*$, min($S \le$ max(S) are the minimum and maximum cardinalities of the structure. These numbers limit the number of values (including duplicates) the associated attributes may have in an instance of the object the attribute relates to.

If min(S) = 0, S defines an optional attribute (with respect to the object the attribute relates to);
if min(S) ≤ 1, S defines a mandatory attribute;
if max(S) = 1, S defines a monovalued attribute;
if max(S) ≥ 2, S defines a multivalued attribute.

- comp(S) = $\{S_i / i \in I \wedge S_i \in S\}$, $I = \{1,2,....,n\}, n \in \mathbb{N}^*$ or $I = \emptyset$ is the composition of the structure. If comp(S) = $\emptyset$, the structure defines an atomic attribute. Otherwise, comp(S) is the set of the structures of the component attributes.
- $d(S)$ is the underlying domain of the structure:

if comp(S) = $\emptyset$ then $d(S) \in ED$ ($d(S)$ is an elementary domain)

else $d(S) \in CD$ ($d(S)$ is a complex domain)

The set of complex values of $d(S)$ is a derived information:

$V(d(S)) = \{ \{(name(S_i),_i)/i \in I\} / \forall i \in I, _i \in P^{min(Si):max(Si)}(V(d(S_i))) \}$

Example : the structure of the *plants* attribute in Figure 3.1.(a) is defined as:

(plants,1,n, { (*pid*,1,1,$\emptyset$,*pid*_domain), (number,1,1,$\emptyset$,number_domain) }, plants_domain).

Entity Types. An entity type is defined by its name, its schema (which is the set of the structures of its attributes), its generic entity types, the set of the entity types with which it is in conjunction, and its population, which is a set of occurrences (entities) with their oids and values.

Let E be the set of entity types. These are defined:

$E \in \mathbb{E} \Leftrightarrow = ($ name, sch, gen, muid , pop $)$ such that:

- name(E) $\in$ NAMES is the name of the entity type
- sch(E) = $\{S_i / i \in I \wedge S_i \in S\}$, $I = \{1,2,....,n\}$, $n \in \mathbb{N}^*$ or $I = \emptyset$ is the schema of the entity type. It is a (possibly empty) set of structures.
- gen(E) = $\{(EG_j)/EG_j \in E\}$, is the possibly empty set of the generic entity types of E.

Let EG be any generic entity type of E, then to each occurrence of E corresponds an occurrence of EG that describes the same real-world object:

soid(E) soid(EG)

must be satisfied at any time; soid(E) is the set of oids of E and is formally defined below.

- muid(E) = $\{ (E_j) /E_j \in E\}$, is the possibly empty set of the entity types bound to E by conjunction.
- pop(E) = $\{(oid, val)/ val \in d(E)\}$ is the population of the entity type. It is a set of entities. Each entity is a couple made up of the entity identity (oid) and its value. The value is an element of the domain of the entity type, $d(E)$, which is a derived information:

$d(E) \in CD$
$V(d(E)) = \{\{(name(S_i),_i)/i \in I\} / \forall i \in I, , S_i \in sch(E) \wedge_i \in P^{mi_i:ma_i}(V(d(S_i)))\}$

where: $mi_i = min(S_i)$ and $ma_i = max(S_i)$

The set of oids of E is called soid(E), and

is formally defined by:

soid(E) = $\{e / \exists v, (e,v) \in pop(E)\}$

Example: the definition of the entity type White Vineyard of Figure 3.1(b) is:

(White_Vineyard, { (heating, 1, 1, $\emptyset$, heating_domain) }, {Vineyard}, $\emptyset$, pop) where pop describes the White Vineyard entities stored in the database.

Relationships Types. A relationship type is defined by its name, the set of entity types it links, with the description of the characteristics of the links (role names and cardinalities), the set of structures of its attributes (which constitutes its schema), and the set of its occurrences. Let R be the set of relationship types. These are defined:

$R \in \mathbb{R} \Leftrightarrow R = $ (name, pet, sch, pop) such that:

- name(R) $\in$ NAMES is the name of the relationship type
- pet(R) is the set of entity types participating in the relationship type. For each entity type, its role and the minimum and maximum cardinalities of its link to the relationship type are specified:

pet(R) = $\{(E_j, role_j, min_j, max_j) / j \in J \wedge E_j \in E \wedge role_j \in NAMES \wedge min_j \in \mathbb{N} \wedge max_j \in \mathbb{N}^* \wedge min_j \leq max_j\}$, $J = \{1,2,....,p\}$, $p \in \mathbb{N}^*, p > 1$,

within the relationship type, the role names are unique:

$\forall (\qquad (E_1, role_1, min_1, max_1),$ $(E_2, role_2, min_2, max_2)) \in (pet(R))^2 ,$
$role_1 = role_2 \Rightarrow (E_1, role_1, min_1, max_1) = (E_2, role_2, min_2, max_2)$

- sch(R) = $\{S_i / i \in I \wedge S_i \in S\}$, $I = \{1,2,....,n\}$, $n \in \mathbb{N}^*$ or $I = \emptyset$ is the schema of the relationship type. It is the (possibly empty) set of the structures of its attributes.
- pop(R) = $\{(oid, poc, val)\}$ is the population of the relationship type. It is a set of relationships. Each relationship is a tuple made up of the relationship identity (oid), the set of the linked entities (poc) and the relationship value (val).

$\forall r \in R$, poc(r) = $\{\{ (E_j, role_j, e_j) / (E_j, role_j, min_j, max_j) \in pet(R)\} / \forall j \in J, e_j \in soid(E_j)\}$

$\forall j \in J, \forall e_j \in soid(E_j)$, $min_j \leq card(\{r / r \in pop(R) \wedge (E_j, role_j, e_j) \in poc(R)(r)\}) \leq max_j$

The value of a relationship is an element of the domain of the relationship type,

$d(R)$, which is a derived information:

$d(R) \in CD$ $V(d(R)) = \{\{(name(S_i),_i) /i \in I\} / \forall i \in I, S_i \in sch(R) \wedge_i \in P^{mi_i:ma_i}(V(d(S_i))) \}$,

where: $mi_i = min(S_i)$ and $ma_i = max(S_i)$

The set of oids of R is called soid(R), and is formally defined by:

soid(R) = $\{e / \exists v, \exists role, (e, role, v) \in pop(R) \}$

Example: the relationship type Harvest of Figure 3.1.(b) is defined by:

(Harvest, { (Vineyard, V, 0, n) , (Wine_Grower, W, 0, n) }, { (year, 1, 1, $\emptyset$, year_domain), (qty, 1, 1, $\emptyset$, qty_domain}, pop) where pop describes the set of occurrences stored in the database.

Attributes. An attribute is defined by the object to which it is attached, its structure, and its values for each occurrence of its object.

Let A be the set of attributes. These are defined:

$A \in \mathbb{A} \Leftrightarrow A = ($ obj, str, inst $)$ such that:

- obj(A) $\in (E \approx R \approx A)$ is the object (entity type, relationship type, or complex attribute) to which the attribute is attached.
- str(A) $= (name(A), min(A), max(A), comp(A), d(A))$ is the structure associated to the attribute

str(A) $\in S$
if (obj(A) = $E_i \wedge E_i \in E$) then : str(A) $\in$ sch(E_i)
if (obj(A) = $R_j \wedge R_j \in R$) then : str(A) $\in$ sch(R_j)
if (obj(A) = $A_k \wedge A_k \in A$) then : str(A) $\in$ comp(A_k)

- inst(A) is the instantiation of the attribute. It is a total function associating to each value of the object to which the attribute is attached, the component value (which may be a multiset) of the attribute.

inst(A) is defined by:

inst(A): $\qquad V(d(obj(A))) \qquad \rightarrow$ $P^{min(A):max(A)}(V(d(A)))$, such that :
$\forall v \in V(d(obj(A)))$, inst(A)(v) = proj$_{name(A)}(v)$.

Identity Axioms. Let gen*(E) be the set of ancestors of an entity type E in the generalization graph.

Let gen+-(E) be the set of entity types to which an entity type E is connected through a path of the generalization graph.

1. There is no cycle in the generalization graph:

$$\forall E \in E \; E \notin \text{gen}^*(E)$$

2. Two entity types linked by a path in the generalization graph can share oids. Defining a conjunction link in between is useless:

$$\forall E_1 \in \text{gen+-}(E_2) \; E_1 \notin \text{muid}(E_2)$$

3. Two entity types, E_1 and E_2, which are bound neither by a generalization link nor by a conjunction link, cannot have any common oid:

$$\forall E_1 \in E \; \forall E_2 \in E \; (E1 \notin \text{gen +- }(E_2) \land E_1 \notin \text{muid}(E_2)) \Rightarrow \text{soid}(E_1) \_ \text{soid}(E_2) = \emptyset$$

Objects-manipulation languages

In the preceding section we have formally described the concepts used by the ERC+ model. Most of actual OO data models, extended ER models, and OR models share the same new concepts: object identity, generalization, object with complex structure, composition link, and/or more general relationship link between objects. We next discuss the guidelines and requirements for data-manipulation languages for managing these new concepts; in the following section we describe more precisely the ERC+ algebra operators.

One of the major principles of algebras is the closure property, which requires the result of any operation to be of the same type as the operands. This principle allows us to build expressions involving nested operators. In OO models, where the object class is the main concept, algebraic operators are performed on classes of objects and the result of any operation is a class of objects. Extended ER (or OR) models have several basic concepts: entity type, relationship type, and attribute or value. Because entity types are the main kind of objects, languages provide operators for manipulating them. To keep extended ER languages from being very complex, operations for manipulating relationships are typically not provided by these languages. Instead, attributes and relationships are queried through the entities to which they are bound.

In the data-manipulation languages each new concept generates either new capabilities (e.g., the crossing of reference attributes or of relationships) or modifications of the relational operators (e.g., the union of objects is based upon their oids). Those novelties are discussed hereinafter.

Oids. To include oids in data models we must add a new comparison operation and modify the usual set operations to handle objects with identities. First, to be able to express cyclic queries involving the same object twice, we define a new equality operator. For example, in a chess tournament one could want to verify that no error had gone into the planning by asking: "Is any player scheduled to play against himself or herself?"

Object-oriented DMLs must provide two equality-comparison operators:

- $o_1 = o_2$, which is true when o_1 and o_2 are the same objects (same oid) regardless of their values.
- $o_1 = o_2$, which is true when the values of o_1 and o_2 are the same.

Second, set operators (union $[\cup]$, difference $[\_]$, intersection $[\_]$) of the relational model need to be modified, because their original definition is value oriented. In the relational-data model, a relation cannot contain two identical tuples. In OO data models, each object has a specific identity and thus two objects having the same value can coexist in the same class. Therefore, OO set operators must be based on the comparison of the oids and not on the comparison of values. Consider this example:

- Union in the relational-data model:
R_1: $\{v_1, v_2, v_3\}$
R_2: $\{v_1, v_2, v_4\}$
$R_1 \cup R_2 = \{v_1, v_2, v_3, v_4\}$
- Union in data models with oids:

E_1: $\{<o_1, v_1>, <o_2, v_2>, <o_3, v_3>\}$
E_2: $\{<o_1, v_1>, <o_2', v_2>, <o_4, v4>\}$
where $<o_i, v_i>$ represents an object: o_i is its oid and v_i its value.
$E_1 \approx E_2 = \{<o_1, v_1>, <o_2, v_2>, <o_3, v_3>, <o_2', v_2>, <o_4, v_4>\}$
Using comparison operations based on oids, the union operation may be performed on two classes containing objects that have the same identity but different values. What will be the values of the resulting objects in this example?

E_1: $\{<o_1, v_1>, <o3, v_3>\}$
E_2: $\{<o_1, v_2>, <o_4, v_4>\}$
$E_1 \cup E_2$: $\{<o_1, f(v_1, v_2)>, <o_3, v_3>, <o_4, v_4>\}$

The objects identified by o_1 above represent two views of the same real-world object. For instance, in a university database, E_1 and E_2 may represent a Faculty entity type and a Student entity type, respectively. o_1 represents both a faculty and a student (a Ph.D. student who teaches a course). The value corresponding to the resulting object o_1 in the union of E_1 and E_2 is neither v_1 nor v_2. It is instead composed of both v_1 and v_2. How this resulting value is composed depends upon the data-manipulation language.

Finally, with the relational model, relations used as operands of set operators must have the same type (same set of attributes) to allow their values to be compared. With OO models, on the contrary, set operations are allowed to have operands with different associated types. Existing OO DMLs choose different solutions for defining the type associated with the result of a union: it can be made of either the common attributes of the operands (or the nearest common ancestor in the generalization hierarchy) (21, 34) or the union of all their attributes. In ERC+ the latter solution has been adopted because it provides more descriptive information (see the discussion below about placing the result into the generalization graph).

Generalization and Conjunction. Including the concepts of generalization and/or conjunction in a data model generates two new aspects that must be taken into account by DMLs associated with the model: inheritance of class properties and placement of the result of a query in the generalization graph.

Inheritance applies to attributes and methods as well as to links between object classes. These links are: reference links (or composition links) in OO models and relationship, generalization, and conjunction links in extended ER models. Inheritance through generalization links is usually descending (downward from the superclass to the subclass): each object of a subclass is also an object of the superclass and inherits the properties associated with the objects of the superclass. But ascending inheritance too can be useful. It is a mechanism by which the properties of the subclass object are attached to the corresponding object (having the same oid) in the superclass. For example, in the vineyard database one can wish to produce a list of all the vineyards by listing for each vineyard its properties together with the exposure attribute if it is a red vineyard, or with the heating attribute if it is a white one.

With explicit inheritance, whenever a user wants to use an attribute or a property of a superclass or a subclass, he or she must explicitly refer to the name of the class to which the attribute belongs. By contrast, with implicit inheritance, users can use properties of the super- or subclass and let the system fill in the references of the corresponding classes. Most user-friendly DMLs such as SQL-like and graphical languages support implicit descending inheritance. This tactic lightens the burden of writing queries: users can quote any property of any superclass; the system will look for it upward in the generalization hierarchy.

To get complete DMLs (with descending and ascending inheritance), the ERC+ algebra offers descending and ascending inheritance through is-a links. May-be-a links are not oriented, and so inheritance is also possible in both directions. To solve the ambiguity that may arise when an entity type has several generic entity types having properties with the same name, inheritance in the ERC+ algebra is explicit: an identity-join operator allows users to join two entity types connected by a generalization or conjunction link.

The result of a query is an object class; thus it has to be placed in the generalization graph to express its generalization/conjunction relationships with the other object classes. Two main solutions are available:

1. the result of a query describes new real-world objects. It is a class containing new oids, placed at the top of the hierarchy;
2. the result of a query is another point of view on real-world objects that are already described (with other points of view) in the database. It is a class containing existing oids; that is, a subclass (or a derived class) of some existing class(es).

DMLs of the first type are called *object-generating* languages. The properties of the new class are derived from the properties of the operands (5). In OO models, this result can be achieved by defining reference attributes that point at the operand objects (6). DMLs of the second type are called *object- preserving* languages. The properties of the new class are derived from the operand

through the subclass mechanism (32, 33). The object-preserving solution generates graphs that are clearer and easier for users to understand. ERC+ DMLs are object-preserving. The result of a query, however complicated, involving one or several entity types, is an entity type that is derived from the operand entity types and whose occurrences are derived from those of the operand(s): same oids, derived values.

Complex Types. An extensive research effort has been devoted to DMLs for models with complex types, such as non-first normal form relational models (18, 30), and complex-objects models (9, 5, 36). OO models and extended ER models often support, as ERC+ does, complex attributes, which are composed of other component attributes, and multivalued attributes that can have several values. A multivalued attribute may be set-, multiset-, list-, or array-valued. An example of complex and multivalued attribute is the attribute planting in Figure 3.1(a). Complex and multivalued attributes may include multivalued attributes at several levels of nesting, like the attribute plants in planting.

With complex types, the DML must provide tools for working on a value inside a set (or multiset, list ...) of values and at any depth in the complex type. Usual tools are:

1. set operators ($\in, \subseteq, =$),
2. attribute-variables at each level of multivaluation, associated with a quantifier ($\exists$ or $\forall$),
3. nested queries, one query for each level of multivaluation.

Nesting of queries is a solution commonly used in NF2 relational models where a multivalued attribute can take a nested relation as value (18). The operators that are used to manipulate relations are also used to work on these relation-valued attributes. By contrast, in languages with two different concepts, object (or entity) and attribute, different operators must be defined to manipulate the different concepts. For example, in the ERC+ algebra the selection operator is defined on entity types, and a new operator (the reduction) applies to a multivalued attribute of an entity type, and is used to eliminate in each occurrence of the entity type, inside the multivalued attribute, the values that do not satisfy a given predicate.

Projection is another operator that works on a complex structure. In NF2 relational models, users have to write nested projections when they want to prune a complex attribute. In models using several concepts (such as ERC+), the projection operator is defined on the entity type and a dot notation allows us to define the pruning of component attributes at any level.

Relationships and Reference Attributes. Relationships in ER models and reference attributes in OO models are used to link objects. The associated DML should allow users to select objects based on their links or relationships to other objects. In the vineyard database, a user may want to list all the growers who harvested "Pommard" wine in 1990. Most OO SQL-like languages allow access from one object to related objects through reference links. They often use a dot notation to move across reference- and value-attribute links.

An alternative solution, better suited to algebras, is to respect this principle: each operator manipulates only its operands. Objects that are not explicitly stated as operands of an operator cannot be accessed by it. ERC+ algebra abides by this rule. A query that involves more than one entity type must be formulated as an expression in which operators that gather together into a new complex entity type several entity types linked by a relationship (*r*-join) or by an is-a or may-be-a link (*i*-join), are used at first.

The ERC+ algebra

In this section we present the query operators associated with the ERC+ model. The ERC+ algebra is a set of primitive operators that may be combined in any order into expressions, so that any possible user query on an ERC+ database can be satisfied by an appropriate algebraic expression.

The closure property and the power of the algebra rely on five basic assumptions:

> operands and result are entity types. Each operator is designed to manipulate one (or more) entity type(s) and to build the result as a derived entity type. Thus, the result may serve as an operand for a subsequent operator.

> resulting entity types are complemented with relationship types, generalization, and conjunction links derived

from the ones linking the operands. This procedure allows us to (temporarily) integrate computed entity types into the existing database, so that they may be used in further manipulations, just like normal entity types. Algebraic expressions of any complexity may thus be defined. The ERC+ algebra is closed.

> the algebra is object preserving.

Each occurrence of the result is derived from the operand entities in this way:

It is made up of

- its oid, which is identical to the oid of the operand entity from which it comes. For instance, the oids in the result of this selection:

select [firstname="Paul"] Wine-Grower

are the oids of the Paul wine grower(s);

- its value, which is derived from the values of the operand(s). For instance, the value of the selection above is the value of the corresponding wine grower. The value of an occurrence of this projection

project [lastname] WineGrower

is the value of the corresponding wine grower, restricted to the lastname attribute;

- its relationships, which are derived as equal to those binding the operand;
- its links of generalization and conjunction, which are derived as equal to those binding the operand.

> the algebra is consistent with the model.

Because the model supports complex objects, the operators build their resulting entity types as complex objects. In particular, the product, relationship-join, and identity-join operators (used to collapse different entity types into a single object) use complex attribute structures to insert the information from the other operands into the "main" (the first) operand entity type. Product and relationship-join are nonflat operators: they create one occurrence for each occurrence of the main operand. The occurrences of the other operand(s) are collapsed into one complex multivalued attribute. For instance, the relationship-join of Owner and Vineyard through the relationship Owns:

$O := $ Owner r-join (Owns, Vineyard)

creates a new entity type O, whose schema comprises the schema of Owner augmented by a complex attribute, grouping all the attributes of Vineyard.

This particularity of the ERC+ algebra has two main advantages:

- it fulfills users' requirements to produce nonflat results or forms that show for each occurrence of the main entity all the second-entity occurrences bound to it;
- binary operators with a main operand (product and relationship join) are object preserving: the oids of the result are derived from (are equal to) those of the main operand. With flat operators (as in the relational algebra), this condition would have been impossible.

> inheritance through is-a and may-be-a links is explicit in two ways.

The algebra offers an operator, the identity-join, which allows users to group two entity types linked by either an is-a or a may-be-a link into a single entity type (with all the attributes, relationships, generalization, [?] and conjunction links of both entity types). All the other operators use only the own properties (not inherited) of their operands.

The algebra includes nine primitive operators. Derived operators may also be defined to lighten the writing of queries involving several operators. We briefly present the operators.

- The *selection* operator is similar to the relational one. The operation:

$E = $ select [predicate] E_1,

where E_1 is an entity type,

creates a derived entity type E, whose population is the subset of the population of E_1 for which the predicate is true. The schema of E, the relationships, generalizations, and conjunctions linking E, are derived from (equal to) those of E_1.

The predicate may involve any attribute or component attribute of E. For each multivalued attribute, a variable associated with a quantifier ($\exists$ or $\forall$) must be defined.

Example:

List the vineyards that had a best year in 1983 and one in 1990.

select [$\exists b_1 \in$ bestyears, $\exists b_2 \in$ bestyears ($b_1 = 1990 \land b_2 = 1983$)] Vineyard

- The *projection* operator is similar to the relational one. The operation:

$E = $ project [attribute-list] E_1,

where E_1 is an entity type,

and attribute-list is a list of attributes of E_1 and/or substructures of attributes of E_1,

creates a derived-entity type E, whose oids are the same as those of E_1. The relationships, generalizations, and conjunctions linking E are derived from (equal to) those of E_1. The schema of E is made up of the attributes or subattributes as defined in the attribute list. The substructures of the attribute list are defined by using the usual dot notation. The value of each E occurrence is derived from the value of the corresponding E_1 occurrence, by pruning it according to the attribute list.

Example:

For each vineyard list its label and its planting years.

project [label, planting·year Vineyard

- The *reduction* operator is a new operator. It complements the functionalities offered by the selection and projection operators with respect to the goal of selecting the desired information from an entity type. Although selection and projection allow users to discard occurrences or attributes that do not interest them, reduction allows them to eliminate attribute values that do not conform to a given predicate.

The operation:

$E = $ reduce [A / predicate] E_1

where E_1 is an entity type,

and A is a (direct or component) attribute of E_1,

creates a derived entity type E, whose oids are the same as those of E_1. The schema of E, the relationships, generalizations, and conjunctions linking E, are derived from (equal to) those of E_1. The predicate must involve A or its component attributes. It may also involve other attributes of E_1. It is defined as a selection predicate. The value of each E occurrence is derived from the value of the corresponding E_1 occurrence, by retaining in A only the values that satisfy the predicate; the value of the other attributes is not modified.

Example:

List vineyards, showing in the vineyard best years only the years before 1960.

reduce [bestyears / bestyears<1960] Vineyard

- The *union* operator is different from the relational one, which is value based. It merges the populations of two entity types according to their oids. It is a binary operator with two main operands. The environment of the result (relationships, generalizations, and conjunctions) is derived from both operands. The operation:

$E = E_1$ union E_2

where E_1 and E_2 are two entity types, creates a derived entity type E, whose oids are the same as those of E_1 plus those of E_2. The schema of E is derived by union-fusion of E_1 and E_2 schemas. Each attribute, A_i, of E_1 (and of E_2) is also an attribute of E. If E_2 has no attribute of the same name, the A_i attribute of E is identical to the A_i attribute of E_1 (the only difference is that A_i becomes optional). If E_2 has also an A_i attribute, the A_i attribute of E is the union of both attributes: its domain is the union of both domains, its value is the multiset-union of the two values. In the same way, the relationships, generalizations, and conjunctions linking E are derived from those of E_1 and those of E_2 by union-fusion (fusion of those with identical names and linking the same entity types).

Example: Let us suppose that the vineyard database above contains, in addition to red and white vineyards, green, gray, and other vineyards.

List the red and white vineyards.

RedVineyard union WhiteVineyard

The result of this query is a subclass of Vineyard, which is implicitly linked by a conjunction link with White Vineyard and Red Vineyard, and which has two optional attributes, exposure and heating.

- The *r*-join operator (for relationship-join) is a *n*-ary operator with one main operand. It is used to transform a network of entity types into a hierarchic structure (a single entity type). In a sense, this operator groups into a single entity the information scattered over entities linked by a relationship. From an object-oriented point of view, a *r*-join may recompose as a single object a complex object that has been disassembled into its component objects.

The operation:

$E = E_1$ ü role$_1$ *r*-join ($A : R$, E_2 ü role$_2$, ... , E_n ü role$_n$)

where role$_i$ is the role played by the E_i entity type in the relationship type,

(the specification of the roles is mandatory only in a cyclic relationship)

and A is a name for the new complex attribute that will be created, creates a derived entity type E, whose oids are the same as those of E_1 (E_1 is the main operand). The relationships, generalizations, and conjunctions linking E are derived from (equal to) those of E_1. The schema of E is made up of the attributes of E_1 plus a new complex multivalued attribute named A, which is de-

rived from the schemas of E_2, ... E_n and R. The value of an occurrence of E is made up of the value of the corresponding E_1 occurrence plus the multiset of the E_2, ... E_n and R occurrence values that are linked to E_1 (if there are some).

Example:

List each wine grower with its vineyards.

WineGrower *r*-join (V : Harvest, Vineyard)

The result contains one occurrence for each wine grower.

- The *i*-join operator (for identity-join) is a binary operator with one main operand. It is used to group into a single entity the information scattered over two entities bound by a generalization or a conjunction link. It allows the user to merge two points of view on the same real-world objects.

The operation:

$E = E_1$ *i*-join ($A : E_2$)

where E_1 and E_2 are two entity types bound by a is-a or a may-be-a link,

and A is a name for the new complex attribute that will be created creates a derived entity type E, whose oids are the same as those of E_1. The relationships, generalizations, and conjunctions linking E are derived from (equal to) those of E_1. The schema of E is made up of the attributes of E_1 plus a new complex monovalued attribute, named A, which is derived from the schema of E_2: it groups all the attributes of E_2. The value of an occurrence of E is made up of the value of the corresponding E_1 occurrence plus the value of the E_2 occurrence (if it exists).

Example:

List all the information about the red vineyards.

RedVineyard *i*-join (V:Vineyard)

The result contains one occurrence for each red vineyard, with the exposure attribute plus all the attributes of Vineyard. The opposite *i*-join:

Vineyard *i*-join (R:RedVineyard) would contain one occurrence for each vineyard, either red or not (in this case the exposure attribute in the result is optional).

- The *product* operator () is used to collapse unrelated entity types into a single entity type. This result is similar to a nested NF2 relational product, because each entity from the first operand is associated with all entities from the second operand. It is a binary operator with one main operand (the first one). The product is necessary to allow users to dynamically establish

unexpected links (not expressed by relationship types in the schema) between unrelated entity types.

The operation:

$E = E_1 (A : E_2)$

where E_1 and E_2 are two entity types, and A is a name for the new complex attribute that will be created creates a derived entity type E, whose oids are the same as those of E_1 (E_1 is the main operand). The relationships, generalizations, and conjunctions linking E are derived from (equal to) those of E_1. The schema of E is made up of the attributes of E_1 plus a new complex multivalued attribute named A, which is derived from the schema of E_2. The value of an occurrence of E is made up of the value of the corresponding E_1 occurrence plus the multiset of all the E_2 occurrence values.

The ERC+ algebra also contains two syntactic operators, *renaming* and *simplification*, which allow us to conform the schema of an entity type to the rules of the model or of the algebra:

- the *renaming* operator changes the name of an attribute, to prepare the fusion of similar attributes during a union.

- the *simplification* operator deletes unnecessary complexity in the structures that may be built by other operators, projection in particular. Simply stated, simplification deletes one level in a complex structure whenever a complex attribute has only one component attribute (unless both are multivalued).

Derived operators may be defined to help users write shorter queries.

A *difference* operator (~) may be defined as derived through the appropriate composition of a product, a selection, and a projection. An *intersection* may also be defined as two differences. As usual, the semantics of these operators is to form a new population corresponding to those occurrences from the first operand for which there is no occurrence in the second operand with the same oid (difference), or to those occurrences from the first operand for which there is an occurrence in the second operand with the same oid (intersection). Those two operators have a main operand, the first one.

The *r*-join is equivalent to the outer join of the relational model: the result has one occurrence for each occurrence of the main operand even if it is not linked by the relationship. A useful derived op-

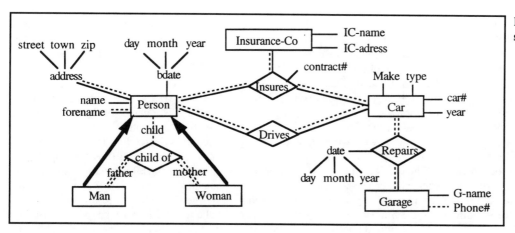

Figure 6. A sample ERC+ schema

erator is the sel-*r*-join, which deletes from the result all the occurrences not linked by the relationship. The sel-*r*-join is equivalent to an ERC+ expression made up of a *r*-join followed by a selection.
Example:
List the wine growers who are children of a family of wine growers:

WineGrower/child-of sel-*r*-join (*F* : Family, WineGrower/parent-of)

In the same way, another derived operator, *v*-join (for value-join), is a NF2 theta-join: it groups into a single entity type the information scattered over two entity types linked by a predicate on their attributes. It is equivalent to an ERC+ expression made up of a product followed by a reduction and a selection.
Example:
List the wine growers who have the same name as a wine label

WineGrower *v*-join [name=label] Vineyard
The result contains one occurrence for each wine grower who satisfies the condition.

ERC+ incorporates two basic languages: the algebra presented above, and a calculus (24). These basic languages are the formal foundations on which user-friendly languages such as SQL-like and graphical languages are built. An ERC+ SQL has been defined (33), and an ERC+ graphical interface, which will be presented in the following sections, is being implemented.

Schema editor

Now that we have discussed the requirements of database applications and shown how the ERC+ model can be used to meet them, we present the SUPER design environment, which is based on the ERC+ model. SUPER is an integrated environment of tools aimed at specifying and developing a consistent set of visual user interfaces for designing and manipulating databases. The tools in the current version of the prototype consist of a graphical schema editor, a data browser, and an editor for graphically specifying database queries and updates. The schema editor is presented in this section and the query editor in the next. Figure 6 depicts an ERC+ schema diagram, which is used as a running example throughout our discussion of graphical editors.

The schema editor is a visual data-definition interface, providing two modes for defining schemas. Each mode has a separate display window, identified by the name of the schema being edited and labeled by the corresponding operation mode. In the *graphical* mode, the designer builds an ERC+ diagram by direct manipulation. The user picks the graphical symbols from a palette and positions them in the workspace provided in the associated window. The symbols in the palette correspond to ERC+ constructs (entity, relationship, attribute, generalization, conjunction). In the *alphanumeric* mode, forms-like representations of ERC+ constructs (called *object boxes*) are provided by the editor for entering data definitions. The different object boxes correspond to the ERC+ constructs. Some are shown in Figure 6.

Figure 7 shows an example of the graphical and alphanumeric windows during schema design. A user working simultaneously on several schemas is provided with both a graphical and an alphanumeric window for each schema. Standard editing operations are available through pull-down menus. "Schema," "Edit," and "Dictionaries" menus are available in both windows, and provide the same functionalities. The "Schema" menu includes the usual operations for opening, saving, creating, ... a schema. The "Edit" menu offers cut, copy, and paste facilities, as well as undo and redo. The "Dictionaries" menu gives access to a global dictionary or any of the specialized dictionaries (entities, relationships, attributes).

The "Options" menu in the graphical window contains purely graphical manipulations (changing the layout, rearrange object disposal, ...) and is therefore specific to this window. Conversely, functionalities for creating a new schema (or modifying an existing one) are provided in the "Creation" menu when in the alphanumeric mode. They are equivalent to defining schema elements through the graphical palette.

Because schema editing is a well-known procedure, we limit this discussion to a few comments on three aspects: displaying, editing, and browsing.

Information Display The graphical representation follows ERC+ guidelines. In a later version of the prototype, users will be able to customize the representation by choosing their own symbols. For user-defined diagrams, SUPER stores the associated spatial information, so that the diagram may later be displayed as it was at creation time. For schemas defined in the alphanumeric mode, SUPER automatically builds and displays the corresponding diagram. Managing this task is complex, and so we did not try to implement a sophisticated algorithm, leaving adjustment of the diagram to users (dragging elements around) if they dislike it. For readability, attributes may be hidden.

Figure 7. shows the schema diagram for a hypothetical Insurance application.

Each object in the diagram was created by first selecting the corresponding graphical symbol in the palette and then clicking in the workspace to position the object. Creating an object activates display of the corresponding object box (alternatively, it may be displayed using the alphanumeric Creation menu). Newly created objects receive a standard name, which can be changed in the corresponding alphanumeric object box. An object box contains text entry areas (e.g., the object's name and comment), radio buttons for predefined choices (e.g., cardinality specification), and list-bars referring to objects directly attached to the current object. The entity box (Person) in Figure 6 shows list-bars for attributes, links, and generalizations defined on an entity type. A list-bar for components of a complex attribute is included in the attribute box (address).

List-bars were chosen as a standard technique for linking objects. Clicking on a list-bar displays the corresponding scrollable list of attached objects. Two such lists are shown in Figure 6, one for links on the Person entity type, one for components of the address attribute. Lists have a standard behavior. They group objects of the same type, attached to the same parent element (the latter is the schema for dictionary lists). Clicking on an object in a list displays its object box. Clicking on the New button in the list box displays an empty object box for adding a new object to the list. Using object boxes, list-bars, and the attached lists, users may navigate through the schema and add or modify objects as needed.

Top-down definition strategies are very easily performed.

Flexibility in designing schemas is enhanced by the possibility of leaving object definitions incomplete. Users may, for instance, define entity types and relationship types, and come back later to these objects to attach attributes or add generalizations. Each user may follow his or her own strategy. Incomplete schema definitions may be saved and reused in another session. At any time, a validation function may be activated to check whether the actual schema definition is consistent with model rules. If inconsistencies or incompleteness are detected, they are reported to the user. As the editor keeps track of what has been validated (and is still valid), users may easily identify which definitions have to be re-

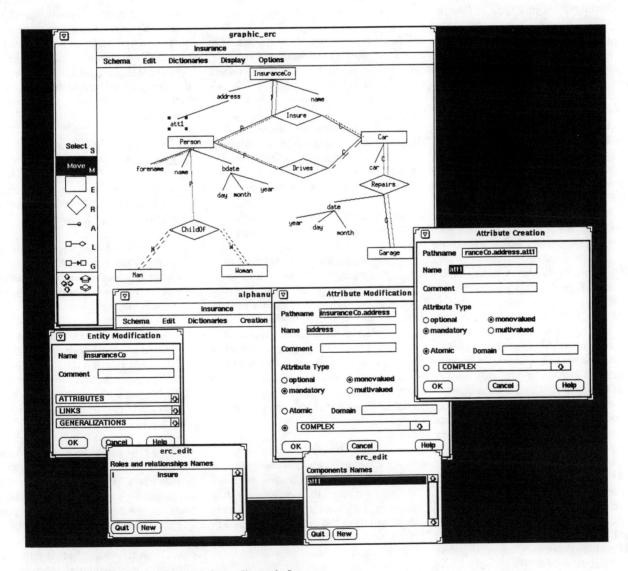

Figure 7. A screen display with schema-editor windows (after a new attribute is created, whose default name is att1)

fined to correct their schema.

Some model rules have to be permanently enforced (e.g., uniqueness of entity names) to avoid ambiguities. These rules are immediately checked by the editor. Default names are, of course, always generated unique.

Finally, users may quit the editor at any time. When they come back to continue schema editing, their work on the schema is reactivated in exactly the same status as at the time of the interruption (open windows and object boxes, selected objects, ...).

Flexibility, Reusability, and Backtracking. Besides the usual editing functions listed above, SUPER includes the facilities of redundancy, reusability, and backtracking to make the user's task as easy as possible.

Redundancy is intended to provide flexibility. It has already been introduced by allowing users to view their schema through two equivalent representations. Accordingly, some functionalities have been implemented redundantly, so that users may access them directly through the representation they are using. For instance, an object may be created graphically (with only one way to do it), or in several ways in the alphanumeric mode. A new attribute can be created either by activating the Creation menu, or by clicking on the New button in the attribute list attached to its parent object. Whichever way we use, it will result in displaying an attribute-creation box, in which users will enter the attribute definition.

This kind of flexibility is sometimes criticized as confusing for users. We believe it may indeed be confusing if the alternatives appear within a single context, and users have no criterion for choosing between them. On the contrary, providing the alternatives along different paths avoids the burden of explicitly moving from the context they are in to the context that provides the desired function. In our example, users can create objects as they navigate through the schema, without having to go to the Creation menu.

Reusability allows users to reuse definitions of objects in the current schema or in another schema. Cut, copy, and paste operations may be used to move an object (i.e., disconnect it and connect it elsewhere), delete it, or create a similar object elsewhere (if needed, because of the uniqueness rule, the name of the object is automatically updated). The ob-

ject here may be a single object (an entity type, an attribute, ...), or a collection of objects (e.g., a set of attributes may be copied from various existing objects and in one shot attached to an entity type), or a subschema (a set of entities, attributes, relationships, and generalizations where the latter two must include the objects they link). A duplicate operation is also provided and creates an object identical to the original one (but with a different name) and bearing the same connections.

Finally, backtracking is supported through undo and redo operations. This procedure allows users to recover from erroneous actions and restore the previous state. Typically, if a user clicks on a Cancel button instead of the nearby OK button, all actions performed on the object are lost. Undoing the erroneous click will give him or her a second chance.

Schema Browsing. The current version of SUPER supports schema browsing. Users may scroll the schema diagram to display the desired part of it. The alphanumeric mode allows schema browsing by navigation from one object to another through existing connections in between. This navigation may use object boxes (as shown in Figure 7) to allow the user to see all informations about the objects on the path. A similar navigation may also be performed using a simultaneous display of the various dictionary lists. For instance, selecting an entity type in the entity types list will automatically display its attributes, relationships, and generalizations/specializations, if any, in the corresponding list. The only information users get in such a navigation, however, are the names of the objects. To know more about a specific object, users have to click on its entry in the appropriate list, to activate its object box (the information in the object box is then available only for inspection, to prevent conflict between different actions on the same object).

Graphical Manipulation Language. SUPER includes two data-manipulation languages, both of which allow querying and updating an ERC+ database: a data browser, and a query editor. We next briefly present the data browser, and in the subsequent section describe the query editor in more detail.

The Data Browser. The SUPER browser provides two modes for visual-

izing data. In the forms-based mode, occurrences are presented with forms-like representations of the corresponding object or relationship type, and in the graphical mode they are presented with entity–relationship-like diagrams showing the occurrences currently being examined. The user can directly manipulate these occurrences.

Regardless of whether forms or diagrams are used, each browsing session has an associated state indicating if the session is in the query mode or in the update mode. In query mode, it is possible to browse the occurrences of a population (one at a time), to examine their attributes' values, and to move from an occurrence to another one belonging to a related population (related via a role or a multi-instantiation link). In the update mode, occurrences can be modified, deleted, and created. At any time during a session the user can switch between query and update mode with a click on a button. For instance we can start browsing the database in the query mode, look for some data to be updated, and switch to the update mode when we find the desired data.

The query editor

We now discuss the query-formulating features in the SUPER query editor. These are the steps followed:

- *Selecting the query subschema*: the portion relevant to the query is extracted from the database schema.
- *Creating the query structure*: the subschema is transformed into a hierarchic structure.
- *Specifying predicates:* predicates are stated on database occurrences, so that only relevant data are selected.
- *Formatting the output*: the editor is provided with data items to be included in the structure of the result.
- *Displaying resulting data.*

The whole procedure may be rather complex and therefore difficult for novice users to master. Because these users are the main target for visual interfaces, we believe visual-query languages should take advantage of the multistep structure suggested above. Indeed, clear separation between the steps alleviates users' mental load and improves their chances of correct formulation. The sequence of steps is logically

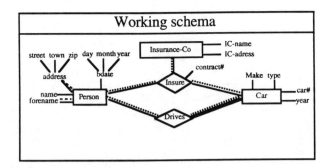

Figure 8. Before disconnection

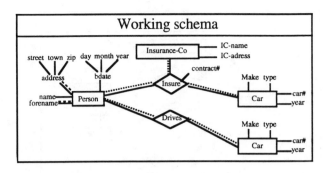

Figure 9. After disconnection

meaningful: for instance, predicates cannot be defined before the query subschema is determined. At any time, users can modify any stated part of the query to correct or refine the current formulation. SUPER implements step separation, by using specific windows for the different steps, as presented here.

Selecting the Query Subschema. This step corresponds to an "open subschema ..." command in textual languages. It configures the schema to include only the objects involved in the query. The diagram corresponding to a schema is displayed in a read-only window, called the *database schema* (DBS) window.

The query subschema is extracted by a sequence of point -and-click specifications. To speed up this sequence, we can tailor the semantics of the clicks to either "keep" or "delete" the designated object. Implicit designation is sometimes used: gql/ER (37), for instance, automatically adds to the query subschema the path between two selected objects (for multiple paths, the "most likely" one is chosen). QBD (10) uses a similar technique, which can be refined with additional constraints (e.g., on the length of the path). It also allows predicates on attribute names to select all entity types with such attributes.

In SUPER, the point-and-click specifications copy objects in a second window, called the *working schema* (WS) window. The user may choose between two modes:

- The most usual mode is a traditional Copy-Paste that transfers previously selected objects into the WS without relating them to objects already in the WS.
- In the second mode, called Expand, users select a start-entity type in the WS and then click on objects in the DBS window for copying them in the WS and reconnecting them to the

start-entity type.

Some automatic selection is embedded in SUPER. If the user clicks on a role, the complete relationship type is transferred in the WS. If the relationship is binary, the start-entity type changes to the new one. Clicking on a distant object is possible if there is a smallest path to the object. For instance, the user cannot click on a relationship that has two roles leading to the start-entity type.

Restructuring the Query Subschema. Once a query subschema is defined, proper query formulation may start. Some interfaces, however, introduce an additional step, to transform the subschema into a specific pattern. In (14) the query subschema is transformed into a hierarchic structure. The root of the hierarchy is selected by the user. Larson (20) follows the same approach, but the transformation is complemented with a generation of nested forms, visualizing the hierarchic structure. QBD provides a querylike transformation language for schema modification.

Graphical data manipulations in SUPER are based on the underlying ERC+ algebra, whose operators produce entities as results. These results are syntactical trees whose root is an entity with constraints expressed as predicates. In Auddino et al. (4), we discuss the use of tree representations of queries. In our editor, the user identifies the root of a query hierarchy. A graph in a tree is transformed by first removing cycles. The removal of cycles could not be automatic. There are as many possible interpretations as there are duplications of entity types involved in the cycle. Such an ambiguity is not acceptable. Because the editor cannot infer which interpretation is the intended one, the user should explicitly direct the transformation to be performed.

In the SUPER query editor, the user can break cycles by removing some vertices or some nodes of the graph or by disconnecting some links. Disconnection means that the designated link is detached from the linked-entity type and attached to a (newly automatically created) copy of that entity type. Figure 8 shows the WS window before disconnection. Disconnecting the Drives—Car link produces the diagram in Figure 9.

If the user wants to express in the query some information about cars, the editor cannot determine where to attach the Repairs relationship type (Figure 10). It is up to the user to direct the editor to "unify" the two Car entity types he or she designates. The diagram resulting from unification is shown in Figure 11.

Disconnection and unification provide most of the functionalities needed for properly defining hierarchic queries over an ERC+ schema. Another facility, pruning, is used to remove objects (attributes, entity types, ...) which are not used in the query—that is, appearing neither in the format of the result nor in a predicate. Some additional facilities like the product or union create an artificial link between two entities.

Specifying the Predicates. Once the user has created a correct query structure in the WS, SUPER builds the corresponding hierarchy as a single-entity type, with all other informations as attributes. This resulting structure is displayed in a third window, called the *selection window* (SW—an example may be seen in Figure 13). If the resulting structure is not what the user expected, he or she can make the appropriate modifications in the WS.

If the resulting structure is correct from the user's viewpoint, he or she will proceed with specifying predicates. Predicates against complex objects may be

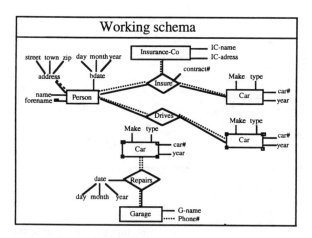

Figure 10. Before unification

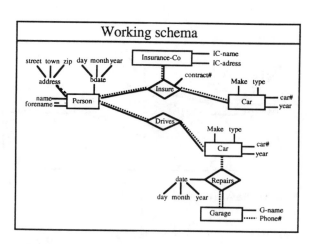

Figure 11. After unification

rather clumsy. For the simplest ones (comparing a monovalued attribute with a constant), a graphical counterpart may easily be defined.

A simple specification technique is to click on the attribute, select a comparison operator from a menu, and finally type the value or choose one from a list. For complex predicates (e.g., involving several quantifiers), there may be no simple way to express the value graphically. Menus are sometimes used for syntactic editing of predicates (14) or ISIS (16). In gql/ER, QBE-like forms are used to specify conditions on the selected nodes. Only a few interfaces allow a graphical formalism to be used for expressing predicates (see, for instance, Pasta-3 or SNAP).

In this chapter we do not want to discuss the best graphical solution for specifying predicates. Rather, we focus on functionalities. Predicates are expressed on the hierarchic structure (entity type) resulting from the preceding step. A predicate is any logical expression involving attributes of the final entity type. The predicate implements the selection operator if it is attached to the root or the reduction operator if it is attached to an attribute. The second step in defining a predicate is defining its domain. The domain is the set of quantified variables. We next show some examples of specifying predicates.

Consider Figure 13 hereinafter. Assume the condition "= 1944" is associated to the year attribute. Year is a monovalued mandatory attribute. The interpretation of the predicate is straightforward: the query will select as resulting entities only those in which year=1944.

Assume that the condition "= Paris" is associated to the town attribute. Town is a 1:1 component of the 1:n attribute address.

Here a quantifier is needed to specify the condition the selected entities have to satisfy. The existential quantifier will select entities for which there is one address value such that town=Paris, and the universal quantifier will select those for which all address values satisfy the condition town=Paris. As in Pasta-3, SUPER assumes (by default) the existential quantifier if none is explicitly defined by the user.

Consider now the selection window shown in Figure 22 hereinafter. Assume that the condition "= Morris" is associated to the G-name component of the Insure-2 attribute. G-name is two levels of multivaluation below the entity type (two multivalued attributes, Insure-2 and repairs, lie along the path leading to G-name). Consequently, two quantifiers are needed to define the query: one to specify whether every repair, or just one, has to be made by Morris, the second to specify whether this condition has to hold for every car in Insure-2, or just one.

Finally, again considering Figure 13, the user may want to select entities such that they have one address with town=Paris and one address with town≠Paris. To state this predicate, the user needs to designate two values for address. In a textual language, this designation is performed by using two variables associated to the same attribute. In SUPER, the user will ask for duplication of the attribute, which will allow both predicates and logical connectors to be specified between (and, or, not). Generally speaking, every attribute that appears several times in one or several predicates must be represented as many times in the selection window.

The predicates can be evaluated in any order. Each intermediate step usually builds a potential query that can be in-

terpreted (a syntactic validation) and executed (a semantic validation on an existing database) in the fourth window.

Formatting the Output. By default, the selection window defines the structure of the resulting entity type. The users may, however, wish to discard some of the attributes, which have been kept up to now only because of some predicate to be defined on them. The selection window has to provide for a "hide" (or, conversely, "show") operation, to define which attributes are to be discarded (or kept in). The hiding (or the showing) of a complex attribute also hides (or shows) all its component attributes.

Displaying Resulting Data. The last phase is displaying instances representing the result of the query. SUPER displays resulting entities according to their hierarchic structure, into a nested tabular form or into an attribute-tree form. To that extent, a fourth window, the *result window,* is used (Figure 18). Users can choose between the two kinds of presentation with a switch-mode radio button.

Relational interfaces display occurrences in tabular form. SNAP provides the user with the choice between the tabular format and a NF2 format, where occurrences are arranged into "buckets." (20) uses the nested-forms representation to display the results of data browsing. GUIDE (35) and VGQF (22) allow the user to choose among formats. In OdeView (2), complex objects can be displayed through a text or picture representation; the user can click on buttons to display all related objects.

Additional Facilities. Additional functionalities supported by SUPER allow us

Select name and address of people who insure a 1984 Ford

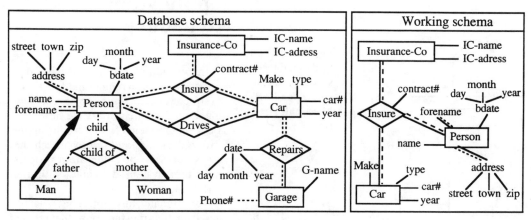

Figure 12. Query-editor windows showing query subschema definition

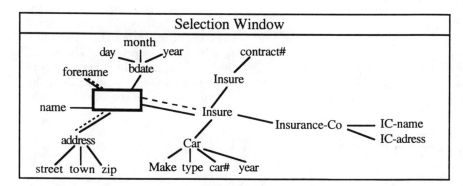

Figure 13. Resulting hierarchic structure, showing the root as an empty box

to store queries for later reuse or modification, as well as evaluation of partial queries. The latter is useful for debugging queries. Suppose the user is confronted with a result different from that expected, without recognizing the problem within the formulation. The query can be broken into two or more separate queries by disconnecting some links. The subqueries can be independently evaluated to identify the changes that have to be made. After this refinement, the original, corrected query can easily be rebuilt by unifying the duplicated entity types created by the previous disconnection.

A Sample Query. In this section we illustrate how queries are formulated in SUPER. Let us assume the user wants to formulate this query on the schema of Figure 6. The corresponding diagram will be displayed in the database window. The user begins by picking the relationship type Insure, which will be copied into the

WS window, together with the linked entity types (Person and Car) and all their attributes (Figure 12).

Next, assume that the user designates Person as the root of the hierarchy. Figure 13 shows the contents of the selection window. This structure includes many attributes the user is not interested in. Consequently, he or she will return to the WS window and prune unnecessary objects. The attributes name and address of Person are needed for result display, and Make and year of entity Car will be used to specify the predicate. Pruning will change the contents of windows, as shown in Figure 14. The predicate is defined through a predicate box displayed in the selection window (Figure 15).

The user designates the attributes (Make and year) involved in the predicate: Make and year. Figure 16 shows the selection window after designation of Make. Because the Insure attribute (to which Make belongs) is multivalued, a

modifiable "exists Insure" clause is automatically generated.

While designating the second attribute, year, the user also has to specify the logical connector between the two predicates. The predicate box now contains all the necessary quantified attributes. The specification is completed by entering the appropriate values: Ford for Make and 1984 for year (Figure 17).

Then the user hides the attribute Insure, which does not belong to the result, and the query is ready for evaluation. Figure 18 shows the resulting occurrences.

Suppose now that the user wants to proceed with specifying this query, very similar to the previous one:

Name and address of persons who insure a 1984 Honda, and who also insure a car that has been repaired in the "Morris" garage.

The user will import in the WS window the additional information needed in the DBS window (the relationship type Repairs). The result is shown in Figure 19. Next, the user will unify the two Cars entity types and prune unneeded objects (Figure 20). Then, he or she can redefine the first predicate to select 1984 insured Honda (Figure 21).

The second condition (insuring a car that has been repaired in the "Morris" garage) involves the Insure attribute, independently from the first condition, for Insure is multivalued. Its specification calls for duplicating Insure. The predicate can now be expanded to include the new condition. By default, Insure-2 and its repairs component have been existentially quantified. The final situation is shown in Figure 22.

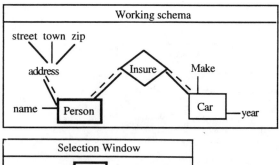

Working schema

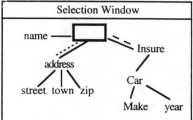

Selection Window

Figure 14. The updated query subschema and corresponding hierarchic structure

Describing application dynamics

In preceding sections we have discussed application requirements in terms of structural modeling and classical data-manipulation operations. We now consider requirements for describing application dynamics and briefly sketch the steps necessary to integrate a process model of system dynamics with the ERC+ model.

Traditionally, this subject has been focused on capturing the events that are significant in the application's life cycle. Events trigger operations on the database, according to preconditions; operations produce postconditions that eventually generate new events. This approach emphasizes the global-control structure of the information/activation flow between the processes composing the application. The Petri-net formalism is a powerful model for describing the control structure of concurrent systems,

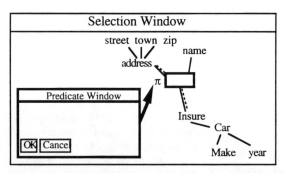

Figure 15. The initial state for predicate definition

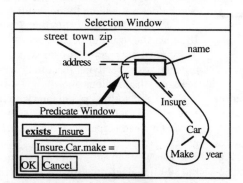

Figure 16. SW after Make is designated

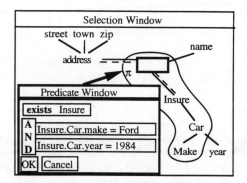

Figure 17. Final state of the SW

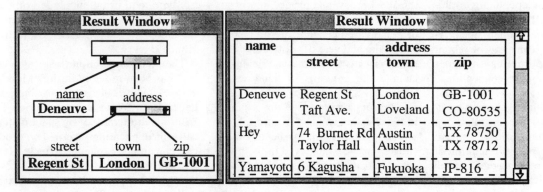

name	address		
	street	town	zip
Deneuve	Regent St	London	GB-1001
	Taft Ave.	Loveland	CO-80535
Hey	74 Burnet Rd	Austin	TX 78750
	Taylor Hall	Austin	TX 78712
Yamayoto	6 Kagusha	Fukuoka	JP-816

Figure 18. Result of the evaluated query in the attribute-tree form and in the nested tabular form

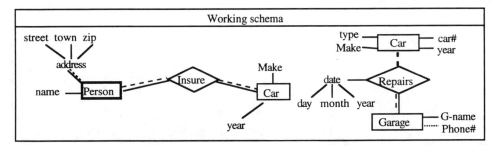

Figure 19. Starting a query modification

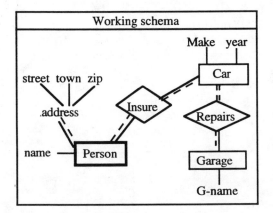

Figure 20. Keep useful objects

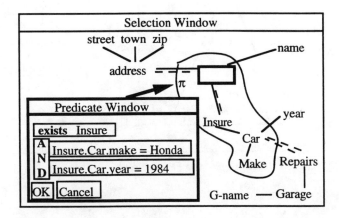

Figure 21. Define a predicate

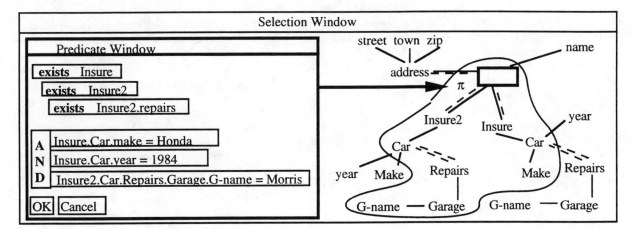

Figure 22. The new query ready for evaluation

and it has been used extensively as a formal vehicle to express this view of the dynamics (27, 28). Unfortunately, for the basic place/transition model the representation of complex systems often leads to very large nets that are difficult to analyze. To avoid this problem, high-level Petri nets have been developed, and are briefly illustrated here by examining one of them, the Predicate-Transition (PrT)-net model described in (15).

The main difference between the PrT-net model and the basic Petri-net model is that tokens in PrT nets can be structured objects and the transition firing is controlled by imposing conditions on the token values. A PrT net consists of these constituents (15):

1. a *directed net* $(P,T;F)$, where P is the set of *predicates* ("first-order" places), T is the set of transitions, F is the set of *arcs*, and:
$P \leftrightarrow T = \emptyset, P \cup T \neq \emptyset, P \otimes T \cup T \otimes P$
F
•$T = \{P|(P,T) \in F\}$ and
•$T = \{P \mid (T,P) \in F\}$
are called the *preset* and *postset* of $T \in$

T, respectively.

2. a *structure* , consisting of some sorts of individuals together with some operations and relations.

3. a labeling of all arcs with a formal sum of tuples of variables, whose length n is the "arity" of the predicate connected to the arc. The zero-tuple indicating a no-argument predicate (an ordinary Petri-net place) is denoted by the special symbol $\mathcal{C}$.

4. an inscription on some transitions, being a logical formula built from the operations and relations of

201

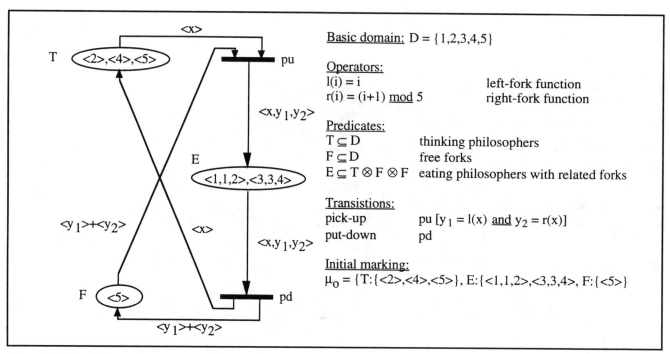

Figure 23. The PrT description of the FP problem

the structure . Variables occurring free in a formula have to occur at an adjacent arc.

5. a *marking M_o* of predicates of P with formal sums of *n*-tuples (*items*) of individual symbols;

6. a function *K*, which assigns to each predicate $P \in P$ an upper bound for the number of copies of the same item that it may carry. *K(P)* is called the capacity of *P*.

7. the transition rule: each element of *T* represents a class of possible changes of the markings of the adjacent predicates. Such a change consists of removing/adding copies of items from/to the adjacent places according to the expressions labeling the arcs. It *may* occur whenever, for an assignment of individuals to the variables that satisfies the formula attached as inscription to the transition, all input predicates carry enough copies of proper items, and for no output predicate the capacity *K* is exceeded by adding the respective copies of items. The occurrence (*firing*) of *T* changes the marking *M* into a new marking *M'*; this fact is denoted by: $M[T > M']$.

The structure can be specified by means of a first-order language *L* that describes the individuals of , their properties and relations. Let be a set of *n*-ary oper-

ators (function symbols), a set of *n*-ary predicates (relation symbols), and *V* a set of symbols (disjoint from and) that will be used as variables. The language *L* consists of *terms* and *formulas*, which are built in this way:

Terms.

a. a variable is a term,

b. if *f* is an *n*-ary operator and $v_1,...,v_n$ are terms, then $f(v_1,...,v_n)$ is a term,

c. no other expression is a term (remark: constants, i.e. 0-ary operators, are terms).

Formulas. A (well-formed) formula is defined as:

a. if v_1 and v_2 are terms, then $v_1 = v_2$ is an atomic formula (or, simply, an *atom*).

b. if *P* is an *n*-ary predicate and $v_1,...,v_n$ are terms, then $(v_1,...,v_n)$ is an atom.

c. if p_1 and p_2 are formulas, then *not p_1* and *(p_1 or p_2)* are formulas.

d. if *x* is a variable and *p* a formula , then $(\forall x)p$ is a formula.

e. no other expression is a formula (remark: the connectors *and*, $\rightarrow$, $\leftrightarrow$, and $\exists$ are derived from *not*, *or*, and $\forall$ in the usual way).

To illustrate this approach, let us consider a simple example, the well-known Five Philosophers (FP) problem (27):

FP: Five philosophers are seated at a round table, eating spaghetti. Next to each philosopher is one fork. To eat, a philosopher must pick up both the fork on his left and the fork on his right. When a philosopher is not eating, he is thinking (and vice versa). The problem is to synchronize the philosophers' activities, for they cannot eat all at the same time because they lack forks.

Figure 23 shows the representation of the FP problem in the PrT-net model.Starting from the state illustrated in Figure 8.1, the transition *pd* can occur with the substitution:
$$\{x/3, y_1/3, y_2/4\}$$
which generates the new marking:
$$_1 = \{T: (<2>,<3>,<4>,<5>), E: (<1,1,2>), F: (<3,4,5>)\}$$

As shown by the PrT net in Figure 23, although the dynamic behavior of the system is expressed in a simple way by using a PrT net, effectively specifying the system requires that the structure and the transaction inscriptions be explicitly defined. In general, this is not a simple task!

Moreover, real-life systems are usually managed by means of large database systems that store data and complex relationships between them. How can a PrT system specification be related to the data structures stored in the database that support the system's operation?

Our aim is to propose a model that will effectively solve this problem. The model relates in a simple way static and dynamics specifications of the system being developed. It integrates a *process model* (which is basically the PrT model) to represent the system dynamics and the ERC+ *data model* to describe data stored in the database. For clarity we use the term ERC++ to denote the model resulting from this integration.

To illustrate the discussion above, consider the classical Five Philosophers problem. It can be described by the ERC+ *data schema* shown in Figure 24, where the initial database state (db-state) DB_o corresponds to the initial marking $_o$ of Figure 23. The relationships Left and Right give, respectively, the left and the right fork of a philosopher.

In the ERC++ model, the system's behavior is specified with PrT nets in which predicates and transitions are described by formulas in the ERC+ algebra (or the ERC+ calculus). Such PrT nets are called *ERC++ nets*. The ERC++ net that expresses the dynamic behavior of the FP system on the database specified in Figure 24 is described by the ERC+ algebra formulas in Figure 25 or the equivalent ERC+ calculus formulas in Figure 26 (only formulas specifying predicates and transitions in the PrT net in Figure 23 are reported).

The OO approach moves the focus from the application as a whole to its objects, seen as independent interacting agents. Dynamics is expressed as a sequence of messages passing from one object to another (hence the expression "active objects"). This arrangement decidedly facilitates control over the integrity of each object in the database. The designer of an object type has to be fully aware of all stimuli to which the objects may have to respond. He or she can then define the appropriate methods to be attached to the object type. Because no agent external to the associated methods can modify the objects, object integrity is guaranteed just by designing each method to be integrity-preserving.

The counterpart of gaining more accuracy and control over the objects is that it becomes difficult to get a global comprehension and overall control of the application, and to enforce integrity rules spanning several objects (global consistency). It is hard to figure out, by looking at methods in objects' definitions, what the application does and how it works. It

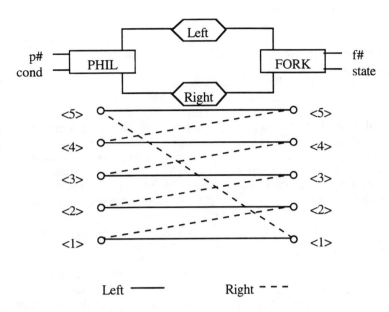

Figure 24. The ERC+ specification of the FP database

T: select [cond='thinking'] PHIL
E: select [cond='eating'] PHIL
F: select [state='available'] FORK
pu: (T sel-r-join (Left, F)) sel-r-join (Right, F)

Figure 25. The ERC++ algebra specification of the FP system

T:\{ $x \mid x \in$ PHIL $\wedge$ x.cond='thinking'\}
E:\{ $x \mid x \in$ PHIL $\wedge$ x.cond='eating'\}
F:\{ $y \mid y \in$ FORK $\wedge$ y.state='available'\}
pu : ($x \in T \wedge y_1 \in F \wedge y_2 \in F \wedge$ Left $(x, y_1) \wedge$ Right (x, y_2))

Figure 26. The ERC++ calculus specification of the FP system

---

is also hard to determine, when designing a new application, which objects and methods may be reused. Often a designer defines new methods for a new application, just because he or she does not know that a similar method is already available or because of slightly different requirements. Also, attempts to reuse methods often create new object types and inheritance structures that are purely artifacts of programming, with no counterpart in the real world.

To sum up, some methods bear clear advantages, but are not easy to use and do not by themselves suffice to cope with all aspects of dynamics. Therefore, the traditional and the OO approaches should be considered as complementing, rather than alternative to each other. The ERC++ model is planned to support both.

For global dynamics (i.e., description of the application's life-cycle), this system will provide support based on high-level Petri nets, as sketched above. To this end, a user-oriented ERC++ lan-guage based on the ERC+ algebra is being developed. The ERC++ language will provide facilities for specifying (more intuitively than algebra or calculus) predicates and transitions of the PrT control net that describe the system's evolution.

On the other hand, the ERC++ language equally provides facilities for attaching specific methods to application objects and for using such methods to describe the change in state of the database related to a given transition. General methods for ordinary access to the information in the objects will also be supported.

Designing methods is one of the most difficult tasks in building OO applications. Little support in the form of methodology or tools is available. In principle, methods have to be developed to express the intrinsic behavior of a set of objects, where by intrinsic behavior we mean the set of operations and request protocol representing a program component common to different applications of the information system. Intrinsic behavior cannot be discovered by looking at one application at a time; in fact, extracting common components is a methodological problem that must be taken into account in an object-oriented methodology for designing an information system. To alleviate this task, SUPER is investigating the concepts needed to build a tool for automatically generating methods specifications from high-level descriptions of different application requirements for processing data.

Conclusion

A lot of research results have documented the advantages of object-oriented concepts for tackling the design of large and complex software systems. Experience gained from using OO models to design database applications has clearly stated the need to combine the primary features of object orientation with concepts for representing explicit relationships among objects and for expressing the integrity constraints necessary to capture the semantics of database systems. We propose in this chapter an object+relationship approach, called ERC+, which is designed to fully support database application requirements. To achieve this aim, ERC+ starts from an accepted semantic-modeling paradigm (the ER approach) and improves its modeling capabilities with constructs for representing complex objects, and OO features (the methods) and Petri-net–based process descriptions for representing behavioral aspects. Moreover, ERC+ provides generic data- manipulation languages for user–DBMS interaction: theoretical languages (an algebra, a calculus) support definition of user-oriented languages (SQL-like, graphical).

Beyond a definition for a modeling approach, we also need integrated tools to support the methodology. To that purpose, we have defined and are currently implementing a design environment called SUPER to support the ERC+ modeling approach. These are the characteristic features of SUPER:

- a graphical schema editor for defining complex objects. The schema editor provides a palette of graphical symbols corresponding to each concept of the ERC+ model: entity types, relationship types, and so on. It allows a designer to build a schema with click-and-pick selections.
- a graphical query editor for manipulating data. The query editor is a tool that allows graphical formulation of data-manipulation operations that are automatically translated into expressions in the underlying ERC+ algebra. Graphical query formulation is achieved by: selecting a query schema, creating a query structure (a template), specifying predicates, specifying the structure of the query results, and displaying the resulting data. The user is allowed to perform these steps in any meaningfully consistent sequence.
- a data browser that allows users to navigate through the database, displaying the visited occurrences either within dynamic forms or as graphical diagrams similar to schema diagrams.

These tools have been implemented in C++. The underlying algebraic language is also implemented. Our current research is focused on specifying a tool to incrementally design objects through view integration. This tool implements a methodology in which complex systems are built by first decomposing the application into a number of small, manageable tasks. Next, a view corresponding to partial perception of the global data description of the application is associated with each task. And finally, the resulting views of the different tasks are integrated to build the application's global schema.

References

1. Abiteboul, S., P. C. Fischer, and H. J. Scheck, eds. *Nested relations and complex objects in databases.* Lecture Notes in Computer Science, 361. New York: Springer-Verlag, 1989.

2. Agrawal, R., N. H. Gehani, and J. Srinivasan. *Ode View: The Graphical Interface to Ode,* ACM SIGMOD International Conference on Management of Data, Atlantic City, N.J. (May 23–25, 1990), pp. 34–43.

3. Albano, A. , G. Ghelli, and R. Orsini. *A Relationship Mechanism for a Strongly Typed Object-Oriented Database Programming Language.* 17th International Conference on Very Large Data Bases, Barcelona, September 3–6, 1991, pp. 565–575.

4. Auddino, A., et al. *SUPER: A Comprehensive Approach to DBMS Visual User Interfaces.* IFIP WG 2.6 2nd Working Conference on Visual Database Systems, Budapest, September 30–October 3, 1991, pp. 359–374.

5. Bancilhon,.F., et al. *The design and implementation of O2, an object-oriented database system.* In Advances in Object-Oriented Database Systems, K. R. Dittrich, ed. Lecture Notes in Computer Science, 334. New York: Springer-Verlag, 1988, pp. 1–22

6. Bertino, E., M. Negri, G. Pelagatti, and L. Sbattella. Object oriented query languages: The notions and the issues. *IEEE Transactions on Data and Knowledge Engineering,* vol. 4, no. 3 (June 1992), pp. 223–237

7. Booch, G. *Object Oriented Design with Applications.* Palo Alto, Calif.: Benjamin-Cummings, 1991.

8. Brodie, M., J. Mylopoulos, and J. Schmidt, eds. *On Conceptual Modeling.* New York: Springer-Verlag, 1984.

9. Carey, M., D. DeWitt, and S. Vandenberg. *A Data Model and Query Language for EXODUS.* ACM-SIGMOD International Conference on Management of Data, Chicago, June 1–3, 1988, pp. 413–423.

10. Catarci, T., and G. Santucci. *QBD: A Graphic Query System.* 7th International Conference on the Entity-Relationship Approach, Rome, November 16–18, 1988, pp. 157–174.

11. Chen, P. P. The Entity-Relationship Model—Towards a unified view of data. *ACM Transactions on Database Systems,* vol. 1, no. 1 (1976).

12. Czedjo, B., R. Elmasri, M. Rusinkiewicz, and D. Embley. A graphical data manipulation language for an extended entity-relationship model. *IEEE Computer,* vol. 23, no. 3 (March 1990), pp. 26–36.

13. Elmasri, R., J. Weeldreyer, and A. Hevner. *The category concept: An extension to the entity-relationship model.* Data and Knowledge Engineering, vol. 1, no. 1 (June 1985), pp. 75–116.

14. Elmasri, R., A. Elmasri, and J. A. Larson. *A graphical query facility for ER databases.* In Entity-Relationship Approach: The Use of ER Concept in Knowledge Representation, P. P. Chen, ed. The Hague: North-Holland, 1985, pp. 236–245.

15. Genrich, H. J., and K. Lautenbach. *System modelling with high level Petri nets.* Theoretical Computer Science, 13 (1981).

16. Goldman, K. J., S. A. Goldman, P. C. Kanellakis, and S. B. Zdonik. *ISIS: Interface for a Semantic Information System.* ACM SIGMOD International Conference

on Management of Data, Austin, Texas, 1985, pp. 328–342.

17. Hohenstein, U. *Automatic Transformation of an Entity-Relationship Query Language into SQL*. 8th International Conference on the Entity-Relationship Approach, Toronto, October 18–20, 1989, pp. 309–327.

18. Jaeschke, G. *Remarks on the Algebra of the Non First Normal Form Relations,* ACM SIGMOD International Conference on Management of Data, Los Angeles, Calif., March 1982.

19. Khoshafian, S. , and R. Abnous. *Object Orientation: Concepts, Languages, Databases, User Interfaces.* New York: John Wiley & Sons, 1990.

20. Larson, J. *A Visual Approach to Browsing in a Database Environment. IEEE Computer,* vol. 19, no. 6 (June 1986), pp. 62–71.

21. Loizou, G., and P. Pouyioutas. *A Query Algebra for an Extended Object-Oriented Database Model.* International Symposium of Database System for Advanced Applications, Tokyo, April 1991.

22. McDonald, N., and H. McDonald. *A multimedia approach to the user interface.* In Human Factors and Interactive Computer Systems, Y. Vassiliou, ed. Norwood, N.J.: Ablex Publishing, 1984, pp. 105–116.

23. Navathe, S., B. Navathe, R. Elmasri, and J. A. Larson. *Integrating User Views in Database Design. IEEE Computer,* vol. 19, no. 1 (January 1986), pp. 50–62.

24. Parent, C., H. Rolin, K. Yétongnon, and S. Spaccapietra. *An ER Calculus for the Entity-Relationship Complex Model.* In Entity-Relationship Approach to Database Design and Querying, F. Lochovsky, ed. New York: Elsevier, 1990, pp. 361–384.

25. Parent, C., and S. Spaccapietra. *ERC+: an object based entity-relationship approach.* In Conceptual Modelling, Databases and CASE: An Integrated View of Information Systems Development, P. Loucopoulos, R. Zicari, eds. New York: John Wiley, 1992.

26. Pernici, B. *Objects with Roles.* IEEE/ACM International Conference on Office Information Systems, Cambridge, Mass., April 25–27, 1990, pp. 205–215.

27. Peterson, J. L. *Petri Net Theory and the Modelling of Systems.* Englewood Cliffs, N.J.: Prentice-Hall, 1982.

28. Reisig, R. *Petri Nets.* New York: Springer-Verlag, 1985.

29. Richardson, J., and P. Schwarz. *Aspects: Extending Objects to Support Multiple, Independent Roles.* ACM SIGMOD International Conference on Management of Data, Denver, Colo., May 29–31, 1991, pp. 298–307.

30. Roth, M., H. Korth, and A. Silberschatz. *Theory of Non First Normal Form Relational Databases,* TR-84-36 Department of Computer Science, University of Texas at Austin, December 1984.

31. Rumbaugh, J. *Relations as Semantic Constructs in an Object-Oriented Language.* OOPSLA Conference, Orlando, Fla., October 4–8, 1987, pp. 466–481.

32. Scholl, M. H., and H.-J. Schek. *A Relational Object Model.* 3rd International Conference on Database Theory, Paris, December 1990.

32. Spaccapietra, S., and C. *Parent. Model independent assertions for integration of heterogeneous schemas.* VLDB Journal, vol. 1, no. 1 (July 1992), 81–126.

33. Sunye, M. *CERQLE: un SQL entité-relation.* 7ème Journées Bases de Données Avancées, Trégastel, September 15–18, 1992.

34. Vrbsky, S. V., J. Liu, and K Smith. *An object-oriented approach to producing monotonically improving approximate answers.* Technical report no. NVY N00014 89-J-1181 Deptartment of Computer Science, University of Illinois, Urbana-Champaign.

35. Wong, H. K. T., and I. Kuo. *GUIDE: Graphic User Interface for Database Exploration.* 8th International Conference on Very Large Databases, Mexico City, 1982, pp. 22–32.

36. Zaniolo, C., and D. Maier. *The Database Language GEM.* ACM SIGMOD International Conference on Management of Data, San Jose, May 1983.

37. Zhang, Z. Q., and A. O. Mendelzon. A graphical query language for entity-relationship databases. In *Entity-Relationship Approach to Software Engineering,* Davis et al., eds. The Hague: North-Holland, 1983, pp. 441–448.

Stefano Spaccapietra, Ecole Polytechnique Fédérale, DI - Laboratoire Bases de Données, IN - Ecublens, 1015 Lausanne, Switzerland Telephone: +41 21 6935210Fax: +41 21 6935195 email: spaccapietra@di.epfl.ch Christine Parent, Marcos Sunye, Kokou Yetongnon, Université de Bourgogne Département Informatique, B.P. 138, 21004 Dijon Cedex, France Telephone: +33 80395891Fax: +33 80395815 email: badine@satie.u-bourgogne.fr Antonio Di Leva, Dipartimento di Informatica, Universita degli Studi di Torino, Corso Svizzera 185 - 10149 Torino, Italy Telephone: +39 11 7712002Fax: +39 11 751603 email: dileva@di.unito.it

Keywords. Object-oriented modeling, object-oriented databases, application requirements, visual programming, user interfaces, entity-relationship model, information systems.

A Multilevel-Secure Object-Oriented Data Model

Sushil Jajodia

Boris Kogan

Ravi S. Sandhu

I ntroduction.

We outline here a new security model that provides mandatory access controls in object-oriented database systems. We depart from the traditional security models, which start with the passive-object, active-subject paradigm. Ours is a flow model, the main elements of which are objects and messages. An object combines the properties of a passive information repository with those of an active agent. Messages and their replies are the basic instrument of information flow. The model we propose combines compatibility with the object-oriented data model and a simple way of stating and enforcing mandatory security policies.

Several security models dealing with mandatory access controls in object-oriented databases have recently appeared in the literature. Although some have much interest and merit (see "Review of relevant research" later in this article for a discussion of related work), they seem to lack intuitive appeal because they ap-

pear to model security in a way that does not take full advantage of the object-oriented paradigm. Our goal is to construct a database security model for mandatory access controls that dovetails naturally with the object-oriented data model. In doing so we seek a set of principles to clearly and concisely help design and implement security policies in object-oriented database-management systems.

The Bell and LaPadula object-subject paradigm (1, 2) is widely used in work on mandatory access controls. An *object* is a data file or, at an abstract level, a data item. A *subject* is an active process that can request access to objects. Every object is assigned a classification, and every subject a clearance. Classifications and clearances are collectively referred to as *security levels* (or classes). Security levels are partially ordered, usually in a lattice structure. A subject is allowed a read access to an object only if the former's clearance is equivalent to or higher (in the partial order) than the latter's classification. A subject is allowed a write ac-

cess to an object only if the former's clearance is equivalent to or lower than the latter's classification. These two rules ensure that subjects cannot directly copy information from high objects to low objects, which can be read by low subjects. Otherwise, because subjects can represent users, a breach of security occurs wherein users get access to information for which they have not been cleared. Of course a system may not be secure even if it always correctly enforces the two Bell-LaPadula restrictions. A secure system must guard against not only direct revelation of data but also violations that produce illegal information flows by indirect means, known as *covert channels* (2) (also see (5) for a brief discussion of this and other issues related to multilevel security requirements in databases).

Our focus in this chapter is a security model, and at this level of abstraction covert channels can be ignored (much as they are in the Bell-LaPadula model). For discussion of some covert channels that can arise in implementing the security

0-8186-6222-0/95 $4.00 © 1995 IEEE

model discussed here, see (17, 18, 21).

Most security models for mandatory access controls are based on the traditional Bell-LaPadula paradigm. Although this standard has proven to be quite effective for modeling security in operating systems as well as relational databases, it appears somewhat forced when applied to object-oriented systems. The problem is that the notion of object in the object-oriented data model does not correspond to the Bell-LaPadula notion of object. The former combines the properties of a passive information repository, represented by attributes and their values, with the properties of an active agent, represented by methods and their invocations. Thus, the object of the object-oriented data model can be thought of as the object and the subject of the Bell-LaPadula paradigm fused into one.

Continuing to examine the object-oriented model from the security perspective, one realizes that information flow in this context has a very concrete and natural embodiment in the form of messages and their replies. Moreover, taking into account encapsulation, a cardinal property of object-oriented systems, messages can be considered the only instrument of information flow.

Let us sketch the main elements in our model. The system consists of objects (in the object-oriented sense rather than the Bell-LaPadula sense). Every object is assigned a unique classification. Objects can communicate, and thereby exchange information, only by sending messages and replies among themselves. Messages are not, however, allowed to flow directly from one object to another. Instead every message or reply is intercepted by the *message filter*, a system element charged with implementing security policies. The message filter decides, upon examining a message (or reply) and the sender's and receiver's classifications, what action is appropriate. It may let the message go through unaltered; or it may completely reject it (e.g., when a low object sends a message to a high object requesting the value of one of the latter's attributes); or it may take some other action (such as restricting the method invocation that processes the message to be "memoryless," as we discuss later).

The principal advantages of the proposed model are its compatibility with the object-oriented data model, and the simplicity and conceptual clarity with which mandatory security policies are stated and enforced.

One comment: Even though all objects are single-level (in the sense of having a unique classification assigned to the entire object and not assigning any classifications to individual attributes or methods), this condition does not preclude the possibility of modeling multilevel entities with multiple single-level objects, as we will demonstrate.

We begin this chapter by introducing our basic object-oriented data model, and then enhance this basic model by adding to it the elements needed for multilevel security. We next discuss how our security model handles information flow due to inheritance in a class hierarchy. Then we show how we can represent multilevel entities within our security model, in which all objects are single-level. Briefly reviewing related research, we give our conclusions and discuss our future work.

Object-oriented data model

An object-oriented database is a collection of objects communicating via messages and their replies. Objects are of two types: primitive and nonprimitive. We postulate a finite set of domains D_1, D_2, ..., D_n. Let D be the union of the domains augmented with a special element nil (whose purpose is explained in this article). Every element of D is referred to as a primitive object.

A nonprimitive object o is defined by its unique identifier i, an ordered set $a = (a_1, ..., a_k)$ of attribute names, an ordered set $\upsilon = (\upsilon_1, ..., \upsilon_k)$ of corresponding values, and a set μ of methods. The uniqueness of object identity is commonly considered a fundamental property of object-oriented systems.

A value is either a primitive object or an identifier. A more general object model would also permit a value to be a set of identifiers and/or primitive values. For simplicity of exposition, however, we forego this generalization in this chapter. The results developed here do not depend on this simplification (8).

Here is the notation we use in the rest of the chapter. For an object o, $i(o)$ denotes its unique identifier, $a(o)$ denotes its attributes, $\upsilon(o)$ denotes the corresponding values, and $\mu(o)$ denotes its methods.

A message g consists of a message name h, an ordered set $p = (p_1, ..., p_k)$, $k \geq 0$, of primitive objects or object identi-

fiers called the message parameters, and a reply r. Similar to the notation used for objects, we let $h(g)$, $p(g)$, and $r(g)$ denote the name, the parameter list, and the reply for message g, respectively.

Each object o has an interface f_o that determines which messages o responds to. Moreover, the interface determines which method, out of the set of methods, $\mu(o)$, defined for object o, is to be invoked, depending on the name of the message. An object will invoke one of its methods in response to a message received from another object. A method invocation can, in turn, carry out one or more of these actions: (1) directly access an attribute belonging to the object (read or change its value); (2) invoke other methods belonging to the object; (3) send a message to another object; or (4) create a new object; eventually returning a reply to the source of the message. (If an object cannot find a method to process this message, we assume a default failure method that returns an appropriate reply.)

An object sends a message g by invoking a system primitive SEND(g, i), where i is the identifier of the receiver object. The reply $r(g)$ is computed by the method activated in the receiver upon arrival of g there and returned to the sender. As we shall see in the next section, sometimes the system's security component will have to interfere in computing $r(g)$ (particularly to ensure that this computation is "memoryless" if so required by security considerations). A special type of object is called *user object*; it represents a user session with the system. User objects can be created only by the system, at login time. User objects differ from regular objects in that, in addition to being able to invoke methods in response to messages, they can also invoke methods spontaneously. The notion of spontaneous method invocation may seem arbitrary at first. It is, however, necessary in order to avoid running into a version of the chicken-and-egg paradox. That is, if a message can be sent only through a method invocation (see property (3) of method invocations) and if a method can be activated only by a message received from another object, then how does any processing in such a system ever get initiated? (One has to insist that either the egg or the chicken come first.) In reality, we want a user to be able to initiate a system activity, for example, by typing a string of characters on the keyboard. This message will serve as a signal for the corresponding user object to initiate a method. We choose to think of this as a "spontaneous" initiation, because the keyboard and any signals that it sends are external to our model.

Objects are used to model real-world entities. We do so by associating properties, or facets, of an entity with attributes of the corresponding object. (More generally, as we will see, an entity may be modeled by more than one object.) The attribute values are, then, instantiations of those properties. For instance, a country can be represented in a geographic object-oriented database by an object o, where $a(o)$ = (COUNTRY_NAME, POPULATION, CAPITAL, NATIONAL_FLAG, FORM_OF_GOVERNMENT) and $v(o)$ = ("Albania," 117, $i(o_1)$, $i(o_2)$, $i(o_3)$). The values of the first and second attributes are a string and an integer, respectively; the values of the rest of the attributes are references to other objects that, in turn, describe the capital, the national flag, and the form of government of the nation Albania.

Notice that an object's methods, unlike its attributes, do not have counterparts in the real-world entity modeled by the object. The purpose of methods is quite different. It is to provide support for manipulating objects, including the basic database functions of querying and updating objects.

A realistic object-oriented model should also include the notion of constraints. For instance, an attribute of an object may be allowed to assume values only from a restricted subset of domains or object identifiers. To simplify the exposition, we disregard here the issue of constraints. It is conceptually simple, however, to incorporate this notion in our secure-data model.

Object-oriented security model

We began with an informal exposition of our security model for objects with unique security-level assignments exchanging messages subject to some security constraints. We next develop a formal model of object-oriented security, in accordance with this general idea.

Security levels and information flow. The system consists of a set O of objects and a partially ordered set S of security levels with ordering relation $<$. A level $S_i \in S$ is said to be dominated by another level $Sj \in S$, denoted by $S_i \leq S_j$, if $i = j$ or $S_i < S_j$. For two levels S_i and S_j that are unordered by $<$, we write $S_i \Leftrightarrow S_j$. A total function $L: O \rightarrow S$ is called the security classification function. In other words, every object o has a unique security level $L(o)$ associated with it.

Characterizing information flows. The main goal of a security policy requiring confidentiality is to control the flow of information among objects. More specifically, information can legally flow from an object o_j to an object o_k if and only if $L(o_j) \leq L(o_k)$. All other information flows are considered illegal.

In the Bell-LaPadula model this objective is achieved by prohibiting read-ups and writedowns. That is, a subject is allowed to read an object only if the subject's security level dominates that of the object. Similarly, a subject is allowed to update an object only if the former's security level is dominated by that of the latter.

In our model, because of its encapsulation property, information transfer among objects can take place either (1) when a message is passed from one object to another, or (2) when a new object is created. In the first instance, information can flow in both directions: from sender to receiver and back. The forward flow is carried through the list of parameters included in the message, and the backward flow through the reply. In the second instance, information flows only forward, from the creating object to the created one, for example, by supplying attribute values for the new object. A transfer of information does not necessarily occur every time a message is passed. An object acquires information by changing its internal state — by changing the values of some of its attributes. Thus, if no such changes occur as a result of a method invocation in response to a message, then no information transfer has been enacted. Then we can say that the forward flow has been ineffective. This situation is analogous to taking pictures with an unloaded camera. The information in the form of light is flowing into the camera but not being retained there. Similarly, if a message's reply is nil, the backward flow has been ineffective.

To eliminate the information channel associated with the receiver object's security level being dynamically changed (the sender can get back a sequence of nil and non-nil replies if it repeatedly sends messages to the same object), we have to require that all security-level assignments be static. That is, the level associated with an object at creation time cannot be changed. (This requirement is similar to the tranquility requirement in the Bell-LaPadula model, whereby the security labels on subjects and objects cannot change (2).) If, however, the security level of the real-world entity modeled by the object must be changed, then a new object has to be created. The new object will be exactly like the one that it replaced, except for the new security level to reflect the desired change. We say that a transitive flow from an object o_1 to an object o_1 occurs when there is a flow from o_1 to a third object o_3, and from o_3 to o_2. All types of flows discussed until now can be called *direct flows.* Now, consider what happens when an object o_1 sends a message g_1 to another object o_2, and o_2 does not change its internal state as a result of receiving g_1, but instead sends a message g_2 to a third object o_3. Further, suppose $p(g_2)$ includes information derived from message g_1 (e.g., by copying some parameters of g_1 to g_2). If, then, invoking the method $fo_3(h(g_2))$ results in updating o_3's state, a transfer of information has taken place from o_1 to o_3. No message is exchanged between o1 and o_3, nor was o_3 created by o_1, therefore this flow cannot be considered direct. Moreover, there may or may not be a flow from o_1 to o_2; therefore this too is not necessarily a transitive flow. This is an instance of what we call an indirect flow of information. Notice that an indirect flow can involve more than three objects. For example, instead of updating its state, o_3 could send a message to a fourth object that would result in updating the latter's state. Both direct and indirect illegal flows of information should be prevented (this rule will also account for all transitive flows) if the system is to be secure.

Primitive messages. We assume that access to internal attributes, object creation (creation by an object of an instance of itself), and invocation of internal methods are all effected by having an object send a message to itself. (Some object-oriented database systems (e.g., GemStone), in fact, use this kind of implementation. At the same time, notice that our model is a conceptual one telling us what needs to be done, rather than how it will be implemented. A correct implementation must demonstrate that it satisfies the model's requirements, even though it may do so without mimicking each aspect of the model, action for action.)

We now define three built-in messages for that purpose. First, however, we must modify the definition of a messagpe. A message g consists of a message name h, an ordered set $p = (p_1, ..., p_k)$, $k > 0$, of message parameters where a pi can be a primitive object or an object identifier or a security level, and a reply r. (The difference, with respect to our earlier definition, is that now a parameter can be a method, an attribute name, or a security level in addition to the previous cases of a primitive value or an object identifier.)

The three primitive messages can now be defined.

1. +A read message is a message sent by an object o to itself, defined as $g = (READ, (a_j), r)$, where $a_j \in a(o)$. A read message results in binding r to the value of attribute a_j. If this result cannot be achieved, say, because there is no attribute a_j, r is returned as FAILURE (which is a reserved symbol with obvious significance).

2. +A write message is a message sent by an object o to itself, defined as $g = (WRITE, (a_j, v_j), r)$, where $aj \in a(o)$. The effect of sending a write message is an update of attribute a_j with value v_j. The reply r is either SUCCESS or FAILURE (SUCCESS, like FAILURE, is a reserved symbol with obvious significance).

3   +Finally, a create message is defined as $g = (CREATE, (v_1, ..., vk, S_j), r)$, where p is a list of attribute values, $v_1, ..., v_k$, appended with a security level S_j. When sent by an object o to itself, a create message results in a new object being created. This new object is assigned an identifier i by the system. The object inherits attributes and methods from o. The attributes are initialized with the values $v_1, ..., v_k$. The new object is assigned security level S_j, as specified in g. If the creation is successful, the identifier i is returned to o as r. Otherwise, FAILURE is returned.

Message-filtering algorithm. The message filter is a security element in the system whose goal is to recognize and prevent illegal information flows. The message filter intercepts every message sent by any object in the system and, depending on security levels of sender and receiver, as well as some auxiliary information, decides how to handle the message. In other words, the message filter is

the system's reference monitor.

The message-filtering algorithm is presented in Figure 1. We assume that o_1 and o_2 are sender and receiver objects respectively. Also, let t_1 be the method invocation in o_1 that sent the message g_1, and t_2 the method invocation in o_2 on receipt of g_1. The two major cases of the algorithm correspond to whether or not g_1 is a primitive message.

Cases (1) through (4) in Figure 1 deal with nonprimitive messages sent between two objects, say o_1 and o_2. In case (1), the sender and the receiver are at the same level. The message and the reply are allowed to pass. The rlevel of t_2 will be the same as that of t_1. Notice that rlevel is a property of a method invocation, rather than a property of an object. We explain the significance of rlevel shortly. In case (2), the levels of o_1 and o_2 are incomparable, thus the message is blocked and a nil reply is returned to method t_1. In case (3), the receiver is at a higher level than the sender. The message is passed through; but a nil reply is returned to t_1, and the actual reply from t_2 is discarded, thus effectively cutting off the backward flow. (Notice that the delivery of this nil reply to t_1 cannot be synchronized with the attempted reply from t_2 to t_1; otherwise information leakage will be associated with the timing of the reply. Therefore, t_1 and t_2 must execute concurrently and asynchronously. For discussion on how to handle this execution securely and correctly, see (17, 18, 21)). For case (4), the receiver is at a lower level than the sender. The message and the reply are allowed to pass. However, the rlevel of t_2 (in the receiver object) is set so as to prevent illegal flows. In other words, although a message is allowed to pass from a high-level sender to a low-level receiver, it cannot cause a "write-down" violation because the method invocation in the receiver is restricted from modifying the state of the object or creating a new object (i.e., the method invocation is "memoryless"). Moreover, this restriction is propagated along with further messages sent out by this method invocation to other objects, as far as is needed for security.

The intuitive significance of rlevel is that it keeps track of the least upper bound of all objects encountered in a chain of method invocations, going back to the user object at the root of the chain. We can show this sequence by induction on the length of the method invocation chain. To do so, it is also useful to show

the related property that $rlevel(t_i) \geq L(o_i)$. For the basis case we assume that the spontaneous method invocation in the root user object has its rlevel set to the user object's level. Inspecting (1), (3), and (4) in Figure 1, we find that the induction step follows. Least upper bound is explicitly used in case (3). (We need to use least upper bound for computing rlevel in case (3) rather than maximum, because the security levels are partially ordered. It is possible for a chain of method invocations to descend in security levels along one branch of the partial order, and then turn around and start ascending along a different branch.) In cases (1) and (4), because of the induction hypothesis and the relative levels of o_1 and o_2, the assignment of rlevel can be equivalently written as in case (3)

We say that a method invocation t_i has restricted status if rlevel $(t_i) > L(o_i)$. In such cases t_i is not allowed to write to o_i (case (6) of Figure 1), or to create an object with security level below $rlevel(t_i)$ (case (7) of Figure 1). A key element in the message-filter algorithm is that the restricted status is propagated along with further messages sent out by a method invocation to other objects (exactly so far as security requires). This step is critical in preventing indirect information flows.

To understand how the message-filter algorithm propagates the restricted status on method invocations, it is useful to visualize how a tree of method invocations is generated, as shown in Figure 2. The root t_0 is a "spontaneous" method invocation by a user. The restricted- method invocations are shown within shaded regions. Suppose t_k is a method for object o_k, and t_n is a method for object on that resulted from a message sent from t_k to o_n. The method t_n has a restricted status because $L(o_n) < L(o_k)$. The children and descendants of t_n will continue to have a restricted status until t_s is reached. The method ts is no longer restricted because $L(o_s) > L(o_k)$, and a write by t_s to the state of o_s no longer constitutes a write-down. This result is accounted for in the assignment to rlevel (t_2) in case (3) of Figure 1.

The variable rlevel clearly is critical in determining whether or not the child of a restricted method should itself be restricted. A method invocation potentially obtains information from security levels at or below its own rlevel. It follows that a method invocation should be allowed to record information labeled only at levels that dominate its own rlevel. For exam-

```
% let g₁ = (h₁, (p₁, . . . , p_k), r) be the message sent from o₁ to o₂
if o₁ ≠ o₂ ∨ h₁ ∉ {READ, WRITE, CREATE} then case
% i.e., g₁ is a non-primitive message
(1)    L(o₁) = L(o₂) :      % let g₁ pass, let reply pass
                            invoke t₂ with} rlevel (t₂) ← rlevel(t₁);
                            r ← reply from t₂; return r to t₁;
(2)    L(o₁) <> L(o₂):      % block g₁, inject NIL reply
                            r ← NIL; return r to t₁;
(3)    L(o₁) < L(o₂):       % let g₁ pass, inject NIL reply, ignore actual reply
                            r ← NIL; r to t₁;
                            invoke t₂ with = rlevel(t₂)← lub [L(o₂),rlevel(t₁)];
                            % where lub denotes least upper bound
                            discard reply from t₂;
(4)    L(o₁) > L(o₂):       % let g₁ pass, let reply pass
                            invoke t₂ with rlevel (t₂) ← rlevel(t₁);
                            r←reply from t₂; return r to t₁;
end case;

if o₁ = o₂ ∧ h₁ in {READ, WRITE, CREATE} then case
% i.e., g₁ is a primitive message
(5)    g₁ = (READ,(aj),r): % allow unconditionally
                            r ← value of aⱼ; return r to} t₁;
(6)    g₁ = (WRITE),(aⱼ,vⱼ),r) : % allow if status of t₁ is unrestricted
                            if = rlevel(t₁) = L(o₁)
                                then [aⱼ ← vⱼ; r ← SUCCESS]
                                else r ← FAILURE;
                            return r to t₁;
(7)    g₁= CREATE,(v₁,. . . ,v_k,Sⱼ),r)$ : % allow if status of t₁ is unrestricted relative to Sⱼ
                            if} rlevel(t₁) ≤ Sⱼ
                                then [CREATE i with values v₁,. . . ,v_k and L(i)← Sⱼ; r← i]
                                else} r ←FAILURE;
                            return r to t₁;
end case;
```

Figure 1. Message filtering algorithm

ple, consider a message sent from a Secret object to a Confidential one (where Secret > Confidential). The rlevel derived for the method invocation at the receiver object will be Secret.

We now discuss the security mediation of primitive messages. Read operations (case (5)) never fail for security reasons, because read-up operations cannot occur. They cannot, because read operations are confined to an object's methods, and their results can be exported only by messages or replies that are filtered by the message filter. Write operations (case (6)) will succeed only if the status of the method invoking the operations is unrestricted. Finally, create operations (case (7)) will succeed only if the rlevel of the method invoking the operation is dominated by the level of the created object. If a write or create operation fails, a failure message is sent to the sender. This failure message does not vi-

olate security because information is flowing upward in level.

The general idea of message filter is similar to that of law filter introduced by Minsky and Rozenshtein (14), although their work has no direct relation to multilevel security. Because its purpose is to enforce security, the message filter is part of the Trusted Computing Base. It is possible, however, to implement the message-filter model on top of a traditional Bell-LaPadula multilevel-secure operating system, without requiring any exemption from the two Bell-LaPadula rules (see (21) for details).

An example of message filtering. We now present a brief example to illustrate the message-filtering algorithm of Figure 1 with the help of a payroll database. Our simple object-oriented database consists of three classes of objects: (1) EMPLOYEE (Unclassified), (2) PAY-INFO

(Secret), and (3) WORK-INFO (Unclassified), with the corresponding attributes as shown in Figure 3. Objects EMPLOYEE and WORK-INFO are unclassified because their attributes (such as name, address, hours worked) represent readily available information about an employee. The object PAY-INFO is secret because its attributes include sensitive information such as hourly rate and weekly pay.

Let us see how cases (1), (3), and (4) in the filtering algorithm apply to the payroll database. Case (1) occurs when the sender and receiver are at the same level and applies to the message exchange between objects EMPLOYEE and WORK-INFO. The message filter allows both messages, RESET-WEEKLY-HOURS and reply DONE, to pass. Case (3) applies to the message exchange between objects EMPLOYEE and PAY-INFO. Because the latter is classified higher, a nil reply is returned in response to the PAY message and the actual reply is discarded. Case (4) involves the objects PAY-INFO and WORK-INFO. Because the object WORK-INFO is classified lower than PAY-INFO, the message GET-HOURS and reply HOURS-WORKED are allowed to pass. The method invocation in WORK-INFO, however, is given the restricted status (because its rlevel is Secret). This step prevents the method from updating the state of object WORK-INFO (which, if allowed, would cause a write-down violation).

Class hierarchy and security. The notion of classes is usually considered very important for object-oriented databases, if not for object-oriented systems in general. Most object-oriented databases support classes. We consider here how our security model deals with information flow because of inheritance in a class hierarchy.

The notion of classes is akin to that of relations in relational databases. Objects of similar structure (types and names of attributes) and similar behavior (methods) are grouped in classes, just as tuples of the same structure, in relational databases, are grouped into relations. The parallel with relational systems does not go very far, however. First, relational databases have no notion analogous to that of object behavior. Second, classes in object-oriented databases are represented by objects that include information on the names and types of attributes of the constituent instance objects of the class as well as the methods common to them. Objects of this kind are called *class-defining object*s, or simply . Thus, object-oriented systems essentially make no distinction in representing data and metadata.

We assume that the reader has basic familiarity with inheritance and class hierarchy (e.g., see (9,24)). A typical class hierarchy has a class OBJECT at its root. It also includes a special class CLASS such that every object defining a class is an instance of CLASS. Earlier we discussed ways in which objects can transfer information to each other, and we mentioned message sending and object creation. We went on to define several types of information flow. With classes and inheritance we now have two more (implicit) ways of transferring information.

Because a class object (i.e., a class-defining object) includes information on structure and behavior for all its instance objects, the latter have implicit read access to the former. Thus, an information flow runs from a class object to an instance object. We refer to this type of flow as a *class-instance flow*.

Classes inherit attributes and methods from their ancestors in the class hierarchy, so that a class object has an implicit read access to all its ancestors. Therefore, an information flow runs down along all hierarchy links. This type of flow is designated *inheritance flow*.

It is easy to see that an inheritance flow is illegal unless the level of a class object dominates that of each of its ancestors. Similarly, a class-instance flow is illegal unless the level of an instance object dominates that of its class.

Our approach in dealing with illegal inheritance and class-instance flows is to implement the

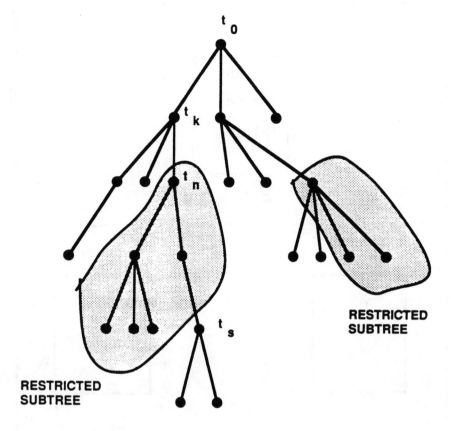

Figure 2. Method invocation tree

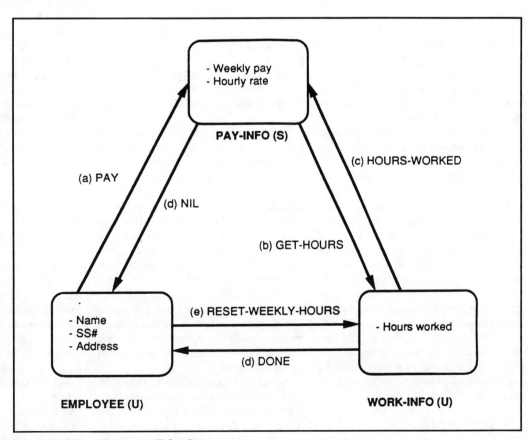

Figure 3. Objects in a payroll database

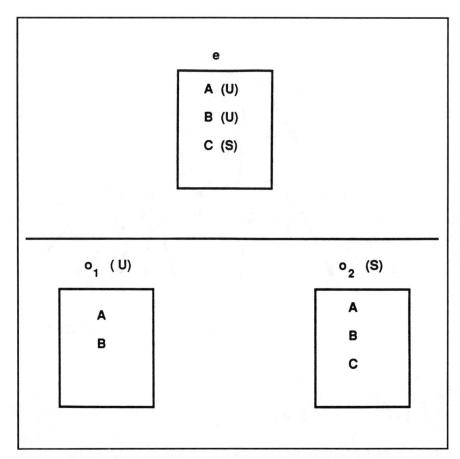

Figure 4. Representing a multilevel entity by multiple single-level objects

included in the algorithm to prevent the illegal direct flow to the newly created object at the creation time rather than the illegal class-instance flow, which can take place at any time after the instance is created. The provision works equally well, however, in both cases. Constraint 2 is not automatically satisfied by the message-filtering algorithm, but the latter could be modified for that purpose. Or the constraint could be enforced by supplying the object CLASS with a method for creating new classes that would include provisions for checking that the security level of the new class is in the prescribed relationship to the levels of its parents. The second possibility is preferable, perhaps, because we want to keep the message filter — which is part of the Trusted Computing Base—as small as possible.

Modeling multilevel entities with single-level objects

In an object-oriented data model, objects are used to model real-world entities. Therefore, it may seem discouraging that our security model insists that all objects have to be "flat" — that is, at a single security level. Much modeling flexibility would be lost if multilevel entities could not be represented in our database. In this section we demonstrate that restricting objects to be single-level does not have to imply that the same type of restriction applies to entities that we are trying to model. We draw this example with a few simple examples. Suppose we have two security levels: U (unclassified) and S (secret), the latter dominating the former.

Consider an entity e characterized by attributes A, B, and C such that A and B are at level U and C is at level S (e could be a collection of information pertaining to an employee, where A is the employee's name, B is the home address, and C is the salary). The intention is to allow access to C only for users with secret clearance. All other users can access only A and B. Entity e can be represented by objects o_1 and o_2 such that a(o_1) = (A, B), a(o_2) = (A, B, C), $L(o_1)$ = U, and $L(o_2)$ = S. Object o_2 is the internal representation of entity e for users with the secret clearance, and o_1 is the representation of e for all other users. The example is illustrated in Figure 4. Attributes of en-

classification and inheritance features by means of message passing. For details about such an implementation, see (14). The purpose we achieve is to make the implicit flows discussed above explicit — that is, they are realized by means of messages. As a consequence, class-instance and inheritance flows can be checked by the message filter, just as forward, backward, and indirect flows are. (Realize that disagreement is rampant about the exact scope of inheritance in a class hierarchy (e.g., see (15)). Because we have chosen to define our security model in terms of information flow among objects, any illegal information flow due to inheritance, regardless of its specific inheritance features, will be prevented as long as these features are implemented by means of message passing.)

It is still a good idea, though, to place the following constraints on the way in which security levels of instance objects and subclasses objects relate to those of the corresponding class objects.

Security-Level Constraint 1. If o_j is an object of class c_j (c_j also denotes the corresponding class object), then $L(c_j) \leq L(o_j)$.

Security-Level Constraint 2. If c_i and c_j are classes such that c_j is a child of c_i in the class hierarchy, then $L(c_i) \leq L(c_j)$.

Understand that the constraints listed above are not introduced for the sake of security, which is still handled by the message-filtering algorithm because all flows, including the class-instance and inheritance flows, are explicitly cast in the form of messages, and therefore violating these constraints will not lead to a violation of security. Instead, a violation of Constraint 2, for example, will break down the inheritance mechanism by creating a situation wherein the message filter prevents a class object from gaining access to a method it inherits from its parent class, because the child's security level does not dominate that of the parent, as required by the constraint.

Notice that Constraint 1 is automatically satisfied by the message-filtering algorithm (see case (7) in Figure 1) at the instance-creation time. It is interesting, though, that this feature was originally

tity *e* have individual security labels (shown in parentheses). This distinction contrasts to objects o_1 and o_2, which have labels only at the object level.

Suppose now that we have an entire collection of entities of the same type as e (*e.g.*, a set of employee entities) — that is, entities with unclassified attributes *A* and *B* and a secret attribute *C*. Let us denote this type of entities *X*. In our model each entity of this type is represented by two objects: one for users with secret clearance and one for all others. Thus, we end up with two classes of objects for one type of entity. The distinction between the two classes is based on security, not semantics, as it would normally be in object-oriented databases. Let *XU* be the class of the unclassified objects and *XS* the class of the secret objects representing entities of type *X*. For modeling it is convenient to relate classes *XU* and *XS* in the class hierarchy. Thus, if *XS* is made a child of *XU*, then it can inherit from *XU* attributes *A* and *B* and add to them a locally defined attribute *C*. Figure 5 shows the relevant segment of the hierarchy. Notice that the class object *XU* is placed at security level *U*, and *XS* at level *S*. The effect is that not only do the uncleared users have no access to the values of attribute *C* in entities of type *X*, but they are not even aware of this secret attribute because access to the class object *XS* is prohibited to them. It is possible to place the class object *XS* at level *U*, while keeping instances of *XS* at level *S*. Then the uncleared users will be aware of attribute C but not of any values of it in instance objects. Notice that such a dichotomy between the class-object level and the level of its instances conforms with Security-Level Constraint 1. The choice of label for *XS* depends on the policy decision.

To carry our example a little further, suppose we have a second type of entities that we have to model, say type *Y*. *Y* consists of the same attributes at the same security levels as *X* plus a new attribute *D* at level *U*. The conceptual class hierarchy (or schema) is shown in Figure 6. In that schema, *Y* is a child of *X*. Let us now address the question of how this schema can be implemented in our model. Using the idea in Figure 5, we arrive at the implementation schema for our database, shown in Figure 7. The implementation schema takes into account security-level assignments to attributes in the conceptual schema, and transforms the latter into the form ready for actual implementation in a system that uses our security

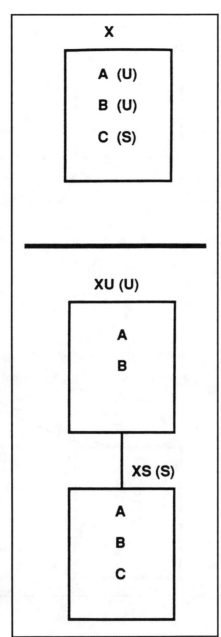

Figure 5. Representing a type of multi-level entities by a hierarchy of classes of single-level objects

paradigm. Specifically, we have four classes in our implementation schema: *XU*, *XS*, *YU*, and *YS*. *XU* represents the view of *X* for uncleared users; *XS*, the view of *X* for users with the secret clearance; *YU*, the view of *Y* for uncleared users; and *YS*, the view of *Y* for users with the secret clearance.

In Figure 7, links between classes represent inheritance relationships among classes. It is helpful to distinguish between two kinds of inheritance in the implementation schema: *semantic inheri-*

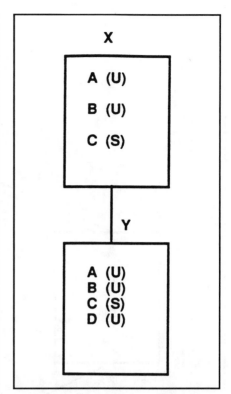

Figure 6. Conceptual schema for types X and Y

tance and *security inheritance*. The actual inheritance mechanism is identical for both cases, but the motivation is different. Semantic inheritance corresponds to the usual notion of inheritance in object-oriented databases. It is intended to represent the semantic relationships among data types found in the conceptual schema. The notion of security inheritance, on the other hand, is introduced solely to represent multilevel entities in our security paradigm. Thus, for instance, *YU* is a subclass of *XU* in the semantic sense because this relationship reflects entity type *X* specialized into *Y* by adding to the former a new attribute *D*. On the other hand, *XS* is a subclass of *XU* in the security sense because *XS* reveals a new attribute of entities of type *X* that is not visible to uncleared users. Notice that the notion of security inheritance agrees with Security-Level Constraint 2, which requires that the security level of a class dominate that of its ancestors.

Instance objects, as discussed earlier in this section, do not have to be at the same security level as their class object. By the same token, instance objects may sometimes be placed at levels different from each other, just as it may be required that real-world entities of the same type have

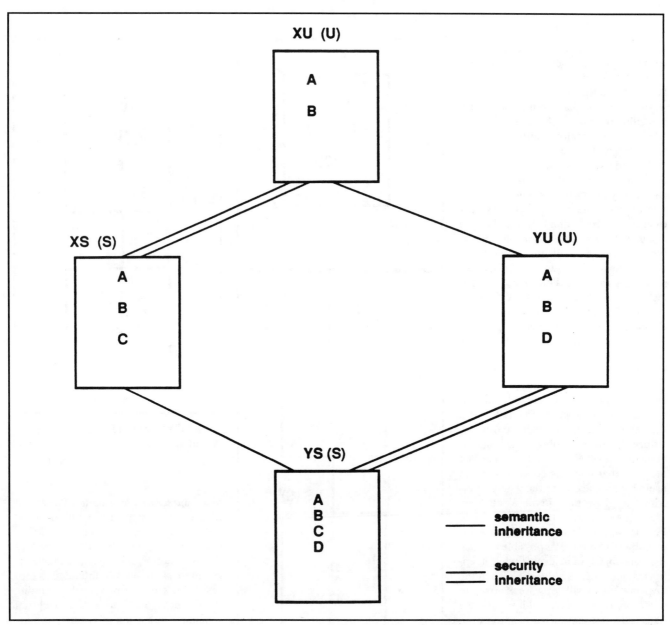

Figure 7. Implementation schema

different security classifications. Our model allows for this flexibility.

Review of relevant research

The object-oriented approach has been a major subject for research in programming languages, knowledge representation, and databases for some years now (e.g., see (9, 19, 24)). Even so, relatively little has been done on security-related issues in the object-oriented databases, although some work appears. Initial efforts in (3, 4, 16) handle only the discretionary access controls. Meadows

and Landwehr (12) are the first to model mandatory access controls using the object-oriented approach, but their effort is limited to considering the Military Message System. Spooner in (20) takes a preliminary look at the mandatory access control and raises several important questions. In (6, 7, 11, 22, 23) objects can be multilevel. Thus, for example, an object's attributes can belong to different security levels, and in turn the security system must monitor all methods within an object. As we argue in the introduction, we consider this condition contrary to the spirit of the object-oriented paradigm. Finally, Millen and Lunt in (0, 13) mention some problems associated with having multilevel objects. In their

model, only single-level objects are permitted; however, the notion of subjects is retained, and subjects are assigned security levels.

Conclusions and future work

Examining the object-oriented data model leads one to believe that it has much — especially in the notion of encapsulation — to make it naturally compatible with the notion of security. Until now, though, relatively little use has been made of this apparent compatibility. This chapter is part of an effort to develop better understanding of the interactions between multilevel security and the object-oriented data model. In our opinion, this interaction can be very subtle, and for that reason we chose a formal approach. We wanted to state precisely all critical assumptions, a necessity if we hope to use this chapter as a departure point for further research.

We believe much more interesting work remains to be done in object-oriented multilevel security. Specifically, we presented in the section "Modeling multilevel entities with single level objects" some ideas for representing multilevel entities using multiple objects at different security levels. These ideas are illustrated by examples. The subject clearly merits further study, and perhaps one should address the issue of designing an algorithm for multiobject representation of multilevel entities. Implementing the class and inheritance mechanisms by message passing is essential to our approach to enforcing security. In a system that follows such an implementation, all information flows are rendered explicit and therefore uniformly controllable by the message filter. Consequently, our future work should address this issue of implementation, as it relates to modeling security, in greater detail.

Acknowledgments

The work of Sushil Jajodia and Boris Kogan was partially supported by the U.S. Air Force, Rome Air Development Center, through subcontract # RI-64155X of prime contract # F30602-88-D-0028, Task B-9-3622 with University of Dayton. The work of Ravi Sandhu was partially supported by the National Security Agency through contract # MDA904-92-92-C-5140. We are indebted to Joe Giordano, Howard Stainer, and Mike Ware for their support and encouragement, which made this work possible.

References

1. Bell, D. E., and L .J. LaPadula. *Secure computer systems: Unified exposition and multics interpretation*. The Mitre Corporation, March 1976.

2. Denning, D. E. *Cryptography and Data Security*. Reading, Mass.: Addison-Wesley, 1982.

3. Dittrich, K. R., M. Hartig, and H. Pfefferle. *Discretionary access control in structurally object-oriented database systems*. In Database Security, II: Status and Prospects, C. E. Landwehr, ed. Amsterdam: North-Holland, 1989, pp. 105-121.

4. Fernandez, E. B., E. Gudes, and H Son. *A security model for object-oriented databases*. Proceedings of the IEEE Symposium on Security and Privacy (May 1989), pp. 110-115.

5. Jajodia, S., and R. S. Sandhu. *Database security: Current status and key issues*. ACM SIGMOD Record, vol. 19, no. 4 (December 1990), pp. 123-126.

6. Keefe, T. F., W. T. Tsai, and M. B. Thuraisingham. *A multilevel security model for object-oriented systems*. Proceedings of the 11th National Computer Security Conference (October 1988), pp. 1-9.

7. Keefe, T. F., and W. T. Tsai. *Prototyping the SODA security model*. In Database Security III: Status and Prospects, D. L. Spooner and C.I. Landwehr, eds. Amsterdam: North-Holland, 1990, pp. 211-235.

8. Khoshafian, S. N., and G. P. Copeland. *Object identity*. Proceedings of the Conference on Object-Oriented Programming: Systems, Languages, and Applications (September-October 1986), pp. 406-416.

9. Kim, W., and F. H. Lochovsky, eds. *Object-Oriented Concepts, Databases, and Applications*. Reading, Mass.: Addison-Wesley, 1989.

10. Lunt, T. F., and J. K. Millen. *Secure knowledge-based systems*. Interim Technical Report, Computer Science Laboratory, SRI International, August 1989.

11. Lunt, T. F. *Multilevel security for object-oriented database system*. In Database Security, III: Status and Prospects, D. L. Spooner and C. Landwehr, eds. Amsterdam: North-Holland, 1990, pp. 199-209.

12. Meadows, C., and C. Landwehr. *Designing a trusted application in an object-oriented data model*. In Research Directions in Database Security, T. Lunt, ed. Berlin: Springer-Verlag, 1992, pp. 191-198.

13. Millen, J. K., and T. F. Lunt. *Security for object-oriented database systems*. Proceedings of the IEEE Symposium on Security and Privacy (May 1992), pp. 260-272.

14. Minsky, N. H., and D. Rozenshtein. *A law-based approach to object-oriented programming*. Proceedings of the Conference on Object-Oriented Programming: Systems, Languages, and Applications (October 1987), pp. 482-493.

15. Nierstrasz, O. *A survey of object-oriented concepts*. In Object-Oriented Concepts, Databases, and Applications, W. Kim and F. H. Lochovsky , eds. Reading, Mass.: Addison-Wesley, 1989.

16. Rabitti, F., D. Woelk, and W. Kim. *A model of authorization for object-oriented and semantic databases*. Proceedings of the International Conference on Extending Database Technology (March 1988), pp. 231-250.

17. Sandhu, R. S., R. Thomas, and S. Jajodia. *A secure kernelized architecture for multilevel object-oriented databases*. Proceedings of the IEEE Computer Security Foundations Workshop IV (June 1991), pp. 139-152.

18. Sandhu, R. S., R. Thomas, and S. Jajodia. *Supporting timing channel-free computations in multilevel-secure object-oriented databases*. In Database Security, V: Status and Prospects, C. Landwehr and S. Jajodia, eds. Amsterdam: North-Holland, 1992, pp. 297-314.

19. Shriver, B., and P. Wegner, eds. *Research Directions in Object-Oriented Programming*. Cambridge: MIT Press, 1987.

20. Spooner, D. L.*The impact of inheritance on security in object-oriented database systems*. In Database Security, II: Status and Prospects, C. E. Landwehr, ed. Amsterdam: North-Holland, 1989,pp. 141-160.

21. Thomas, R., and R. S. Sandhu. *Implementing the message filter object-oriented security model without trusted subjects*. In Database Security, VI: Status and Prospects, C. Landwehr and B. Thuraisingham, eds. Amsterdam: North-Holland, 1993, pp. 15-34.

22. Thuraisingham, M. B. *A multilevel-secure object-oriented data model*. Proceedings of the 12th National Computer Security Conference (October 1989), pp. 579-590.

23. Thuraisingham, M. B. *Mandatory security in object-oriented database system*. Proceedings of the Conference on Object-Oriented Programming: Systems, Languages, and Applications (October 1989), pp. 203-210.

24. Zdonik, S. B., and D. Maier, eds. *Readings in Object-Oriented Database Systems*. San Mateo, Calif.: Morgan Kaufman,1990.

Chapter 10

Computer-Aided Design
and Manufacturing

Object-Oriented Intelligent Computer-Integrated Design, Process Planning, and Inspection

M. Marefat, University of Arizona

Sandeep Malhotra and R.L. Kashyap, Purdue University

Reprinted from *Computer*, March 1993, pp. 54–65.
Copyright © 1993 by The Institute of Electrical and
Electronics Engineers, Inc. All rights reserved.

An integrated manufacturing environment includes a computer-aided design system, a computer-aided manufacturing system, and a vision system. The CAD system is used to design the part, the CAM system to automatically generate a process plan and detailed instructions for machining the part, and the vision system to inspect the finished parts and monitor the execution of operations.[1] These components should all share a common database that correlates and incorporates their data (see Figure 1).

An automated, flexible, and intelligent computer-integrated manufacturing (CIM) system might not be as inconceivable as once believed. Such a system could not only generate the solution (a process plan or an inspection plan) automatically, but it could also provide tools and friendly interfaces to simplify access to the system's knowledge. Moreover, it could provide information to help the designer and the operator with decision making. For the system to be flexible, its knowledge and domain should be expandable without reprogramming. Finally, an intelligent CIM system should reason about the tasks it performs. In process planning, for example, reasoning about alternative valid interpretations of a part could lead to alternative plans for machining it. In inspection planning, the strategy for measuring a component's attributes could be determined by considering the interactions between the component's shape features (slots, pockets, etc.).

Our research objectives focus on issues and techniques in developing automated, flexible, and intelligent manufacturing based on object-oriented design and analysis principles. Our goal is a system in which design, process planning, and inspection are integrated. We chose a purely object-oriented environment because, according to Stefik and Bobrow, "objects are a uniform programming element for computing and saving state, and are ideal for simulation problems where it is necessary to represent collections of things that interact." Information structures required to represent the system's knowledge (interpretations, features, machining processes and tools, etc.) and procedures are encapsulated in objects and their associated methods.

> A prototype implemented using Smalltalk-80's object-oriented environment shows that an automated, flexible, and intelligent computer-integrated manufacturing system may not be inconceivable after all.

The contributions of our work stem from

- object-oriented representation of the knowledge, and modeling of the behavior of the individual components in the design, process planning, and inspection tasks;
- effective development of the required data models, interfaces, and other necessary components to achieve a truly integrated environment;
- new, innovative approaches to achieve individual system functions, including the development of a case-based methodology for process planning of three-dimensional prismatic parts, and the development of a knowledge-based geometric reasoning approach for automated inspection planning and intelligent sensing; and
- development of a prototype and experimentation with the system on the basis of the ideas and methodology presented here.

This article discusses the methodology for developing intelligent integrated computer-aided design and manufacturing systems based on object-oriented principles. We provide examples and discuss how the application of these principles affects the nature of these systems. Our discussion details the implementation of an automated, intelligent, and flexible CIM system prototype using an object-oriented programming environment — Smalltalk-80, Version 4.0.

A CIM system includes CAD, a process planner, and an inspection planner. We discuss each of these components individually in the following sections.

CAD

Our modeling environment integrates and takes advantage of two modeling paradigms: (1) solid modeling with a boundary representation output to provide maximum flexibility in design, and (2) feature-based modeling[2-4] to provide a capability for modification and/or design with composite entities. The first paradigm describes the part in terms of the three low-level entities: faces, edges, and vertices. However, process planning and inspection planning consider the same part as a set of relatively

abstract entities such as features, with interrelationships between them. This mismatch in the abstraction level of the elements in the domains of design, process planning, and inspection planning makes integration of the domains nontrivial.

We describe a feature extractor that transforms the low-level representation of the part into an abstract description (that is, features and their relationships). The part's abstract description can take advantage of the solid modeler's output. The feature extractor allows integration of the solid modeler with the CIM system's other components.[5]

Feature-based modeler. In feature-based design, the designer uses the manufacturing-oriented features directly when designing or modifying the part.[6]

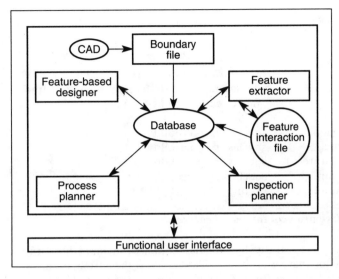

Figure 1. The intelligent computer-integrated design, manufacturing, and inspection system architecture.

The design kernel is a menu-driven 3D interactive design environment. A user starts designing by selecting a workpiece from a set of workpieces and then adding shape features to the workpiece or removing some from it. The design phase is facilitated by exploiting shape features as design primitives.

The object-oriented design kernel comprises several categories of classes. The classes in these categories together constitute a framework that contains all the classes that embody the essential characteristics of a design environment, such as interaction with a user (graphical display, picking, etc.), maintenance of a database that represents a design, and input/output. The features in the design kernel are represented as classes. At the top of the class hierarchy is class *Feature* (see Figure 2). This class

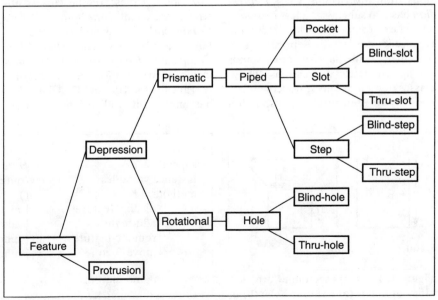

Figure 2. The design kernel feature hierarchy.

```
class                    Feature
superclass               Object
instance variables       ()
subclasses               (Depression, Protrusion)
interface protocol       (display-feature, add-feature, remove-feature,
                           move-feature, name-feature)

        display-feature      subclass responsibility
        add-feature          subclass responsibility
        remove-feature       subclass responsibility
        move-feature         subclass responsibility
        name-feature         { return "feature" }
```

Figure 3. The interface protocol for class *Feature*.

represents the concept of features by specifying the behavior that an entity must have to be considered a feature.

The interface protocol for class *Feature* is shown in Figure 3. The second line identifies class *Object* as the superclass of *Feature* (class *Object* represents the notion of objects in the object-oriented methodology). Class *Feature* has no instance variables but specifies five messages in its interface protocol: display-feature, add-feature, remove-feature, move-feature, and name-feature. The actions of these messages are implicit in their names. Only one of the five methods is implemented, since at this high level of abstraction not enough information exists about the shape features.

The subclasses of the class *Feature* represent the next level in the feature hierarchy shown in Figure 2 — *Depression* and *Protrusion*. These classes add specifications that distinguish depressions from protrusions. Class *Depression* has two subclasses: class *Prismatic* and class *Rotational*. Class *Prismatic* represents a prismatic depression in a workpiece, while class *Rotational* stands for axisymmetric depressions. These classes don't have any instances either, and they are used purely for abstraction

of the common behavior of the features.

The classes at the bottom of the hierarchy are more specialized and correspond to shape-feature instances, which are actually created during design.

Inheritance, along with encapsulation, eases the addition of a shape feature to the feature-based modeler. Adding a new shape feature involves

- finding an existing feature that best resembles the behavior of the new feature,
- creating a subclass for the class of feature found above, and
- implementing the methods in the interface protocol of the class *Feature*.

For instance, consider adding countersink holes to the system's domain (see Figure 4). The first step is to identify the existing feature in the feature hierarchy that best shares attributes with countersink holes. Holes are the closest abstraction to countersink holes, and class *Countersink-Hole* is added to the system as a subclass of class *Hole*. Class *Countersink-Hole* must define two new instance variables for the outer radius (r2) and the total depth (d2). Class *Hole* has implemented all the methods de-

scribed in the interface protocol of features. Three of these messages, display-feature, add-feature, and name-feature, should be reimplemented. The other two need not be changed and are simply "inherited" by class *Countersink-Hole*, shown in Figure 5.

Thus, object-oriented methodology is used to alleviate the extensive coding and maintenance that result if each facility develops a system dependent on its own ever-changing processes and requirements. Encapsulation and inheritance minimize the modification effort involved in making changes to the system as the needed processes change; they also aid in customizing the system for a particular facility or environment.

Both the solid modeler and the feature-based modeler are integrated with the entire system. Such an architecture has the advantage that the solid modeler can be used creatively to design a component, yet the design can be fixed or modified by adding new features and by modifying or removing existing features. Modeling a component with the solid modeler produces the boundary representation for the component. A feature identification and extraction module[5] is invoked, producing an abstract description of the component in terms of its shape features and their relationships. The hierarchical representation of the component, consisting of both the abstract description and the lower level detailed information, is stored in the database to be used for reasoning and processing by other components.

Process planning

Process planning is the act of preparing detailed processing instructions for manufacturing a part. An automated process planner must be able to

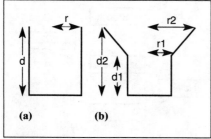

Figure 4. The cross section of two kinds of holes: (a) a simple hole; (b) a countersink hole.

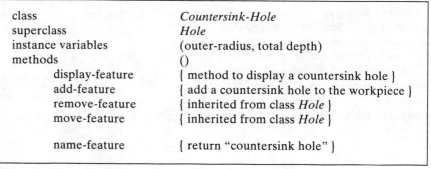

```
class                    Countersink-Hole
superclass               Hole
instance variables       (outer-radius, total depth)
methods                  ()
        display-feature      { method to display a countersink hole }
        add-feature          { add a countersink hole to the workpiece }
        remove-feature       { inherited from class Hole }
        move-feature         { inherited from class Hole }

        name-feature         { return "countersink hole" }
```

Figure 5. Class *Countersink-Hole*.

- sequence the features of each interpretation in the order they are manufactured,
- determine appropriate processes and tools to produce each feature, and
- find an optimal machining operation sequence with respect to a suitable criterion.

Most existing computer-aided process planning systems have generally used either a variant or a generative approach. Although several knowledge-based process planners have been implemented, the only other attempt to develop a case-based approach to process planning is the one described by Tsatsoulis and Kashyap.[7] The system they describe for rotational parts considers the machining surfaces one at a time. Our work is essentially different because our method is developed for general 3D prismatic parts. We have addressed issues that deal with groups of surfaces with certain properties (features), geometric reasoning about the different aspects of the part, and representation models and the similarity measures for analogical reasoning with abstract global characteristics of a part. Treatment of these issues is fundamental for the development of practical automated process planners for 3D parts using a case-based approach.

Underlying case-based planning is the idea of planning as remembering.[8] A typical case-based process planner[9] must be capable of

- retrieving past experiences from the plan memory,
- modifying the old solution fragments for the new part, and
- abstracting and storing the newly generated plan in the plan memory.

Figure 6 shows a schematic representation of the components in the case-based process planner.

Solution characteristics. An automated process planner should not only generate the process plan for machining a part automatically but also provide tools

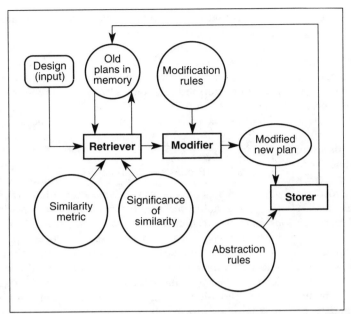

Figure 6. A schematic representation of a case-based process planning system.

and a friendly interface that enhance the display of the generated process plan. This allows easy access to the system's knowledge, enabling the user to inspect, modify, and tailor the knowledge of the process planning system. For instance, the engineer could inspect the system's machining processes by selecting the option "Inspect Processes" on the interactive graphical user interface. This interface also offers the user the option of generating alternate process plans for machining the same part through active exploitation of the alternate valid interpretations of the component.

For a CAM system to be efficient, its domain and knowledge should be dynamic.[10] The system should be flexible and extensible. This is partially addressed by the different kinds of features the system can handle. For example, the system's manufacturing capabilities might be extended so that it can address processes for drilling holes in the workpiece. The system's knowledge — machining processes, tools, etc. — should also be easily extensible and accessible. This requirement is addressed by developing an object-oriented hierarchical process and tool kernel that captures the knowledge about machining processes and tools.

The CAM system must be intelligent. Defining a part as an integration of individual features does not sufficiently describe the part. Alternate actions may

be taken in machining a part if the alternative sets of features describing that part are considered. These different sets of features form valid alternative interpretations of the part. Therefore, an intelligent process planner should not only consider the alternative strategies and select the best method for making the part but also intelligently modify or adapt appropriate portions of the plan as needed. Furthermore, an intelligent process planner should be able to generate alternate processes, tools, and plans for machining an entire feature.

Process planning overview. Machining a part consists of taking a piece of stock and performing processes or operations on it to transform it into a component conforming to the desired specifications. Process planning is the task of determining a plan of action for how to machine the part. Because the problem is complex, existing process planners typically characterize a part as a collection of machinable features and plan for each of these features individually. Our system describes the part as a collection of alternate valid interpretations,[11] each composed of a set of features. A process plan for each of the interpretations needs to be developed with some measure of quality and accuracy. Let's look at the approach involved in generating a process plan for each interpretation.

The methodology for developing an appropriate process plan for machining a component includes the following steps:

(1) Generating a process plan for each interpretation. This involves

- sequencing the features in the order of machining on the basis of their accessibility and the interactions between them;
- determining machining processes for each feature, using case-based reasoning;
- computing certainty values for the subplans used for each feature;
- selecting the appropriate tools for each process; and

• generating a global plan for the part.

(2) Determining the cost, quality, and accuracy of the developed process plans for the different interpretations.

(3) Selecting the most appropriate process plan for machining the part.

Object-oriented process planning kernel. Process planning is a function in a manufacturing facility that assigns a sequence of manufacturing processes to a design. However, the operations of a process planning system depend on the manufacturing processes of a *particular* manufacturing facility. This dependency reveals the inapplicability of a particular process planner to a wide range of manufacturing environments and the inability to easily update or modify the knowledge or capabilities of a process planner. Nevertheless, object-oriented techniques can be applied effectively to the design of a process planner to minimize this dependency on particular manufacturing facilities and therefore maximize their utility.

Figure 6 shows the schematic structure of the case-based process planner, which consists of three basic modules: Retriever, Modifier, and Storer. Each of these modules has submodules, each of which performs a specific task. For instance, the Modifier contains process selection and tool selection modules. These are used for selecting machining processes and tools in a case where the retrieved plan must be modified. Thus, the CAM system consists of many such modules that need to be integrated. Object-oriented design techniques enable self-contained partitioning that leads to a stable model. In other words, all these modules can be encapsulated as individual classes. The sole assumption that the planner makes about these

classes is that they would respond to a given set of messages defined in their protocols. For instance, the class *Process-Selector* represents the process selection module. Figure 7 shows some messages defined in class *Process-Selector*. A loop in *getAllProcesses: aFeaturesCollection*, as shown below,

aFeaturesCollection do:
  {:aFeature |
      self getProcessesFor: aFeature }

gets all the processes that are essential for machining the features in *aFeaturesCollection*. It is the responsibility of the message *getProcessesFor: aFeature* to modify the best existing plan selected by the retriever for a particular feature. The code's modularity makes it understandable and easy to modify to maximize the process planning capabilities.

Important leverage is gained by reducing the repetition of code. Explicit representation of commonality generates inheritance hierarchies, which reduce the code. All the features — slot, blind-slot, step, blind-step, hole, and pocket — have some common behavior. Thus, a superclass, *Gen-Feature*, contains the information common to all the features. The subclasses representing each feature reflect information that differentiates one feature from the others. To highlight a feature in the graphical interface, we need to determine and change the thickness of all the feature's edges. The message *getFeatureLines* in class *Gen-Feature* returns the edges of a feature — regardless of the feature's shape or type. The subclasses representing specific types of features inherit this ability from their superclass *Gen-Feature*. In a conventional programming language, the programmer would have to write similar functions for each of the different feature types. Thus, effective

use of abstraction makes system code more reusable and adaptable.

Another advantage of object-oriented design is the structured representation of the system's knowledge. A comprehensive case-based process planner requires knowledge about machining processes and tools; previous experiences; an abstract-level representation of the part, including features and their interactions (declarative knowledge); and a process plan generation methodology (procedural knowledge). In an object-oriented process planning system, the system's declarative knowledge is encapsulated in objects. The knowledge of machining processes forms the backbone of the system's declarative knowledge. The advantages of using object-oriented design methodology for a structured representation of the system's knowledge are illustrated in terms of the knowledge for the machining processes and tools in the "Process planning kernel process taxonomy" sidebar.

Process plan generation. The generated process plan, an instance of the class *Process Plan*, is displayed on an interactive graphical user interface (see the top window of Figure 8). The interface depicts the process plan both pictorially, in a tree, and textually with regard to its different aspects, such as the order of processes and which processes and tools should be used to produce different features. The features list in the subwindow to the top left of "Menus" corresponds to the machining order of the features. In Figure 8, the order of machining the features is Slot1, Slot2, Slot3. The machining order, emphasized in the tree representation of the process plan, is vertical from top to bottom in the second level of the tree. Therefore, horizontal movement across the tree corresponds to further detailing of the

class	*Process-Selector*	
superclass	*Object*	
class methods		
getAllProcesses: aFeatureCollection	{ get processes for machining all the features in aFeaturesCollection }	
instance methods		
getProcessesFor: aFeature	{ select processes for machining aFeature }	
getProcessFor: aFeature at: aLevel	{ get the best process for aFeature at aLevel }	
getProcessAt2for: aFeature	{ get the best process for aFeature at level 2 of the hierarchical representation of the machining processes (see Figure A in the sidebar "Process planning kernel process taxonomy") }	

Figure 7. Some messages defined in class *Process-Selector*.

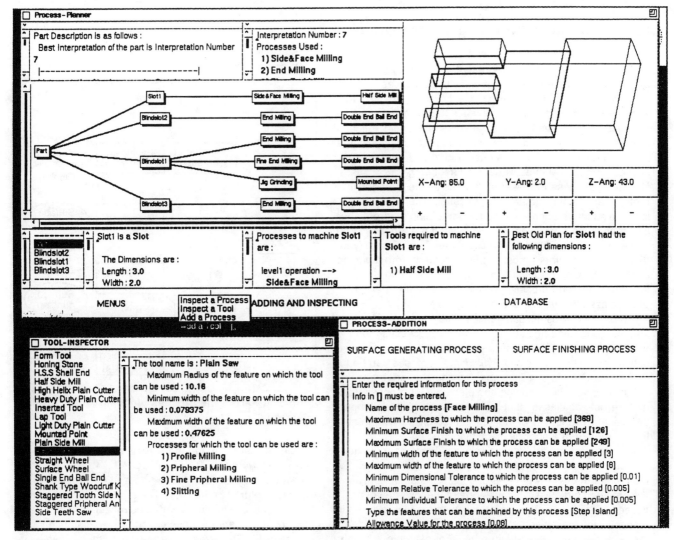

Figure 8. The process plan interface: (top) the "Process-Planner" window; (lower left) the "Tool-Inspector" window, used for tool addition/inspection/modification; (lower right) the "Process-Addition" window.

plan; vertical movement corresponds to the sequential order. Processes and Tools options in the "Adding and Inspecting" subwindow to the right of "Menus" allow inspection and modification of the pieces of the machining processes and the tools knowledge. The "Database" and "Menus" subwindows provide options to query the system about the different aspects of the generated plan or to recall the plans for a different part (or component).

Inspection planning

The functions of an intelligent inspection system can be logically divided into two parts. The first part can be regarded as the generation of an inspection plan, which is typically performed off line. The second part is the use of the inspection plan, together with sensors and other resources, to execute the inspection, which is performed *on* line. The inspec-

tion system must search for the measurable entities, such as particular object edges, and determine their inspection-relevant parameters (such as length, angle, etc.) robustly and efficiently once the sensor data is available. Inspection planning consists of determining plans and instructions for measuring the dimensions and tolerances of the object's different attributes. A typical automated inspection planning system must be able to

- find the abstract shape information (higher level features) in a part,
- determine the relationships between the features,
- determine, on the basis of the above information, the physical entities (edges, etc.) to be measured,
- determine the possible sensor locations and viewing directions, and
- minimize sensing operations while achieving successful measurement of all entities (optimization).

One of the major difficulties with current vision systems is that their knowledge and reasoning are encoded in the system, and it is difficult to extend their scope or modify their knowledge. Since inspection systems should be developed to operate with different designs (that is, the set of objects and the set of sensors they work with are not fixed), it is important that they be flexible. Extensibility, flexibility, and effective use of knowledge in vision systems have been emphasized by DARPA's image understanding researchers, too.[12] We will show how object-oriented design techniques can be exploited effectively to make the knowledge and reasoning capabilities of these systems extensible and easily modifiable without much reprogramming.

Overview of approach. Inspection planning consists of preparing the inspection knowledge base, generating the inspection plan, and optimizing sensing and processing operations. Preparation

Process planning kernel process taxonomy

Machining processes are represented by the class *Process*, which is the abstract superclass of all classes representing different machining processes[1] (see Figure A). Class *Process* specifies the list of messages that all processes must respond to. The instance variables of *Process* reflect all the common attributes of all machining processes. Messages add- and remove-process are used to add and remove processes from the list of available manufacturing processes. Note that the class *Process* implements all the methods in its protocol except for add-process, because different kinds of lower level information are required for adding different specific machining processes. For example, if the process to be added is a surface-finishing process, then it is necessary to determine what other processes must occur before it can be applied. Thus, at this level of abstraction, it is impossible to implement the add-process method. Some of the messages of the class *Process* are shown in Figure B.

Machining processes can be classified in two categories: surface-generating and surface-finishing processes (see Figure A). To embody this classification, class *Process* has two subclasses: *Generating* and *Finishing*. Processes can be further categorized into milling, shaping and planing, broaching, fine milling, and fine shaping and planing. Our process planning kernel has classes that represent each of these types of processes. The leaves of the tree in Figure A, shown in ellipses, represent a specific machining process.

The *Generating* and *Finishing* classes implement the add-process message. The user is requested to provide the information about the new process that is essential for applying the process and classifying it as one of the lower level processes in the abstraction hierarchy shown in Figure A. An instance of the classified process is then created and added to the system's database for future use. For example, the information required to add a new surface-generating process to the system's knowledge is shown in the "Process-Addition" window of Figure 8 (lower right) in the main text. The system determines internally the classification of the process' level and type in the abstraction hierarchy by manipulating the provided information. For example, the information shown in Figure 8's "Process-Addition" window is classified as a milling process, and an instance of the class *Milling* is instantiated with the user-entered information. The new process in-

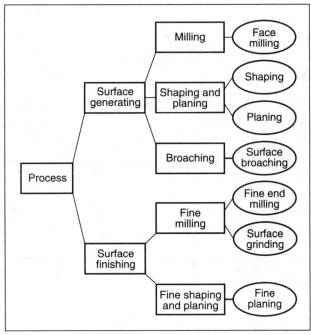

Figure A. Part of the process planning kernel process hierarchy.

stance corresponding to the "Process-Addition" window is shown in Figure C.

Like the process knowledge, the system's tool knowledge is captured in the class *Tools* in the process planning kernel. The instance variables reflect the attributes of the tool necessary for its selection. These instance variables include the name, type, maximum radius, width range of the feature for which the tool can be used, and the list of processes for which the tool is applicable. Figure D shows some messages of this class. Similarly, the old plans are abstracted and stored in the system's plan memory.

Reference

1. M. Stefik and D.G. Bobrow, "Object-Oriented Programming: Themes and Variations," *AI Magazine*, Winter 1986, pp. 40-62.

---

of an inspection knowledge base entails listing

- visible features and the methods to inspect them,
- potential viewing directions and camera locations, and
- visible edges from each viewing direction and location.

Determining a list of visible features and their inspection methods corresponds to determining the measurable entities of the part. There is more than one way to inspect an attribute. For example, as shown in Figure 9a, a non-interacting slot has four edges that can

be used effectively to determine its length. If there are interactions between the features, each method for inspecting an attribute may need more than one entity (currently an edge). For example, as Figure 9b shows, if a slot is perpendicular to another slot, then computing its length actually consists of measuring three edges.

The higher level shape-feature information is extracted from the CAD solid models using a geometric reasoning mechanism described in our earlier work.[5] This information is used to determine the different attributes to be measured and the different strategies

for measuring each attribute. Reasoning with the shape of the features and the relationships between them leads to (1) a set of physical entities (currently edges) of the part to be measured and (2) the method by which the individual entity measurements should be combined to compute the desired attributes.

The list of possible camera locations and viewing directions is calculated using the individual physical entities to be measured. Then, using a reasoning mechanism based on the primary visible faces and the secondary visible faces from each viewing direction and location, each camera location and viewing direction

```
class                        Process
superclass                   Object
instance variables           (type, name, hardness, surFinMin, . . . , allowance)
messages
    remove-process           { method to remove a process }
    addProcess               { subclass responsibility }
         .
         .
    features                 { return the features for which process can be used }
```

Figure B. Some messages of the class *Process*.

```
instance            face-milling
class               Generating > Milling
initialization
       type         milling          { type of the process }
       name         face milling     { name of the process }
       level        1                { level at which the process is applicable }
       hardness     369              { maximum hardness of a raw material }
       surFinMin    126              { minimum surface finish of a raw material }
       surFinMax    249              { maximum surface finish of a raw material }
       widthMin     3                { minimum width of the feature }
       widthMax     8                { maximum width of the feature }
       dimtol       0.01             { dimensional tolerance achievable by a process }
       reltol       0.005            { relative tolerance achievable by a process }
       indtol       0.005            { individual tolerance achievable by a process }
       features     (step island)    { features that a process is applicable to }
       allowance    0.08             { allowance of a process }
```

Figure C. The new process instance corresponding to the lower right window of Figure 8.

```
class                    Tools
superclass               Object
instance variables       (name, radiusMax, . . . , widthMax, listOfProcesses)
methods                  (addTool, listOfProcesses, widthMin, widthMax,
                          getToolsFor: , . . . , getBestToolFor: for: from: with: )
       addTool           { add a tool to the database }
       name              { return name of the tool }
         .
         .
       listOfProcesses   { return the processes for which the tool can be employed }

comments on instance variables
       name              name of the tool
       radiusMax         maximum radius of the tool
       widthMin          minimum width of the feature to which the tool can be applied
       widthMax          maximum width of the feature to which the tool can be applied
       listOfProcesses   processes for which the tool can be employed
```

Figure D. Some messages of the class *Tools*.

is linked with a list of all the entities it can successfully inspect. The different combinations of the proposed camera locations and viewing angles are systematically explored (currently in breadth-first order), and a simple verification procedure is performed to determine whether a minimum set of required entities of the part could be measured from the particular sensing combination. The best combination of camera parameters (locations and viewing directions) that passes the verification procedure is used to construct an inspection plan. The final step required after construction of the plan is to logi-

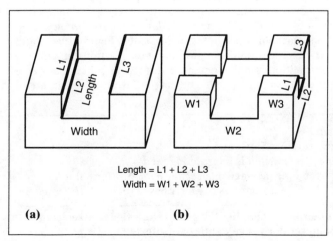

Figure 9. (a) Attributes and corresponding entities (length) in a simple noninteracting feature (slot); (b) entity (length) in interacting features (slot with slot).

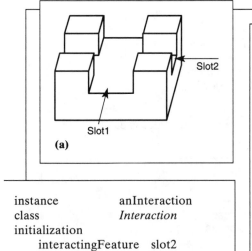

instance	aSlot	
class	*Slot*	
superclass	*Gen-Feature*	
initialization		
name	slot1	{ id for the feature }
length	10.0 (1.0 0.0 0.0)	{ magnitude and direction }
width	2.0 (0.0 0.1 0.0	{ magnitude and direction }
depth	1.0 (0.0 0.0 0.1)	{ magnitude and direction }
position	(1.0 4.0 0.0)	{ relative position to the }
		{ origin of the part }
faceCollection	(F131 F132 F130)	{ id of the faces that make the feature }
appCollection	((0.0 1.0 0.0))	{ collection of approach directions }
feedCollection	((0.0 0.0 1.0))	{ collection of feed directions }
.		
.		
interactions	((anInteraction))	{ list of instances of *Interactions* }

(a)

(b)

instance	anInteraction
class	*Interaction*
initialization	
interactingFeature	slot2
typeOfInteraction	'intersecting'

(c)

Figure 10. Representing a slot shape feature for a component with two intersecting slots: (a) an object with two slots; (b) an instance of a feature slot (note: length, width, name, depth, and position are actually defined in the superclass *Gen-Feature*); (c) an instance of the class *Interaction*.

cally represent and appropriately update the inspection data and procedures in an integrated database to be used by other components, including executing modules.

Object-oriented inspection planning kernel. A major component of an inspection planning system is its knowledge. This includes declarative knowledge about the problem (information about the part, camera, plan, etc.) and procedural knowledge about how to solve the problem (rules in the If_Then form and methods invoked by messages sent to the objects implementing them). Declarative and procedural knowledge constitute the system's problem-solving knowledge.

Geometric knowledge consists of a hierarchical description of the part to be inspected. The low-level part description includes the object's CAD boundary representation, which consists of the description of its faces, edges, and vertices. Since this information is not sufficient for the required reasoning at a higher abstraction level, information about the part's location and its type of shape features, such as slots and holes, and the relationships between these features, is represented and appropriately tied with the lower level descriptions.

Inheritance can be exploited naturally and advantageously in modeling this knowledge. The abstract behavior common to all features is captured in the abstract class *Gen-Feature* (generic feature), which has no instances but holds the common protocol about features. Each shape feature, such as a slot, is a subclass of *Gen-Feature*. New shape features can be implemented by simply adding new subclasses to *Gen-Feature*, and new specializations of existing shape features (such as a T-slot) can be implemented by creating appropriate subclasses of the existing classes (such as *Slot*). Figure 10b shows an instance of the class *Slot* for a part containing two intersecting slots (Figure 10a). Information about the relationships of a particular feature with other features of the object is described declaratively using instances of the class *Interaction* (Figure 10c). Two important instance variables of the class *Interaction* are *interactingFeature* and *typeOfInteraction*, which represent, respectively, the other interacting feature and the interaction type (perpendicular, parallel, nested, etc.) between the two features.

The reasoning mechanism that applies the interaction knowledge is represented procedurally as rules in methods. Figure 11 shows an example of a rule that applies the generic knowledge associated with intersections to find out how the edge entities of a slot are affected (related to its inspection). New types of feature interactions, or modifications to the old ones, are achieved through new messages without having to make significant changes to any other aspect of the system.

To determine which geometric entities should be used during inspection, the system should know the abstract features' attributes that need to be inspected and how they relate to the geometric entities of the part. This information is captured in the instance variables of the generic class for features, *Gen-Feature*. Because of their importance, the attributes width, height, and length have individual instance variables associated with them. However, other attributes of a feature also can be inspected using the instance variable *measurableEntities*, which is used to

if *feature* is SlotA and
    if *interactingFeature* is SlotB and
        if *typeOfInteraction* is intersecting then
            send the message *intersectingWith: SlotB* to SlotA
            to get edge entities of SlotA based on *typeOfInteraction*.

Figure 11. Example of a rule that applies the generic knowledge associated with intersections to learn how a slot's edge entities are affected.

model the collection of attributes to be measured for a particular feature. The information for determining which geometric entities should be used for each attribute's measurement is represented by rules in another object — Entity — and this information is retrieved as needed. These rules basically determine the different strategies one can use for an attribute's inspection and are instrumental in reasoning with the abstract information about the part.

The system's inspection knowledge consists of the collective knowledge of the different inspection elements, such as cameras, views, plans, and rules for determining an optimal plan. The camera knowledge is declarative and is represented by an object called Camera. Currently, the simplest model of camera, the pinhole-camera model, is used to represent a camera sensor. Once instantiated, this object contains the location of the camera relative to the origin of the part, which is also assumed to be the origin of the global coordinates, the viewing direction of the camera, and the entities (edges, etc.) on the part expected to be visible from the camera's viewing direction. This effective use of encapsulation in modeling the sensor knowledge allows for the easy use of other camera models (if desired) without affecting other reasoning aspects of the inspection planner.

Different aspects of the inspection knowledge (camera knowledge, view information, etc.) are encapsulated in objects that are instance variables of the abstract class *Inspection Data*. With this approach, the inspection variables of the system can be easily modified or extended, and they are localized. Hence, for example, if we know that the camera may not be less than 20 inches from the part, this information can be modeled as a constraint on the *z* axis of the representation for the view information.

Inspection planning progresses by determining what attributes need to be inspected and which geometric entities could be used to measure the dimensions needed for each attribute. On the basis of this information, a set of different views is generated. For each view, an instance of the object HypPlan (hypothetical plan) captures the intermediate planning information and represents the sensor setting and all the entities (not attributes) that can be measured from that particular setting. Subsequently, an optimization procedure is used on the generated HypPlans to create the final inspection plan with a minimum number of sensing operations. The top window in Figure 12 shows a picture of the inspection planning user interface, which in our prototype can also graphically simulate the generated inspection

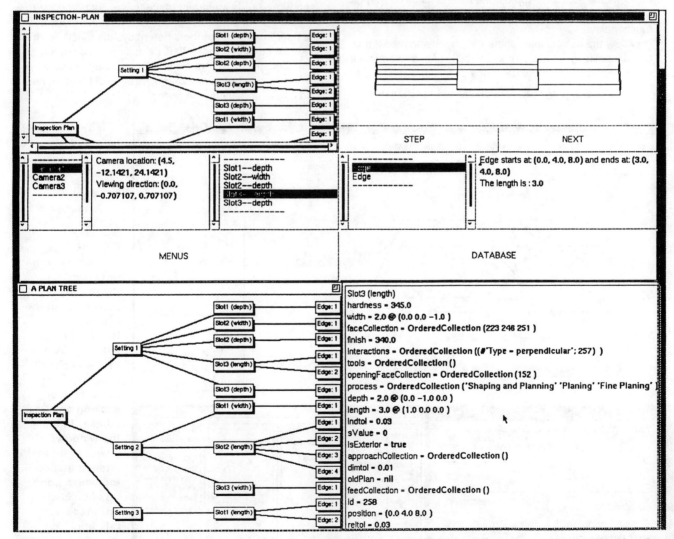

Figure 12. The inspection plan interface: (top) the "Inspection-Plan" window; (lower left) an expanded tree showing the plan; (lower right) detailed information about Slot3 obtained by clicking on box slot3(depth) in the plan tree.

plan (see the "User interface" sidebar). The user interface includes a hierarchical tree representation and also a textual representation of the generated inspection plan. The tree window (Figure 12, lower left) can be expanded to alleviate the cluttering when several sensing operations are needed.

We have described the methodology and example implementation solutions for the design of flexible and intelligent computer-integrated design and manufacturing systems based on the object-oriented paradigm. The fundamental approach has focused on

- developing techniques for modular representation and modeling of the different kinds of complex data present in a manufacturing environment,
- designing the system such that its knowledge and domain are extensible and flexible,

User interface

A user interface helps the user navigate graphically through the system and interact with the different tasks through its functionality. An appropriate user interface should

- Intelligently lay out all the information pertinent to the task in an organized fashion using a combination of graphical displays, trees, and text.
- Provide the user with a comprehensible set of primitives and tools, such as pop-up menus, graphical input tools, switches, etc., to interact with the underlying model. This provides the user with appropriate mechanisms for stepping through the necessary choices to accomplish a particular functionality.
- Allow the user to interrogate the underlying model and the system's knowledge. This capability aids and enhances the user's ability to make decisions.

A human-computer interface should produce reliable (consistent) results. Its efficiency is measured by its functionality and usability. Functionality reflects the system's capabilities. Usability indicates ease of use (a subjective rating of how easy or difficult the interface is).

Design, process planning, and inspection are important tasks underlying our system. The database is essentially the data manager, acting as an intelligent integrating agent (see Figure 1 in the main text). Each of the three tasks mentioned above has its own interfaces, arranged like cards on top of each other. The top card (see Figure E) is a user interface that is not particular to any task, but it provides options to invoke the tools and the user interfaces for the different system functions. Invoking a particular tool brings its user interface to the front to display different aspects of information and to allow the interrogation and/or modification of the information model underlying the task.

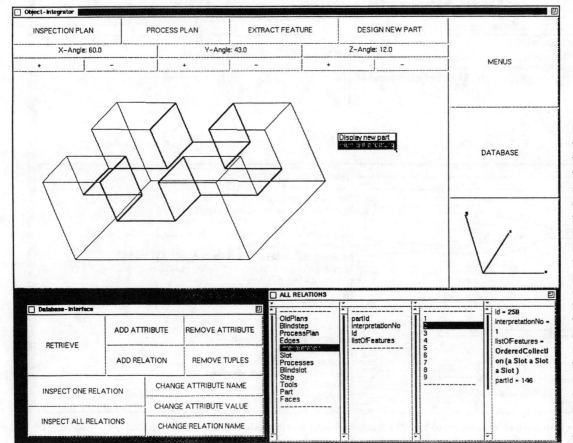

Figure E. The topmost user interface card for the prototype system: (top) the overall user interface; (lower left) the "Database-Interface" window, which pops up upon clicking on "Database" in the top window; (lower right) the relation inspector, which pops up upon clicking on "Inspect all relations" in the "Database-Interface" window.

- applying abstraction, encapsulation, and inheritance to significantly reduce the amount of software and the development time through effective reuse, and
- developing design solutions that allow incremental construction and evolution of the system.

The prototype system developed in our lab shows the application of the methodology to the development of an intelligent computer-integrated design, process planning, and inspection environment that can respond quickly to technological advances. The objects provide modular data structures for the system's declarative knowledge (part description, inspection plan, process plan, etc.). Message passing captures the system's procedural knowledge (rules, procedures). Encapsulation facilitates the integration of all the individual modules, which is difficult in a conventional programming language because of the many different complex types of data necessarily present in a CIM environment. Inheritance reduces the need to specify redundant information, helps with systematic reuse of code, and simplifies updating and modification of the system. Most of all, encapsulation and inheritance enhance the flexibility of the system to adapt to changes and/or extensions of its knowledge.

We plan to extend the system's domain to include other classes of parts. This incremental development strategy is remarkably simple, thanks to an effective design based on object-oriented methodology. ∎

Acknowledgments

This work has been partially supported by NSF Grant DDM-9210018 to M. Marefat, and by NSF Grant CDR-8803017 to the Purdue Engineering Research Center for Intelligent Manufacturing Systems.

References

1. T.C. Chang, D.C. Anderson, and O.R. Mitchell, "QTC — An Integrated Design/Manufacturing/Inspection System for Prismatic Parts," *Proc. ASME Computers in Eng. Conf.*, Am. Soc. Mechanical Engineers, New York, 1988.

2. D.C. Gossard, R.P. Zuffante, and H. Sakurai, "Representing Dimensions, Tolerances, and Features in MCAE Systems,"
IEEE Computer Graphics and Applications, Vol. 8, No. 2, Mar. 1988, pp. 51-59.

3. C.R. Luby, J.R. Dixon, and M.K. Simmons, "Design with Features: Creating and Using a Features Database for Evaluation of Manufacturability," *Computers in Mechanical Eng.*, Vol. 5, No. 3, 1986, pp. 25-33.

4. J. Shah and M. Rogers, "Functional Requirements and Conceptual Design of the Feature-Based Modeling System," *Computer-Aided Eng. J.*, Feb. 1988.

5. M. Marefat and R.L. Kashyap, "Geometric Reasoning for Recognition of Three-Dimensional Object Features," *IEEE Trans. Pattern Analysis and Machine Intelligence*, Vol. 12, No. 10, Oct. 1990, pp. 949-965.

6. A.A.G. Requicha and S.C. Chan, "Representation of Geometric Features, Tolerances, and Attributes in Solid Modelers Based on Constructive Geometry," *IEEE J. Robotics and Automation*, Vol. 2, No. 3, Sept. 1986, pp. 156-166.

7. C. Tsatsoulis and R.L. Kashyap, "A Case-Based System for Process Planning," *Robotics and Computer-Integrated Manufacturing*, Vol. 4, No. 3/4, 1988, pp. 557-570.

8. C.K. Riesbeck and R.C. Schank, *Inside Case-Based Reasoning*, Lawrence Erlbaum Associates, Hillsdale, N.J., 1989.

9. M. Marefat and R.L. Kashyap, "Automatic Construction of Process Plans from Solid Models," *IEEE Trans. Systems, Man, and Cybernetics*, Vol. 22, No. 5, Sept. 1992, pp. 1,097-1,115.

10. A. Kusiak, *Intelligent Manufacturing Systems*, Prentice Hall, Englewood Cliffs, N.J., 1990.

11. R.R. Karinthi and D.S. Nau, "Using a Feature Algebra for Reasoning About Geometric Feature Interactions," *Proc. 11th Int'l Joint Conf. Artificial Intelligence*, Morgan Kaufmann, Palo Alto, Calif., Aug. 1989.

12. J. Mundy et al., "The Image Understanding Environments Program," *Proc. DARPA Image Understanding Workshop*, 1992, pp. 185-214.

M. Marefat is on the faculty of electrical and computer engineering at the University of Arizona, where he founded the Intelligent Systems Laboratory. He has been the principal architect and developer of IDP, an integrated system for design, process planning, and inspection. His research interests include geometric modeling, knowledge-based software engineering, CAD/CAM, machine perception, and automation.

Marefat received a BS in electrical and computer engineering and a BA in mathematical sciences at Rice University in 1986, and MS and PhD degrees in electrical engineering from Purdue University in 1988 and 1991, respectively. He is a member of the IEEE and the IEEE Computer Society.

Sandeep Malhotra is working toward a BS in computer and electrical engineering at Purdue University. Since 1991 he has been working as an undergraduate research assistant at Purdue's Engineering Research Center for Intelligent Manufacturing Systems. His research interests include CAD/CAM, robotics, and computer graphics. He is a member of Eta Kappa Nu and a student member of the IEEE and the IEEE Computer Society.

R.L. Kashyap is a professor of electrical engineering and associate director of Purdue University's Engineering Research Center for Intelligent Manufacturing Systems. His research interests include pattern recognition, image processing, intelligent databases, random field models, and intelligent manufacturing systems. He has authored more than 100 refereed journal articles and served as area editor for several journals.

Kashyap received his PhD from Harvard University. He is a fellow of the IEEE and the Institute of Electrical and Telecommunication Engineers in India, and the recipient of the 1990 King Sun Fu Award for fundamental contributions to pattern recognition. He is also a member of the IEEE Computer Society.

Marefat's address is AI-Simulation Group, Department of Electrical and Computer Engineering, University of Arizona, Tucson, AZ 85721, e-mail marefat@ece.arizona.edu. Malhotra and Kashyap can be reached at the School of Electrical Engineering and Engineering Research Center for Intelligent Manufacturing Systems, Purdue University, West Lafayette, IN 47906, e-mail {malhotra, kashyap}@ecn.purdue.edu.

Bibliography

Balzer, R., T.E. Cheatham, and C. Green, "Software Technology in the 1990s: Using a New Paradigm," *Computer*, Vol. 13, No. 11, Nov. 1983, pp. 39–45.

Barker, V.E., and D.E. O'Connor, "Expert Systems for Configuration at Digital: XCON and Beyond," *Comm. ACM*, Vol. 32, No. 3, Mar. 1989, pp. 298–318.

Bihari, T.E., and P. Gopinath, "Object-Oriented Real-Time Systems: Concepts and Examples," *Computer*, Vol. 25, No. 12, Dec. 1992, pp. 25–32.

Boehm, B., "Improving Software Productivity," *Computer*, Vol. 20, No. 9, Sept. 1987, pp. 43–57.

Brooks, F., "No Silver Bullet: Essence and Accidents of Software Engineering," *Computer*, Vol. 20, No. 4, Apr. 1987, pp.10–19.

Buchanan, B., and E. Shortliffe, *Rule-Based Expert Systems*, Addison-Wesley, Reading, Mass., 1984.

Building Expert Systems, F. Hayes-Roth, D. Waterman, and D. Lenat, eds., Addison-Wesley, Reading, Mass., 1983.

"CAIS, Military Standard Common APSE Interface Set," US Department of Defense, MIL-STD-CAIS, 1985.

"CAMP: Common Ada Missile Packages: Reusable Software Parts," Tech. Report MDAC-STL, McDonnell-Douglas Astronautics Co., St. Louis, Missouri, 1987.

Coad, P., and E. Yourdon, *Object-Oriented Analysis*, Yourdon Press, Prentice-Hall, Englewood Cliffs, N.J., 1990.

Comerford, R., "Technology 1993: Software," *IEEE SPECTRUM*, Vol. 30, No. 1, Jan. 1993, pp. 32–33.

Computer, Special Issue on Inheritance and Classification in Object-Oriented Computing, Oct. 1992.

Cox, B., "There Is a Silver Bullet," *Byte*, Oct. 1990.

Davis, R., "Expert Systems: Where Are We? And Where Do We Go from Here?" *AI Magazine*, Summer 1982.

DeMarco, T., *Structured Analysis and System Specification*, Yourdon Press, Prentice-Hall, Englewood Cliffs, N.J., 1979.

Egbert, P.K., and W.J. Kubitz, "Application Graphics Modeling Support through Object Orientation," *Computer*, Vol. 25, No. 10, Oct. 1992, pp. 84–91.

Fichman, R.G., and C.F. Kemerer, "Object-Oriented and Conventional Analysis and Design Methodologies," *Computer*, Vol. 25, No. 10, Oct. 1992, pp. 22–39.

Fonash, P., *Characteristics of Reusable Software Code Components*, doctoral dissertation, George Mason University, Fairfax, Va., 1993.

Gold, J., "Reusability Promise Hinges on Libraries," *IEEE Software*, Vol. 13, No. 1, Jan. 1993, pp. 86–92.

Grimshaw, A.S., "Easy-to-Use Object-Oriented Parallel Processing with Mentat," *Computer*, Vol. 26, No. 5, May 1993, pp. 39–51.

Grochow, J.M., "Developing Strategic Business Systems Using Object-Oriented Technology," *Hotline on Object-Oriented Technology*, Vol. 3, No. 11, Sept. 1992, pp. 1–12.

Guttage, J., and J. Horning, "The Algebraic Specification of Abstract Data Types," *Acta Informatica*, Vol. 10, No. 1, 1978.

Harandi, M., and H. Lubars, "Automating Software Specification and Design," in *Artificial Intelligence and Software Eng.*, D. Partridge, ed., Ablex Publishing, Norwood, N.J., 1991.

Hoare, C.A., "Proof of Correctness of Data Representations," *Acta Informatica*, Vol. 4, 1972.

Hurson, A.R., S.H. Pakzad, and J. Cheng, "Object-Oriented Database Management Systems: Evolution and Performance Issues," *Computer*, Vol. 26, No. 2, Feb. 1993, pp. 48–60.

IEEE Software Eng. Standards, IEEE, New York, 1984.

Ishikawa, Y., H. Tokuda, and C.W. Mercer, "An Object-Oriented Real-Time Programming Language," *Computer*, Vol. 25, No. 10, Oct. 1992, pp. 66–73.

Kang, K., et al., "Feature-Oriented Domain Analysis Feasibility Study," Tech. Report CMU/SEI-90-TR-21, Software Engineering Institute, Pittsburgh, Pa., 1990.

Koenig, A., "Why I Use C++," *J. Object-Oriented Programming*, Vol. 1, No. 2, June 1988.

Lee, S., and S. Sluizer, "An Executable Language for Modeling Simple Behavior," *IEEE Trans. Software Eng.*, Vol. 17, No. 6, June 1991, pp. 527–543.

Lenz, M., H.A. Schmid, and P.F. Wolf, "Software Reuse through Building Blocks," *IEEE Software*, Vol. 4, No. 4, July 1987, pp. 34–42.

Lientz, B., and E. Swanson., *Software Maintenance Management*, Addison-Wesley, New York, 1980.

Liskov, B., and S. Zilles, "Programming with Abstract Data Types," *Proc. ACM SIGPLAN Conf. Very High Level Languages, SIGPLAN Notices*, Vol. 9, Apr. 1974.

Lubars, M., "Code Reusability in the Large versus Code Reusability in the Small," *ACM SIGSOFT Software Eng. Notes*, Vol. 11, No. 1, Jan. 1986.

Marefat, M., S. Malhotra, and R.L. Kashyap, "Object-Oriented, Intelligent Computer-Integrated Design, Process Planning, and Inspection," *Computer*, Vol. 26, No. 3, Mar. 1993, pp. 54–65.

Meyer, B., "Applying 'Design by Contract,' " *Computer*, Vol. 25, No. 10, Oct. 1992, pp. 40–51.

Meyer, B., *Object-Oriented Software Construction*, Prentice-Hall International Series in Computer Science, Prentice-Hall, Englewood Cliffs, N.J., 1988.

Meyer, B., "Reusability: The Case for Object-Oriented Design," *IEEE Software*, Vol. 4, No. 2, Mar. 1987, pp. 50–64.

Nicol, J.R., C.T. Wilkes, and F.A. Manola, "Object Orientation in Heterogeneous Distributed Computing Systems," *Computer*, Vol. 26, No. 6, June 1993, pp. 57–67.

Nishida, F., et al., "Semi-Automatic Program Construction from Specifications Using Library Modules," *IEEE Trans. Software Eng.*, Vol. 17, No. 9, Sept. 1991, pp. 853–871.

Parnas, D.L., "On the Criteria to Be Used in Decomposing Systems into Modules," *Comm. ACM*, Vol. 5, No. 12, Dec. 1972.

Partsch, A., and R. Steinbruggen, "Program Transformation Systems," *ACM Computing Surveys*, Vol. 15, No. 3, Sept. 1983, pp. 199–236.

Pfleeger, S., *An Investigation of Cost and Productivity for Object-Oriented Development*, doctoral dissertation, George Mason University, Fairfax, Va., 1989.

Ponder, C., and B. Bush, "Polymorphism Considered Harmful," *Software Eng. Notes*, Vol. 19, No. 2, Apr. 1994.

Prieto-Diaz, R., "A Domain Analysis Methodology," *Proc. Workshop Domain Modeling Software Eng.*, 13th Int'l Conf. Software Eng., Austin, Texas, 1991.

Prieto-Diaz, R., "Classifying Software for Reusability," *IEEE Software*, Vol. 4, No. 1, Jan. 1987, pp. 6–16.

Prieto-Diaz, R., "Domain Analysis for Reusability," *Proc. CompSAC 87*, IEEE CS Press, 1987, pp. 23–29.

Research Directions in Object-Oriented Programming, B. Shriver and P. Wegner, eds., MIT Press, Cambridge, Mass., 1987.

Rine, D., "Domain Modeling Requirements of an Expanded MIS Using a Formal Approach," Tech. Report, CS Department, George Mason University, 1991.

Rine, D., "Fuzzy Object-Oriented Design of Databases and Expert Systems," *Proc. Third Int'l Fuzzy Systems Assn. Conf.*, IFSA, IEEE, 1989.

Rine, D., "Principles for Object-Oriented Development," *ACM SIGSOFT Software Eng. Notes*, Vol. 16, No. 1, Jan. 1991.

Rine, D., "Retrainable Software: Software Engineering and Machine Learning," *Digest of Papers AIDA-88 Conference*, George Mason University, Nov. 1988.

Rine, D., "Software Perfective Maintenance: Including Retrainable Software in Software Reuse," *Information Sciences, An International J.*, Vol. 75, No. 1, Dec. 1993.

Rine, D., "The Use of Object-Oriented Construction to Develop an Expanded Management Information System," *Cybernetics and Systems: An Int'l J.*, Vol. 22, 1991.

Rine, D., and H. Wechsler, "Object-Oriented Programming (OOP) and Its Relevance to Designing Intelligent Software Systems," *Proc. 1988 Int'l Conf. Computer Languages*, IEEE CS Press, 1988, pp. 242–248.

Sing, L., "Interview with Bjarne Stroustrop," *C++ J.*, Vol. 1, No. 3, 1991.

Sommerville, I., *Software Eng.*, 3rd ed., Addison-Wesley, New York, 1989.

Swangwanna, S., and J. Zytkow, "Real-Time Decision Making for Autonomous Flight Control," *SAE Tech. Paper Series*, 891053, General Aviation Aircraft Meeting and Exposition, Wichita, Kan., Apr. 1989.

Udell, J., "Component Ware," *Byte*, May 1994.

Ungar, D., et al., "Object, Message, and Performance: How They Coexist in SELF," *Computer*, Vol. 25, No. 10, Oct. 1992, pp. 53–64.

Van Lamsweerde, A., et al., "The Kernel of a Generic Software Development Environment," *Proc. ACM SIGSOFT and SIGPLAN Symp.*, ACM, New York, 1986.

Wechsler, H., and D. Rine, Chapter in *Progress in Object-Oriented Databases*, J. Prater, ed., Ablex Publishing, Norwood, N.J., 1990.

Wegner, P., "Capital-Intensive Software," *IEEE Software,* Vol. 1, No. 3, July 1984, pp. 7–45.

Wegner, P., "Dimensions of Object-Oriented Modeling," *Computer,* Vol. 25, No. 10, Oct. 1992, pp. 12–20.

Wegner, P., "The Object-Oriented Classification Paradigm," in *Research Directions in Object-Oriented Programming,* B. Shriver and P. Wegner, eds., MIT Press, Cambridge, 1987.

Weicker, R., "Dhrystone: A Synthetic Systems Programming Benchmark," *Comm. ACM,* Vol. 27, No. 10, Oct. 1984, pp. 1013–1030.

Wells, D.L., J.A. Blakeley, and C.W. Thompson, "Architecture of an Open Object-Oriented Database Management System," *Computer,* Vol 25, No. 10, Oct. 1992, pp. 74–82.

Zilles, S., "Introduction to Data Algebras," in *Abstract Software Specifications,* Springer-Verlag, New York, 1979.

Contributing Authors

Dimensions of Object-Oriented Modeling

Peter Wegner
Department of Computer Science
Brown University
Providence, RI 02912

Object-Oriented and Conventional Analysis and Design Methodologies

Robert G. Fichman
Chris F. Kemerer
Massachusetts Institute of Technology, E53-315
Cambridge, MA 02139

Applying "Design by Contract"

Bertrand Meyer
Interactive Software Engineering, Inc.
270 Storke Road, Suite 207
Goleta, CA 93117

Object, Message, and Performance: How They Coexist in SELF

David Ungar
Randall B. Smith
Sun Microsystems Laboratories, Inc.
2550 Garcia Ave., MTV 29-116
Mountain View, CA 94043

Craig Chambers
Department of Computer Science and Engineering
Sieg Hall, FR-35
University of Washington, Seattle, WA 98195

Urs Hölzle
University of California
Santa Barbara, CA 94305

Easy-to-Use Object-Oriented Parallel Processing with Mentat

Andrew S. Grimshaw
Department of Computer Science
University of Virginia
Charlottesville, VA 22903

Architecture of an Open Object-Oriented Database Management System

David L. Wells
Jose A. Blakeley
Craig W. Thompson
Texas Instruments Inc.
P.O. Box 655474, MS 238
Dallas, TX 75265

Object-Oriented Database Management Systems: Evolution and Performance Issues

A.R. Hurson
Simon H. Pakzad
Department of Electrical and Computer Engineering
Pennsylvania State University
University Park, PA 16802

Jia-bing Cheng
IBM-Research
Triangle Park, PA
(Contact A. R. Hurson A2H@ecl.psu.edu)

Object Orientation in Heterogeneous Distributed Computing Systems

John R. Nicol
C. Thomas Wilkes
Frank A. Manola
GTE Laboratories, Inc.
Computer and Intelligent Systems Laboratory
40 Sylan Road
Waltham, MA 02254

Design and Construction of a Software-Engineering Environment: Experiences with Eiffel

Chris Bosch
Hassan Gomaa
Larry Kerschberg
Center for Software Systems Engineering
School of Information Technology and Engineering
George Mason University
Fairfax, VA 22030-4444

An Object-Oriented Real-Time Programming Language

Yutaka Ishikawa
MITI Electrotechnical Laboratory
(Contact H. Tokuda)

Hideyuki Tokuda
Carnegie Mellon University
School of Computer Science
5000 Forbes Avenue
Pittsburgh, PA 15213

C.W. Mercer
Carnegie Mellon University
School of Computer Science
5000 Forbes Avenue
Pittsburgh, PA 15213
(Contact H. Tokuda)

Object-Oriented Real-Time Systems: Concepts and Examples

Thomas E. Bihari
Adaptive Machine Technologies
1218 Kinnear Rd.
Columbus, OH 43212

Prabha Gopinath
Sensor and System Development Center
Honeywell, MN 65-2350
3660 Technology Dr.
Minneapolis, MN 55418

Application Graphics Modeling Support through Object Orientation

Parris K. Egbert
Department of Computer Science
Brigham Young University
3328 TMCB
Provo, UT 84602

William J. Kubitz
Department of Computer Science
University of Illinois at Urbana-Champaign
1304 W. Springfield Ave.
Urbana, IL 61801

ERC+: An Objects + Relationships Paradigm for Database Applications

Stefano Spaccapietra
École Polytechnique Fédérale
DI — Laboratoire Bases de Données
IN — Ecublens, 1015
Lausanne, Switzerland

Christine Parent
Marcos Sunye
Kokou Yetongnon
Université de Bourgogne
Département Informatique, B.P. 138
21004 Dijon Cédex, France

Antonio Di Leva
Dipartimento di Informatica
Università degli Studi di Torino
Corso Svizzera 185-10149
Torino, Italy

Multilevel-Secure Object-Oriented Data Model

Sushil Jajodia
Boris Kogan
Ravi S. Sandhu
Department of Information and Software Systems Engineering
George Mason University
Fairfax, VA 22030-4444

Object-Oriented, Intelligent Computer-Integrated Design, Process Planning, and Inspection

M. Marefat
AI-Simulation Group
Department of Electrical and Computer Engineering
University of Arizona
Tucson, AZ 85721

Sandeep Malhotra
R. L. Kashyap
School of Electrical Engineering and
Engineering Research Center for
Intelligent Manufacturing Systems
Purdue University
West Lafayette, IN 47906

Author Index

About the Author

David C. Rine is a professor of computer science as well as information and software systems engineering at George Mason University, and a senior researcher in the university's Center for Software Systems Engineering. At CSSE, his research has focused on object-oriented development, software maintenance and reuse, and software development environments.

Rine received his PhD in mathematical sciences in 1970 from the University of Iowa. He has published more than 140 papers and received numerous awards including the IEEE Centennial Award, the IEEE Computer Society's Pioneer Award, Meritorious Service Award, and Special Award. He has coauthored several computer texts and is presently associate technical editor for *Computer Journal*, area editor for object oriented computing, and editor for the IEEE Computer Society's *Readings in Computer Science and Engineering* series.